# *The* THOUSAND YEARS *of the* APOCALYPSE

# THE THOUSAND YEARS OF THE APOCALYPSE

Aspects of Western History as foretold
in the Christian Scriptures

Thomas R. Sharp

Copyright © Thomas R. Sharp 2023

The right of Thomas R. Sharp to be identified as author of this work has been asserted by him in accordance with section 77 and 78 of the Copyright, Designs and Patents Act 1988.

Published April 2023 by Frintonbrook

Paperback ISBN-978-1-7392511-0-9

All rights reserved. No part of this publication may be reproduced, reprinted, or utilised in any form or by any electronic, mechanical or other means, without **written** permission of the copyright owner.

Produced in the United Kingdom

Cover and layout design by www.spiffingcovers.com

In memory of my maternal grandmother,
Beatrice Annie White, née Lynn

## Contents

| | |
|---|---|
| Preface | ix |
| 1. History and the Apocalypse | 1 |
| 2. Ten barbarian Kingdoms of the West | 32 |
| 3. The Demise of Rome and the Genesis of the West | 62 |
| 4. The Word of God in the Carolingian Renaissance | 91 |

Three Aspects of the Christian West –

| | |
|---|---|
| 5. I: The Faustian Society | 121 |
| 6. II: The Cult of the Saints | 154 |
| 7. III: The millennial Reign of Christ | 185 |
| 8. The End of the thousand Years: Satan let loose | 220 |
| 9. Strands of Apostasy in the nineteenth Century | 255 |
| 10. The Hosts of Gog and Magog are as the Sand of the Sea | 288 |
| Epilogue: Prophecies fulfilled | 316 |
| References | 323 |
| Bibliography | 344 |
| Index of personal Names | 354 |

*Preface*

The inspiration for this book owes its origin to a number of years of personal turmoil which I experienced in my younger days, and which left me harbouring a dissatisfaction with the society in which I lived. The outcome was to investigate the condition of that society, which eventually led me to form the hypothesis that Western civilization had reached a serious, almost critical, situation, and this was confirmed for me after reading the two-volume work of the German historian Oswald Spengler, entitled *The Decline of the West*. A second discovery was even more compelling, namely, that the history of Western civilization bore a close affinity with the later chapters of the Book of Revelation in the New Testament, also known as the Apocalypse.

The decision to write a book rather than continue merely to contemplate a closely held hypothesis was made over fifteen years ago. This was not an easy matter for me as a first-time author. To begin any venture in old age requires a leap of faith and to persevere to the end requires a huge effort, particularly if the main theme is almost certainly going to be a highly controversial one. Contrary to what many readers may think, once the theory had taken shape, reason was the guide, enabling me to select and marshal historical data, a process which gradually enabled me to formulate my ideas more lucidly. Our ancestors claimed that God spoke through revelations which would have manifested themselves in dreams and visions. The modern way is to rely primarily or solely on the great goddess Reason, but reason may just as well serve the same purposes as revelation.

In this book, no claim is being made that all the historical research has been culled from primary sources. On the contrary, much of the data that I have gathered and presented in the narrative – facts, figures, dates, arguments – are derivative, that is to say, I have culled them from secondary sources. I have been anxious to ensure that, so far as possible, my interpretation of the later chapters of the Apocalypse can be related to the historical facts and commentaries that I obtained from my studies, and in so many instances the relevant authorities have unwittingly laid bare the evidence to support my thesis. In effect, historical research has been pressed into the service of an ancient prophecy. This book therefore is a tribute to all those authorities who have made contributions, however small, and I beg forgiveness if by oversight I have omitted to make appropriate acknowledgments of other writers' material.

The reader may be astonished that historical detail and a book of the Christian Bible have been treated in this way. Nevertheless, we are left with a story which is all the more powerful for being based on biblical texts and on historians' opinions, and not on the suppositions of myth-makers in search of the Holy Grail or some mysterious centuries-long conspiracy. It is common nowadays for some authors to denigrate the Christian faith, by uncovering such conspiracies. I wish to propose no such sinister agenda. Perhaps the Holy Grail will after all turn out to be the history of the Christian West, which so faithfully seems to mirror the apocalyptic prophecies.

The book is not intended to be an historical textbook. Readers can ascertain the bare historical facts for themselves from their own reading, and a copious bibliography appears at the end of the book. However, to understand history in its proper sense we need to get beyond the empirical standpoint altogether and approach it in quite another way. The historian should ask 'why?' for to do so is to satisfy the wish to probe below the surface of historical phenomena in order to discover the reality which undoubtedly underlies them.

One commentator and friend, Dr Rodney Dean, who has scrutinized much of my work, gained the impression from perusing my narrative that in some parts of the book, I was writing a theology, not a history. This was not my original intention, but I rest content with his analysis. However, the book is not intended as an exegesis of the Book of Revelation itself.

Some of the chapters have also been reviewed in advance by other friends and colleagues also, and much of their advice has been studied, and incorporated into my narrative. They have been more than generous with encouragement, and I thank them for their critiques and assistance. As well as Dr. Rodney Dean, I must thank my friends John and Rosemary Davis, who have also rendered financial support, Roland and Eleanor Young who have assisted with proof-reading of the first draft, a former work colleague John Hudson, and Mark Burrell. I also am grateful to the Reverend Robert Bashford, Janet Hartnoll and Peter Drewry for their comments on theological matters. I am certain that, without their various contributions, my book would have been the poorer.

In the following text, dates before the Christian era are written as B.C., otherwise all dates quoted are those within the Christian era.

All biblical quotes and references are taken from the Revised Standard Version published by Thomas Nelson and Sons Limited for the Division of Christian Education of the National Council of the Churches of Christ in the United States of America, London, 1965.

March 2023

CHAPTER ONE

*History and the Apocalypse*

"Time does not respect what is done without him." *Paul Morand*

WHAT IS the definition of history and how do we understand its discipline? What is its purpose and what constitutes its subject-matter? What kinds of things does history discover? Does it possess a logic and how does it proceed? There would seem to be as many different answers as there are questions concerning history, and to a greater or lesser extent different people would answer these questions in different ways. "History," said the nineteenth-century historian John Bagnell Bury "is a science, no less and no more."[1] For a discipline to conform to this particular terminology, it must comprise an organized body of knowledge, and *a fortiori* it must always be organized in a particular way.[2] Thus, history appears to be a science of some special kind.

By engaging in the pursuit of history, the aim is to produce a record of, and to interpret, past events, and the theologian Reinhold Niebuhr stated that it is through our memory of past events that we can understand what is real to us in the present.[3] Saint Augustine also maintained that the past must be identified with memory, just as the future must be identified with expectation. Past and future, however, can be thought of only as present. From this he deduced that there are three 'times': the present of things past as memory, the present of things present as sight, and the present of things future as expectation.[4] Historians conclude from this that time is part of the essence of history, the more so since human protagonists are themselves subject to the flow of time, and whatever they achieve decays and passes away. The relationship between meaning and time renders history mysterious, with time and meaning inextricably bound together, a mystery which Saint Augustine himself confessed that he could not explain. The concept of time is subjective, existing in the human mind, which remembers, considers and expects.[5]

Many commentators who are not involved in the discipline of history, see history as just a confused hotchpotch of discrete events, and indeed historical facts considered individually cannot speak for themselves in isolation from each other. The quest for meaning in history would be futile if it was manifested overtly in individual events, or even in the mere succession of them, and so the historian is motivated by the sheer lack of a clear meaning.[6] He contributes to knowledge by studying events, discerning their inherent meaning and the human motives associated with them, and creatively reorganizing them in order to bring that meaning to the surface. Particular events may be selected which are relevant for their own particular narrative, and it is these which enable historians to attain an adequate comprehension of the whole. Accordingly, some structure is required which will allow individual events to be slotted into place in a comprehensive story. The historian Jacques Barzun stated that facts gain significance only in the manner in which they are selected and arranged.[7] Another answer to our questions would be to view history as the past actions of men and women, and so history deals with human affairs, and its conclusions are of a different order from many other intellectual disciplines. The theologian Ernst Troeltsch stated that, whereas natural science seeks to generalize and formulate laws, history comprises the systematic treatment of that which is unique and particular and, by selecting appropriate facts, history entails the construction of values in the wider sense with a view to constructing individual 'value units' *(Wertganzen)* out of them.[8]

The historian gathers evidence from his authorities and selects from them whatever he considers important and true, rejecting what is regarded as irrelevant for his purposes, and introducing into them conclusions which are not explicit from the bare evidence. In this way the historian becomes his own authority by selecting, constructing and criticizing, and interpreting the evidence contained in the documents of the past. It is he, and not his authorities, that is responsible for what is included in his analysis, and so his work is to that extent autonomous. By its very nature, the evidence of historical science is always partial and thereby reflects to a certain degree the mystery in human motives, attitudes and decisions.

Certainly, evidence is a vital ingredient, but imagination is also needed to embellish the primary texts. The historian investigates not mere events but human actions, and so he must think himself into such actions. All history becomes therefore the re-enactment of past events in the historian's own mind. For the historian, the events whose history he is studying are not mere spectacles to be watched from the outside, but experiences to be lived through. Therefore, the historian has to stand within history and be involved in the interpretation of events to the extent that a particular understanding of the subject matter is presupposed. The Swiss historian and philosopher Wilhelm Dilthey maintained that there should always be a connection between the author of an historical document and the historian as its interpreter, who must likewise possess a prior understanding of the subject matter in question. In addition, written history becomes an ongoing dialogue between historians, not just about events themselves, but why and how those events occurred.

We may further enquire whether the history of humanity possesses something, which we may call a comprehensive plan, an overarching narrative or superstructure, that lies beyond all the apparently arbitrary, individual events. Rudolf Bultmann posed the problem, when he asked whether history contains an underlying core which provides it with relevance, and without which every sequence of events remains meaningless.[9] Such an idea might be called a metaphysical structure that is independent of events, whatever events they may be, whether social, political or spiritual, and these events may be derived from that structure. Just as we have stated that neutral historical facts cannot speak for themselves, so likewise they cannot provide an interpretation of the historical process itself. Should historians therefore indulge in system-building in order to find or construct an overall purpose in the huge clutter of events that appear before them? The historical discipline is often complex and historical events rarely transparent, and since human thought cannot function to any degree in chaos, a coherent framework is certainly necessary. Such a task would be classed as philosophy of history, and may be accomplished by assigning one continuous force or a predestined goal as a motif, which at the end of history would bring mankind to some paradisiacal or disastrous end. Examples which can be shown to be such a motivating or generative force are: the progress of freedom, the class struggle, divine Providence, secular progress, or mankind's advancement towards rational self-sufficiency. All these would provide a pathway to some kind of destination, be it the ideal society, a workers' paradise, or that which the philosopher Immanuel Kant designated as an ethical commonwealth.

All attempts at system-building up to the present have been ineffectual or invalid because historians have tried on diverse occasions to assign a single cause to history. Those writers who propounded grandiose theories, as the eighteenth-century Enlightenment *philosophes* did, were also, in their own way, engaged in the construction of philosophies of history. They too were attempting to trace a pattern in the course of historical change. Not to put too fine a point on it, they were convinced that history was 'going somewhere', with their desire to discover a reality or overall plan, which they believed lay underneath historical events. Despite their many differences from contemporary theologians, the writers of the Enlightenment felt the same need to demonstrate that the miseries which men and women experienced were not in vain. We must entertain the possibility that historical events really do reflect some kind of structure, so that we return to the question that we posed at the beginning: is there a logic or meaning to history and can the individual historian realize that meaning as history unfolds?

## History in pre-Christian Times

Ancient man had no awareness or appreciation of history. His narratives could not be considered as history but rather as myth. Only when a people were transformed into an organized entity through its history did historical experience beget an historical consciousness and a historiography. The phase of chronicles and tales was then abandoned and men began to search for connections between various historical events. This arose first among Greek storytellers, when the idea of history developed in the fifth century B.C. as a branch of knowledge in which attempts were made to understand history as well as that of nature. It was continued by their Roman successors, but initially the historiography was primitive, being partly poetry and partly prose. Such accounts may be called sagas, but the Greeks perceived the world as static, a completed cosmos, and for them history was regarded as equivalent to nature. Its one characteristic was the idea of recurrence, which they had already discerned in the natural world. In the long run, events that were happening at any one time would be repeated over and over again, and so their history was not progressive but cyclical. The view of history held by the historian Theucydides was typical. He saw movement in history in the same way as cosmic movement, in which all change was simply the same thing in new arrangements. Just as a new year followed the old, just as the seasons go round, all past events would recur again and again. History therefore was not considered distinct from nature, so that a true philosophy of history was alien to the aesthetic ponderings of the ancient world.

In the Old Testament, Judaism's faith was an historic one from the earliest times and the Jewish people considered that history derived its meaning from God's guidance and education. The Old Testament relates how God came to be recognized first and foremost as the God of History.[10] Such a view potentially entailed eschatology, the doctrine of the last or final things, or the end-time, which might include terrible events as signs of the end, such as war, famine and epidemics. In early Judaism this eschatological element in the true sense is missing. Later on, the notion of history decisively changed as reflected in the apocalyptic literature of the Old Testament, which came to imply that history had a meaning and a purpose more important than events considered individually.[11] God, as the ruler of history, was now seen to lead history to an ultimate end or *telos* with a plan through His interaction with men and women.[12] The end of the old world, and the inception of the new, was to be brought about by divine judgment at a time determined by God. The Jewish conception of history as progressive replaced the Hellenic conception of history as cyclical, but even so the Old Testament was not considered to be an historical document, but rather consisted of books of revelations.

## Christianity is an historical Religion

Unlike any other religion, apart from its Judaic precursor, Christianity is destined as an historical religion, and this explanation reflects two complementary aspects. In the first instance, the New Testament does not record the teaching or the meditations of the prophets or the wise as its primary aim, although these aspects are very important. It appeals to events which can be dated, because belief in Christ as Redeemer always implies the conviction that God acts in history, at least in some way. The Bible states that Jesus was born during the reign of Herod Antipas. Luke chapter 2, verses 1-2 states, "In those days a decree went out from Caesar Augustus that all the world should be enrolled," that is, for a general registration throughout the Roman world. "This was the first enrolment, when Publius Quirinius was governor of Syria." We learn of the life and ministry of Jesus, His condemnation to death by Pontius Pilate, the acts of the apostles, the missionary journeys of Saint Paul. These are all examples that are intended to place biblical events in an historical framework, and link Christianity firmly to unique historical events. Christianity will stand or fall on historical events such as these. Furthermore, Christianity in the West remained thoroughly historical in its view of the world, and for this reason Christianity made a philosophy of history possible.

Because some historical events are believed to have a spiritual significance, Christianity asserts that it is an historical religion. The theologian Wolfhart Pannenberg contended that the revelation of God is bound to history, and in the Israelite tradition, God was thought to be revealed through his actions in history. Similar to Judaism, the Christian history of salvation developed as a result of nurturing a belief in a final purpose. Historical thought is therefore an inextricable component of Christian thought, and its theology has always reflected this. The sociologist Maurice Halbwachs asked how one could explain the fact that the Christian religion promotes itself as a permanent institution, in such a way that it claims to be outside of time, and yet Christian truths must simultaneously be historical,, that is, inside of time, as well as eternal.[13] Christianity, by staking a powerful claim to be an historical religion, surpasses all other religions in this respect. Other religions might lay claim to a storehouse of wisdom which may be invaluable in itself, but it excludes history. Christianity could not take that route, for it revealed that mankind had a single historical fate, which had a beginning and will have an end.

In the period of the early church, Greek and Old Testament traditions became blended together, and two main elements emerged. First of all, the emphasis gradually veered towards an apocalyptic disposition which eventually prevailed over all others. The Pauline understanding of history, for example, was defined in this way. The Book of Revelation was an inevitable outcome of this apocalyptic period. Between the fourth and fifth centuries, the Christian idea of history was modified in a revolutionary way as Christian thought developed further.[14] Its historiography became characterized by four elements or principles: universal, providential, apocalyptic and periodized. In Western culture particularly, this view of history triumphed over Greek and Roman ideas when it became apparent to historical commentators that the classical doctrine of cyclical recurrence rendered it impossible to cope with the multifarious novel situations that arose in the passage of time.

The second element, however, concerned the effect occasioned by the disappointment in the early church when Christ's *parousia*, or second coming, failed to occur. This feeling did not take place suddenly and not everywhere at once, but Christians gradually became accustomed to waiting. The idea of a universal eschatology was still retained, but interest amongst Christian believers shifted to the salvation of the individual soul, and the development of religious ceremonies and the sacraments. The longer the *parousia* was delayed and the further into the future that the end of history was out of necessity postponed, the more the church discovered that it had a history in the present world, and so it developed an understanding of the philosophy of history and fostered an interest in historical studies.

Saint Theophilus the Penitent of Antioch, who lived at the end of the second century, was regarded as the oldest historical commentator. About 220 the historian Sextus Julius Africanus wrote comments on the Bible which included the idea that the history of the world was a matter of importance to Christians. Next, the chronicle of the theologian Hippolytus of Rome ran from the creation of the world until the year 234.[15] The scholar and historian, Eusebius, bishop of Caesarea, in his *Chronicle* written at the end of the third century, set church history in the framework of a world history. For these writers, a new Christian chronology considered the birth of Christ to be at the centre of history, time was reckoned backwards and forwards from this event, and history now had a meaning, but this meaning was not inherent in the process of history itself. Rather any meaning that it may have had was imposed by divine Providence, and so a teleological view of history began to develop.

Saint Augustine's works were to mould the minds of the peoples of the Christian West more than anything else. He disputed the classical world's interpretation of the historical process as comparable with nature. For him time had a beginning, for it was created by God, and it will have an end which God has also determined. He saw all history as a struggle between two dynamic spiritual principles that manifested themselves throughout the ages in the unceasing conflict between two separate societies, the City of God and Babylon, the *Civitas terrena* or City of Confusion, the latter often depicted as no better than a *Civitas Diaboli*, a city of the Devil. The struggle between the two was enacted in the history of individual protagonists, in which the problem of free will now appeared for the first time, and from this new understanding of man a new conception of history developed.

Medieval historiography continued to reflect this distinctive character. It too believed that the meaning of history could be known by detecting the divine plan within it, not as immanent in history but as imposed upon it by God. Medieval man looked forward to the end of history as something foreordained by God, of which mankind was given foreknowledge through revelation. History was separated into epochs, and the most notable exponent of this mode of thinking was the twelfth century theologian Joachim of Fiore, whose tripartite division according to Father, Son and Holy Ghost became the most celebrated.

### The later Development of historical Studies

The Renaissance thinkers, by adopting a more profane view of history, concluded it was man, not God, that motivated the historical process and so they abandoned millennial thinking and the idea of an eschatological conclusion to history. For them history became the story of human passions. From the sixteenth to the eighteenth centuries, the main thrust for new knowledge led to the early endeavours of modern natural science, and by contrast historical thought was always simple or rudimentary.[16] Indeed, the philosopher René Descartes' radical ideas concerning knowledge contributed little to historical thought, because he did not believe history to be a branch of knowledge at all. It was the historian Giambattista Vico in his *Scienza nuova (New Science)* (1725) who may be said to originate the philosophy of history in its modern sense, but the term was also used by the philosopher François-Marie Voltaire, as distinct from the theological interpretation of history. In his work *Essai sur les Moeurs et l'Esprit des Nations (Essay on the Manners and Spirit of Nations)* (1756), the will of man and human reason was the predominating factor rather than divine Providence.

From the mid-eighteenth-century onwards, history gradually came to be written in a dogmatically more or less neutral way. The Christian idea of teleology remained, but history became secularized. Its course came to be understood as progress from a previous dark era to an era of enlightenment under the sovereignty of reason, which would lead ultimately to a Utopian state of perfection. The men of the Enlightenment, the *philosophes*, from this time onwards became interested in the secular past. The historian Edward Gibbon in his celebrated work *The History of The Decline and Fall of the Roman Empire* (1776-1788) accounted for historical events by means of other historical events. In other words, he adopted the notion of cause and effect in history. Immanuel Kant continued the idea that world-history was a teleological process. He saw historical development as a progression towards rationality, and the education of mankind would have a major role to play in this process, but for him the truths of the Christian faith and its view of history were interpreted as philosophical truths.

For the historian and philosopher Georg Wilhelm Hegel the divine plan which gave history its unity was described as the 'Absolute Mind', realizing itself according to a law of dialectical movement. Progress occurs when two opposing ideas or forces, the thesis and the antithesis, terms derived from the philosopher Johann Fichte, combine to forge a new proposition or synthesis, as a resolution of their conflict. The 'Cunning of Reason' replaced God's direction of human history. The concept of eschatology was replaced by the historical process itself. At the same time, Leopold von Ranke, a key figure as a professor of history at the University of Berlin from 1824 onwards, revolutionized the study of history, which now emerged as a new academic discipline. By pursuing historical studies with the maxim *'wie es eigentlich gewesen'*, *('how it really was')*, in other words, by examining original data in the search for an accurate narrative of historical events, he maintained that the historian could discover what really happened.

The Hegelian dialectic of history was transformed into dialectical materialism by the philosopher Karl Marx, by turning Hegel's theory of dialectical movement on its head. In Marx's case, the motivating force was not ideas but socio-economic conditions. A boundless secular faith in progress and the progressive mastery over nature were rendered possible by the development of science and technology. The economist Robert Turgot and the politician Pierre-Joseph Proudhon were also advocates of this idea, replacing divine Providence by the natural law of progress. For them, Providence was nothing but the human collective instinct, thus completely contradicting Christian belief. Through the influence of Romanticism, historiography in the nineteenth century eventually arrived at some form of relativism. The consensus of nineteenth and twentieth century opinion, derived from those such as Wilhelm Dilthey and the philosopher Benedetto Croce, seemed to be that no individual could view his or her historical context as thought from the outside. We have no option but to live within our own context. The philosopher Auguste Comte believed that history would become the 'sacred science of humanity', in which humanity will become more conscious of itself, through the study of its past intellectual and moral activity.[17] Historians with penetrating and powerful minds, exemplified by Oswald Spengler and Arnold Toynbee, saw history essentially as an analytic study of comparative civilizations and their cultures, in which history essentially has no beginning and no end.[18] As a result, modern historical academic scholarship disapproves of anything at all that speaks of, or concerns, the idea of Providence.

If the term 'philosophy of history' signifies an explanation of history in which historical events are directed towards an ultimate meaning, a theological interpretation is being imposed upon history. In such a case, the philosopher Karl Löwith remarked that such a philosophy of history cannot be considered a true science, for it would pose the virtually impossible problem of verifying belief in salvation on scientific grounds.[19] The absence of such a scientific basis and at the same time the quest for it, caused modern philosophers and even theologians to reject altogether the pre-modern, Christian treatment of history.

### Providence in History

It is an oft-repeated fact, and a curious irony, that in history the results of man's willed actions on many occasions do not conform to his intentions, a situation which we may call, for want of a better term, the 'law of unintended consequences'. People oftentimes do not know what they are doing until they have done it. They may even be horrified at what has actually occurred, vowing that they had not expected such an outcome. Does this situation indeed reveal something, perhaps an inner logic, which overrules the will of man?[20] Such notions assume a motivating and driving force for the historical process which is more potent and omniscient than any human agency.[21] It would seem to follow from this that man's achievements do not depend upon his own will and intellect but upon something other than himself. Important historical changes can then be viewed as enabling a structure to be conferred upon the historical process.

It is an axiom of Christian thought that ultimately the whole course of history can be understood if we consider the guiding hand of Providence. Christian literature about the past concerned itself with plotting events along a teleological trajectory in which God's purpose was worked out in history in accordance with His plan, in order to reach an eschatological destination, which led to the redemption of mankind. History was moving towards a point at which God's kingdom was transferred from heaven to earth as the final event at the end of history. The Bible records God's actions in history, and biblical faith included the notion that God reveals His purposes by means of significant and powerful events and situations. The chemist, theologian and philosopher Joseph Priestley maintained a providential view of history, and that the study of history enabled mankind to understand better God's natural laws. Moreover, to thinkers such as Jacques Bossuet, Rudolf Bultmann and Giambattista Vico, God guided the development of the human race by intervening directly in history, a situation which resembled a drama.[22] In this case, the historical process was not the accomplishment of man's purposes, but rather of God's. Human actions are from time to time fulfilled in accordance with pre-conceived plans only because they conform to God's purposes.

In his celebrated work, *Discours sur l'Histoire universelle (A Discourse on universal History)* (1681), Jacques Bossuet defended against the sceptics the traditional notion that divine Providence is also the law of history. For those of the Christian faith, what seemed to outsiders to be disorder in history revealed itself on the contrary as an order in which all events were directed by Providence to carry history onwards to its end, and that the actions of men served the divine plan, although they may not have been conscious of what it was. Giambattista Vico was also guided by the same idea, but he took the matter one stage further by viewing the historical process as a development which was natural as well as providential. He called his new science a rational theology of divine Providence. The course of history had its own inner necessity given to it by God, and so God need not interfere with it. In this case Providence worked as a *lumen naturale* or hidden light. Such an understanding vitiated the idea of eschatology, since he returned to the idea of a cyclical format for history, but in contradistinction to the ancient world's idea of simple recurrence, Vico asserted that the cycles of history followed each other in a spiral progression. The Lutheran church historian Johann Lorenz von Mosheim, a spokesman of the early Enlightenment, believed firmly in divine Providence, and maintained that God had so arranged matters that the first apostles should be uninformed, illiterate men (sic) so that their writings would be viewed as of divine, not human, origin.[23]

The concept of revelation became contentious in the modern world from the eighteenth century onwards, when the *philosophes* of the Enlightenment confronted society with the choice between revelation and autonomous reason, and their views concerning the historical process were ruled by reason. However, at the time not all these men thought in this way. For example, the philosopher Johann Georg Hamann, a through-going opponent of the French Enlightenment, considered that everything was indeed revelation, and causality was illusory. Friedrich Schelling in his book *System des transcendentalen Idealismus (System of transcendental Idealism)* (1800) also subscribed to the notion that the entire history of the world was the progressive and never completed self-disclosure of God. Wolfhart Pannenberg too provided the insight that such revelation did not consist of just one event, but rather of the totality of history, and it developed as a continuing process arising from the sequence of historical events, in which God continually provides guidance. A similar sentiment was expressed by Gotthold Lessing in his work *Über den Beweis des Geistes und der Kraft (On the Proof of the Spirit and the Power)* (1777). He held that God had indeed entered the historical process. Such an interpretation would include cultural changes, and we shall see how true this will be with respect to the Christian West as its story unfolds in the following chapters.

## Regarding Apocalypses generally

In contemporary usage, the word 'apocalypse' has two meanings. First of all, it is the name given to the last book of the New Testament, and therefore the last book of the Christian Bible, the work known as the

Revelation of Saint John. But the word has come to mean not only the 'revelation of things secret', but also a widespread final catastrophe, which has become a common usage for this word. In the Christian tradition, astonishing events are expected to usher in the end of the present world and its replacement by a new world to come, or what might be considered the end of history. Apocalypses are promoted during periods of intense change, when a great variety of conditions generate feelings of crisis,[24] and this would include social disorder, persecution, conflicts and wars, plagues, famines and so on.

The Greek word *apokálypsis* means 'unveiling', or the uncovering of what has been hidden. The root is the verb *kalypto*, which means to cover or to hide; the prefix is the preposition *apo* which means 'away or from'. So *apokalypsis* means to take the covering away from that which had previously been secret or hidden, thereby revealing what had previously been invisible. In the ancient world some revelations that were unveiled in an apocalyptic form concerned the heavenly world, but most apocalypses concerned the destiny of this, our temporal, world.

Apocalyptic writing was characterized by descriptions of dreams and visions, apparitions, ecstatic states or heavenly raptures whereby the seer or prophet was shown other-worldly secrets. They were related to everyday life in a variety of ways, as warnings, prophecies, or important encounters with the sacred, and this would carry implications for daily conduct. With respect to their status, it might seem that in them the realities of ordinary existence had been unquestionably abandoned.[25] However, throughout the greater part of human history, and no doubt in New Testament times, these other-worldly 'appearances' were taken quite seriously as realities, albeit of a different kind from daily, waking states. They might be composed of several visions or 'tableaux' which followed one another within a number of parts or sections. Although these were bound to each other by various links, yet they were presented as discrete episodes, and were to be interpreted accordingly.[26] Apocalypses have conventionally been thought to be about history and eschatology, but they would also have consisted of several other components which would be described as epistolary, prophetic, proverbial or liturgical. They would have been written in a narrative which included metaphor, allegory and symbolism, in order to portray religious experiences. Ancient peoples would undoubtedly have ascribed to them a much higher cognitive status than we would today.

### The Environment, Date and Authorship of John's Apocalypse

The origins of the New Testament *Apocrypha*, known as John's Apocalypse cannot be examined without taking into account the status of Christian people under the Roman Empire during the first century of Christianity's existence, a status which was inextricably linked to John's writing. To many Christians at the time, the Empire was considered wicked, with oppression and evil in abundance. From almost the first years of its existence, the church had been regarded as an unpopular Judaic sect without any legal status,[27] but according to Pliny the Younger, a Roman governor writing at about the year 110, there was no empire-wide Roman law, which actually criminalized Christianity. Christianity's principles were misunderstood and membership of the sect could put a person in danger. As a result, the Christian minority found itself the object of continuous suspicion and its members, if denounced to the authorities, were oftentimes persecuted, sometimes punished. Some Christians were killed for their faith. It was precisely this kind of situation at the end of the first century to which John of Patmos responded. His Christian faith could not be reconciled with submission to the Roman authorities of the time, because he believed that God's rule conflicted with the Empire's own political rule. John was attacking the political ideology of the Roman Empire with a view to encouraging the young Christian churches to engage in attacking it as well.

The Christian Church was comprised of a number of communities within the Roman Empire. They considered themselves to be congregations of the elect that had distanced themselves from what they regarded as the contaminating outside world, which meant in practical terms the menacing secular Roman state, and this task long remained an urgent concern among Christian groups. Throughout the Roman Empire, the imperial cult or emperor worship flourished from the time of Caesar Augustus onwards. Indeed, a number of successive emperors, such as Nero, Domitian or Diocletian, assumed the role of a living emperor-God. The Christians' beliefs prohibited them from offering sacrifices to this semi-divine emperor, but such refusal bore a sacrilegious and treasonable flavour, and those who questioned the regime or refused to take part in the imperial cult risked serious trouble. Moreover, the author of the Apocalypse himself, as an itinerant preacher in Asia Minor, must have witnessed at first hand the problems which the Christian community faced there, since few provinces were more intent on celebrating the emperor-cult than this one. Pagans were also suspicious of the Christian refusal to sacrifice to the Roman gods, because they viewed this as an insult to their own gods, and it potentially endangered the Empire which they saw fit to protect.

Pliny the Younger called Christianity a superstition taken to extravagant lengths. Similarly, the historian Publius Tacitus called it a deadly superstition, and the historian Gaius Suetonius called Christians a class of persons given to a new and mischievous superstition. Persecutions tended to be triggered by particular events, or during periods of crisis. Christians as a group were the primary targets for horrible persecution during the reign of the Emperor Nero, for example. In the year 64, a colossal fire broke out in Rome, destroying much of the city. Rumours abounded that Nero himself was responsible. Perhaps to divert attention from himself, Nero ordered that Christians should be rounded up and killed. Some were torn apart by dogs, others burnt alive as human torches.

Christians were not only a growing state within a state but the acknowledgement of God's rule was incompatible with submission to Roman authority, especially its idolatry. What better proof could there be of their seditious nature? It was hardly surprising, therefore, that the early Christian community was an apocalyptic one, with persecution from the Roman state on one side and on the other the eschatological expectation that God would call forth the *perousia* or return of Christ. In early Christian writings, the most violent expression of this perilous situation was reflected in John's Apocalypse.

During the Middle Ages, there was agreement by most commentators that the Apocalypse had been written on the desolate Greek island of Patmos at about the year 70 by Saint John the Divine, the author of the fourth Gospel, also known as the apostle John of Zebedee. The intention was to render the text authoritative as written by the disciple 'whom Jesus loved'. Such attribution, however, went back much further, being accepted by various first- and second-century Fathers of the church, and was partly responsible for the inclusion of the book of

Revelation in the New Testament canon. Even today this attribution is accepted by some scholars, who argue the case for dating the book shortly after Nero's death. Yet the book could not have been written in its present form around the year 68 when Nero died. The identification of Rome with Babylon provides some evidence for settling on a later date. For the most part, this identity occurred after the year 70, when Rome was thenceforth described as Babylon once the Roman army had destroyed Jerusalem and its temple. There is no hint of apostolic authorship in the narrative, and more cogently, it would imply that the apostle composed the work, when he had attained the age of 85 years or more. Additionally, the style, vocabulary, intense language, and theology of the Apocalypse are so different from the Gospel of John that common authorship is improbable. The author's style lacks elegance and he frequently breaks the rules of grammar. From the point of view of eschatology, the apostle John in the fourth Gospel tends to emphasize the present significance of the Christ event in Christian life, whereas the John of the Apocalypse promotes an eschatological atmosphere which is latent in the future events that he is describing.

Some historians maintained that it might have been the crisis resulting from the drastic Roman persecution of Jews and Christians under the Emperor Domitian that encouraged John of Patmos to compose his work. It was in all probability written as a reflection of this crisis, towards the end of Domitian's reign which lasted from the years 89 to 96. Other historians, however, have maintained that there was little or no persecution of Christians during Domitian's reign. Without any consensus on the matter, it would be reasonable to conclude with most historians, when all the evidence has been appraised, that the Apocalypse was written sometime between the years 92 and 96.

Those of the church Fathers who attributed authorship of the fourth Gospel, but not that of the Book of Revelation, to the apostle John, did not consider the writer of the latter book to hold the same status. Contemporary scholars are generally in agreement with this conclusion. The personal identity of the author of the Apocalypse will probably never be known, for the name 'John' was common in the early church. He was in all likelihood an itinerant Christian prophet-teacher, affiliated to the Christian community at Ephesus, in the Roman province of Asia, an area which comprised, approximately, the

Mediterranean coast of present-day Turkey. We shall consider a little more evidence for his peripatetic way of life in chapter 3. The author was clearly a Christian of Jewish and Palestinian origin, because the strange and ungrammatical Greek, in which the book was written, suggests that he normally thought in the Hebrew or Aramaic languages.

Apocalypses were usually written in a fictitious name, or perhaps the name of some illustrious predecessor, but at the start of the Apocalypse, John states his own name. The claim for John was that he was a prophet, and it was on that fact that he claimed his right and authority to speak. He did not call himself an apostle, as Saint Paul did, nor did he appear to have any official or administrative position in the church. He received the message in a series of prophetic dreams and visions of overwhelming power and related his experiences in his book. The only status John claimed for himself was implied in the description of his book as a prophecy.[28]

## A Description of the Book and John's Concerns for it

From among all the texts of the Christian Bible, the Book of Revelation is the most enigmatic and controversial. Martin Luther wrote that Saint Jerome had praised the book highly, but "that there are as many mysteries in it as words."[29] The theologian Arthur Wainwright succinctly stated that although the word *apokalypsis* implies the disclosure of secret truths, John's Apocalypse often seems, on the contrary, to keep them secret![30] The Protestant historian John Bale said of it, "The very complete sum and whole knitting up is this heavenly book of the universal verities of the Bible…He that knoweth not this book, knoweth not what the church is whereof he is a member."[31]

All the books of the New Testament deal with early Christian teaching, with the glaring exception of this one. One must wonder why such a strange piece of writing was included in the New Testament at all, but included it was. This is the only full-length Christian Apocalypse, and the only prophetic book to have been admitted into the Christian canon. What did the church Fathers discern in this book that was so important to them? Some might say that it has no place in the Christian Bible, being included only after some hesitation. Martin Luther also did not accord the Apocalypse the same status as the other books and letters of the New Testament, and even cast doubts as to its suitability to be a book of the Bible at all, stating: "to my mind, it bears upon it no marks of an apostolic or prophetic character."[32] As the last book of the New Testament, the Apocalypse ended the canon in both east and west, but the Eastern churches were even more reluctant to include it at first, and its status with them was subject to debate for some while. It was not until the fifth century that the Greek and Syrian churches recognized it as part of the New Testament, and the Armenians not until the twelfth. Even today, some Christians in the East are unwilling to accept it as part of the Christian canon.[33]

Some commentators held the view that the book assumed only the appearance of Christian writing because its text has been influenced by Old Testament apocalyptic literature. Many early Christians explained the book in this light. For example, there are parallels with Ezekiel's vision and direct quotations from the Book of Daniel. The scholar Robert H. Charles pointed out several parallels from the non-canonical book of Enoch. As a consequence, it has been claimed that the Apocalypse is to a certain extent a product of assimilation.[34] However, many others came to the conclusion that it is a profoundly Christian work throughout. This must have been one of the justifications for its inclusion in the Christian canon.

The seer introduces his work as a 'Revelation of Jesus Christ', which had been communicated to him through Christ's messenger, an angel, and so John was witness to the Word of God. John's book describes symbolically the final events of the Judeo-Christian myth. We encounter a series of visions which are descriptions of a sort, but they do not necessarily imply that they are intended to be actual occurrences. Moreover, the great majority of Christian exegetes have insisted that the Book does not provide us with a chronological outline of future events, for the book is principally concerned with allegory. Moreover, the Christian Church has never really determined the book's significance, and this has unsurprisingly given rise to multifarious interpretations of it. John's aim is to depict events that are about to happen: 'the time is near', and 'what must soon take place', as stated in Revelation 1:3 and 22:6. With these two verses in mind, such a revelatory narrative could not be considered abstractly or as mere allegory, for it concerned the description and meaning of events that were prophesied to happen within actual historical time. Furthermore, there is the inescapable fact that for the Christian community at the time when John wrote his book, the Empire's rule was certainly no mere allegory. On the contrary, imperial rule for the Christians of John's time was oppressive and terrible.

There is the danger that the interpretation being presented in this book might overlook the significance of what it meant to its first readers. John communicated his prophecy to his own contemporaries in the early Christian churches, the only readers he explicitly addressed, as the theologian Richard Bauckham has commented.[35] They could not have profited much from a text if John's concern was exclusively for readers of later periods. He perforce had to write in such terms as they were able to understand. On the other hand, one could contend that any reader of the book, in any era, would have found it one of the most puzzling of all the books of the Bible, not just for ourselves, not just for a medieval scholar, but for the early Christians too. The puzzle is compounded by John's practice of withholding the names of the protagonists in his prophecies, whether it be the 'great harlot', the 'Bride of Christ', the 'Rider on the white horse', the 'hosts of Gog and Magog', or he who sat upon 'a great white throne' in Revelation 20:11. Except for the last-mentioned which is beyond the book's remit, we shall attempt to decipher these distinctive titles as they are encountered and become relevant in the historical text.

John was grappling with what he believed to be a crisis of faith in his own time. The Roman Empire's sovereignty was absolute, and according to John many of its citizens were lured by its deceit and the exploitation of its peoples. He was alerting the Christian churches to their dire situation by exposing this deceit, and was preparing them to participate in the perilous task of censuring the Empire. John wished to proclaim the victory of the Lamb which would put an end to the power of the beast, the false prophet and Satan, and as a result establish God's kingdom upon earth. When he describes the end times, he does not imply that the physical world will come to an end, but rather the cessation of all idolatrous political power.[36]

However, the book would seem to be redundant, unless there was a suspicion that it did deal with future events that were to occur within historical time. The theologian Adolf Harnack put the matter as follows in *Das Wesen des Christentums (The Essence of Christianity)*: "If the

Christian message is inextricably linked with the world-view and cultural assumptions in which it was first transmitted, then it does not belong to our era." He continued: "There are only two possibilities here: either the Gospel is in all respects identical with its earliest form, in which case it came with its time and has departed with it, or else it contains something which, under different historical forms, is of permanent validity."[37] Richard Bauckham signalled his agreement, when he stated that John's prophecies were included in the Christian canon, because their relevance was not restricted just to the Christian communities of the first century, but they held an important message for future readers as well.[38]

John may not have originally intended his book to have any theological pretensions. Nonetheless it does possess a theology, if only in the sense that the thousand-year period, the central object of this study, should be understood as being linked to the *parousia*. This event signifies the destruction of all evil, but it occurs only after the delay of a thousand-year interval, at which time the Devil will share the same fate as the beast and the false prophet, as described in chapter 20 of John's book. Disclosure of this somewhat esoteric message comes through visions which are special revelations that God communicates to John. John's concerns are mainly prophetic and so it would be best to call his work a prophetic apocalypse or an apocalyptic prophecy.[39] John claims that the visions which he experiences come from God, and so the reader must assume that his word is faithful and true. John's intention is to act solely as mediator, with a divine rather than his own impress, so that the visions are described as if they are being communicated directly between God and the reader.[40] Such a task could then be understood as an attempt to enable John's readers, as with John himself, to visualize world history from a divine perspective, and to convey to his readers what the ultimate outcome of history would be.

### The historicist Interpretation

If anyone in our own times had stated that he or she had received prophetic dreams and visions foretelling the history of the world, or a significant part of it, for the next two thousand years, that prophecy would at best be considered preposterous, and at worst utter foolishness. Why should anyone bother to read such a narrative and, *a fortiori*, why should anyone take the writing of such an author seriously? Nevertheless, from the twelfth until the nineteenth century under the influence of Joachim of Fiore, a number of interpreters did indeed treat the Apocalypse as a prophecy of the future course of history.

The author Handley H. Edlin considered that the apocalyptic narrative spans the entire history of the Christian church,[41] and this book will interpret the Apocalypse as a forecast of Western history, in which the claim is made that such history has unfolded to a surprising degree in the manner which John of Patmos prophesied in his apocalyptic narrative. Such an analysis must be considered an unashamedly historicist position. Put succinctly, the present work is therefore the history of Western society told in a particular way, with the aim of mapping events in its history to the later chapters of John's Apocalypse. Sir Isaac Newton was convinced that the prophecies of Scripture are nothing else than 'histories of things to come'.[42] One must search for a conclusive answer to the question as to whether the facts of history really do parallel in some way the prophecies narrated in the Apocalypse. Clearly, for the theory to work, there must be a good correspondence between John of Patmos' prophecies and actual events in Western history. The question, though, remains, how much should we expect? One would not hope, perhaps, for there to be a complete agreement, for, after all, the author John of Patmos was writing many centuries before the events which he describes were to occur.

The *New English Bible* demarcates the book of Revelation into various sections. Chapters 14 to 22 are sub-titled *Visions of the End* of which chapters 17 to 20 form the subject of our scrutiny. In this part of John's book, the historical mode appears to be in the ascendant, encompassing the downfall of Rome, the descent of the 'Word of God', the thousand years, and lastly the period, or season, when Satan is let loose from the abyss. The fall of Rome paved the way for the emergence of Western civilization, which in turn led into the thousand-year period. However, allegorical imagery and historical prophecy are so intertwined, that it is often difficult to discern what is being described, and the problem is how to extricate the one from the other. The task is to ascertain whether actual historical events do fit the prophecy, not only with respect to the downfall of the ancient world, but also to the emergence and eventual triumph of the Christian West, and the ensuing chapters will make this clearer. This period signified the civilization of the West for Arnold Toynbee, the culture of the West for Oswald Spengler.

We have discussed the notion that Providence preordained the course of human history, of which the most important and central event was the life and ministry of Jesus Christ. Earlier events, which R.G. Collingwood called periods of darkness, prepared for it, and later events developed from it. Further sub-divisions would divide history into epochs, each having peculiar characteristics of its own and each being marked off with an event which may itself, for want of a better term, be called a pivotal point in history.[43] Thus, it will be demonstrated that the culture of the Christian West can be demarcated as starting around the year 800 and ending around the year 1800, thereby lasting for a thousand years. Whether we consider only the symbolism of these two actual dates, or the vitally important historical changes which occurred within periods of about two generations prior to these two dates, the reader cannot fail to note that the thousand-year period stands out in a remarkable and conspicuous way.

Immediately there will be protests. Some readers will maintain that even where the course of events in Western history appeared to correspond with John's text to some extent, the similarity is entirely fortuitous, superficial or coincidental. Others will make the objection that any selection of historical events in Western history would be arbitrary and must have been distorted to underpin the thesis. Yet others will maintain that many of John's descriptions in the later chapters are described in too broad an outline to be really meaningful for the purpose of historical comparisons. Additionally, allegory in John's book has been intertwined to such an extraordinary degree with prophecy as to make any analysis on the lines stated impossible or unfeasible. Christian believers and exegetes will say that the Apocalypse itself cannot be read or studied in such a manner and the book cannot be treated as an actual historical prophecy. The central core or message of the Apocalypse is being overlooked or marginalized. It is a mystery and should remain so. Such a view fiercely conflicts with the opinion of Sir Isaac Newton, who was a theologian as well as a scientist. He stated that "if (these prophecies) are never to be understood, to what end did God reveal them?" It must surely be maintained that God's communication of prophecies to John of Patmos was an act that made no sense unless their meaning could ultimately be deciphered. Additionally, there would, after all, be no point in formulating, or indeed for others to heed a prophecy of future events, unless there was some strong supposition that they would eventually occur.

Another possible objection is encountered with R.G. Collingwood, who maintained that the past cannot be understood by theological thinking, because it has as its subject matter a single infinite object, whereas events in history are finite and plural.[44] In opposition to this, the Christian idea of fulfilment and salvation enables history to be interpreted in a theological manner.[45] Moreover, the nature of the present book entails that this enterprise will concern not only historical analysis, for it will become apparent that the subject matter virtually amounts to a theology itself, and so a theologizing exposition cannot be avoided.

### Commentaries on, and Interpretations of, the Apocalypse

Work on the Apocalypse was spread widely throughout the early church, and provided a basis for future interpretations of its text, as well as establishing it as a separate book. It retained some appeal for the Christian church during its early struggles, but when the church had become an accepted institution of the Roman Empire, the book seemed no longer to have any relevance to the church's situation, and was to a certain extent considered eccentric.[46] The earliest interpreters explained the Apocalypse in relation to the Roman Empire's contemporary persecution of Christian communities, but after Constantine's conversion to Christianity, commentators linked the book's narrative to history only in a general way. Commentaries on the text of the Apocalypse were first written by Hippolytus of Rome early in the third century in Rome, and by Saint Victorinus, bishop of Pruj (Pettau) in Slovenia, whose text was edited in a new version by Saint Jerome. Later came the late fourth century commentary of the North African Donatist writer Tyconius. In the sixth century Saint Caesarius, archbishop of Arles, wrote eighteen homilies on the Apocalypse which together constituted a treatise. Primasius, bishop of Hadrumetum in North Africa, also wrote an influential commentary.

When considering the relationship between John's prophecies and historical events, a major area of disagreement between commentators arose. The crucial question was, should the Apocalypse be interpreted literally or spiritually? In the early centuries, a literal interpretation prevailed. Papias of Hieropolis, Justin Martyr, Saint Irenaeus and the second-century church father Quintus Tertullian all believed that the first six verses of chapter 20 prophesied Christ's earthly kingdom which would follow His second coming, and which would last a thousand years. They were called Chiliasts from the Greek *khilias*, meaning 'thousand'. Origen of Alexandria, on the contrary, interpreted these prophecies figuratively,[47] an interpretation that was also apparent in the works of Tyconius, who considered the Apocalypse as the struggle between good and evil in relation to the history of the church.

It was Saint Augustine in the fifth century who acted as an intermediary between the two opposing views, but he indicated that Jesus' forthcoming ministry should be interpreted in a figurative manner. He often commented on texts from the Apocalypse in other works, stating that from chapter 20 the thousand years would indeed become the Age of the Church, to be followed by Christ's second coming. As the crises which had assailed the church in its early years had now come to an end, he considered that the church's success was itself the commencement of the thousand years ruled by Christ from heaven.

The Venerable Bede relied heavily on his predecessors' interpretations, sometimes incorporating Saint Augustine's commentaries, but he made an original contribution by dividing the Apocalypse into seven parts. Later, in the ninth century, the monk Berengaud explained the book as a narrative of the whole of history from the creation until the *parousia*. From Bede's day onwards the Apocalypse had a growing impact on Western Christianity's formative centuries. Many commentaries appeared, their numbers increasing after the end of the eleventh century. Some of the important ones were written by the mendicant friars, who considered the book to be suitable as a prophetic narrative for their own missions. An anonymous Wycliffite commentary served much the same purpose. One work considered pertinent for the book's exegesis, which had much influence though not an actual commentary, was produced by Adso of Montier-en-Der *De Ortu et Tempore Antichrist (On the Origins and Timing of the Antichrist)* (949-954). In the twelfth century and thereafter, the Apocalypse began to be translated into the many national languages that were developing in Europe.[48]

Although Saint Augustine's views continued to find support throughout this period, at the end of the twelfth century the theologian Joachim of Fiore produced one of the most remarkable and distinctive contributions to the study of the Apocalypse that seriously modified Saint Augustine's account. He conceived a new interpretation of the thousand years that assigned a terrestrial reign for Christ under the direct inspiration of the Holy Spirit. Such a view came to be described as the 'church-historical' interpretation, which linked the apocalyptic narrative to the major events of the church. He used the principle of recapitulation in which the various prophecies in the Apocalypse referred to the same event. Significantly for our present thesis, his exposition of the later chapters of Apocalypse led him to a further innovation. He was the first to propose that, following an earthly millennium, Satan would be released once more for a final assault.[49] The immediate result of his work was the rapid growth of the belief that the Apocalypse could be regarded as a prediction of the course of history, and this would later engender the widespread expectation that a future millennium would actually occur. Such an interpretation became influential throughout Europe. Furthermore, his teaching on the dawning of the new age of the Spirit was said to have prepared the way for the Enlightenment's confidence in historical progress in the eighteenth and nineteenth centuries.

Following Joachim of Fiore's work, interpretations emerged that continued to treat the Apocalypse as a chart of the course of history, but a new method came into popularity. The Franciscan commentator Alexander the Minorite in the thirteenth century rejected Joachim's principle of recapitulation and replaced it with an explanation that treated historical development as linear and continuous by connecting the prophecies with historical events in a chronological sequence. During the later Middle Ages, Peter Aureolus and John Wycliffe adopted this approach, and its most famous exponent was the Franciscan Nicholas of Lyra. All these commentators claimed that the book prophesied events from New Testament times until their own particular era, whenever that happened to be.[50] From the fourteenth century onward this church-historical, or historicist, method, whether the principle of recapitulation was accepted or not, dominated interpretations of the Apocalypse. During the Reformation this idea continued to win adherents among both Protestants and Catholics. Martin Luther accepted the historicist approach by interpreting the Apocalypse as a book which concerned the future. One major reason for this was that he considered that Satan was about to be unleashed upon the world, and that Christ would come in judgment. Thus, in his *Vorrede zur Offenbarung Johannes* (*Preface to the Revelation of John*) written in 1522,[51] he read into this book the history of Christianity, and in so doing, set the pattern for all Protestant readings of the Apocalypse until the nineteenth century.

The millennial worldview remained popular amongst Protestants after the Reformation, and in these conceptions of the Apocalypse, sacred and secular history became intermixed, thereby bestowing on the book a prestige which it had not previously enjoyed.[52] In 1508 Albrecht Dürer finished producing fifteen graphic illustrations using an engraving process for an edition of the Book of Revelation. One of these illustrations is depicted on the front cover. Thenceforth, John's apocalyptic visions had an undeniable fascination for European intellectuals throughout the sixteenth, seventeenth and eighteenth centuries, which included interpretations of the book of Daniel. Between 1498 and 1650 over 750 editions of the text or commentaries on the Apocalypse were published, and it remained central to the faith of a learned cleric.[53] Jacques Bossuet believed that one of the ways in which one could understand the Apocalypse was the moral issue, which Saint Augustine had expounded. This alone, however, would not have been sufficient to have ranked John of Patmos among the prophets. His work could be treated as a genre of prophetic literature only by the knowledge which was imparted to him to predict future things and in particular what was soon to happen both in the early church and in the Roman Empire.[54] Those commentators such as Joseph Priestley, Edward Bickersteth, and Thomas Birks, who expected Christ to return at the beginning of the millennium, also treated the book as a prediction of the course of history, and were described as premillennialists, a term that we shall meet later.

Many and wondrous have been the subsequent chosen time-frames during which the millennium was supposed to have taken place. Martin

Luther said that the thousand-year period began about the time that the Apocalypse was written, and ended with the rise of the Turks.[55] In his book *The Ruin of Rome* (1798), the Anglican Arthur Dent averred that it began during Christ's ministry and therefore ended in the tenth century.[56] The sixteenth-century Calvinist scholar Franciscus Junius the Elder maintained that it also extended from the time of Christ until Pope Gregory VII, who reigned 1073-1085. The martyrologist John Foxe declared that the millennium itself lasted from the time of the Emperor Constantine the Great until the time of John Wycliffe,[57] and for the Czech philosopher Jan Huss it lasted until the Ottoman Empire began to threaten Europe. When that time had passed, the enemy was progressively let loose to seduce the church into error. Then in the time of the Reformation, the Devil was definitively cast out of the church. Foxe's partisan reading of the Apocalypse entailed difficulties with chronology and hermeneutics, but it did not prevent this view from becoming influential. In his publication *Succession and State of the Christian Churches* (1613), James Ussher set out to prove what was almost the same point, but was more meticulous with regard to the calculation of dates. In his book *A Paraphrase and Notes on the Revelation of St. John* (1737), Moses Lowman developed an influential following by maintaining that the Apocalypse predicted events in church history chronologically. John Napier, the inventor of logarithms, the biblical commentator Thomas Brightman and the scholar Johann Bengel even suggested that there were two distinct millennia, the first one having a similar timescale to Foxe's scheme, and the second one being either the eternal reign of the saints or the life of the church on earth. Lutherans in Germany worked the Apocalypse into their vision of church history. The historian Johannes Lampadius divided up the Christian era in terms of the prophecy of the seven trumpets in chapters 8 and 9 of the Apocalypse. Sir Isaac Newton employed the church-historical method in explaining prophecies that he believed to be fulfilled, but wisely refused to make conjectures about the future. God, he argued, did not intend people to reach a complete understanding of His prophecies until after the events which they predicted.[58]

Much energy continued to be expended on prophetic activity during the seventeenth century, for the most part caused by the devastation wreaked upon Central Europe during the Thirty Year's War. The belief in a future millennium became even more popular in Protestantism, and those that championed the Apocalypse treated it synoptically as church history. The Calvinist Johann Alsted wrote a treatise with a millenarian interpretation *Diatribe de mille Annis Apolyptica (Diatribe of the thousand Years of the Apocalypse)* (1627) that was among the most influential of works. Millenarianism now became firmly entrenched, and attracted Protestants in England, Germany, the Netherlands, and amongst French Huguenots. According to several scholars, Johann Bengel was the person most responsible for reviving chiliasm amongst scholars in Germany in the eighteenth century, and he insisted that the thousand years of Revelation, depicted in chapter 20 should be taken literally.

In the mid-nineteenth century a group of German scholars launched a last-ditch defence of the church-historical approach. Sometimes known as 'kingdom history', the Apocalypse was considered to be predicative of the main periods of history. Its most important exponent was the theologian Ernst Hengstenberg, a professor at the University of Berlin from 1826 onwards and a Lutheran pastor. Historians and theologians had previously positioned their 'apocalyptic moment' at different eras, for example, the invention of printing, the scientific revolution of the seventeenth century, the Enlightenment, the French Revolution or even the Liberal movement of the nineteenth century. Most intriguingly for the thesis in this present book, Ernst Hengstenberg adopted a different scheme by dating the start of the thousand years of John's Apocalyptic narrative at the year 800. He cautions his readers, however, that we cannot in all truth "historically point out with precision the thousand years, and we must satisfy ourselves with being able to fix on a period that somewhat nearly corresponds to it".[59] This scheme was identical to the one presently being adopted, and one which has remained ignored or buried for over one hundred and seventy years.

With the triumph of the eighteenth-century Enlightenment, the popularity of this type of literature began to wane, and it gradually became recognized as a refuge for the eccentric or the artist.[60] It was administered a severe setback when conservative Protestants reinstated the theory of Futurism under the initiative of the Spanish commentator and archbishop Saint Juan de Ribera, who asserted that most of the John's apocalyptic writing dealt with the future.[61] It was left to the proponents of historical criticism in the nineteenth century finally to banish the church-historical interpretation from academic circles.

The historicist theory has had supporters amongst later authors, who have interpreted the Apocalypse in a broadly similar way and such views can indeed make the book meaningful for our times. The theologian Alexander Bukharev created an interpretation which was a product of Eastern Christian and Slavophile mythology. He believed that it placed the Orthodox Church at the centre of world history. His main argument was that, once again, the Apocalypse concerned the course of human history and was therefore comprehensible to human beings. For him, chapters 15 to 20 prophesy events which were beginning to unfold in his own time. He emphatically compared the whore of Babylon in Revelation, chapter 17, with the Turkish Empire which the Slavic East will destroy. Considering how contrived this arrangement was, it is hardly surprising that his book has provoked vigorous criticism![62]

The philosopher Rudolf Steiner, the psychologist Carl Jung and his disciple Edward Edinger have offered psychological and anthropocentric explanations. Emmett O'Regan, as a result of studying a prophetic vision experienced by Pope Leo XIII in 1884, has concluded significantly that, given the prevailing situation, the millennium or the age of the church has come to an end and that Satan and his forces have been let loose. The religious educator Beatrice Neall adopted an historicist position because she also viewed the Apocalypse as an outline of the course of history.[63] With such an auspicious list of interpretations, we can only remonstrate that it would seem appropriate to perform a similar task of deciphering John's text, but now employing the fruits of modern historical research.

\* \* \* \* \* \* \* \*

John's Apocalypse may therefore be considered as a series of prophecies concerning the course of history, both as a forecast of the future and about the meaning of certain events that were to occur within historical time. When the events recorded in the Bible are corroborated by history, it gives them a far greater degree of credibility. The Revelation of John, as Alexander Bukharev understood it, draws aside the curtains on this historical drama. We have described the long tradition in the church-historical approach to the Apocalypse, and these interpretations all claimed that the book in some way provided a map of history from the Christ-event onwards. However, some scholars, in rejecting this tradition and with it the theory that it predicts church history, maintain that the prophecies of the Book of Revelation relate to events that happened during the first century, namely the early years of the church. These scholars are oftentimes called Preterists from the Latin word 'praeter', meaning beyond or past. Modern historical critics are close in their outlook to this group, since they examine the Apocalypse only in the light of the situation in which it was written. They consider that its contents are not prophetic at all, but reflect symbolically those events which have already taken place. Yet another group hold what is called the futurist interpretation, and these commentators maintain that most of the visions are concerned with the last days. According to this view, the text of the Apocalypse refers to events around the return of Christ, which will occur sometime, or eventually, in the future. Finally, there was the idealistic or symbolic viewpoint, which considered the Apocalypse to refer symbolically to the 'conflict of good and evil' in any age, at any time, and is not really a part of history at all.[64] We shall meet similar variations on these themes later when considering the various millennial approaches to the Apocalypse.

Leaving aside for a moment the book's probable prediction of the course of history, it undoubtedly illustrates God's involvement in human affairs.[65] It sustained the Western concept of time, in which the meaning of history was defined linearly in terms of its relationship to eternity. There runs through the whole book an expectation that the end will come quickly. In Revelation 1:3 and 22:10, the usage of the word *kairos* is understood as meaning near at hand. In both places the word signifies the end of world history and the sudden onset of God's kingdom. The concept of an existence outside of time is totally foreign to the book.

We cannot meddle with John's prophecies, but we can alter how we envisage historical events by means of new perspectives regarding the way that history has progressed. This is indeed the metier of the historian. The present work is not primarily designed as a biblical exegesis, nor as an historical textbook, but perhaps should be considered as a European, and Christian, 'meta-history'. Contrariwise, we should perhaps turn the thesis on its head and say that the course of Western history followed a trajectory extraordinarily similar to that outlined in the Apocalypse. In the ensuing chapters we shall map the historical events of the West together with John's prophecy to ascertain what correspondences can be achieved between the two. In this modern age we can survey the events which occurred subsequent to the thousand years, as well as take advantage of modern historical research, advantages which previous exponents of the church-historical thesis would not have had.

It has been said that the book of Revelation is 'a theology of power', albeit power exercised in love, for it is the slain Lamb who triumphs, and that power has been, and will continue to be, exercised through history. In his essay *Idee zu einer allgemeinen Geschichte in weltbürgerlicher Absicht (Idea for a universal History with a cosmopolitan Purpose)* (1784), Immanuel Kant argued that Nature or Providence might be construed as unravelling a hidden plan in history as a result of which humanity would be raised from the 'Dark Ages' to an illumination or enlightenment.

CHAPTER TWO

*Ten barbarian Kingdoms of the West*

JOHN OF Patmos condemns the Roman Empire and everything that it represents. He considers it to be oppressive and describes it as a harlot. In Revelation 17:3 he writes: "I saw a woman sitting on a scarlet beast which was full of blasphemous names," and that she ruled over its citizens by means of sorcery and deception. She represents the city as the mistress and centre of the Empire. For almost a century after the Apocalypse was written, the Empire continued to rule as a mighty power, and indeed, it was not long after John's text was written that it reached the zenith of its territorial expansion under the Emperor Trajan in 117, when Dacia and Mesopotamia were added to its territory. This situation lasted until the death of Emperor Marcus Aurelius in 180. A period of war, disorder and instability followed, and the Empire's decline may be said to begin at this date.

Our historical survey begins at Revelation 13:3, which describes the beast with a mortal wound on one of its seven heads, but which had healed. Richard Bauckham suggested that this verse might allude to the tumultuous and chaotic events in the year 69 which threatened the Empire's survival, but from which it managed to recover.[1] Chapter 16 refers to seven plagues, which might correspond to the epidemics which were reputed to have hit Rome in the second century, and in which large numbers of people perished. The severe and protracted Antonine plague, also known as the plague of Galen, started around 165. For about twenty years, waves of one or more diseases, including possibly the first ever outbreaks of smallpox and measles, swept through the Empire. Epidemics of a similar nature occurred in the third century.

Revelation 16:19 states: "The great city was split into three parts." We can consider this statement in several ways with respect to Rome. A geographical split in late antiquity came to reflect the huge difference between life along the frontiers of the Empire and that centred around the Mediterranean. As a second possibility, it might strain credulity to compare this statement with Arnold Toynbee's description of civilizations in decline. Their populations fragment into three elements: a dominant minority or the elites, an internal proletariat or the masses, and an external proletariat.[2] In the case of the Roman Empire, the latter would refer to the barbarian tribes which had long been amassing along its borders, and which became increasingly threatening as time progressed. For Toynbee, a civilization declines at the point when the elites, in the case of the Roman Empire the patrician class, no longer command the support of its masses, and cease to lead effectively. The masses become estranged from their leaders, and the latter then employ force to maintain their authority as a substitute for their erstwhile attractive power. The eventual downfall of that society is often aggravated by the aggression of the external proletariat.[3] Whether such an eccentric explanation is viable in John's description of Rome, this triple division is the first hint in the Apocalypse that the downfall of the Empire was going to be anything but peaceful.

John does indeed predict the fall of the Empire, although the reasons for this have been debated many times by historians. Of this event, the seer could not have had any knowledge apart from the revelation that he received. Indeed, if any Roman citizen had disseminated such seditious ideas, he or she would have put themselves at risk of incurring serious trouble with the Roman authorities. John takes the step therefore of referring to the Empire indirectly by various lurid descriptions, for example in Revelation 17:5, "Babylon the great, mother of harlots, and of earth's abominations." It is generally agreed amongst biblical exegetes that such descriptions are indeed that of the Roman Empire.

In John's narrative, the second half of chapter 17 depicts the end of the Empire, and we shall discover that his descriptions were astonishingly accurate when placed against the historical chronology of events as they unfolded. Apart from calling her a harlot, John further obliquely describes Rome as the 'scarlet beast' which had seven heads, a reference to the seven hills on which the woman is seated, a clear allusion to the seven hills of the city of Rome. He continues with a brief description of seven kings in Revelation 17:10, whose identity has caused speculation. They may relate to seven Roman emperors, to seven civilizations or empires, or to seven forms of Roman government. Whatever may be the case, our story begins with the barbarian tribes, peoples that would eventually develop for themselves significant roles in Western European society.

In referring to ten horns or kings in chapter 17, John employs an Old Testament prophecy from the Book of Daniel.[4] He is using this as an analogy, or a form of symbolism to describe the fate that the Empire would ultimately suffer. The kings could refer to the ten territories over which the Emperor Constantine ruled, or the phrase could be interpreted as ten Roman emperors. Furthermore, John describes two beasts in chapter 13. The first arose from the sea and represents the imperial powers. The second arose from the earth and set up an image of the first beast for the people to worship. For John the first beast represents the Roman establishment, the second represents the message.[5] The epithet beast might justly apply, not only to the religion practised within the Empire, but also to the paganism practised by the barbarian tribes living beyond its borders or *limes*.

### The barbarian Tribes are the 'ten Horns' of John's Prophecy

Alternatively, the phrase ten 'horns' could refer to the barbarian tribes that invaded the Empire and eventually established successor kingdoms on Roman territory. Originally, for reasons of size alone, they would hardly have formed kingdoms, for they would have comprised groups of families. They were, for the most part, peoples of long standing, with their own traditions; they were barbarians not savages.[6] Compared with the peoples of many ancient empires, even to describe them as barbarian would hardly apply, for many were farmers. In the course of time many of these tribes formed alliances or confederacies with other tribes, and certain it was that from the middle of the third century onwards they posed an ever more serious threat to the Empire. John describes the ten horns as this very same threat, and which are referred to in Revelation 17:12 as ten kings. It would be hazardous at best to identify the ten horns or kings mentioned by John with the barbarian tribes of late Antiquity were it not for further apocalyptic text, namely, verses 12-14 of chapter 17, in which John provides fuller descriptions of their roles and activities. We can interpret these descriptions as criteria that makes identification with them feasible.

For the first criterion there must be ten kings, or a number approximating to ten, since the ten horns of John's prophecy should represent the kingdoms which eventually established their rule on the Empire's territory. As with the Roman emperors, the ten were not as yet kings for their time was yet to come. Secondly, they must oftentimes have participated in, or co-operated with, the Empire's government.

The description of the kings given by John in Revelation 17:12-13 is apposite, and states: "And the ten horns that you saw are ten kings, who have not yet received royal power, but they are to receive authority as kings for one hour, together with the beast." Instead of receiving their power and authority *from* the beast, as we might expect, they give their power and authority *to* the beast. The third criterion, specified in Revelation 17:14 is that the kings will "make war on the Lamb, and the Lamb will conquer them." The Lamb does not fight or wage war in the world by physical force of arms, but conquers by the Word of God. Furthermore, the kings themselves cannot be overthrown at this point, since the Apocalypse states a little later that it is they who will destroy the Empire, for, fourthly, they will make war on the Empire, dismembering it to the point of annihilation.

### Early History of the barbarian Tribes

To identify John's ten kings with ten barbarian tribes is a complex matter because there were originally a great number of them living beyond the *limes* of the Empire. Over 300 have been identified. They varied greatly in size, and even the larger tribes mentioned in Roman sources were confederacies with limited permanency, since new groupings would arise from time to time as a result of fresh military strategies.[7] It becomes apparent, after perusing relevant texts, that the same tribal names crop up continually in their conflicts with the Empire, namely, Salian Franks, Ripuarian Franks, Ostrogoths, Visigoths, Vandals, Alans, Burgundians, Suebi, Alemanni, Lombards, Huns, Heruli, Saxons, Frisians and Thuringii.

The Frankish tribe was the most important. It embraced at first several small groups, mentioned in the Augustan *Historia*, and the term has also been found in primary sources of other Roman authors and Saint Gregory of Tours.[8] They lived initially north of the river Rhine delta, and north of the *limes* of Roman Gaul, which itself also ran along the Rhine. They were divided into the Salian and Ripuarian branches. The Salians consisted of elements of tribes which had formerly lived between the Rhine and the Ijsselmeer (present-day Netherlands). Their territory extended eastwards as far the river Weser. The Ripuarians originally lived on the right bank of the Rhine, later known as Franconia. They, too, had coalesced from a few smaller tribes, and were recorded for the first time around the year 50 when they invaded the Empire across the Rhine, being mentioned as both allies and enemies (*laeti and dediticii*).

They eventually established themselves among the urban peoples living on the left bank of the Rhine.

The Ostrogoths and Visigoths were branches of the nomadic tribes of Germanic peoples referred to collectively as the Goths. Roman sources employed the terms 'Vesi', the Latin for Visigoths or 'Tervingi', and 'Austrogothi', the Latin for Ostrogoths or 'Greutungi'. They were divided into these two large blocks from the end of the third century, and thereafter they were considered as separate tribes. The Visigoths, or western branch, were most likely derived from the Gutones, possibly originating from Scandinavia. The vast majority of them settled between the rivers Oder and Vistula until, according to legend, overpopulation forced them to move south and east, where they settled north of the Black Sea. The Ostrogoths, as the eastern branch, migrated southward from the Baltic Sea in the third and fourth centuries. They established a kingdom on the shores of the Black Sea between the rivers Don and Dniester. Some of them continued migrating into what is now Romania, which brought them into proximity with Dacia, the only province of the Roman Empire situated on the north bank of the Danube.

The Vandals were an East Germanic group of tribes, divided in the second century into two tribal groups, the Silingi and the Hasdingi. who first enter the historical records in the second century as living in Silesia. The Hasdingi branch moved south from the second century onwards into the lower Danubian area. The Vandals were attacked by the Goths and migrated to Pannonia (approximately present-day Austria) and western Dacia, where about 330 Constantine the Great granted them permission to settle. The Alans were an Iranian nomadic pastoral people. They migrated westwards in the first century and settled in the region north of the Black Sea by the early second century. The Burgundians were a large East Germanic group of tribes of Scandinavian origin but were believed to have emigrated to the Baltic island of Bornholm. By the end of the fourth century, they appeared in the Vistula basin. The Suebi were also divided into many distinct tribes, according to Roman authors, occupying a substantial portion of Germania in or near what is present-day Hessen, and some moved from the areas around the Baltic Sea and the Elbe, again becoming a threat to the Empire on its Rhenish and Danubian frontiers.

The Alemanni also probably constituted a loosely-knit confederation of smaller tribes. They originated from the upper Rhine and were first mentioned by Roman authors in 213, for in that year they came into conflict with the Empire, somewhere between the Danube and Elbe, and they later expanded into Alsace, northern Switzerland and the Austrian Vorarlberg. The Lombards descended from a small Germanic tribe called the Winnili who dwelt in southern Scandinavia before migrating, according to the Lombard historian Paul the Deacon in his work the *Historia Langobardorum (History of the Lombards)* (790s). In the mid-second century, they appeared in the Rhineland. Claudius Ptolemy mentions the 'Laccobardi' to the north of the Suebian territories, indicating a Lombard expansion from the Elbe to the Rhine. The Herules, or Heruli, believed to have originated in Scandinavia, lived north of the Black Sea near the Sea of Azov, in the third century. They were mentioned by Pliny the Elder, and later moved to central Europe on the Danube.

The Huns were a group of nomadic people who first appeared in Europe from east of the river Volga, with a migration intertwined with the Alans. In the second century, they migrated from the Caspian Sea to the south-eastern area of the Caucasus. The Saxons are believed to have originated in Albingia, which is approximately present-day Holstein. Some Saxons raided and settled in Britain during these centuries, but many remained in continental Europe. They were organized into loose, and changing, confederacies of warrior bands, combining with other groups as the need arose. The Frisians lived in what is now part of the Netherlands, being noted occasionally in the accounts of Roman wars against the tribes living in the region. The Thuringii or Toringi did not appear in the historical records until late in the fourth century, occupying the Harz Mountains of central Germania, still called Thuringia. They seemed eventually to have acquired an extensive kingdom from the Elbe to the Danube by the sixth century.

Many commentators, such as Saint Jerome and Saint Gregory of Tours, Pliny the Elder, Julius Caesar, and Publius Tacitus, recorded a multitude of lesser tribes. Most of the these lived on the fringes of the Empire, and when they crossed the frontier or fought the Roman armies, they did so in collaboration with the larger tribes. Many were absorbed by other tribes, thereby losing their identity, and the moves towards larger federations occurred especially during the third century, for example, the Gepids, Rugii, Dacians, or Carpi, Sarmatians, Scirii, Valagoths, Dani, Suiones, Gotlanders, Varangians, but they were minor players, or non-players, in the saga of the 'decline and fall' of the Empire.

Mention should be made at this juncture of the series of wars between Rome and the Parthian empire, which lasted for over 250 years, and posed a huge threat to the Empire's eastern provinces. It would certainly have appeared to John and his contemporaries that these conflicts would be destined to cause Rome's eventual downfall. Therefore, we might expect that John would mention such an empire in his prophecies, but he does not. The Persian dynasty of the Sassanids succeeded the Parthian empire from the 220s onwards. Equally powerful, aggressive and well organized, they pushed back the Roman army from the Euphrates and from parts of Armenia and southeast Turkey, causing some concern in Rome and Constantinople. According to the British diplomat Robert Cooper in his book *The Breaking of Nations* (2003), it was not this empire either that brought about the fall of Rome, but the Germanic barbarians. Similarly, Ernst Hengstenberg stated that we must think solely of the Germanic tribes as having contributed to Rome's ultimate downfall,[9] and so John's prophecy in this respect is completely vindicated.

### Incursions of the barbarian Tribes into the Roman Empire

Barbarian incursions into the Empire's territory led to the eventual establishment of successor kingdoms upon Roman territory with or without the consent of the Roman authorities. Tribes had been in contact with Rome from at least the third century B.C. Even before Caesar's time, they had crossed the Rhine into northern Gaul, and warfare along this frontier occurred so frequently that the Roman government came to the conclusion that the barbarians posed a dire threat. In addition, the establishment of a firm Roman boundary on the lower Danube established a barrier which disrupted the ancient migration of peoples.[10]

From the first century onwards, tribes caused turmoil by amassing in strength along the Empire's *limes*. In the middle of the second century, conflict broke out on the middle Danubian frontier involving many barbarian peoples. The ensuing Macromannic wars provided a portent of future incursions. What is now called the 'Great Migrations', a sudden irruption, began during the first half of the third century, but it is still largely uncertain what drove the barbarian tribes forward. John's text states in Revelation 17:17: "for God has put it into their hearts to carry out his purpose by being of one mind and giving over their royal power to the beast, until the words of God shall be fulfilled." Henry Sheldon wrote that it may be as if they were called by God to hasten toward the risen light of Christianity.[11] On a more prosaic note, they may have been displaced from their lands under pressure from other migratory tribes, such as the Tartars or Magyars from Southern Russia or by the Huns from Central Asia, forcing those tribes living on the Empire's *limes* to risk full-scale immigration into the Empire. Other reasons might include overpopulation or an economic motive which aimed to participate in the Empire's wealth.

A Frankish confederation probably began to coalesce in the 230s leading to the first bout of prolonged incursions when the Salian Franks made their first serious foray into Roman territory. The Empire was unprepared for this event. In 257 the Franks crossed the Rhine, and penetrated as far as Tarraco (present-day Tarragona) in Spain, plaguing this region for about a decade before they were expelled. Incursions continued so frequently that in 288 the Emperor Maximian launched a successful military campaign against them. To exert control, he settled some of them in Germania Inferior, roughly present-day Belgium, as the first Germanic tribe to settle permanently on the Empire's territory. In 297 the remaining Franks were settled on the island of Batavia at the mouth of the Rhine, where they were able to control the river Scheldt, and disrupt transport links to Britain. Although Roman forces managed to pacify them, they failed to expel them, and the Franks continued to be feared as pirates for some decades. In 358 the Emperor Julian the Apostate permitted their settlement in Toxandria, (approximately present-day Noord-Brabant and Antwerp).[12] Other Franks, from Moguntiacum (present-day Mainz) to Duisburg, carried out raids across the Rhine and acquired the name Ripuarians, or 'river people'. Both branches remained distinct until the Frankish leader Clovis I united them in the sixth century.

The Alemanni took advantage of the Empire's troubles to launch devastating raids on the its Rhenish *limes* for over twenty years commencing in 233, and they occupied areas of south-western Germany between the Rhine, Danube and Main in about 260, to include Alsace and the northern Alps.[13] They launched a major invasion of Gaul and northern Italy in 268, in which they were routed and forced back into Germany in a battle near Lake Benacus (present-day Lake Garda). Their most famous battle against the Empire took place at Strasbourg in 357, when they were defeated by the Emperor Julian.[14] Around 366 to 370, they yet again crossed the frozen river Rhine in large numbers to invade Gaul, this time being defeated at the Battle of Solicinium by Emperor Valentinian.

In 286 Claudius Mamertinus recorded the Emperor Maximian's victory over a group of Heruli who attacked Gaul. In the 270s, along with the Goths the Heruli attacked Greece from the Black Sea, and plundered the Southern Balkans. In the late third century the Burgundians, having migrated westwards towards the Roman *limes* along the Rhine valley, moved with the Suebi into the Agri Decumates (present-day Swabia). It was the Goths that became the object of such dread that Roman emperors were obliged to make peace with them by the expedient of paying tribute. They invaded southward across the Danube from the Baltic Sea into the Roman province of Moesia in 238, and built up an empire stretching from the Black Sea to the Baltic. Overpopulation led to the settlement of these tribes, including the Heruli, within the Roman province of Dacia around 260. They caused a trail of destruction which led to their defeat and reduction to client status in 332. A war in the years 367-369 did result finally in pacification.

A terrifying new enemy now appeared on the scene. During their migrations, the Huns had subjugated the Alans, and both tribes plundered Gothic settlements in 376. During the Goths' flight, one of their leaders, Fritigern from the Tervingi tribe, appealed to the Roman Emperor Valens to allow his people to gain refuge on the other, south, bank of the Danube. Valens agreed, but in due course, the local administrators were unwilling either to relieve a famine or to release land which the Goths had been promised. Open revolt led to six years of plundering and destruction throughout the Balkans. At the decisive battle of Adrianople in 378 a large Roman army was slaughtered, and Valens was killed.[15] This was the first shock to the Roman world and forced the Romans to negotiate peace. In 395 the Huns began their first large-scale attack, but at the end of 398 a force composed of Romans and Goths succeeded in restoring peace.[16]

The death of Emperor Theodosius in 395 and succession by his incompetent sons with dynastic infighting provided the incentive for fresh barbarian offensives. Events now moved rapidly. The Huns reached the Rhine in 400 or 401 and defeated the Franks. Soon after, the Visigoths led by Alaric, invaded Italy, and occupied tracts of northern Italy. In 405, various tribes under Alaric crossed the Danube and the Alps, and were repulsed by the Romans near Florence. The Ripuarian Franks conquered the valleys of the Meuse and the Moselle. The Vandals, Suebi, and Alans crossed the frozen river Rhine to invade Gaul in 406. The Vandals and some Suebi worked their way into the south of France, and the Alans settled in the upper Rhône valley. The Huns under Uldin crossed the Danube in 408 and ransacked Thrace. The Alemanni appear to have crossed the Rhine, conquering, and settling, in Alsace and a large part of the Swiss Plateau.[17] Various Suebian groups moved south from the Baltic Sea and the Elbe, threatening the Empire on its Rhine and Danube frontiers. In 408-409, Alaric and his Visigothic army laid siege to Rome and Ravenna. From this series of invasions, the military frontier on the Rhine collapsed in chaos, and as a result, power gradually passed into the hands of the Franks, although the Empire still retained nominal authority.

Roman rule ended for different parts of Britain at different times. In 401 or 402, the military commander Flavius Stilicho stripped Hadrian's Wall of troops to strengthen military manpower on mainland Europe. In 407 Emperor Constantine III withdrew the remaining troops from Britain and in 410, the Emperor Honorius advised the Romano-Britons to provide for their own defence. The romanized British population was now exposed to invasions, first by the Picts and afterwards by the Saxons and Angles, the latter two tribes participating thereafter in the Anglo-Saxon settlement of Britain.

### Settlements after the Sack of Rome

The Visigoths sacked Rome in 410, an event which made an enormous impression on contemporaries, as it was the first time since the Gallic invasions of the fourth century B.C. that the city had fallen to a foreign enemy. While Rome was no longer the official capital of the Western Empire, which had been moved to Ravenna for strategic reasons, the city's fall sent shock waves across the Empire even greater than Valens' defeat in 378. The event was viewed as a turning point in the Empire's decline, for now its weakness was fully recognized, and provided further impetus for barbarian settlement on Roman territory. Rome had been revered as the 'Eternal City' and it was inconceivable that a civilized state might not have Rome at its head.

After crossing the Pyrenees into the Roman province of Hispania in 409, the Vandals, Alans and some Suebi established a peace by dividing the province among themselves, the Vandals in Asturia, and Hispania Baetica (south central), the Alans in Lusitania (present-day Portugal) and Hispania Carthaginensis, the Suebi in Gallaecia (present-day Galicia and northern Portugal). In 411, the Burgundian King Gundahar, in co-operation with Goar, king of the Alans, seized land on the left bank of the Rhine, namely, Borbetomagus (present-day Worms), Speyer, and Strasbourg. The Emperor Honorius later officially granted them this land. Burgundian raids into Roman Upper Gallia Belgica became intolerable and were ruthlessly brought to an end,[18] when the Roman general Flavius Aëtius called in Hun mercenaries in order to destroy the Burgundians' Rhineland kingdom in 437.

Visigothic resistance in Italy collapsed in 416. They originally aimed for Africa and Spain, but settled in Aquitaine in 418, a large loss to the Empire. The Vandals were defeated in 419 by a joint Roman-Suebian coalition,[19] and together with some Alans crossed over to North Africa in 429 at the request of Comes Bonifatius, the military ruler of the region, and expanded their kingdom into Provence. After losing a battle against the Ostrogoths in 469, those Suebi that had not settled in the Iberian Peninsula migrated to southern Germany. The Hunnic Empire under the brothers Attila and Bleda raided the Balkans, Gaul and Italy, and then turned their attention to the west. In 451, Aëtius, now de facto ruler of the Western Empire, called upon his Germanic allies to help fight off this invasion, and at the decisive Battle of Châlons, also called 'The Battle of the Catalaunian Plains' the Huns were defeated, ending the Hunnic threat to Europe.

The Goths, after the wreckage left by the collapse of the Hun empire in the 450s, expanded slowly westwards and southwards, and were settled on lands in Pannonia. They entered Italy under King Theodoric the Great to fight the Empire's enemies. In the second half of the fourth century, the Lombards embarked on their own migration, probably due to bad harvests, settling in Bohemia and Moravia. In 505, some moved south into the old Roman province of Noricum (most of present-day

Austria and Slovenia). In the 540s, King Audoin led them across the Danube once more into Pannonia, where they received Imperial subsidies, as Emperor Justinian encouraged them to fight the Gepids.[20] From Pannonia, Italy was invaded by the Lombards from 568 onwards. By 572 they had conquered all northern Italy, but they failed to take Rome and Naples. The last known location of the Heruli seems to have been in the area around present-day Belgrade as a settlement within the Eastern Empire and under Roman control. The Saxons that had remained behind on the continent were scattered. Some were permitted to settle in the Rhineland as farmers, some in Italy and in 573 in Provence, and yet others in various other locations in Gaul.

### The Barbarians 'are to receive Authority as Kings'

John states in Revelation 17:12 that the ten horns "...are to receive authority as kings for one hour." Whilst barbarians had already been successfully absorbed into Roman structures of power centuries before, in the context of the Empire's decline, they eventually enjoyed a relationship with the Empire, which entailed co-operation with, and participation in, its government. This occurred at various times from the late fourth century onwards with most of the major tribes. As a strong force in support of Rome, the exercise of royal authority would take a variety of forms in either a military or civilian capacity.

Successive waves of Germanic migration put pressure on the Empire to find ways to deal with the situation, and the most common means was by settling the Germanic tribes as *foederati*. The word was derived from the Latin *foedus*, indicating a treaty of mutual assistance between the Empire and another tribe. It served to identify those tribes which were bound by such treaties but were not beneficiaries of Roman citizenship. In this way, barbarians became allies of the Empire, which at first repaid assistance in the form of subsidies, such as money or food, an offer sometimes extending to entire tribes. The usage of the term *foederati* later embraced tribes that could no longer be expelled from Roman territory. An alternative means had to be found of containing the menace, and the solution was achieved by exchanging freedom to settle within the Empire's borders for co-operation in maintaining peace. As tax revenues dwindled in the fourth and fifth centuries, the *foederati* were billeted on local landowners, and this was interpreted as permission to settle on Roman territory.

One of the main ways in which the barbarians served the Roman Empire was by providing contingents of fighting men when trouble arose. Often the Empire accepted the barbarians as mercenaries and in exchange rewarded them with a gift of land,[21] giving them property rights in the Empire. Ever since the days of the Republic, many barbarians had served Rome in this way. Barbarians served in the ranks, and their leaders held commands in the Empire's armies. They were employed to hold, defend and expand swathes of Roman territory, and with a military career a route to political power would be ensured. During the third and fourth centuries the Empire, attracted by the barbarians' fighting abilities, increasingly relied upon hiring them rather than Roman citizens to form its army. Since the Empire now lacked the wealth needed to pay and train a professional army, by the late fourth century the army was composed mostly of hired barbarians, and Western Roman military strength became almost entirely reliant upon *foederati* units. Barbarians came to exercise senior commands within the Roman army, and there were several elite units, such as the scholae, which had similar duties to the earlier praetorians, and consisted largely of Germans. The result was no less than the complete barbarisation of the army, and the surrender by the emperors of all effective power into the hands of barbarian chieftains. The Heruli, for example, became well known as soldiers in various Roman armies and it is probable that from 268 the Romans instituted a Herul auxiliary unit. One Herul chief, Naulobatus, became the first barbarian to be granted the high-ranking status of *ornamenta consularia*, that is, to receive imperial insignia. Horsed warriors from the Alans were also sometimes brought into Roman service.

From the middle of the third century onwards, Frankish tribes allied themselves fleetingly with the imperial government, whilst preserving their independence. In 297 after the Saxon attacks, some Franks were recruited by Constantius Gallus and joined the Roman troops in Gaul, even defending the Empire from other Frankish raiders. The Salian Franks become a powerful ally of Rome, providing many imperial generals, notably Flavius Salia and Arbogastes. Later, in 358 the Salian Franks and their allies were conquered by the Emperor Julian the Apostate and accepted into the Empire as *foederati* in Toxandria, the first on imperial soil, according to the Roman historian Ammianus Marcellinus.

In the war with the Persians in 238, Goths assisted the Roman armies. They were probably already *foederati* of Rome, but a treaty struck with them in 382 confirmed their status. They increasingly participated in the Roman armies in the fourth century, oftentimes being granted prominent positions. Alaric began his career leading a band of such Gothic *foederati*. The Ostrogoths had been granted *foederati* status whilst in Pannonia in the middle of the fifth century. On settlement in Aquitaine, the Visigoths were also granted this status. From here they fought as Roman allies against the Vandals, Alans, and Suebi in Spain. The settlement formed the nucleus of the future Visigothic kingdom that would eventually expand across the Pyrenees.

After the invasions of the 370s, the Huns begin to be noted both as *foederati* and as mercenaries, and were allowed to settle in Pannonia in 380. Uldin, the first Hun known by name, headed a group of Huns and Alans fighting against King Radagaisus in defence of Italy. After the Burgundians' Rhineland kingdom had been destroyed, they were resettled by Aëtius in 443 in the region of Sapaudia (present-day Savoy) as Roman allies and granted *foederati* status a second time. In 456, apparently confident of their growing might, they even negotiated a territorial expansion and power-sharing arrangement with the local Roman senator. The Suebi, having settled in the Roman province of Gallaecia, were granted autonomy as *foederati*. In 435 the Romans signed a treaty with the Vandals accepting them also as *foederati* in North Africa. Frisian mercenaries were also hired to assist the Roman invasion of Britain. According to Roman sources, by the beginning of the fourth century, individual Alemannic soldiers were regularly employed in the Roman forces.

Individual warriors of German race, put themselves at the command of the emperors, and became allies and deputies of the Empire. Most of the barbarians considered themselves citizens of the Empire and quite several of their leaders received titles from the imperial authorities.[22] There were even barbarian emperors from the third century onwards. Those who led military expeditions were often subsequently promoted to positions of power. Many were extensively romanized and many became Christians, playing a significant role in the Empire's internal politics. In 397 Alaric was awarded the title of *magister militum*, a top-level military command, of the eastern Illyrian prefecture by Emperor Arcadius. One of the greatest chieftains to defend the Empire against his own kind was the Vandal, Stilicho, half Germanic. Married to the niece of Emperor Theodosius I, he acted as regent to the Emperor Honorius. Arbogastes and Mellobaudes were Franks, and Flavius Ricimer was a Suebian. The Empire's historical relationship with the Germanic tribes was sometimes hostile, at other times co-operative, but ultimately it was fatal, because the Empire was unable to prevent these tribes from assuming a dominant role in the relationship.

One of the most successful and lasting fusions of the dual character of Romans and barbarians was achieved by King Theodoric the Great, the greatest of the Ostrogoth leaders, who ruled from 493 to 526. As a child he had received a Roman education which gave him an excellent grounding in imperial government. He gained the rank of *magister militum*, and became king of Italy at the end of the fifth century, declaring his aim of preserving Roman civilization and the Roman traditions of law and government, by arms if necessary. He held the title of patrician and consul from the Eastern emperor in Constantinople and envisioned himself as a Roman ruler, becoming a patron of Roman art and literature. He may be considered the successor, though without any imperial title, of the Western emperors, but remained the national Ostrogothic king.

The Franks integrated well into Roman society. Many of them rose to high office, speaking Latin and obtaining Roman citizenship. Some were even promoted to consular and senatorial ranks by the emperors for their competence. Franks were mentioned in the undated *Notitia Dignitatum*, which detailed the administrative organization of the Empire. In 351, Gaiso became the first Roman consul of Frankish blood, followed by Silvanus in 355, Vitta, a personal friend of Julian the Apostate, in 362, Merobaudes in the 370s twice as consul, an exceptional honour, Richomer in 384 and Bauto in 385. Arbogastes acceded to the role of *magister militum* in the west under Emperor Valentinian II after 388. Some were even granted the Imperial family name of 'Flavius'.

King Athaulf the Visigoth abandoned his early opposition to Roman law and decided to use Gothic power in the service of Roman society. At least one Burgundian princeling, Hariulf, attained high imperial service in the emperor's bodyguard and in 443 his people earned the status as *foederati* in order to control the Alpine passes, thereby serving the Empire faithfully. Apart from their participation in the battle of Châlons in 451, reported by the historian Jordanes, there is no record of the Ripuarian Franks participating in either the imperial government or army. Likewise, the Saxons appear to be one of the few major tribal groups that did not enter into any treaty or friendly relationship with the Empire.

### 'The Lamb will conquer' – Christian Conversion of the Barbarians

Revelation 17:14 states that the ten kings "will make war on the Lamb, and the Lamb will conquer them." Such a war might well allude to the pagan religions of the barbarian tribes, before they encountered Christianity. The beast of John's narrative could then be interpreted as various forms of paganism. The proffer of faith to the barbarians began during the decline, and continued after the fall, of the Western Empire. In the course of time the Salian Frankish political elite would be one of the most active forces in disseminating Christianity over Western Europe.

The barbarians' religion consisted of polytheism in various forms. Their gods stood in a close relationship to nature, but in time a cult of warlike deities also evolved. Most of the pagan deities were associated with local cult centres, for example, sacred groves, but temples and images became a feature somewhat later. The goodwill of the gods was solicited by sacrifices, though such tribute was not particularly lavish.[23] The Byzantine poet Agathias of Myrina in his book *The Histories* stated that the Alemanni worshipped mostly nature deities in whose honour they sacrificed animals. Roman authors also noted seasonal festivals and the fabrication of statues of wooden gods as additional practices. The Salian Franks, after conversion, maintained their highly ritualistic veneration of ancestors. The one essential institution of the barbarian tribes was their conception of kingship. A Germanic leader was not only a political ruler, but was considered to be of divine descent, and this sacral status made him responsible for his tribe's religious cult, and the cult of a god or gods of war would come to assume great importance.

By the time of the barbarian tribes' main infiltrations into the Empire, Christianity had become the Empire's official faith once Emperor Constantine had granted it a favoured status. Conversion of the barbarians was partly facilitated by the prestige in which they held this Christian Empire. However, the Romano-Christian world felt no obligation to evangelize the pagans beyond its borders. Not until the 'Great Migrations' occurred did any contact take place between a Christian leader and the barbarian tribes.[24]

The barbarians had no tradition of higher learning or literature of their own, and were unable to assimilate Christian theology. They had observed a cult of heroes, and so the practical lives and acts of Christian saints and ascetics, who seemed to them endowed with supernatural qualities, impressed them. As a mode of teaching, this was well suited to assisting the church's spiritual conquest and could act as a safeguard against any future relapse back to paganism. A pagan god might have a popular shrine, and bishops realized that it was preferable not to destroy it, but to replace the original object of worship with a saint.[25] Furthermore, Christian feasts could be substituted for pagan saturnalia.

Christian communities among the barbarians developed outside the imperial frontiers through diverse ways as a result of trade, diplomatic contacts, cross-frontier marriages, converted barbarian veterans returning from service in the Roman army, or Christian prisoners exiled from their homelands after barbarian raids. Both branches of the Goths were the first of the Germanic tribes among whom Christianity had any degree of influence, unsurprisingly because they were among the earliest of the Germanic peoples to invade the Empire's territories. Consequently, they were also the first to be brought into continuous close contact with the Christian faith, which was probably introduced to them by Christians whom they had captured during third-century raids. Carried away into slavery, these captives, some of them ecclesiastics, would have retained their faith as a solace. Their most famous missionary was one of their own, Salminius Ulfilas. By intercourse with their captors, Christianity would have gradually become established among the Goths, and many individually converted. Christianity spread actively among the Visigoths first of all, and from them it made headway among the Ostrogoths and the Vandals.

In some instances, conversion was made a condition of settlement upon imperial territory. An example of this was an explicit agreement negotiated between the Visigothic leader, Fritigern and the Emperor Valens in 376. In gratitude for permitting resettlement, according to the church historian Sozomen, Fritigern and his people under his rule accepted Christianity. However, the opposite might have been the case.

The Goths had perforce to accept the empire's Christian faith as a *quid pro quo* for their resettlement, a pattern that was to be repeated several times. Vandals, Burgundians, Ostrogoths and Suebi all adopted Christianity within a generation or two after resettlement. By accepting the Catholic Christianity of the provincial population among whom they settled early in the fifth century, the Burgundians were one of the first Germanic people to accept this form of Christianity. Subsequently, though, they converted to the Arian form of Christianity.

Royal conversion was an important way in which Christianity took root amongst the barbarians. From the time of Saint Augustine, missionary efforts were directed first of all at royal families, but it was a complicated business. The elements in the conversions of kings and tribal leaders were oftentimes repeated: a Christian wife, admiration for the superior power of the Christian God and the allure of Christian and imperial Rome.[26] A Christian queen could play a significant role, for there were instances where she encouraged her husband's conversion, Bertha of Kent being one example. There was an appropriate scriptural reference for this in 1 Corinthians 7:14: "For the unbelieving husband is consecrated through his wife." As a starting point, the king might regard the Christian God with some favour, but be unaware that this would entail the believer's exclusive loyalty. Baptism and full entry into the Christian community would ensue, but royal hesitation was a notable feature, and the journey from the first to the last stage could take several years with plenty of pauses in between.[27]

In Germanic paganism the king was charged with interacting with the divine on his people's behalf, the latter accepting that their mode of worship should be chosen for them. Accordingly, the king's conversion was a crucial element. If he considered it appropriate to adopt Christian belief, the rest of his tribe would be likely to follow his initiative. It was critical that missionaries should convert the barbarian aristocracies as a first step, because of their influence in imposing the faith upon their subordinates. Unlike the early history of Christianity, therefore, conversion of the Germanic tribes generally took place from the top downwards. After the conversions, the church sought the barbarian leaders' support in the church's mission of creating a Christian society.[28]

A cogent example of this conversion process occurred with the Franks. In north-eastern Gaul the Frankish invasions and settlement had obliterated much of the Christian culture of the region, and so Bishop Remegius of Rheims organized a mission to bring the people back into the Church. A decisive reason for a Germanic king-as-commander to adopt Christianity was the spiritual battle aid he might receive, if he could attribute his victories to the Christian God. In 496 whilst waging war against the Alemanni, King Clovis found himself hard pressed. He prayed to Christ, promising to convert and undergo baptism in return for victory. The Alemanni were indeed decisively defeated at the battle of Tolbiac. With encouragement from his queen, Clotilde, a Catholic Christian, Remegius began to instruct Clovis, but secretly, because Clovis feared that his subjects would not permit their king to forsake the ancestral gods. His apprehensions proved baseless. Clovis was baptized into the Catholic faith by Remigius and according to Saint Gregory of Tours, 3,000 of his armed followers also. Since a pagan such as Clovis could ask Christ for help, this demonstrated that Germanic polytheism could be adaptable, for the pagans had no concept of the Christian doctrine of religious exclusivity.[29] If the pagan god failed, well, one could give Christ a chance instead! Clovis' conversion to Catholicism would prove to have an enormous effect on the course of European history. At the time the Franks became virtually the sole Catholic Christian group amongst the barbarians. Later they became not only increasingly powerful, but also developed an amicable relationship with the Church of Rome.[30]

A full-hearted commitment to the new faith would entail a considerable amount of time, persuasion and effort during the following centuries. In the fourth and fifth centuries the Alans were at least partially christianized by Arian missionaries. The Suebian king, Rechiarius, together with other Suebian leaders, was the first of those Germanic kings who had settled in the Empire, to become an orthodox Catholic Christian by the time of his accession in 448. His people remained mostly pagan until Ajax, an Arian missionary, converted them in 466. The Alemanni were formally converted to Christianity by Saint Columbanus and his disciple Saint Gall in the early seventh century. Members of the Alemannic elite such as King Gibuld may have been converted to Arian Christianity as early as the fifth century. The continental Saxons were converted from the seventh century onwards.

The Lombards' first conversion to Christianity in Pannonia had been incomplete until the middle years of the seventh century. At one point, they were Catholics allied with the Byzantine Empire, but converted to Arianism when they invaded Italy. By the reign of Emperor Justinian in the sixth century, many Heruli had also become Arian Christians. There seemed to be no record that the Huns ever became christianized. There had been a limited conversion to Christianity among the Thuringii in the fifth century, but full conversion took place later, along with the Frisians. Saint Gregory the Great sent a team of missionaries to convert King Ethelbert and the English Saxons in the spring of 597, and by July 598 a large number of converts had been made. The king of the east Angles, Redwald, was converted on a visit to Ethelbert's court but was talked out of the Christian faith by his wife. The east Saxons accepted Christianity and a bishopric was founded for them at London in 604. King Edwin of Northumbria presented a formidable challenge to an Italian priest, Paulinus of York, but was converted in the end. True to form, Ethelbert and Edwin both took their time. From Kent and Northumbria, Christianity spread into adjacent regions.[31]

A feature of these conversions was that almost all the barbarians at first espoused the heretical, Arian, as opposed to the Catholic, form of Christianity with the exception of the Franks, who had adopted, and kept, the Catholic form of the faith from the outset. Arius, a priest of Alexandria, taught that Christ was not one with God the Father, but instead created by God, in effect denying the divinity of Christ, and making the Son inferior to the Father. This formulary stood in direct opposition to the creedal Trinitarian beliefs of the Catholic Church.

Importantly, most of the Empire's original inhabitants had remained faithful to Catholicism, and the Catholic Church's organization at both episcopal and parochial levels had remained in place. Many of the Burgundian people had reconverted by the early sixth century. The governing circles in the Vandal kingdom decided to convert to Catholicism, when it was reunited with the Empire by Emperor Justinian in 533-534. According to the *Historia Suevorum (History of the Suebi)* (619-624) of Saint Isidore of Seville, the conversion of the Suebi in Gallaecia by Saint Martin occurred after the year 550. The Visigoths of Spain were reconverted in 587. The Lombards' changeover to Catholicism took place between 588 and 662. Once again, this was due partly to the pressure of their queen, Theodelinda, and partly to the heroic efforts of Irish monks. Justinian appears to have pursued a policy of attempting to convert the Heruli to Roman Catholic orthodoxy. By the reign of Saint Gregory the Great in the 590s, the Catholic Church had established an ascendancy, since almost all the barbarian kingdoms had adopted its faith.

The Lamb had conquered and the barbarians were received into the Christian church. In this respect, too, John's prophecy had been fulfilled. However, conversion did not entail only a change in religious belief and observance. The barbarian newcomers gradually assimilated with the Empire's existing population, and adopted its language, but much greater cultural changes would have to follow over the course of the next centuries before the start of the thousand years.

## Political Dismemberment of the Roman Empire

The next event in John's prophecy concerns the dismemberment of Rome, and he writes in Revelation 17:16 the ten horns and the beast "will make her desolate and naked, and devour her flesh." After their settlement, local barbarian kings ventured to replace Roman Imperial power, and as a result, a host of new successor kingdoms, came into being. The barbarians' original motive was not to subjugate the Empire, but rather to join it in order to participate in its wealth. They did not consider that they were conquering Roman territory, but merely settling within its boundaries in the capacity of allies or *foederati*. It was only later after settlement that they took it over piecemeal by carving out territory, and thus claiming authority, for themselves. Those parts of the Western Empire which remained under direct Roman rule gradually diminished in the course of time.

In describing the 'decline and fall' of the Western part of the Empire, it would therefore be more appropriate to say that it was destroyed by dismemberment, for the barbarians apportioned its territories out under new administrations. This transformed the fundamental nature of Roman civilization, for in due course of time the Empire's ethos essentially became no longer Roman in any real sense at all. Often it was not clear exactly when the transformation would have occurred from tribal status, with a chieftain as leader, to something akin to permanent kingdoms. Kingship developed amongst the Germanic peoples when the unity of a single military command occurred, and successful leadership in war might entitle a ruler to adopt such a title to reflect his personal supremacy. This would be unlikely to occur during the tribe's migratory travels, but at the point when settlement in a particular territory had been accomplished, a hierarchy of sorts would evolve. Successor states were founded in some instances by the tacit consent of the imperial authorities, for example, the Burgundians, Ostrogoths and Visigoths, but other tribes acted without the Empire's agreement. The inescapable conclusion is that the Western Empire met its demise because too many tribal groups made permanent settlements on its soil and subsequently expanded their territorial holdings by warfare. By so doing they deprived the Western Empire of its longstanding tax base.[32]

The Franks formed a kingdom, acknowledged by the Empire, in 358, although it was a confederation of smaller tribes. Otherwise, the Suebi established the first barbarian kingdom in Western Europe.[33] Under their King Hermeric, they established a de facto kingdom in the Roman province of Gallaecia, which lasted until 584 when it was integrated into the Visigothic kingdom. It proved to be relatively stable and prosperous. In the 450s the Visigothic army turned against the remaining Roman provinces in Spain and Lusitania, and the Visigoths' King, Euric, in 475 forced the Empire to grant independence. At this point, the Visigoths were now the most powerful of the Western successor states. By 500, the Visigothic kingdom, centred at Toulouse, controlled Aquitaine and Gallia Narbonensis and most of Spain excepting the Suebic kingdom in the northwest and small areas controlled by the Basques and Cantabrians. The Visigoths quickly crushed the Alans and forced them and the Vandals under King Geiseric to cross over to Africa in 429. Geiseric made Hippo Regius the first capital of the Vandal kingdom after a siege, during which Saint Augustine died. A peace treaty was concluded between the Romans and the Vandals in 435, which Geiseric broke in 439. He moved eastward and captured Carthage, which he made his capital. He now styled himself Rex Wandalorum et Alanorum (king of the Vandals and Alans). By conquering Sicily, Sardinia, Corsica and the Balearic Islands, he built his kingdom into a powerful state. The separate ethnic identity of the Alans then dissolved.

The Ostrogoths, under Theodoric the Great settled in the Po valley in Italy in the 490s. Theodoric was given a commission by the eastern Emperor Zeno the Isaurian to recover Italy from King Odoacer. By 493 Ravenna had been captured and had become the capital of the Ostrogothic kingdom of Italy.[34] It was notable for the harmonious co-existence within it of Goths and Romans. Theodoric the Great was forced to become regent of the kingdom of Toulouse, so that his power extended over a large part of southern Gaul too. By the mid-sixth century, Emperor Justinian was able to defeat the Ostrogothic kingdom, and the leadership of Western Europe henceforth passed to the Franks. The Burgundians were resettled by Aëtius in the region of Sapaudia. Eight kings ruled this kingdom until they were conquered at Autun by the Franks in 532. The Alemanni formed kingdoms which were mostly situated along the Rhine between Strasbourg and Augsburg until 496, when they too were conquered by the Franks. In the spring of 568, the Lombards under Alboin migrated to Italy and the next year, they conquered Milan, the main Roman centre of northern Italy. Pavia fell after a siege of three years, in 572, becoming the first capital city of the new Lombard kingdom.

By the beginning of the fifth century, a considerable body of Franks had settled over a wide area on the left bank of the Rhine, and these settlements eventually became established as minor kingdoms within the Empire. Tournai came under the rule of the Salian Franks in 446, becoming their centre. They established a royal dynasty, known as the Merovingians. Other settlements covered areas around Le Mans (North-Western France), Cambrai (Northern France), Trier (Rhineland-Palatinate), and Deutz (North Rhine) along with some groups of Suebi, and they became a strong supporter of Rome. When Clovis I succeeded to the Salian Frankish throne in 482, his kingdom was still confined to the territory around Tournai, but his prowess was such that in the next ten years he brought the other Frankish kings under his sole sovereignty, ending the loose Frankish confederation. Clovis pressed on to destroy Roman rule in the Loire valley and defeated the Roman general, Syagrius, the last imperial military commander in Gaul at Soissons. Clovis turned his forces next against the Burgundians and the Visigoths, defeating the latter at the battle of Vouillé near Poitiers, ending Visigothic rule in Aquitaine, though not in Spain. Thus, by the start of the sixth century the Salian Franks had gained possession of a large kingdom, which included most of Gaul, together with the Netherlands south of the Rhine and Belgium.

The year 434 witnessed the rise of the Hunnic Empire led by Attila and Bleda, who raided the Balkans, Gaul and Italy. Even though they ruled a massive empire in central Europe, their administration was amorphous and ill-defined. After the battle of Châlons in 451, their empire broke up, after which they soon disappeared from historical records. The Heruli established their own kingdom. They became known as sea raiders on the Atlantic coast, before themselves also suffering the same fate. It is of some doubt whether the Frisians ever formed a self-contained political unit which might be called a kingdom, and whether any portion of their territory was ever under Roman jurisdiction. This also applied to the Thuringians, who eventually acquired an extensive kingdom from the Elbe to the Danube by the sixth century outside the Empire's territory, and this was conquered by the Franks in 532.

After the final withdrawal of Roman imperial administration by about 409, Britain was left vulnerable to the invading Saxons and Angli, who began to settle permanently from about 440 onwards. In the succeeding centuries Germanic warrior aristocracies established themselves as the dominant groups over much of eastern Britain, and from the fifth century onwards a number of small Anglo-Saxon kingdoms and sub-kingdoms flourished.

### The Process of Dissolution was violent and unpleasant

We noted earlier that Goths were resettled on the Empire's territory by explicit agreement with the Emperor Valens, but apart from this one occasion, every barbarian invasion and subsequent settlement was accompanied by conflict and violence, notwithstanding the fact that a diplomatic agreement of sorts might follow.[35] This, too, reflects John's narrative in Revelation 18:21: "So shall Babylon, the great city, be thrown down with violence and shall be found no more."

Western civilization could be said to have developed out of the ashes of the ancient world. And ashes it certainly appeared to be according to contemporary observers. The Western Empire had been stricken by a dreadful catastrophe as a result of the barbarian invasions. "The whole of Gaul burnt just like a torch," the Christian poet Saint Orientius remarked woefully, surveying the damage and despoliation of property that had been caused.[36] John writes in Revelation 17:16 and 18:9: "the ten horns...shall burn her with fire," and again: "And the kings of the earth...shall weep and bewail themselves over her, when they shall see the smoke of her burning." Ernst Hengstenberg commented that the lamentation of the kings is not that of their love of the Empire but the grief that arises from self-interest.[37]

According to the Roman clergy, the fury of the barbarians raged with every day that passed, and that their whole life was occupied in beating off the war-bands that surrounded them. Henry Sheldon's language was just as colourful: "By strokes of barbarian fury the Empire was reduced to a feeble and tottering power."[38] Similarly the Lombard invasion of a large part of Italy with incessant warfare, brought misery to the native population. The savage Lombards were considered a plague to rank with those of the Old Testament. They burned churches, slew the clergy, robbed monasteries, violated nuns, and desolated cultivated fields. Saint Gregory of Tours, commenting on Gaul, wrote that the Frankish triumph was now characterized by continual warfare, at one and the same time as pointless as it was destructive, and by rape and murder.[39] He commented in one of his homilies on Ezekiel shortly after his accession, "Everywhere do our eyes behold sorrow; at all times are our ears assailed with groans. Cities are destroyed...the country turned into a desert...of the people, some we see led into captivity, some maimed, some slain...Rome herself...beaten to the ground on all sides by its ever-increasing woes, by the desolation of its citizens, and by the attacks of the enemy...we who remain are daily exposed to the sword...the very buildings we behold crumbling around us."[40] Rome came under siege repeatedly by a succession of barbarian conquerors. It could be said that the Catholic Church and its people paid a high price just to survive, but survive they did. The reference to widowhood in Revelation 18:7 denotes not the loss of empire, but the state of helplessness and humiliation which the Empire had experienced.

Once the barbarian incursions began in the third century, pillage and looting became commonplace. When the Franks and the Alemanni invaded Gaul in 257, they plundered it at will. The Alemanni caused widespread damage with their raids when they broke through the Roman *limes* between 258 and 260. In the 260s after the Goths, along with other Germanic tribes, had invaded Asia Minor from the sea, they left a trail of destruction in Greece, Macedonia, and Italy, plundering many cities on the way, and pillaging Troy and the temple of Artemis at Ephesus. The Vandals, Suebi, and Alans ravaged Gaul in 406, and plundered their way westward and southward. Alaric's troops pillaged Rome for six days in 410, though Alaric forbad rape and the desecration of Christian property. In the 420s, according to the writer Hydatius, the Vandals created widespread havoc by pillaging the western Mediterranean. In 441, the Huns razed the cities of Margus,

Singidunum and Viminacium (all three in present-day Serbia) during the Hunnic war with the Eastern Empire. In 455, the Vandals from North Africa pillaged Rome, carrying off as much treasure as they could in the space of fourteen days.[41] The Suebian kingdom, too, from 411 inflicted a horrific catalogue of raiding, war, destruction of cities, and enslavement. Some historians have recently reassessed the barbarian invasions, by claiming that they were a peaceful accommodation. Some evidence does support this view, for often pillage was followed by stabilization once the barbarians had established themselves on Roman territory.[42]

Mention is made once again in Revelation 18.8, of the plagues or pestilences that beset Rome. It was during the resettlement of the barbarian tribes that the first instance of bubonic plague may have occurred, called the 'Plague of Justinian'. Recurrent epidemics caused decreases in population, perhaps by as much as a third, and contributed to the Empire's precipitous decline. Everyone suffered equally from further outbreaks in the 540s, which may have originated in Egypt. From Alexandria it was carried to Constantinople and then it ravaged Italy and Gaul, leaving countless dead not only in the cities, but even throughout the countryside. Saint Gregory of Tours in his *Historia Francorum (History of the Franks)* (seventh century) mentioned the cities of Clermont, Lyons, Dijon, Narbonne, Avignon and Marseilles. The survivors were left in fear and anguish, perhaps a reference to mourning in Revelation 18:8. Europe may have recovered only when the population, through natural selection, had gained some resistance to such infections.[43] Famine, too, would have become a problem in such circumstances.

What does it mean when John writes in Revelation 17:17 that the barbarian tribes will give 'over their royal power to the beast' to make Rome desolate? Perhaps it alludes to the barbarians' essential, primeval nature. Converted to Christianity they may have been, but they retained their pre-Christian attitudes, for it is doubtful whether the first generation of barbarian converts properly understood their new faith. Henry Sheldon stated that they had not ceased their barbaric conduct after conversion, adequately describing their rule as characterized by violence, polygamous excess, unrestrained licence, intrigue and assassination, and this continued right up until the Carolingian renaissance.[44] Barbarian administration too was primitive, and that same barbarism had even infiltrated the church.

## Ten tribal Groups that fit the Criteria

The tribes that fulfilled substantially the criteria stipulated earlier, were the Salian Franks, Ostrogoths, Visigoths, Vandals, Alans, Burgundians, Suebi, Alemanni and Lombards. The following table lists them, with the relevant items checked if the criteria were applicable, with the ten most likely candidates appearing first. The Heruli have been included as one of the ten tribes rather than the Huns, for the Hunnic empire in central Europe, established in the middle of the fifth century, was ill-defined and short-lived. Rather, as noted earlier, the Huns were destined to provide the catalyst for some of the other Germanic migrations. Most continental Saxons lived outside the territory of the Roman Empire, and it is doubtful whether their lands were ever under Roman jurisdiction.

| Tribal Group | Status as *Foederati* | Conversion to Christianity | Successor Kingdoms on imperial Territory | Germanic in Origin |
|---|---|---|---|---|
| Salian Franks | ✓ | ✓ | ✓ | ✓ |
| Ostrogoths | ✓ | ✓ | ✓ | ✓ |
| Visigoths | ✓ | ✓ | ✓ | ✓ |
| Vandals | ✓ | ✓ | ✓ | ✓ |
| Alans | ✓ | ✓ | ✓ | no |
| Burgundians | ✓ | ✓ | ✓ | ✓ |
| Suebi | ✓ | ✓ | ✓ | ✓ |
| Alemanni | no | ✓ | ✓ | ✓ |
| Lombards | ✓ | ✓ | ✓ | ✓ |
| Heruli | ✓ | ✓ | ✓ | ✓ |
| Huns | ✓ | no | ✓ | no |
| Frisians | ✓ | no | no | ✓ |
| Saxons | no | ✓ | no | ✓ |
| Thuringii | no | limited | no | ✓ |
| Ripuarian Franks | no | not known | ✓ | ✓ |

Making due allowance for the confusion which occurred during the centuries of the Empire's decline, John's prophecies are confirmed to a substantial degree. It is remarkable that the major barbarian tribes harassing the Empire totalled about ten in number. It raises questions concerning the astonishing prescience of John's prophecy, or have historians and Roman commentators underplayed the significance of the many lesser tribes that existed at the time?

\* \* \* \* \* \* \* \*

That Christianity had become a *religio licita* from the fourth century onwards would appear to contradict John's prophecy, for in Revelation 17:5 he depicts the Empire as the 'harlot of Babylon', certainly not a Christian one, and we must delve further. When the Empire was overrun by the barbarians, its own peoples, the Gallo-Romans for example, made little or no effort to stave off its final collapse. Joseph Tainter stated that many people living in the Empire at the time might have preferred this outcome,[45] with the result that they were perfunctory in their attempts to save it. The leaders of the community, who might have made attempts to tackle the situation, were reluctant to serve the administration, thereby creating a vacuum of sorts which the barbarians were only too eager to fill.[46] Edward Gibbon in his celebrated book also blamed the Empire's demise on the loss of civic virtue among its citizens.[47] Moreover, church and state were often at loggerheads. Pious Christians in the West despised the Roman government and its administration as worldly evils and felt compelled to forsake the business of the world and cloistered themselves in monasteries and hermitages in order to pursue their own salvation without being distracted by the brutality and decadence of the 'earthly city'. This was accepted as the Christian ideal during these centuries, and it contributed to the Empire's fall.[48] It is a moot point how much Saint Augustine's writings may have encouraged such sentiments. For him, not only did baptism entail abandoning secular activities completely,[49] but that the only salvation was to be found in the 'heavenly city'.

As a result of this dereliction of civic duty, effective government diminished to the degree that the Empire gradually lost the ability to cope with its traditional responsibilities. Christianity may have eventually become the religion of the Empire, but by then it was too late to save it, stricken as it was by instability, civil war, fiscal chaos, and as a last straw, outbreaks of various diseases. It can also be argued that the Empire collapsed from its own inertia, for it was too large to retain adequate control of its own territory. As a result, some commentators have asserted that the Christian faith, or rather the withdrawal by those of the Christian faith, could be construed as a significant cause in the Empire's decline.

It may have occurred to the reader that Rome's downfall occurred after the Empire had embraced the Christian religion. The question that arises is whether it was credible that God would have punished Christian Rome for the sins that had been committed by heathen Rome. Ernst Hengstenberg provided an answer that the period when God's judgment on the Empire began to be executed, heathenism still reigned uncontrolled, and that it continued to maintain a deep root amongst the Empire's subjects. Perhaps Constantine despaired of extirpating heathenism completely in Rome, and it may have been one reason why he transferred the seat of the Empire to Byzantium. Heathenism had penetrated so deeply, that the Roman state was no longer capable of regeneration, and the protecting grace of the Christian faith could take effect only on individuals.[50]

According to Christopher Dawson, when the barbarians ravaged the Empire in the fourth and fifth centuries, they stumbled upon a situation which was undergoing a movement for change anyway. The West was on the verge of a long regression in social, economic and political life that came to characterize the early Middle Ages. Richard Fletcher stressed that the Empire did not suddenly disappear from history in the fifth century, nor could one single date be assigned to the Empire's final 'fall', nor did it succumb after one cataclysmic battle. With the deposition of the last Emperor Romulus Augustulus in 476, there may not have been a Western emperor thereafter, but no one living at the time could have foreseen that this state of affairs was anything more than a temporary one. Theoretically, authority would have reverted to the emperor at Constantinople, where the Eastern Empire would continue for almost another thousand years.

However, by the end of the fifth century it had become evident that the Roman Empire in the West had lost its power and its cultural leadership. Saint Gregory of Tours traced this gradual deterioration of the western portion of the Empire together with its accompanying fragmentation into barbarian successor states, where the barbarian invaders lived parasitically upon the original populace of the Empire, and the great institutions of that Empire continued to decline. A wealthy urban society was being replaced by a rural culture that would eventually generate the rise of medieval feudalism.

The barbarians infiltrated the Empire, settled on its territory, and shared in its rule. Having converted to Christianity, they proceeded to dismember the Empire piece by piece by usurping its political and military functions. The historian André Piganiol famously declared that Roman civilization did not die a natural death. Its demise was more in the nature of an assassination.[51] The barbarians may have wielded political power, but for everything else, for example, moral authority, social care, learning and culture, the church took such responsibilities upon itself.[52] The barbarians brought with them nothing that could be of advantage to the Empire. Their whole social and political background, and *Weltanschauung* were of no value whatsoever to the Roman society which they entered. The historian Peter Brown succinctly stated that they came as "impoverished squatters taking up residence in an ancient palazzo."[53]* For Rome itself, only her final economic downfall remained, and to this we turn in the next chapter.

---

\* © 1996, 1997, 2003 Peter Brown. Reproduced with permission of the publisher and licensor John Wiley & Sons Limited through PLSclear.

CHAPTER THREE

*The Demise of Rome and the Genesis of the West*

AS PART of his apocalyptic narrative, John has correctly prophesised the end of Rome, all the while describing it as the great city, holding sway over the nations of the earth, and portraying it in Revelation 17:5 as "Babylon the great, mother of harlots and of earth's abominations." This Empire, formerly a pagan one, had incurred the wrath of God, its fate having been decided in heaven, and it was to be punished by the seven angels with seven plagues. Revelation 19:2 states, "for his judgments are true and just; he has judged the great harlot who corrupted the earth with her fornication, and he has avenged on her the blood of his servants." Edward Gibbon commented that it was a prerequisite for the Roman Empire to be destroyed before a new civilization could replace it, and he described the Empire's fate as "the greatest, perhaps, and most awful scene in the history of mankind."[1]

We have described in the previous chapter how the barbarian invasions were the major factor in Rome's political downfall, and we demonstrated that John's Apocalyptic narrative accurately predicted these events, with its description as to how the kings, ten of them or thereabouts, of the main barbarian tribes, invaded the Western Empire's territory, settled upon it, and dismembered the Empire. The Apocalypse, however, does not by any means conclude the account of Rome's demise at this point. One last important factor in the Empire's plight remains, for John implies that political dismemberment was not the final act. Further troubles were to come in the form of economic ruin, and in chapter 18, from verse 11 onwards, John elaborates on this theme.

### A Description of Rome's Economy

John envisaged Rome as the successor to Tyre regarding its economic activities which would have included its excessively luxurious living, echoing the Old Testament prophecy foretelling the destruction of this city, and using it as a kind of model to compose a similar doom-laden prophecy for Rome. Tyre had been the greatest trading centre in the Old Testament period, and John likens the commercial enterprises of both Tyre and Rome with prostitution because their hallmark was the persistent exploitation of other lands for the sake of their own profit. Put simply, they both acted as plunder economies.

In order that the Empire should function successfully, trade was essential. The Empire cost an enormous amount of money to run and trade brought in much of that money. Perhaps this is the reason why John dwells on this point so emphatically in his narrative. He realized the important link between the decline of the Empire and the commerce that was involved in it, and, as we shall discover, that decline was reflected most eminently with reference to its trade in luxury articles. Several places in the apocalyptic text make mention of those who also had a vested interest in Rome's economic well-being, namely, the kings, the merchants and the mariners. They too were exploited, but as Richard Bauckham suggested, they all failed to recognize their situation, being so much in awe of Rome's glory and seduced by her economic benefits.[2]

Chapter 18 gives the unmistakable impression that John understood the significance of Rome's commercial activity connected with the sea. Apart from the reference to merchandise or cargo, in verses 11 and 12, we meet specific mention of Rome's sea-borne trade as well in verses 17 and 19: "And all shipmasters, and seafaring men, sailors, and all whose trade is on the sea...where all who had ships at sea grew rich by her wealth!" John is correct in both historical and economic terms. The Empire was fundamentally a maritime one, centred around the Mediterranean. Whilst there were numerous routes overland facilitated by the roads which the Romans constructed, in particular for moving their army and for trade purposes, horses were too expensive and other pack animals too slow to accommodate the mass flow of goods. Trade on the Roman roads connected military posts, not markets, and were rarely designed for wheeled transport. It was about sixty times cheaper to send goods by sea than by land, and ships could accommodate much larger volumes of cargo. The sea, therefore, not only provided the means for political administration and military supervision but also for trade, and her underlying economy depended upon cross-Mediterranean traffic. In conclusion, therefore, throughout the Empire, travel by sea was always found to be equal to, or superior to, travel on land. This was just as true for North Africa as it was for the southern European shores and Egypt where commerce was maintained by boat and barge upon the river Nile. Indeed, bulky low-valued commodities, such as grain and construction materials were carried only by the sea routes. Almost all trade was contained within the confines of the Mediterranean, Black and Red seas, by means of which such trade was transported to Rome. There is still evidence today of this maritime activity from the infrastructure remains of harbours, breakwaters, warehouses and lighthouses at ports such as Civitavecchia and Ostia. Maritime archaeology and ancient manuscripts from classical antiquity also show evidence of vast Roman commercial fleets.

Alexandria's two large sea harbours lay open to all vessels,[3] and the voyage to Rome took between nine and nineteen days, that from Crete took three or four days and that from Rhodes three. A trading vessel took less than one month to complete a trip from Gades (present-day Cadiz) to Alexandria via Ostia, spanning the entire length of the Mediterranean. From the African coast, the voyage to Rome could be completed in four days. As a result of this maritime trade, coastal towns were encouraged to pursue commercial activity, and it was from these urban centres that the hinterlands adjacent to these towns also profited. For example, harbours and anchorages were dotted along the coastlines of Syria and Asia Minor where an active commerce was maintained, with the important harbour of Berytus (present-day Beirut) serving Damascus. The Roman emperors also deliberately fostered the sea voyage to India, rather than land routes because the latter ran through Parthian territory. As a result of this policy, all tolls and harbour dues would fall into Roman hands instead of benefiting Parthian and Arab officials.[4]

### The Significance of John's List of Commodities

In chapter 18, verses 12 and 13, of the Apocalypse, John constructs an impressive, though by no means exhaustive, list of some of the commodities that were traded within the Pax Romana: "cargo of gold, silver, jewels and pearls, fine linen, purple, silk and scarlet, all kinds of scented wood, all articles of ivory, all articles of costly wood, bronze, iron and marble, cinnamon, spice, incense, myrrh, frankincense, wine and oil, fine flour and wheat, cattle and sheep, horses and chariots, and slaves, that is, human souls." The list is modelled on Ezekiel verses 27:12-24 with respect to Tyre's commerce. In a biblical text whose content was concerned principally with allegory and prophecy, we might well wonder why John made such a specific description of Rome's commerce. His narrative at this point has received scant attention, most biblical exegetes taking little notice of these passages, glossing over the text with few remarks, as if perplexed by it. The reason for John's narrative is not, however, so difficult to discern as it appears at first sight. It points assuredly towards a condemnation of Rome's economic exploitation, with the aim of providing yet another and ingenious aspect of John's hostility towards the Empire.

John's list demonstrates well his knowledge of Roman commerce, but its hallmark is the highly selective nature of the items. The commodities have by no means been chosen at random, since most of the merchandise was shipped to Rome, and the arrangement of the list accords with the types of cargo that were so shipped. Furthermore, most of them will be recognized as appertaining to the luxury class of goods, which only the richer and extravagant sections of Roman society could afford to purchase. Many of the items are first-rate examples of luxury, with decadence, opulence and 'conspicuous consumption' rivalled only in modern times. John's aim, no doubt, was to emphasize the importance not only of Rome's once considerable trade but also of the calamity that the cessation of that trade would cause, particularly to the privileged, ruling minority of Roman society, the patrician class. Many Roman writers mentioned the way that luxurious living had corrupted the Empire's upper classes. John wished to denigrate this minority, many of whom were responsible for, or apathetic to, the Empire's corruption, its paganism and its persecution of Christians living in the Empire. He is therefore at pains to prophesy that terrible economic calamities would befall them, and that their wealth would perish with them.

It would be reasonable to assume that John's commercial knowledge emanated from his own personal experience. As an itinerant preacher travelling around the eastern Mediterranean, his missionary activity would undoubtedly have entailed contact with all classes of people, and this would have included the merchants and manufacturers who traded there. The conversations which he must have had with them would have yielded knowledge of the Empire's commercial activities. How much detail John gathered from such sources, and how much of the description in the Apocalypse is prophecy as told to him by the angel, we do not know. What we can, however, investigate is whether the afore-mentioned commodities listed by John bear any resemblance with what historical research has actually revealed concerning Rome's commercial activities, not only in Asia Minor, but also in Egypt, Greece, and even further afield. These provinces are those which John might well have visited, or heard about, on his travels. Indeed, the Middle East was a central trading area for the import and export of goods to and from the Far East. The Silk Road was an important route connecting Asia with the Mediterranean world, and this trade passing through Asia Minor would undoubtedly have been familiar to John. Clearly, though, he could not have known about the increase in the Empire's economic prosperity during the second century up to the end of Emperor Marcus Aurelius's reign which occurred after his lifetime. Some of the economic activities described below developed further after John's time, for example, marble quarrying in Asia Minor and the contribution which Britain made to Rome's economy.

### Description of the Commodities listed by John

Gold and silver were found at Darum, Crenides and on Mount Pangaeus in Greece,[5] and to the south of Syria, and silver was also found on Cyprus. Precious metals were found in many other parts of the Empire, in the far south of Egypt, in Asturia and Galicia in north western Spain and around the river Tagus. Pliny the Elder, in his *Naturalis Historiae (Natural History)* (78-79), declared that Spain had mines of lead, iron, silver and gold.[6] At the same time, Pliny considered that gold, together with silver, ivory and precious stones, had become the hallmark of excessive luxury and greed among the wealthy families of Rome, and as evidence of the moral degeneration of Rome in his day. Also, according to Pliny, vast quantities of plate and *objets d'art* were made from silver, as examples of extravagance carried to extremes. Indeed, Pliny bewailed the vast amounts spent on all the luxuries that Roman commerce could offer, and made reference in several places in his writing to luxurious living in the Empire, for example books xxxiii, xxxiii and xxxv. At the height of the Empire, a range of metals were in use, including gold, silver, copper, tin, lead, zinc, iron, mercury and antimony. As a consequence, Rome had a very developed coinage system, with an abundance of gold, silver, brass and bronze coins in circulation throughout the Empire.

Some precious gems and jewels were found in Cyprus, in the mountains to the east of the Nile, and along the Egyptian desert road to Berenice in Upper Egypt, but they were imported mainly from China and India, the trade from these regions flourishing from the reign of Emperor Caesar Augustus onwards. Likewise, pearls were imported mainly from India,[7] but the Red Sea and the Persian Gulf also contributed. Once again, Pliny considered that the use of precious stones, particularly pearls, had grown into an extreme obsession. For him they had become the epitome of extravagance, and he mentioned the practice of swallowing them at banquets, dissolved in vinegar, just for the sake of the thrill of consuming such a huge expense at a single gulp.

Next John mentions fine linen in verse 18:12. Linen is woven from flax, which in Roman times was grown in the eastern Mediterranean, especially Egypt, and garments were made from it. Tyre, Sidon, Damascus and the country around the port of Laodicea in Syria also produced fine linen. Flax was also woven around Patras, brought to it from the fields of Elis,[8] further south, as well as exported from Spain.[9] In due course of time linen tended to replace wool as clothing in Rome. The terms 'purple' and 'scarlet' to which John refers could signify either the commodities used for dyeing cloth or the robes themselves, worn by wealthy people. Garments of these two colours were featured in tariff-lists drawn up by Roman officials. All around the Phoenician coast was to be found the murex, the shellfish from which a purple dye, called 'Tyrian purple' was extracted, and Tyre and Sidon despatched robes of purple and other dyed cloths to all quarters of the Empire. Vast numbers of these tiny shellfish were needed to make only small quantities of dye, hence its exorbitant price. Scarlet dye was obtained not only by the Egyptians from a variety of shellfish, but also from an insect parasite of the kermes oaks, or coccus plant, which grew in Greece and Asia Minor. Purple-fishing and dyeing were also extensively carried out in the Peloponnesian peninsula, near Corinth and at Thyateira, (present-day Akhisar), where the dyeing trade still continues. Pliny once again recorded how the Romans developed an insane craze for purple clothing. Since the shellfish from which most dyes were extracted were considered unclean as food for God's people, purple and scarlet came to imply a connection with unrighteous people who displayed sinful behaviour, as in John's description of those who wear clothing of these colours. Shellfish therefore became, for Pliny, the greatest single badge of moral corruption.

Silk featured amongst the highly prized exotic goods imported from India and China, confirmed by the Roman craze for this fabric which started in the first century B.C. during the reign of Emperor Caesar Augustus. At the central mart in Damascus, the minerals of the west were exchanged for the silks from the east, and Berytus, Tyre and Sidon were celebrated for their silken garments manufactured from the raw material. As regards 'all kinds of scented woods', Asia Minor was well supplied with resin-bearing and incense trees. Stobrum, a tree with scented wood, was mentioned by Pliny and was the subject of commercial transactions in the Empire. Once the Syrian elephant had been hunted to virtual extinction for its ivory, Abyssinia became the main centre for the ivory trade, conveyed into Egypt from the Red Sea ports,[10] whilst ivory from India, which tended to replace both Syrian and African sources, was taken to the workshops of Alexandria. Ivory seems to have been a commodity which was almost universally used in Roman homes, for example, for statues, beds, chairs, hilts, chariots, scabbards, doors, combs, brooches, bird-cages, floors, the list is almost endless. At Cappadocia, in Central Anatolia, there was also a white stone of an ivory-like surface which was used to make dagger handles and for ornamentation.

Wood was the basic building material in the Empire, employed in the floor and roof structures of Mediterranean houses. Along the southern coast of the Black Sea were vast forests of oak, fir, maple and larch. Wood from the forests of Lebanon with their tall cedars was reserved for the Roman fleets. The finer kinds of wood, for example citrum, expensive citrus wood, were used for making articles of furniture for the rich, since some species were valued for their colours and patterns created by their veining properties, which lent themselves to veneering. This came originally from all along the North African coast, but by Pliny the Elder's time the best quality trees were confined to Morocco. Roman carpenters also valued ash from Gaul for its resilience. Good timber was also to be had in Macedonia,[11] and cedar and cypress, the favourite woods for making palatial doors, were found in Syria. Tables made from citrus wood became an expensive and manic fashion, introduced during the later years of republican Rome. Ebony came from Africa and India, but costly maple wood was more popular.

Bronze, an alloy of tin and copper, requires a supply of both these metals for its manufacture and this provided the main industry on

Cyprus. It was one of the few places in the Mediterranean where copper was obtainable in any quantity. As the Romans came to control Galicia in Spain and Cornwall in Britain, both areas main sources for the supply of tin, the production of bronze was facilitated. Veins of copper lay also in the mountains of the Sinai Peninsula and in Spain. Iron or iron ore in large quantities was obtained from Elba, Cappadocia,[12] Pharnacia (present-day Giresun on the southern shore of the Black Sea) and near Syene (present-day Aswan) in Egypt, whilst iron was imported from Abyssinia. Lead was present in abundance in Britain.[13]

The mining and quarrying of stones constituted the largest of the Empire's industrial and manufacturing activities. Whilst the most famous marble quarries were to be found at Luna and Carrara in Central Italy where carving was also carried out, marble and stone for building were also found in Greece,[14] in Egypt to the east of the Nile, at Sidon in Syria, and in Asia Minor. Later, the island of Marmara in the sea of that name, situated between the Black and Mediterranean Seas, had an export trade in marble due to its quarries at Proconnesus and its excellent harbour. Once more, examples of extravagance can be found in the use of marble for Rome's public buildings and, according to Pliny, in the ostentatious and ridiculous use of marble for the private buildings and chattels of the rich.

Spices came from Arabia, China and India and initially, this trade was conducted mostly by camel caravans over land routes, some imported through Asia Minor. Later, Alexandria became the dominant trading centre for Indian spices entering the Greco-Roman world. The marts of Antioch and Damascus also traded in spices and cinnamon, the latter probably coming from the cassia plant. Perfumes, frankincense and incense, the latter being used as a medicine, in religious rites and for perfuming the rooms of the rich, were also imported together with frankincense, myrrh and fragrant gums,[15] all of which emanated from India, the Arabian merchants acting as middlemen for such trade.

There was an incentive to plant vines and develop the wine trade once the Romans had acquired a taste for wine. Technological advances in, and burgeoning awareness of, winemaking and viticulture spread to all parts of the Empire and it became a highly profitable trade. The economic opportunities presented by the wine trade drew merchants to do business with enemy and ally alike from the Carthaginians and peoples of southern Spain and Sicily, to the Celtic tribes in Gaul and Germanic tribes of the Rhine and Danube. Syria, Galilee and Judea, and the southern coast of the Black Sea produced wines, much of it being exported to Alexandria. Olives, cypress, castor and sesame plants were all cultivated in Egypt in order to extract their oil.[16] Olive trees were cultivated in Syria, Galilee and Judea, having overtaken Italy as the major suppliers to the Roman populace. Further south at Petra, the oil of sesame was used instead. The climate of Asia Minor was well suited to the cultivation of the olive, and it grew in almost every district. There are records of the olearii or itinerant merchants and dealers in oil, who passed by way of the Cyclades, a Greek island group in the Aegean Sea, to Rome.

The staple cereal crop was spelt, an inferior species of wheat, and bread was the mainstay of every Roman table. The people living in the city of Rome, estimated at almost one million, constituted a huge market for the purchase of food produced on Italian farms, with Sardinia and Sicily originally the leading producers of wheat, but in the later Empire, the valley of the Nile, North Africa and Syria also sent their grain across the sea to Rome and Constantinople. Thousands of ships were involved. John makes no mention of spelt but it is significant, that he refers to 'fine flour and wheat', as opposed to spelt, and in accordance with his stress on luxury, he would have wished to denote this foodstuff as a costly item, since the best kind of bread was made from this. The inclusion of wheat, in contrast to the other luxury items mentioned by John, suggests that Rome was parasitic upon the resources of the whole empire to support the growth of its inhabitants.

The Empire's inhabitants kept sheep and cattle on a wide scale, but there was also importation of animals to Rome. The import of cattle was unlikely to have been for meat, since they were kept mainly as working animals and for milk. Pliny wrote at length about sheep, and Strabo mentioned wool production in Celtic Gaul. The Romans kept sheep on a large scale and were an important agent in the spread of sheep for breeding through much of Europe. In the south of Syria, horses were bred in large numbers. Arcadia and the plains of Thessaly also provided good pasturage for them. A market for horses was to be found at Amasea, located in Northern Turkey, but it was the more mountainous areas of the Iberian peninsula that were particularly renowned for their breeds, in Lusitania, and in Asturia from which came a famous breed of chariot horse. The reference to chariots was probably to do with the quadriga, a vehicle comprising a team of four horses used by the rich. The extensive timber production throughout the Empire already mentioned, must have facilitated their manufacture, particularly in Gaul. In Asia Minor, timber was used for small, light boats which would also have been ideal for constructing chariots.

Foreign wars and conquests, penury caused by debt, people selling themselves into slavery, and kidnapping, made slaves increasingly cheap and plentiful, and by the late Republic, they played an important role in society and the economy. Slaves are estimated to have constituted from around ten to twenty per cent of the Roman Empire's population, and this reflected the growing prosperity of the wealthy classes. As John hints, transactions in slaves themselves were considered a profitable enterprise. From tariff lists dating from the second century, Emperor Caesar Augustus imposed a two percent tax on the sale of slaves, giving an indication of about 250,000 sales annually. Slave markets may have existed in every city of the Empire, but outside Rome the major centres were Ephesus. Delos, Palmyra in Syria, and Zarai, situated in the Roman province of Numidia in what is now Algeria, also became important market venues for slaves. They could also be obtained from India and Britain. John has placed the slave trade significantly at the end of his list, appearing to be almost confounded by it, and obliquely alluding to the contempt for human life which was involved.[17]

As examples of manufacture, Roman records provide evidence that papyrus for book production was imported from Sicily and scrolls were imported from Egypt, where papyrus grew. A kind of paper was produced from it. Egyptian cotton and glass products manufactured in Alexandria were also some of the major export items from this area. Large quantities, and a wide variety, of high-quality pottery were manufactured in various regions of the empire and these had a significantly wide geographic distribution, suggesting a sophisticated and specialized system of production and distribution.

The Romans put their reputation for austerity behind them when their Empire grew, resulting in a widespread consumer market, and the trade in so many luxury goods gave a firm indication of a complex market economy. Tribute flowing into Rome fed an appetite for luxuries of every kind, including fine furniture, elegant tables and sideboards of exotic woods with marble tops and inlays of ivory and tortoiseshell. There should now be no doubt that John's list of commodities was amply attested by Martin Charlesworth, even though the list omits the more staple products of Roman trade. John's items correspond exactly to what was traded within the Empire, providing confirmation of the apocalyptic narrative. Moreover, some exegetes have queried whether John was really referring to Rome, or whether other cities and empires could be the target of his attack, for example, Jerusalem or Tyre. The accurate description of Rome's economic activity given by John should leave us in no doubt that it was Rome to which he was alluding.

### Henri Pirenne's Thesis and Rome's economic Decline

Although John does not specify any particular time-scale, it is clear from his narrative that Rome's economic woes would be concomitant with, or would occur after, the barbarians' dismemberment of the Empire. Understandably, there must have been a link between the latter circumstances and the disintegration of Rome's economy. This issue has been explored by many historians, but most have concentrated on the period before the fall of the Empire, in order to establish the theory that declining economic prosperity had weakened the Empire's capacity to repel the barbarian invasions. The historian Henri Pirenne focussed, however, on the events after the barbarian invasions. He formulated the thesis that the demise of the classical world was postponed until Rome's economic activity was brought to a standstill some while after the Germanic invasions of the third to sixth centuries. This would not be the reason for the downfall itself, but it provided the best evidence possible to show that Rome and its Empire had finally succumbed.

For Pirenne, the economic life of the Empire overall continued with remarkable persistence after the barbarian invasions in the same manner as before them. The idea of the economic unity of the Empire had continued even though its political unity had been dissipated. Sea-borne Navigation continued to provide articles of current consumption for the barbarian kingdoms, for example, the organization of the ports, the minting and circulation of money, and the importation of oriental products. Vibrant commercial activity endured in the cities, where there were merchants by profession. The barbarians, in dismembering the Empire, had not disrupted the unity of Europe, for such unity did not depend solely on a political system. It also depended on commerce, and the activity of its cities was sustained by such commerce. The intention was, no doubt, to provide a signpost to the unity of Europe by postulating commerce as the bond which continued to hold Western Europe together after the barbarian kingdoms had established themselves on Roman territory. Martin Charlesworth, in setting forth his study of the Empire's commerce, made a similar point by quoting Pliny the Elder to the effect that the Empire's might had conferred unity upon the world,[18] and it carried the implication that commerce continued to make an important contribution to that unity.

Pirenne's ideas sounded similar to what John presages in chapter 18 of the Apocalypse, where Rome's economic troubles are recounted, and which follow on when political doom had struck the Empire. He stated that it was possible for a Roman way of life to survive in Western Europe, and especially in its Mediterranean regions, for centuries after the Roman Empire itself had succumbed to barbarian invasion. There was, no doubt, in the commercial sphere as in other departments of life, a certain deterioration of manners due to barbarization, but he maintained that there was no definite rupture with the Empire's former economic life. The same situation could be applied to agriculture, which continued as the basis of economic activity, alongside which commerce continued to play an essential role, both in daily life by the production and distribution of various commodities, as well as in political and social life.[19]

Pirenne therefore dated the end of *Romanitas*, as he called it, to the eighth century, because, he argued, only then was its underlying economy destroyed. The cause was not the incursions and settlement of the barbarian tribes, but rather the Muslim invasions of the seventh and eighth centuries which closed off the Mediterranean Sea to Christian shipping wherever the Byzantine fleet was unable to protect it. The decline of commerce would have begun about the year 650, during the period when hostile Moslem conquests were starting to overwhelm the Mediterranean littoral, thereby blocking the sea-borne trade routes. Only then was the erstwhile unity, formerly enjoyed by the ancient world, destroyed.

Henri Pirenne's claimed therefore that Rome's final economic decline was deferred until after the Empire's political dismemberment, and that the Mediterranean had continued as a thriving trading region for several centuries after. However, his timing poses somewhat of a problem in comparison with John's narrative. It would be reasonable to assert that in John's version, economic ruin occurs at, or soon after, the point of Rome's political demise Furthermore, Pirenne made no allowances for an adequate time-interval between the end of the ancient world and the emergence of Western civilization which began in the eighth century. Later historical scholarship, however, challenged Pirenne's thesis. The cause of this revision stemmed from archaeological research which demonstrated that the reduction in the economic activity of the Empire occurred at an earlier date, in all likelihood by end of the sixth century, not later. Modern scholars were not challenging the idea that trade was the lynchpin of the former unity of the empire, but they were now querying the date of its terminal decline.

Many and diverse were the reasons for the Empire's economic decline. One interpretation maintained that the Roman state had been enfeebled as a legacy from the crises caused by the barbarian invasions, which had begun in the third century. The markets and resources on which the Mediterranean economy had depended began to disappear and so were any imperial revenues that helped fuel that economy. The replacement of the bureaucratic Roman political system by Germanic tribal elites must have led to a massive diminution of local taxes. In this respect, the Empire received a serious blow with the reduction in its tax flows when the Vandals occupied Carthage, which had been Rome's major supplier of wealth and grain. This same problem was repeated later by the loss of tax revenues from Syria, Palestine, and Egypt when these areas fell to the Arabs in the seventh century. Edward Gibbon also mentioned catastrophe through war, famine and pestilence.[20]

Rome's economy and trade were similar to today's global economy, although on a smaller scale. A skilled labour force was able to mass-produce goods, and a sophisticated network of transportation and trade was able to distribute those goods to other provinces, however distant. A high degree of interdependence existed between all the regional economies of the Empire because of local specialization and consequent economies of scale. With close links between the different shores of the Mediterranean, the result was economic complexity and wealth in good times. These same factors, however, would later prove to be fatal weaknesses once the Empire's trade went into decline. Its prosperity was rendered vulnerable if one regional economy collapsed because other regional economies relied upon that region's goods. This would lead in turn to the decline of other regional economies through a domino effect. In bad times, therefore, problems of one region could have a damaging effect on the prosperity of others. Already fragile since the reign of Emperor Marcus Aurelius at the end of the second century, the economic prosperity of the West started to unwind radically once the barbarian invasions during the fifth century gathered pace.

It seems that the political and military difficulties exacerbated the situation in regional economies, irrespective of whether they were flourishing or already deteriorating. As the Empire declined, the government was increasingly unable to pay its soldiers, thus impairing the whole economy, as well as its inability to defend its frontiers. At the end of the fifth century there was no longer an imperial government in the West anyway to maintain roads and protect sea-borne trade from piracy. Trade continued during this time, but became increasingly difficult. Rather than collapsing all at once, the Mediterranean economy went downhill by degrees, the northern frontier provinces' trade, which included Britain, collapsing first by 500. The north had less deeply rooted cities than the provinces centred around the Mediterranean. Britain was the Empire's most recently civilized region. Its economy in particular was especially dependent on the imperial government for money to pay the legions. Once those were withdrawn, it reverted to a level of economic simplicity similar to that of the bronze age, with no coinage, and only hand-shaped pots and wooden buildings.

The western Mediterranean economy folded in the sixth century, particularly in Italy and North Africa, the Aegean area went next, and finally the economies of the main areas of the Empire imploded. Consumers on the northern and western shores of the Mediterranean were badly hit by the resulting insecurity, leading to gradual impoverishment. It is safe to conclude that the organization of markets was disappearing at the same time in the Frankish Merovingian kingdoms. Traders became few and far between, and in the second half of the seventh century trans-Mediterranean commerce was reduced to an almost prehistoric scale. As trade declined, so did the Mediterranean cities decline *pari passu* as the great caravans ceased to call. Marseilles, deprived of her ships, was dying of suffocation. According to the *Vita* of Saint Didier of Cahors, the city, flourished during his episcopacy, but later atrophied after his death. Similarly, Lyons, where one great merchant was still noted in 601, fell into a frightful state of decadence.[21]

In less than half a century all the cities in the south of France had lapsed into the same state, witness the disappearance of papyrus in Gaul. Mention of this commodity and also of spices disappeared from texts of the early eighth century. The wine trade also ceased. Trade, no longer fed by sea-borne traffic, came to a standstill, and the middle class disappeared throughout the province.

In North Africa and the Levant, village settlements vanished into thin air as their oil and grain were no longer exported, because Rome, now impoverished and depopulated, ceased importing goods from her provinces. Although the export of large quantities of fine tableware and olive oil from the African provinces continued into the succeeding three centuries, the quantity of goods exported gradually shrank, until by the seventh century it was only a trickle in comparison with fourth century levels.

With markets and the apparatus of government diminished to such an extent, farmers were compelled to provide not only their basic necessities but also to make manufactured goods for themselves which earlier had been acquired by purchase or barter. As a result, long-distance trade collapsed, and in the western portion of the Empire, the structure of its society and economy were undermined, its wealth absorbed by two centuries of intermittent warfare pursued by the barbarian kingdoms. The sharp decline led to the closure of the trade-routes to the north, so that from the mid sixth century onwards imports from the Mediterranean to northern areas were rare.

Can the foregoing description of Rome's economic woes compare with the Apocalyptic narrative? From chapter 18, verse 11 onwards, John describes the economic consequences of Rome's downfall, and these verses contain descriptions similar to what has been described above. Without the power of Rome, who would be willing to buy what was produced in the Empire's regions? The Apocalypse remarks upon the erstwhile trade managed by the Empire's merchants, a trade now completely abandoned. Verse 18:11 states, "And the merchants of the earth weep and mourn for her, since no one man buys their cargo any more." The inevitable consequence of the virtually total cessation of trade produced a similar decline in industrial activity as well, apart from a few local industries, such as the weaving of cloth, which still survived in Flanders. Few remains of pottery have survived from this period.

Such failure is mentioned in the Apocalypse too at Revelation 18:22: "...and a craftsman of any craft shall be found in thee no more; and the sound of the millstone shall be heard in thee no more."

Furthermore, money no longer circulated, and the Mediterranean became a dangerous place for merchants due to the activities of pirates who marauded as far north as the English Channel. Henri Pirenne stated that the sea no longer stimulated the spirit of enterprise in the countries of the West. Men looked seawards no longer except in terror, lest enemy sails should appear on the horizon. From the eighth century onwards, Western Europe lived for three hundred years virtually cut off from other lands overseas.[22]

### The Interregnum during the Dark Ages

Rome's downfall as regards both its political and economic circumstances was followed by an interregnum of sorts between the disappearance of the Hellenic world and the emergence of the new Western society. The activities of two institutions filled this span of time.[23] They were the Christian Church together with the monasteries, and the barbarian successor states or kingdoms, carved out from imperial territory, as described in the last chapter. Of this twofold outcome, Edward Gibbon lamented: "I have described the triumph of barbarism and religion."[24] The Apocalypse too has an interlude between the downfall of Rome and the next vision, from Revelation, verses 19:1 to 19:10. This is filled with paeans of praise and thanksgiving from "the mighty voice of a great multitude in heaven", celebrating Rome's demise.

The political unity of the Roman state had been shattered by the barbarians, but they established themselves on Roman soil with no intention of deliberately destroying classical civilization. What the barbarian kingdoms did wreck was the Imperial government itself in the western portion of the Empire. Their settlement was accompanied by a process of serious degradation, politically, economically and socially. The impact of the barbarian invasions was even more disastrous for intellectual culture than for material concerns. Whatever standards the ancient world had achieved were no longer maintained, indeed they had greatly changed for the worse. Since the third century, in every intellectual sphere, be it science, the arts or literature, an increasing decadence revealed itself.[25] The educational institutions of the Roman Empire were swept away by the barbarian invasions, or became moribund as the city culture of the Latin world declined. An exception can be seen in the work of Flavius Cassiodorus, the scholar-bureaucrat turned monk. For a brief period, in the middle of the sixth century, he carried the aristocratic ideal of cultivated leisure into the monastery and library which he founded on his estate at Vivarium in southern Italy, so that classical culture and the writings of classical authors, the so-called Latin classics, could be preserved.

The Frankish Merovingian kings had not abandoned their barbaric behaviour by becoming Christians. Apart from their vigour, and an intense love of personal liberty, the barbarians brought nothing new to the Empire's table. On the contrary, the decadence resulting from their ungoverned impulses and ignorance appeared to be in the ascendant. Modern commentators have somewhat idealized their native culture, by claiming that they brought creativity and new life to a dying civilization. Those in the Christian world who actually had to deal with them during the Dark Ages would have intensely disagreed, for they witnessed the barbarian conflicts and violence which brought in its train destruction of property. This emphasizes the point that Christianity made little, if any, difference to the manner in which barbarian rule was exercised until the eighth century. For them, Christianity was professed but without commitment. Saint Gregory of Tours wrote to the emperor that he reigned over men, the barbarians over slaves.

The period has consequently been popularly described as the 'Dark Ages'. The concept originated with the Italian scholar Francesco Petrarch (Francesco Petrarca) in the 1330s, and was originally meant to describe the period as a contrast to the supposed 'light' of classical antiquity.[26] Later historians equated the period to a general lack of cultural achievements and intellectual stagnation, mainly because of the lack of written sources. The historian Edmund Bishop described the period thus: "The three centuries that elapsed between Caesarius of Aries and Alcuin of York are the darkest of West European history."[27] Modern archaeological discovery has led historians to take a more cautious view of the matter, emphasizing instead some of the age's positive cultural achievements. Henceforth, the term 'Dark Ages' was used, if it was used at all, specifically to refer to the Early Middle Ages, or Late Antiquity just after the collapse of the Empire. As a static or stagnant period when compared to a later, more dynamic one, this state of affairs persisted for some two centuries until the Carolingian Renaissance.

### The Western Church as a 'Bride of Christ'

Surrounded by such decadence, the Catholic Church was the only moral force that remained. Christianity had become the official religion of an Empire that had collapsed, but as far as the church was concerned the Roman Empire still existed. It had developed under this Empire, and it continued to preserve the same traditions after the barbarian invasions. Whilst the old, Hellenic, world was coming to an end, a very different world was destined to emerge. The warlike society of the barbarian kingdoms with their cult of heroism and aggression on the one hand contrasted with the peaceful society of the Christian church on the other.[28] The vital challenge which the church faced in these circumstances was how it would respond to this new situation, since it was no longer dealing with a wealthy Roman senatorial class, but with barbarian kings.

Left to their own devices, the barbarian kings were incapable of preserving the heritage of the ancient world, since their crude and clumsy management was quite unequal to the task. This vacuum was filled by the church because it had the organization which the barbarians lacked, to prevent Europe from sinking even further into barbarism. Since it was organized on the pattern of the former Roman administration, it was able to preserve its structure in the midst of this disorder, with its hierarchy intact, and it attempted to preserve whatever had survived of Rome's ancient culture. Though it may have become somewhat decadent itself, the church was not only the great civilizing force of the time, it was the only such force. Its ecclesiastical institutions created a solid framework for learning and the cultured arts that later ages could use to build a rebirth. For the Western peoples, and in particular for the barbarians, the church possessed the leadership, and retained the loyalty of its people, in contrast to the situation that had prevailed in the final centuries of the Empire.[29] As the inheritor of the Western Empire, the medieval church found its *raison d'être* by keeping the torch of culture alive during the hazardous period between the dying embers of the ancient world and the genesis of the new Western,

Carolingian, society, but it was not its original conscious intention to do so.

After Flavius Cassiodorus, the most pressing task for the bishops of the age consisted in furthering basic literacy, not indulging in cultivated leisure. With the disappearance of widespread literacy, writing appertained exclusively to the church. The monastic schools, libraries and scriptoria became the chief, and virtually the sole, organs of higher intellectual learning in Western Europe, with the task of conserving ancient culture. Certain it was that monasteries helped to shape every aspect of medieval life, and they were a major factor in countering and subduing barbarism in Western Europe. They would ultimately provide a foundation for later renaissances. As a consequence, Western monasticism also had perforce to assume cultural leadership, a role which was alien to its original intentions.[30] The Catholic Church in the West became a closed elite, similar to a colonizing power in underdeveloped territory, regarding itself as obliged to impose its views on the unregenerate world. From this, we can understand the manifest contrasts in the society of that period, namely, the intellectual world of the monasteries and the church with its clergy on one side, and an uncultivated laity on the other.

At the point when Rome finally met its demise, a significant passage in the Apocalyptic narrative at Revelation 19:7 confirms the sentiment of a new beginning: "for the marriage of the Lamb has come, and His Bride has made herself ready." The church considered as a 'Bride of Christ', the Lamb's wife, is a traditional allegory, and is a term referred to in various verses in the Bible, namely, in the Gospels, the Epistles and the Apocalypse. Ephesians 5:22-33 compares the union of husband and wife to that of Christ and the church, and for over fifteen hundred years the majority of Christians have always identified the church as the bride betrothed to Christ. Adolf Harnack concurred when he stated, in connection with the ever-present dangers of believers falling back into heathenism and Gnosticism: "...the institution, together with all its forms and arrangements, became more and more identified with the 'Bride of Christ'...and accordingly was even itself proclaimed as the inviolable creation of God and the fixed and unalterable abode of the Holy Ghost."[31] Henri Pirenne, too, referred to the church as the Bride of Christ, *la Fiancée de Jesus-Christ*, Christ's representative on earth, the mystical source of grace and salvation.[32] A new bride must necessarily concern herself with her new situation, and this occurred in a similar way for the Western church. Matters which had been of little concern to Christians in the ancient world, or which had affected them in an entirely different way, came to take a more prominent place.[33]

What did John himself intend by his mention of the 'Bride of Christ' at this particular place in his narrative? Did it presage the creation of a new church and even a new society? After all, Christian churches and communities were starting to appear almost immediately after Christ's death, and had been in existence for some years by the end of the first century when John wrote his Apocalypse, witness his messages to the seven churches in Asia Minor in the opening chapters of his book. Therefore, the reference in chapter 19 of the Apocalypse must carry some additional significance. Certain it is that we shall witness a new era, described thereafter in the Apocalypse as the inauguration of the thousand years' reign of Christ. The church's ability at adapting to this new environment during the 'Dark Ages' and thereafter, aptly fitted the apocalyptic description of a bride making herself ready.

### The Transformation in the seventh and eighth Centuries

The seventh century is acknowledged as being crucial to the development of Western Europe. Its own version of Christianity was created between 550 and 650 and not before. It was precisely during this period that the Catholic church underwent crucial changes whereby Western Christianity would take on features which would settle the religion of the West for the future thousand years. A new culture was emerging as well, such that eventually every trace of the Roman state would disappear, and in its place a society would emerge that would preserve the family community, with all the moral, legal, and economic ramifications that this involved.[34]

Many of the characteristics of the medieval church were created in this period.[35] In Gaul and Spain, the emergence of the Romance languages reflected the final death of cultures that had existed since pre-history. The Christian church inherited the results of this change. Both East and West had shared the culture of Christian Rome, but a distinct and important break occurred between them. From the reign of Saint Benedict in the early sixth century until the establishment of the monastic system of northern Gaul in the course of the seventh, a different cultural milieu in the West from that in the East emerged. The church developed its own hierarchy, and although national churches came into existence, each with its own particular concerns, ecclesiastics in the new church shared, and were partly defined by, a common framework.

It could be said that the religion of this emergent society represented a new form of Christianity, or was it just a slow but irreversible change in orientation or emphasis? Whatever the case, it was to be distinguished from both ancient Christianity and the Eastern Orthodox Church. Two principles, sin and repentance, would assume overwhelming importance in the West. In the Celtic churches, any infraction of the moral law was absolved by a penalty determined by the appropriate authority, be it the abbot or the confessor. Codes of such penalties were carefully and minutely developed, and were known as the 'Penitentials'. It was a precise calibration of sins, but it was destined to be replaced subsequently in the West by the practice of auricular confession.

The concept of the 'Bride of Christ' therefore confirmed another of John's predictions in an historical sense, if we link this to the transformation of the Christian church in the West during Europe's 'Dark Ages'. The church became a new institution in its own right, and new leaders certainly emerged as well, for the Latin Fathers, such as Saint Ambrose of Milan, Saint Augustine, Saint Leo the Great, Saint Benedict and Saint Gregory the Great, were in a real sense the fathers of Western culture. We shall discuss three of these leaders, because, more than any others, their work and writing encouraged innovation and reform to the extent that affirmed the emergence of a new church. As the different peoples of the West were being incorporated into this spiritual community, so they too began to share in its culture. It was in this period, when the Roman Empire had ceased to function as a political force, that the concept and the ideal, of 'Christendom' emerged.

### Three Fathers of the Church

There is one book of **Saint Augustine** (354-430), especially, which became one of the most influential works for Western thought, and was important even in the political sphere, *De Civitate Dei (The City of God)*. It was written between 412 and 427, and in it Saint Augustine developed a comprehensive Christian scheme of history. What was noteworthy was the concept of the separation between church and state and the resulting divergence between cultural leadership and political power which was a new development in the history of civilization. That church and state should be perceived as distinct and often competing institutions became a critically important feature of Western society, and it carried the implication that only by submitting to the church in all questions of religion could the state be part of the City of God. The work became enormously influential throughout the Middle Ages, and for a thousand years it served as a kind of manual for the rights and obligations of Western peoples towards the state. The church was exalted as a potent social force and explains Christian social philosophy, including the importance of moral freedom and individual responsibility.

Apart from the above work, Saint Augustine was a voluminous writer, both for his philosophy and his theology. He produced stimulating and inspired works on the Trinity, the Incarnation, and the theory of salvation. His genius would influence anew the piety of the new Christian society. In the succeeding centuries medieval Catholicism relied upon his intellectual heritage. He wrote of the 'kindly harshness' that the church should employ to bring unwilling souls into the fold of the church,[36] and to achieve this end, repression and violence could be condoned in an imperfect world. This introduced a fresh concept into Christianity which would also profoundly influence later Western development.

One of the results of the 'Dark Ages' was the rise of monasticism in the West, permeating the church and the life of the people by their educational and religious influence, of which **Saint Benedict (480-547)** was the founder. This resulted in one of the very greatest of Catholic inventions, namely, the monastic life according to the 'Holy Rule' of Saint Benedict, and it became a social force of the first magnitude. Earlier monastic rules had been very brief. Now, for the first time, a fulsome practical code came into being, which dealt with every aspect of the monk's life, a code which itself created a way of living and would, ultimately, create a new type of monk. Henceforward, the 'Holy Rule' would provide an integral set of guidelines. In the ensuing centuries a whole host of monastic communities based on this Rule were founded which became autonomous and self-sufficing, noted for their own centres of economic and social life no less than of religion. Furthermore, the abbeys' trade became important, they fostered arts and crafts, and they developed a social role.

**Saint Gregory the Great** (c540-604) was pope from 590 until his death, a member of an ancient Roman senatorial family, a statesman of the first rank, and the first pope to come from the monastic orders. He acceded to a troubled heritage but the difficult times offered great opportunities to such an able statesman. Partly by developing the ideal of the Christian pastor, and partly owing to his personal qualities, he was able to assert his authority in reforming abuses in the church. He has also been credited with a tradition of generous service for the public welfare, with a sense of responsibility and care for dependants. He combated with energy and wisdom the sources of the troubles which he inherited, and exercised his administrative talent for the benefit of the church. Similar to Saint Augustine, he was a prolific writer. His books included the *Moralia*, a practical guide to the spiritual life, *The Homilies*, a book of sermons, and *The Dialogues*, which contained a vision of the punishments that we shall suffer when we die. His most important book was the *Liber Regulae pastoralis (Book of pastoral Rule)* (590), written to train and instruct bishops. and to improve the quality of the episcopate, and it came to have great influence throughout the Middle Ages. It helped to end the dependence of the clergy and secular rulers of Western Europe on the Eastern Empire, for the book gave them clear and multifaceted rules and a code of conduct.

### 'The righteous Deeds of the Saints'

After the passage announcing the Bride of Christ, John continues in Revelation 19:8: "...it was granted her to be clothed with fine linen, bright and pure – for the fine linen is the righteous deeds of the saints." The righteous deeds mentioned here may be interpreted in the first instance as a social force which was generated within the early church. Throughout the early stages of its development, the church became well known for its social work. It set up a system of care for the poor, the sick, and widows and orphans. Many commentators, both Christian and non-Christian, remarked upon its success in caring, not only for its own members, but for the poor who were not Christian as well.[37] The level of provision and of giving within the early church was quite astonishing. This was something new, for such a thing had hardly been seen before. One of Quintus Tertullian's famous remarks was his account of a pagan exclaiming: "See how the Christians love one another."[38] As an example, when the Imperial commissioners investigated a relatively small church in North Africa in 304, the church's storeroom contained almost 200 articles of clothing and 11 containers of oil and wine, a valuable store of charity.[39]

In the Roman Empire, civic philanthropy had been based on the generosity of local benefactors, and the wealthy considered it a civic virtue to offer assistance. It is recorded that Pliny the Younger and the Emperors Tiberius and Severus Alexander, to take only three examples, gave help to many people.[40] The towns had oftentimes special funds for the assistance of the poor. However, when the Roman Empire became unable to cope with its traditional responsibilities, Christian bishops stepped in to fill the gaps, and Christian charity provided thereafter many areas of welfare, including hospitality for travellers, support of the poor, medical assistance, and education.[41] This would have included such diverse services as prison visiting, ransoming of captives and the provision of public entertainments. In theory, medieval charity was made one of the chief acts of piety. The churches of Rome had large estates, and one third of their income was given quarterly to the clergy, papal domestics, monasteries, and charities. After the church had become legitimized, it set up or expanded poorhouses, homes for the aged, hospitals, cemeteries and orphanages.[42]

Such activities afforded the bishops an opportunity to provide leadership in their respective communities, and this continued after the barbarian invasions. Saint Gregory made it clear to his subordinates that their duty was to dispense poor relief, and so by the late sixth century the church had developed a system for circulating consumables to the poor. On the first of every month, Saint Gregory distributed to the poor corn, wine, cheese, vegetables, oil, fish, meat, clothes, and money.[43] The bishop of sixth century Gaul was the chief personage in the social life of his diocesan city and its neighbouring territory. If the bishop was responsible for temporal administration, he would oversee the provision of public works, for example, dykes, canals and fortifications and would provide for the destitute with registers, poor-houses and hospitals. From 513 onwards, the property of the church became inalienable because it was considered to be the property of the poor, of which the bishop acted only as administrator.

Western monasticism too came to possess a strong consciousness of its social responsibility and, as we shall learn in the next chapter, its missionary functions. In most monastic traditions, social goals interacted with spiritual ones. The monasteries fed the hungry and poor, took care of the sick and dying, and were asylums for the unfortunates.[44] Monasteries also often served as comprehensive social-service agencies, acting as hospitals, homes for the aged and orphanages. They were a place where travellers could stay as there were very few inns during that time, and they provided education to boys in the local community. By and large, monastic institutions may have aided the progress of civilization, even though they have often been blamed for obstructing and retarding it.

### Arnold Toynbee's Thesis on the Genesis of Civilizations

We have described how the ancient world centred on the Mediterranean finally disintegrated when the last remnants of Rome's central imperial control collapsed, and how her economic prosperity and unity disintegrated thereafter. These events occurred from the fifth and sixth centuries onwards, contemporaneously with the political dismemberment of the Empire by the Germanic barbarians. Revelation 18:19 states, "Alas, alas, for the great city where all who had ships at sea grew rich by her wealth! In one hour she has been laid waste."

A new civilization might arise spontaneously and begin its life independently from any and every society that had preceded it. Alternatively, it could arise as a result of a transformation from a previous society which was undergoing its final, dying stages. Western civilization conformed to this latter pattern by emerging from the disintegration of the Hellenic world, and inheriting some elements from that earlier civilization, a social and cultural process which Arnold Toynbee labelled 'affiliation'.[45]

The Western church, John's 'Bride of Christ', took advantage of the opportunity, and possessed the capacity, to assist in the genesis of this new society. The barbarian successor-states were not assigned this role, for, as we have noted, their contribution to the creation of the nascent Western civilization was quite insignificant in comparison with that of the Christian church. With respect to its aspirations, this would not have been the church's original purpose nor its intended function. Both Toynbee and the German sociologist and historian Max Weber were of the opinion that religion had a positive role to play in the development of societies, but far from acting as the generative instrument which ignited the fire of a new civilization, Toynbee considered that the western church was but the means through which this new civilization emerged. We need to delve backwards a little, and ask the question, what other factor or factors were necessary to initiate the generative process? What were the circumstances which might engender a new civilization out of a 'Dark Age' of stagnation and decadence?

It would be impossible to find a solution to such a difficult question in purely historical terms. As a prosaic explanation, it may be said that civilization came into existence at the moment when man as hunter, for the first time, refrained from devouring his prey on the spot and took it home, thereby postponing his immediate pleasure. Such divorce of pleasure from need has become a characteristic feature of civilization. Perhaps, on the other hand, geographical conditions favoured the development of agriculture. Arnold Toynbee, in his major work *A Study of History* (1934-1961), was looking for an answer of a completely different kind, and supplied it by recourse to the language of mythology. He described a static situation in a pre-civilized existence as living in a perfect state, and employed as the primordial example Adam and Eve in the Garden of Eden, who were without blemish. We might also say that Faust, the subject of the famous Western legend to be discussed in chapter 5, was a compatible example, for he sought to attain the utmost degree of knowledge. But Toynbee considered that such states of perfection within their own terms of reference could be changed only by an external impulse or motive. Another protagonist would have to be brought on to the scene from the outside, an external adversary who could generate a fresh start, with force if need be, by instilling distress, discontent, fear or by sowing doubts.[46] The function of the intruding factor was to supply a stimulus of the right kind for a humanity that was indolent by nature, to evoke further creative variations in the most potent way. This was the role of the serpent in the Book of Genesis, and of Mephistopheles in the legend of Johann Wolfgang von Goethe's Faust. The theologian and philosopher Pierre Teilhard de Chardin put the matter succinctly. The individual had to be given a shock, and he must be released from the extant structures that bind him, shattering them if necessary. In order to achieve this, it was indispensable that he should be provoked from the outside.[47]

With constant renewal, God's creation may be allowed to change and grow, but this does not entail that God has failed in His original creation. On the contrary, a fresh act of creation will lead to something new and which, within the terms of this new setting, will be equally good. Thus, the works of creation may be perfect but they can indeed be changed, as the biblical text at 2 Corinthians 3:18 states, from "one degree of glory to another". Toynbee, in his mythical scheme, conceived such a process of renewal as an encounter between two personalities. We need an enemy to sow tares in the field, or weeds among the wheat (Matthew 13:24), and this is personified by the Devil, or the Adversary, who intrudes into God's universe. If the Devil's intervention really is necessary in order to accomplish the transition from a static to a dynamic state, for Toynbee this might take the form of a wager between God and the Devil. However, the supposition that God should be obliged to accept or even contemplate such an idea must be seen at best to be misguided. The Devil, if He exists at all, must always remain subordinate to God, and God is not required or impelled by His nature to accept such an invitation, or indeed to perform any task whatsoever. Indeed, the Devil is able to act only at God's behest.

Again, according to Toynbee, the next stage of such a process comes through an act, performed under temptation from the Devil, by God's creatures, who serve as pioneers and this enables God Himself to continue His creative activity.[48] Theologians have drawn the conclusion from this that God permits the Devil to tempt human kind for the greater good to come. In a similar vein, Saint Augustine, in his aforementioned book *De Civitate Dei*, stated that God foreknew the sins of devils, but also their use in improving the universe as a whole. "For God would never have created any Devil…whose future wickedness He foreknew, unless He had equally known to what uses in behalf of the good He could turn him, thus embellishing the course of the ages."[49] Furthermore, Immanuel Kant preserved in a secularized form the Christian idea that human history originated in the fall of Adam, and that it consisted in the struggle between good and evil. Whilst he denied the notion of the Devil as an independent being, nevertheless, according to him, it was evil which brought the historical process into movement.[50] The Devil's role will be considered further in later chapters, but for the moment, if we wish to consider Toynbee's thesis at all in our description of the West's development, we can describe the Devil's task as a catalyst in accomplishing the necessary transition from the stagnant interregnum of the barbarian successor states to a new, dynamic civilization. However, it has to be stated that the widely held and antithetical view is that God is capable of new activity without any intermediary whatsoever. Rather, if God chose to modify His creation, it would be at His own volition.

\* \* \* \* \* \* \* \*

The Roman Empire had been split into two parts politically, with the construction of a new 'Rome' at Constantinople, this city eventually becoming the centre of the Byzantine Empire. A tripartite partition of the territories of the former Roman Empire ensued, and Western civilization's unique characteristics emerged as a result of how these factors interacted with each other.[51] The successor barbarian states in Western Europe, and in particular the Frankish kingdom, carved out one portion situated on its western and north-western flanks. Secondly, the Byzantine Empire continued to survive in the east. Thirdly, the rapid and unexpected Islamic conquests, beginning in 632, swept quickly and decisively over Asia Minor and North Africa during the seventh century and later, creating the Moslem Caliphate. As a result, the Western lands were effectively blockaded and forced to live upon their own resources, and for Henri Pirenne this in turn was the cause of the final break with the traditions of antiquity. It marked the separation of East from West and the end of any possible unity, political, cultural or religious, which would once again be centred on the Mediterranean. The relationships between all three forces, Frankish-Papal, Byzantine, Islamic, were to be important for the eventual establishment of Western civilization. Never again during the thousand years would one power base or religious culture unite the world that had belonged to Rome.

We have noted that it was during the decisive seventh century that Western Christianity adopted its own, idiosyncratic form. From the middle of that century, Western society effectively began to cast off its romanized character. An important factor which helped to distinguish Western Europe from the two other successors of the Hellenic world was the rise of feudalism. The process was complete, or nearly so, by the middle of the eighth century. It was the same population, but it was no longer the same society.[52] New ideas were accumulating which had existed only in an amorphous form in the Christianity of the Empire, and they came together with decisive clarity of focus during the seventh and eighth centuries. They accompanied the first stirrings of Western civilization.

The axis of society was now beginning to shift northwards away from the Mediterranean and towards the Seine and the Rhine, and for many centuries it remained there. As historian and jurist Rudolf Sohm stated, the horizon of mediaeval church history was not just a Christian one, but in all essentials that of the West, for world history was shifting its centre of gravity westwards.[53] The decadence into which the Frankish Merovingian monarchy had lapsed gave birth in due course of time to a new dynasty, the Carolingian, whose original home was in the Germanic north. The Germanic peoples, which had hitherto played only a negative part as usurpers and destroyers, were now called upon to play a positive part in the construction of this new Western society. It was the consolidation of the Frankish state which defined what Western Europe would become. Islamic expansion around the eastern and southern shores of the Mediterranean had brought to an end a Europe which had lived the life of the ancient world and of barbarism. The Carolingian Renaissance finally turned Europe towards a new orientation, possessing an identity of its own. The Carolingians found themselves in a situation which they did not create, but they were able to exploit it further, and by so doing ushered in the thousand years of Western civilization.

CHAPTER FOUR

*The Word of God in the Carolingian Renaissance*

"In the beginning was the Word, and the Word was with God" *John, verse 1:1*

**JOHN OF** Patmos foretells the last days of the Roman Empire, and it is indeed extraordinary to come across a prophetic narrative which predicts historical events several centuries in advance, and even more so, to find one which is able to achieve this with any degree of accuracy as to detail. In the preceding two chapters, however, we have described, not only the demise of the Roman Empire – perhaps many could have foreseen that event anyway given the decadence and turbulence into which that Empire had fallen – but also the fulsome circumstances which accompanied that demise in both political and economic terms. The actual events almost perfectly matched John's prophecies, and serve completely to validate his prophetic narrative. If we can conclude that the detail that John is disclosing in his earlier prophecies is significant and accurate, we will surely have a much greater confidence in his prophecies that follow. Such narrative therefore serves as an appropriate introduction to our main topic, namely, the thousand years of Western civilization.

Many exegetes would vehemently insist that the Apocalypse cannot be interpreted in an historicist manner onwards in time from the point at which the Roman Empire fell, and almost everyone would find it difficult to accept that John's apocalyptic text finds its counterpart in Western history. Furthermore, in common with many forecasts, historical or otherwise, we have reached the point where the more distant the future events are which John sets before us, of necessity the less detailed they must become. Once Rome had 'fallen', and a transformed Western church had emerged, acknowledged as a 'Bride of Christ', some commentators might contend that the ensuing events described in the apocalyptic narrative would take place eventually, but at a future unspecified time, or alternatively that the final chapters describe only allegory. If it is conceded that John has correctly prophesied the fall of Rome as a series of actual historical 'tableaux' in chapters 16 to 18, it would be somewhat bizarre if the following chapters, 19 and 20, were to change their character. Such an interpretation would suffer from the major defect that it conflicts with what John is actually telling us, for he states in Revelation 1:1: "The revelation of Jesus Christ, which God gave him to show to his servants what must soon take place." The phrase 'what must soon take place' is noteworthy and significant, for with this choice of words, God was imparting to the seer His plan for the future. It could be argued that the term 'soon' or its synonym 'shortly' which appears in other biblical texts, covers only events concerning the demise of the Empire, and not those which succeed it. This cannot be the case, because John mentions the word 'soon' yet again after he has narrated most of the prophetic events described in his book, at Revelation 22:6. "These words are trustworthy and true. And the Lord, the God of the spirits of the prophets, has sent his angel to show his servants what must soon take place."

We must investigate what John infers from this wording. Does it mean a few years, several centuries, or many millennia hence? Perhaps it signifies immeasurable periods of time extending far into the future. The word 'soon' cannot bear this latter meaning in human terms. An alternative explanation would be that the word should be interpreted as one that is of indeterminate duration.[1] As Psalm 90:4 states: "For a thousand years in thy sight are but as yesterday when it is past, or as a watch in the night." This seems unlikely, as according to Ernst Hengstenberg, God always speaks to men according to their own mode of understanding. Gotthold Lessing in his work *Die Erziehung des Menschengeschlechts (On the Education of the Human Race)* (1780), wrote in similar terms, namely, that the message God conveys to us at each step reflects the degree of development of mankind's reason at that time.

Is it possible in some way to delimit the word 'soon' in John's text, so that we can determine an appropriate time-frame? The Empire's 'decline and fall' occurred between the fifth and the seventh centuries within some hundreds, not thousands, of years after the Apocalypse was written in the 90s. This fixes the meaning of the words 'soon' or 'shortly' in human terms. Alternatively, if John were to imply a change of time-scale from 'soon' to something else, surely he would have said so. Must we take 'soon' to mean in the one case of the Roman Empire's demise a few hundred years, and in other, later, cases in his book possibly many millennia hence? This would be tantamount to accusing John of inconsistency or caprice. It would not be reasonable to assign one meaning, or timescale, to the word 'soon' in one part of John's narrative and another, completely different one, for the remainder of it, unless John so indicates. If one part of the prophecy was fulfilled a few hundred years after it was written, we should not have perforce to wait many millennia more for the fulfilment of the remainder of God's plan, with a timetable which is intended to be postponed for an indefinite future period, thousands of years away. The appropriate time-scale therefore consists of hundreds, not thousands, of years stretching into a distant future. Furthermore, it is noteworthy that the seer frequently prefaces many passages in his narrative with the word 'then' when introducing a new episode or 'tableau' into his text. There are too many occurrences of this word in the Apocalypse to list them all, but the important verses for our purposes are Revelation 17:1, 18:4, 19:6, 19:10, 19:11, 19:17, 20:1 and 20:4.

There is a strong inference where this word appears, that the historical sequence of events continues without undue interruption or break, suggesting at the very least that the event or events in question follow each other without long intervals of time between them. That John uses the formula "then I saw" strongly implies that the events which he is describing are taking place, not only in a chronological sequence, but in close juxtaposition to each other.[2] The start of Revelation 19:11 does not differ from this pattern, referring once again to the Revised Standard Version: "Then I saw heaven opened." After the Roman Empire departs from history, John's narration of events follows on in quick succession.

Alternatively, it could be argued that, rather than representing an historical time-scale, the word 'then' refers only to the successive sequence of visions or dreams that John experienced. The events which are depicted in them might occur in subsequent periods in discontinuous time-frames and therefore in John's case, the word 'then' inserted into the text at frequent intervals does not appertain to an uninterrupted chronology of historical events. This suggestion does not seem to possess either much merit or feasibility. If the thousand years of the Apocalypse have indeed not yet come to pass and are to be deferred *sine die*, what are we to make of the present age, the time which extends from the fall of Rome, so correctly prophesied by John, up to the age in which we are now living? Why does John not give us some kind of description for this period too? There is only one conclusion that we can draw from an unwarranted interpretation which places the later of John's prophecies from chapter 19 onwards in the Apocalypse into an indeterminate future time-frame. We would be living at the present time in an historical limbo, awaiting the next sequence of events which are described in John's text and which are to take place at some date far into the future. In short, if John does intend a huge hiatus, or interval of time, in his prophecies at this point, he does not say so. Why should we now assume that there will be an enormous gap in the historical narrative such that we have perforce to wait for a very long time before the occurrence of the next collection of prophecies in chapters 19 and 20? To conclude, John's Apocalypse has made a faithful prophecy, and he has marshalled his text, in which he prophesizes the dismemberment of the Roman Empire by the ten principal barbarian 'kings' or tribes, their conversion to Christianity, the Empire's final economic collapse and the rise of a new church, which he describes as a 'Bride of Christ'. All these events follow each other consecutively and with great accuracy as to historical detail. The text of the Apocalypse, after describing the fall of Rome, does not indicate in the slightest way a different treatment from, nor a long break before, the next sequence of prophecies.

## The Rider on the white Horse

John's next vision begins in Revelation 19:11 in which he beholds a white horse, followed by the armies of heaven, who make war on the beast, the kings of the earth, and the armies of the earth. The description of a white horse appears earlier in the Apocalypse at Revelation 6:2, in which its rider was designated a conqueror. The colour white is symbolic of righteousness and the absolute purity of God, and the word 'conqueror' was an ancient title of Christ which signified his victory over sin and death. Saint Irenaeus was among the first to interpret this horseman as Christ himself.[3]

In chapter 19, the Rider who sits upon the white horse is now assigned additional attributes. He is called 'Faithful and True' and on his robe and on his thigh, he has a name inscribed 'King of kings and Lord of lords'. There is no gainsaying the fact that these titles belong to Christ, and so the appearance of the one who is thus described in this passage was taken by many exegetes to represent Christ's second coming. In the next chapter we will discuss both pre- and postmillennialism, and adherents of these two camps divide over the question of whether the second coming of Christ will take place before or after the thousand years. Certainly, we must agree that there is a coming of sorts described in this passage. The conqueror is described as coming first in chapter 19, and the thousand years follow in chapter 20. The question remains, how are the verses 11 to 16 in Revelation, chapter 19, to be interpreted, verses in which is described therein the 'Word of God', a description which has led some commentators to believe that it is at this point in the apocalyptic narrative that we witness the return of Christ.

Is there additionally, or alternatively another, return of Christ at the end of the thousand years, tantamount to a third one? Some commentators, such as the postmillennialists, maintain that Christ will not appear visibly until the thousand years have ended and that the resurrection before the millennium, namely the second one, will be spiritual, along with a spiritual resurrection of the martyred saints. This resurrection should not therefore be interpreted as a physical return to earth for the period of the millennial reign. The resurrection at the end of the thousand years will be the physical one. Many interpreters have debated whether Christ will reign visibly or invisibly during the thousand years, a point discussed further in chapter 7. Those commentators who believe that Christ will visibly inaugurate this period in person are designated premillennialists.

It is curious that, despite the several titles ascribed to the Rider on the white horse which allude to Christ Himself, nowhere in this passage is Christ's name actually mentioned as such. Is this a slip on John's part or is the omission intentional? Having posed the question, it would be reasonable to conclude that what is being described in this passage is not the advent of Jesus personally, but simply the triumph of 'the testimony of Jesus' in the world. Mathias Rissi stated that verses 11 to 16 in chapter 19 do not depict the physical appearance of the Rider, so much as describe his characteristics and functions.[4] By way of reiteration, Revelation 6:2 introduces the rider whose function is to conquer. Together with the vision in chapter 19, therefore, we see before us a picture of the rider on the white horse which represent the victorious progress of the Gospel of Christ,[5] a conclusion attested by the postmillennialists. The alleged resurrection preceding the thousand years is consequently to be understood as a spiritual renewal, or development, of the church.

According to the theologian Aaron Hills, the assumption that a literal battle is being depicted, fought on the earth by Christ in person, riding on a white horse, with a sharp sword protruding from His mouth, is absurd.[6] We are not to interpret this as manual fighting or a literal war. The sword by which God's victory is won is not a physical weapon, but issues from the Rider's mouth as the Word of God which overcomes all opposition as described in Revelation 19:15 and 19:21. Just as the ten barbarian kings and their peoples were conquered by the Lamb, so in this instance the forces of evil are overpowered through the faithful witness of the spoken word, not by force of arms. Therefore, if the Rider is to prevail over his enemies, the only weapon he needs is the proclamation of the Christian Gospel, the 'Word of God'.

It would be apposite at this point to introduce the idea of progressive revelation. Each cycle of events after the advent of Christ reflects the escalation of the conflict against Satan and the development of the Christian faith. Each of these events culminates in a stage higher for God and a stage lower for Satan. This is especially true in chapter 20 of the Apocalypse. As the book's narrative moves forward, there is more than recapitulation, for Christ is progressively more victorious and Satan's power is progressively weakened.[7] Thus the kingdom of Christ and the reign of the saints develop by degrees. The purpose of the first centuries of Christianity, designated ancient Christianity, would be interpreted as formulating, agreeing and settling the tenets and creeds of the faith by means of ecumenical councils. A religious faith could not, after all, undertake the work of extensive mission and conversion unless its doctrines had been firmly established. Next comes the dissemination of the 'Word of God'. This phase would be reflected in the Carolingian Renaissance, in which the 'Word of God' became an all-important, even vital, feature of the period, and it initiated the thousand-years' reign of Christ and the saints, an epoch which must be understood as the era of the church. There would be a resurrection at each end, the first spiritual and the second physical. It seems that the righteous were to be raised at the first resurrection and the wicked at the second. The first resurrection would consist of the blessed and holy, namely, the saints, as opposed to the rest of the dead, who would be raised at the end of the thousand years.

We can now apprehend the connection between the foregoing narrative and the Carolingian Renaissance. We left the last chapter with the emergence of a new Western church and with it, the dawn of a new civilization centred around the Frankish monarchy. With regard to the Apocalyptic narrative from chapter 19, verse 11 onwards, we shall explore the 'Word of God' and the way in which the Frankish kingdom during the reign of Emperor Charlemagne made it its primary and essential task to spread the Word of God. This can be witnessed not only in the way that it wholeheartedly pursued the encouragement of a more Christian way of life for its own peoples, but also in the way that it undertook renewed and extensive missionary endeavour in Western Europe. It was destined to be the crucible for carrying the Word of God ever further afield into those peoples of Europe that were pagan and therefore still remained to be converted to the Christian faith.

### The Background to Carolingian Rule

Conversion to the Christian faith made little difference to Frankish, or indeed any barbarian, rule before the eighth century. From the sixth century onward, the Frankish kingdom during the Merovingian dynasty was characterized by perpetual, aimless and destructive wars, by rape, murder, pillage, lawlessness and sheer incompetence. We have already noted that Saint Gregory of Tours chronicled with much sadness and trepidation this era of treachery and corruption. Yet it was this same Frankish kingdom which became ultimately the vehicle for refashioning Western Europe. Out of the remnants of the Roman Empire, its ethos shattered, its political hegemony destroyed, a cultural transformation was to take place during the next two centuries in the formative period of the new, Western civilization and the thousand years.

It is tempting to speculate whether this was indeed an example of Providence acting in history, and whether it was a case where the sheer depravity and criminality of the situation acted as a catalyst for change in the manner described in the previous chapter. Royal authority in the Frankish state had declined, to the point where the Merovingian kings had become weak and impotent. It was the mayor of the palace, the king's chief household official, supported by the aristocracy, who became the effective ruler over the passage of time. In 750, with the approval of Pope Zacharias, King Pepin III, the then mayor, usurped the throne by deposing the last Merovingian king and appointed himself king of the Franks, thereby inaugurating a new dynasty, the Carolingian. There were essential differences between the two dynasties, of which the most notable was the relationship with the church. Pepin accepted the royal crown by a religious ceremony at Soissons in 752, in which the oil of consecration was held to bestow on the monarch a new sacred nature. The power of the Merovingians had been purely secular, but that of the Carolingians in stark contrast now displayed a profoundly religious imprint.[8] A new ideal of kingship emerged, for the new ruler was such by the grace of God. Thus, from the beginning the new Carolingian monarchy was regarded as being divinely appointed. After 754, Pepin was invariably referred to as *spiritualis compater*, literally, spiritual cofather.

The events that took place in this period would eventually be considered so important as to have marked a new era in Western history. It was but a period of gestation on the way to the all-important year 800, which witnessed the imperial coronation of Charlemagne and signified the commencement of the thousand years. The same interval of time, about 50 years, was to prove significant once again when it occurred exactly one thousand years later. In that part of Western Europe which extended from the Seine valley towards the north and east regions in the vicinity of the old *limes* of the Roman Empire, a new economy, separate and different from the former Mediterranean economy of the ancient world, had for some time prospered. As a result, the Frankish monarchy had been able firmly to establish itself, and henceforth become the centre of Western culture.

A decision was made in the course of the eighth century to convert peoples living outside the Frankish kingdom to Christianity. With the idea of using force if necessary to accomplish this task, Pepin's ensuing military campaigns could be interpreted as a series of crusades. It would be interesting to know if the decision to employ military force was in some way inspired by the Apocalyptic text. The integrity of the church and the blessings of the clergy were important to ensure the continued protection of God and the saints, which in turn would assist in securing the success of these campaigns. This description has echoes of the Apocalypse in chapter 19, verses 11 onwards, but the similarity should not be over-stressed. In the present case, we are speaking of military campaigns rather than peaceful conversion by the Word of God.

## The Emperor Charlemagne and his Rule

To comprehend the nature of the Carolingian Renaissance, both the personality of Charlemagne and the nature of his rule must be considered. Charlemagne succeeded to the Frankish throne together with his younger brother King Carloman, but became sole ruler on the latter's death in 774. Charlemagne's Christian faith was to have an appreciable influence on the history of the church. Whilst his greatness was built on military success, he had a breadth of vision that elevated him from the rank of war hero to an enlightened ruler. Charlemagne made it clear that he laid his faith in a Providence deeply involved in human affairs, with a divine mission to act as the steward of a great inheritance and not just as a military conqueror. He considered that his prime responsibilities for enlightening his people were the extension of the kingdom of God, the care of the church in his dominions, and the correct teaching of the faith. A Christian emperor, ruling as the protector of the church and having responsibility for its welfare, could serve not merely as Christ's ally in the great war against evil, but at his coronation he would come to be hailed as something even more spectacular: the representative on earth of Christ himself. A man of immense energy and ambition, though illiterate until late in life, he attached great value to learning. He gave a new and biblical dimension to what was meant by living under the law, and attached importance to private and extra-liturgical prayer. The church was to him not only the visible representative of Christ on earth, but as an instrument of government, it was also an organ of civilization.

It would be an intriguing exercise to compare Charlemagne with the rider upon the white horse described in Revelation 19:11. That there are parallels cannot be denied, but the temptation must be resisted. Rather we should offer descriptions which he gave of himself or were given him by his contemporaries. Charlemagne and his courtiers used biblical names in their correspondence with each other, and Alcuin in particular described the king as the second David, who was charged with responsibility for the salvation of his people. In a letter to Charlemagne at the beginning of his reign, Cathaulf referred to him as God's earthly representative, and he advised Charlemagne to use the Book of Divine Law as his guidebook for government.[9] The Spaniard

Bishop Theodulf of Orleans and Saint Angilbert called Charlemagne by such terms as 'head of the world', 'august' and 'pacific', and reminded Charlemagne that he now ruled over a Christian Empire and a Christian people. Charlemagne himself wrote to Pope Leo III in 796, stating that he was 'lord and father, king and priest, chief and guide of all Christians'. These terms reflected the underlying conceptions which Saint Augustine had made in his treatise *De Civitate Dei*, Charlemagne's favourite book after the Bible.[10]

That Charlemagne was preoccupied with a civilizing mission and the religious life of his people was attested by the circle of clerical and lay scholars that he gathered at his court, and these were the most learned and eminent men of his time. They congregated around a monarch renowned for his intellectual curiosity, and they came from every part of Western Europe, and included the Northumbrian Anglo-Saxon Alcuin who had been educated at York, the Italians Peter of Pisa and Paulinus of Aquileia, and Theodulf of Orleans. Other great men, such as Leidrade of Lyons, Einhard, Agobard of Orleans, Saint Paschasins Radbertus, Rabanus Maurus and John Scotus Eriugena Hincmar were connected with the school which Charlemagne had founded in his palace at Aachen, either as teachers or as pupils. He valued Christian learned and cultured men for themselves, and not just as officials who were able to help him with the administration of his empire.[11]

Most were theologians, but their interest did not exclusively lay in this domain. Their talents covered many disciplines and a broad range of learning: as poets, philosophers, statesmen and practical administrators. The French statesman, François Guizot, writing in the nineteenth century, deduced from the emperor's choice of companions that "his predominating idea was the purpose of civilizing his people."[12] The Empire's cultural achievement was largely dependent on the contribution of these independent scholars. They thought of themselves first and foremost as Christians and their culture did not need to be reborn for the simple reason that they did not think that it had died in the first place. Their chosen term, therefore, was *correctio*,[13] which was intended to improve all aspects of life, including, *inter alia*, a programme for reforming moral behaviour. One defect which may be attributed to the Carolingian Renaissance in contrast to the later fifteenth century Renaissance was that its intellectual horizon was bounded by the Latin Fathers and the extant traditions of the church.[14]

The basis of the Carolingian monarchy followed that put forward by the seventh-century Spanish encyclopaedist Saint Isidore of Seville in which the Christian monarch was recommended to show himself not only in authority, but also in humility, and must benefit the people, not oppress them. In this, the idea of Christian leadership was paramount.[15] When Charlemagne waged wars on the northern and eastern frontiers of his kingdom in order to subdue the warlike Saxons, he aimed not only to incorporate their lands into the Frankish kingdom but to convert them to Christianity by stamping out their paganism. He considered it justifiable to use force by 'preaching with the iron tongue', namely with the use of the sword.

After these campaigns, much of Western Europe was now under Charlemagne's rule, almost a reincarnation of the former Roman Empire in the West. The Papal possessions in Central Italy were essentially a Frankish protectorate, and the small Anglo-Saxon and Spanish kingdoms, which lay outside Charlemagne's direct rule, were negligible, but they paid the Carolingian monarchy a deference which practically amounted to protectorate status. With the alliance of Church and state, Henri Pirenne was able to describe the monarchy as one that would be coterminous with what he called Western 'Christendom' directed and inspired by the spiritual authority of the Roman papacy. For him, Caesar and Napoléon alone enjoyed a comparable universal fame. The comparison with Napoléon is intriguing, for Charlemagne's rule stood at the commencement of the thousand years, Napoléon's at its end. Charlemagne could now be justifiably called Carolus Magnus, Charles the Great, a title which he conferred upon himself. He was claimed by both France and Germany as a founding father, the inspiration for the Holy Roman Empire.

With the idea of *correctio*, and in the task of ensuring that this 'corrected' Christian order was upheld, Charlemagne invoked the assistance of the entire governing class of his realm. Each group was given its own law, was urged to live by it, and faced the serious consequences of imperial disfavour should they fail to do so. In matters of religion, the true 'Christian Law' was universal in the sense that all baptized Christians participated in, and obeyed, it. Following the theme

Territory of the Carolingian Empire at the end of the eighth century
William R. Shepherd: *Historical Atlas*, Henry Holt and Company, 1923

of the 'Word of God', significantly, this was a written law. It was contained in texts, in the Bible in the first instance, then in written liturgies, in the rulings (canons) of the Councils of the Church, and lastly in the works of the Latin Fathers of the Church. It was to be disseminated by a largely new group of persons drawn from the monasteries and the clergy throughout the empire, who were to be the means by which society was itself to be trained for the service of God. A rare combination of the fear of God's displeasure and the confidence that the Christianity of their times could be 'corrected' from the top downwards impelled a movement that has been named the 'Carolingian Renaissance'. The ideal was to ensure that the divine precepts prevailed on earth, and to govern in accordance with Christian morality, that is, in accordance with the Church. In effect, Charles wished to prepare for the reign of the Catholic Church, not by destroying any national traditions, but by imbuing a fresh energy into ancient forms.[16] This was the ideal which Saint Boniface had presented to Pepin, and this ideal was bequeathed to Charlemagne.

Charlemagne's legislation was intended to protect orthodoxy and to eradicate heresy and theological error, and so he carried out a systematic programme for the reform of clerical education. He took care to ascertain that suitable men were nominated to high office in the Church. His capitularies, which were Frankish royal ordinances, underlined the responsibility of the clergy to live a religious life and to forswear secular pursuits and in their turn to ensure that the monasteries observed the rule of Saint Benedict.

During the 'Dark Ages' of the West, rural lifestyles replaced the once-dominant urban lifestyle.[17] Cities had shrunk dramatically into a moribund state, and were replaced by the monasteries. Unsurprisingly, therefore, in its turn the entire Carolingian developed monastic characteristics to a certain extent. Churches and monasteries received enormous endowments everywhere in Charlemagne's realm, and the first business that was undertaken after conquering a new territory was the formation of dioceses and the construction of churches. The great monasteries in their capacity as cultural centres were greatly to assist Charlemagne's plans for ecclesiastical and liturgical reform.

In all the Frankish provinces the Christian Church had a monopoly of ritual. Charlemagne's reforms furthered the unanimity of Catholic doctrine and practice and the introduction of the Roman liturgy, and his substitution of the Roman for the Frankish mode of chanting. Charlemagne asked Pope Adrian I for a book of canon law in 774. Intent on regulating the life of the clergy, at his request, Adrian sent him an expanded copy of the *Collectio Dionysio-Hadriana*, a set of ecclesiastical laws. For Henri Pirenne, the Carolingian Empire, or rather the empire of Charlemagne, provided the framework for the Middle Ages.[18] Whilst the state upon which it was founded was extremely weak and would presently crumble, the Empire would survive by being transformed into what we now recognize as the civilization of the West.

## The Word of God: the Bible and Christian Literature

The Rider on the white horse in chapter 19 is described as having a sharp sword issuing from his mouth, with which to smite the nations, and is named as the 'Word of God'. The Carolingians firmly believed that it was through the medium of the written 'Word' rather than through imagery, that knowledge of the Christian faith could be enhanced. The religious world of Charlemagne's advisors and their colleagues was dominated by written text, and this meant that faith and morals were promoted through the 'Word of God' from the books of holy Scripture. The Bible and Christian literature, therefore, became prominent features of the Carolingian period, as the basis of a wide-reaching reform of piety. With the firm intention of providing official and authorized texts for his subjects, as early as the 780s, and through the widespread use of the Bible, especially in preaching, sermons and learning, Charlemagne's subjects were able make a start in comprehending the Scriptures. It fostered an ethos in which the Bible was considered the ideal source of instruction and wisdom. Medieval society after the Carolingian period was to continue this practice. It inspired contemporary ideas, not only in religion, but also in literature, art, law, politics, and social policy.

The best-known Bible from this period is the manuscript of the *Codex Amiatinus* produced in England, but the first known Carolingian Bible was that of Angilramus, bishop of Metz, who produced a single-volume Bible. However, there were numerous different Bible translations available in the eighth century, some being based on St. Jerome's Vulgate, others from pre-Jerome versions, with English missionaries contributing yet more variations. Charlemagne had wanted biblical manuscripts that were reliable, an easy source of reference, and a normative biblical text so that Carolingian priests could be provided with one, authoritative, version. To this end, he commissioned Alcuin of York and Theodulf of Orleans to produce a revision of the Vulgate Bible with a view to correcting the many scribal errors that had crept into past versions. As Charlemagne's chief scholar in residence, Alcuin despatched a team to search for reliable biblical manuscripts.

Master copies of the new Bible were produced and distributed throughout the empire as examples of textual correctness and high standards of production. From the ninth century onwards, large bibles were produced at the abbeys of Saint Martin and Marmoutiers at Tours.[19] This project would have also included a revision of the Gospels, and many luxurious gospel books were produced in the scriptoria. Emphasis was placed upon faithful transcription and correction, so that the industry of experienced scribes ensured that their version of the Bible would indeed become the standard for the Catholic Church.

However, biblical culture and the study of the Bible were placed to a great extent in cathedral and monastic schools. As a result, this fund of learning was accessible only to the small literate and intellectual elite that existed in Carolingian society. Accordingly, a further exegetical tradition developed as a response to the needs of student beginners, monks, nuns and priests, and all those who were literate and who needed to be schooled in both the vocabulary of the Bible, and the first steps in its exegesis. The ecclesiastical councils of Frankfurt (794), Riespach (798), Aachen (816), Meaux (845) and Pavia (850) decreed that bishops were required to study the Bible and instruct their own clergy.[20] So far as ordinary people were concerned, biblical culture was mediated by the liturgy and preaching, and not by direct contact with Scripture, this being to a great extent standard practice until the Reformation.

Besides biblical study, that of classic literature was also revived, in order to make this heritage accessible to the clergy and monastic orders.[21] Early on, excerpts were not taken directly from the church Fathers but from biblical anthologies, because Carolingian exegetes were not prepared to engage with the patristic tradition without the aid of intermediaries. Biblical, devotional and secular texts were included, the latter to assist progress in the liberal arts. There was also an expansion in the copying of pandects, or compendiums. Many patristic scriptural writings, sermons, homilies, treatises and handbooks were recovered and worked on to provide consistent, continuous commentaries on almost the entire Bible as an introduction to it. For example, Alcuin of York was a major exponent of the works of Saint Augustine, Saint Benedict, Flavius Cassiodorus and Saint Gregory the Great. Lengthy commentaries of Saint Augustine on the book of Psalms and of Saint

Gregory on the book of Job, became standard in monastic and cathedral libraries. Late antique Latin translations of exegetical works by Origen of Alexandria, Saint John Chrysostom and the Cappadocian fathers were also widely copied. The theological writer Wigbod's *Commentary on Genesis* was dedicated to Charlemagne himself, and was an encyclopaedic text composed of excerpts from the works of more than eight church Fathers. Additionally, in a circular sent to religious institutions, Charlemagne continued the work of Flavius Cassiodorus by emphasizing the need to cultivate letters. By making a huge effort, nearly the whole of the patristic literary inheritance was retrieved, and this scholarship brought the church Fathers their first significant readership. It also resulted in instruction in the proper binding and preservation of books.

Charlemagne wanted the liturgical texts to be as accurate as possible, and to achieve this end, Alcuin ordered from Rome a standard documentary so that the Mass would be everywhere celebrated in the correct manner. The Gospel Capitulary, *Capitulare evangeliorum de Circulo Anni*, was a chapter list of each Gospel arranged according to the liturgical year. The so-called Rhenish *Weissenberg Catechism*, named after the Alsatian monastery's library where it was finally kept, contained texts in German of the Lord's Prayer and a commentary, the catechism, a list of the principal sins, the text of the Christian creeds and the *Gloria in Excelsis*.[22] This substantial collection was probably dated from around the time of Charlemagne's coronation in 800.

The monasteries played their part in this scholarship and book production. For example, the monks of Fulda worked on a German translation of a 'gospel harmony', called the *Codex Sangallensis*. In it, the four gospels were combined into a single coherent narrative, and it dates to about 830 when Rabanus Maurus was master and afterwards abbot of the monastery school at Fulda from 804 to 842. He also provided students with a complete series of commentaries on the Bible, which gained a leading place in biblical exposition from the 820s onwards.

Charlemagne collected many of the most important Christian writings in his library at Aachen, works necessary for what might be called 'applied Christianity', and established the professional study of Latin for a better understanding of the Bible, as well as encouraging a standardized Latin. In this way the varied heritage from the whole of the new Christian West could be shared in a universal Latin culture. Medical, astronomical, agricultural, musical, architectural, and military manuscripts were also studied for technical guidance. The works of several authors were studied, such as Priscian and Donatus, for the purpose of training in grammar, and the *Psychomachia*, a poem by the Latin poet Clemens Prudentius, used as a manual for moral teaching. There can be no doubt that the 'Word of God', as evidenced by the Carolingian era's studious work on the Scriptures and Christian literature, lay at the heart of its Renaissance, and established uniform standards for the ensuing centuries.

### The Word of God: Missionary Activity

The spread of Christian culture in the early years of Christianity had taken place from the Hellenistic cities of the Levant to the less advanced peoples of the West. A fresh wave of missionary activity flowing eastwards from the Christian populations of Ireland and England to the European Continent from the sixth century onwards reversed this process.[23] In Northumbria a new and remarkable type of missionary activity emerged, and it was destined to target and benefit the Germanic peoples of Western Europe. Whereas most religious revivals decline after a few decades, this one lasted until the arrival of the invaders from Scandinavia during the tenth century. Fired with an unquenchable zeal, these men planned and launched extensive evangelistic crusades. The ascetic ideal of pilgrimage, *peregrinatio*, was primarily what motivated this movement, or it could be said, represented a form of martyrdom, which entailed leaving one's homeland and wandering for the sake of God.

By the early eighth century, the recently established Anglo-Saxon churches in Britain had developed to a point where they could provide such missionary wanderers who possessed the necessary motivation. Noteworthy here were such names as Saint Patrick, Saint Columba, Saint Aidan, Saint Columbanus, Saint Fursey, Saint Clement (Willibrod), Saint Walpurga (Walburga) and Saint Boniface (Wynfrith), the 'Apostle of Germany'. As with the Western church of which he was a member, Saint Boniface stood for a new form of Christianity, unencumbered by the past. Supported by the monastic base in Ireland, Scotland, and Northumbria and an established Episcopal hierarchy in

Anglo-Saxon England, these missionaries crossed the Channel into those parts of Europe which were still pagan.

Christian missionary activity has often been considered a purely nineteenth-century phenomenon, but the Carolingians tackled missionary activity in an impressive way. Unlike the achievements of his Celtic predecessors, Saint Boniface's mission to Germany was not an isolated one, but formed only one part of a greater programme, for the conversion of these German peoples was the first time that Christianity had been extended to new territories outside the ill-defined frontiers of the Frankish empire. It might seem that the conversion of a few tribes of German barbarians was insignificant, but the work of Saint Boniface and his Anglo-Saxon companions on the northern flank of the empire contributed greatly in setting the groundwork for the future expansion of Western culture. Missionary activity now became a vital component of the church's endeavours. The faith was preached with much success, and the lands over which the Western church presided were effectively extended once the conversion of peoples in the western and southern German lands had taken place. The Anglo-Saxons were not the only protagonists in this task of conversion. Somewhat earlier, from elsewhere, including the surviving Christian areas of Spain, came Saint Emmeram of Regensburg, Rupert of Salzburg, and Saint Corbinian. Also of note were St. Amandus' work in Flanders and Saint Gregory the Great's role in the conversion of England.

The great abbeys situated near the frontiers of the empire had important roles to perform in this missionary enterprise. As well as evangelising the newly conquered territories, they had the additional tasks of maintaining local aristocratic support for the Frankish dynasty and to take part in the governance of the Empire. The list of monasteries and abbeys that were established during this period was impressive: Murbach (founded in 727 by Saint Pirmin), Fritzlar (founded about 732 by Saint Boniface), Ohrdruf (founded about 725 also by Saint Boniface), Amorbach (founded in 734), Benediktbeuern (founded in 740 by Lantfrid, Duke of Alamannia, Abbot Waldram and Abbot Eliland) and Reichenau on Lake Constance (founded in 724 by Saint Pirmin). The latter abbey promoted a number of other monastic centres, such as Fulda in 744, Gorze about 757, Lorsch in 764 and Gegenbach, and on several of the Austrian and Bavarian lakes, such as Chiemsee and Mondsee. Further foundations followed one another rapidly, for example, Saint Gall in Switzerland, Altomünster (about 760), Schäftlarn (762), Lorsch and Ottobeuren (764), Tegernsee in Bavaria (765), Hersfeld (769), founded by Saint Boniface's successor Saint Lull, Innichen (769), Kremsmunster in Austria (777), Frauenchiemsee and Herrenchiemsee (782) and New Corvey in Saxony (822). All these efforts are ample testimony to the Carolingians' missionary enterprise.

The see of Rome gave its support and encouragement in a co-operative enterprise between the Anglo-Saxon missionaries themselves, the Papacy and the clerical elites, and the rulers of the Frankish kingdom. The timing was significant. Here two historical situations follow one upon another. We discussed in chapter 3 the gradual emergence of the transformed Western church during the sixth to eighth centuries, and now in the eighth century itself the new missionary movement gathered momentum. The movement was to continue until it had converted the whole of Western Europe by the fourteenth century. The parallel with the apocalyptic narrative is notable. In Revelation 19:7, John writes of the 'bride' of Christ and immediately following in Revelation 19:11, John's narrative proclaims the 'Word of God' and the Rider with his armies who go forth to smite the nations, which can be interpreted as missionary activity.

The conduct, however, of the Frankish dynasty itself, especially during Charlemagne's reign, was inspired to a great extent by political motives. Frankish kings understood that the most effectual means of countering the barbarism of the outsiders, thereby rendering them less dangerous as neighbours, was to begin by converting them to the Christian faith, and so Charlemagne took a great deal of interest in the missionaries' plans. That the papacy legitimated the Carolingian dynasty was also of assistance in establishing Frankish leadership of this missionary work, and contributed to strengthening the growing Carolingian ascendancy and influence over the new political culture of Western Europe.

Historians have adopted the view that the Christian West was more zealous with regard to missionary work in the eighth and ninth centuries in contrast to the situation that had prevailed earlier in the Christian era.[24] We must enquire why this should have been so, even if we momentarily put aside the suggestion that the timing of Carolingian missionary activity exactly paralleled John's apocalyptic prophecy regarding the 'Word of God'. It was only in this period that a definite concept emerged and explicit decisions were made to pursue missionary work in Western Europe. Earlier, Christians had been slow to draw the conclusion that their faith should encompass all peoples of the globe, so that, in the main, Christians on the European mainland had not felt the need to convert peoples who lived outside their own lands. We must recall the earlier remark that the Romano-Christian world did not feel at all obliged to evangelize outsiders beyond its borders. The situation was now completely reversed from the point of view of the Anglo-Irish missionaries, for the role of missionary developed an identity of its own just before the Carolingian age. Furthermore, it must have become widely accepted that the Papacy should become intricately involved with missionary work, and as a result, the West became much more conscious of a missionary responsibility towards non-Christian peoples. Furthermore, the strength and power of the Frankish state itself in the eighth century underpinned Christian missionary enterprise and provided the necessary stimulus for the 'Word of God' to be disseminated.

Both Saint Boniface and Saint Pirmin appreciated the importance of books which led to the planning of missionary literature. Sources of practical advice were to be found in manuals and model sermons, for example, Saint Martin of Braga's *De Correctione Rusticorum (On the Correction of rural People)*, and the *Indiculus Superstitionum et Paganiarum (Small Index of Superstitions and Paganism)*, this latter consisting of capitularies identifying and condemning superstitious and pagan beliefs, emanating from Germany in the eighth century, but was possibly dated much earlier. Such missionary expansion did much to spread Christianity and restore monastic life throughout Western Europe during this period, and it had the effect of setting the culture of the West apart from other civilizations. We may conclude *tout court* that missionary work was accorded a new prominence in the Carolingian age, compared to earlier centuries. Consequently, the image of the missionary was changing from that of an itinerant, holy miracle worker to become principally a teacher of the Christian faith,[25] establishing centres for contemplation and study, which would assist the revival of education.

## The Word of God: Teaching and Education

Besides missionary activity, a no less important aspect of this period was the domestic policy of teaching and education to impress the 'Word of God' upon the empire's own subjects. To achieve this end, books and writing were crucial components of Carolingian culture from its earliest days. The Scriptures had to be taught, explained and understood, and so education was considered by the Carolingians to be of great importance. The eighth century began to witness a significant change in the attitudes of the church's elites, for they adopted a rationale to civilize and convert. Education now became as important as miracles and it began in the Carolingian Empire itself. Churchmen in previous centuries, such as Saint Augustine, Saint Caesarius, Saint Gregory, Saint Isidore of Seville and the Venerable Bede had wanted to strengthen what they often saw as the nominal faith of the laity. The reformers of the Carolingian Renaissance were given a greater opportunity to carry out this policy, in part because they were the legatees of the efforts of these earlier churchmen, and in part because new resources had become available.

Much of the resurgence in education and scholarship can be credited once again to royal initiative. Hardly any rulers have surpassed Charlemagne in their understanding of the value of education, not just for the clerical order but for the laity as well. In the Palace School at Tours directed by Alcuin of York and continued by the great Carolingian abbeys, centres for higher study were established. Their main achievements were educational as well as literary or philosophical, by preserving the traditions established by the Palace School, and such traditions were transmitted to their pupils in turn. Together with individual assemblies of officials, both secular and ecclesiastical, Charlemagne undertook a methodical project for Christian teaching, clerical standards and instruction, consisting of capitularies. Now it was possible to understand and conduct Christian ceremonies in the correct manner and this would extend to prayers. The *Admonitio Generalis (General Admonition)*, discussed below, by ordering the establishment and maintenance of schools and libraries in monasteries and cathedrals, marked the very beginnings of a tradition of higher learning, a true renaissance.

Schools, with distinguished scholars presiding over them, now became dispersed over the empire, usually connected to monasteries and cathedrals, for example, Alcuin at Tours, Theodulf at Orleans, Rabanus Maurus at Fulda and Mainz, and later Hincmar of Rheims and Remigius of Auxerre. Alcuin saw that the chief need was to train teachers and so successful was he in his training programme that after fifteen years, when he retired, universal free education had become a viable prospect. In an important official document, the *De Litteris Colendis (On the Cultivation of Letters),* probably drawn up between 781 and 791 by Alcuin of York or Angilramnus of Metz and addressed to Baugulf, abbot of Fulda, Charlemagne encouraged monasteries and bishoprics to promote learning and to be zealous in teaching others. The renewed interest in the texts of Saint Caesarius of Arles from the early sixth century reflected Charlemagne's wish to make preaching one of the major elements in his reforms. It would have made an important contribution for promoting religious education.

In the task of disseminating the 'Word of God', a parallel, graphological revolution occurred with the introduction of the 'Carolingian miniscule'. Charlemagne understood the value of good writing for efficient administration, since universal application of the law was dependent *pari passu* on a universal script. The literate now came to expect that Latin texts should be easy to use and understand, and so the development of a new script became the handmaid of Carolingian learning. The new miniscule was clear, uniform and attractive, smaller and so much more regular and more legible than its predecessors, making it easier to read and copy manuscripts. It would be no overstatement to say that it became one of the great success stories of the Carolingian era. By the end of the eighth century texts began to be written out in such a way as to guide the voice of the reader. They were now punctuated and divided up into paragraphs. Text and comments could thereby be separated, which improved the layout when it was employed for teaching purposes. Next, punctuation warned the reader immediately when a sentence ended and how the sentence fell into separate parts, with capital letters marking its beginning. Even doubt and certainty, indicated by cadence of voice, could now be written in textual form, and the question mark directly originated from this. Books began to be produced more in a form that we recognize today. The first dated example of the Carolingian miniscule appeared in the evangeliary written by Godescalc between 781 and 783, at Charlemagne's request. The monastery of Tours became the centre for the spread of the new miniscule, which was to influence the whole of later scriptural development in the Middle Ages,[26] and it formed the origin of all modern western European printed alphabets. Alcuin was also concerned with grammar and spelling, and these features were apparent in the careful copying of the Maurdramnus Bible (772-781), the earliest known use of the Carolingian miniscule.

### The Word of God: Councils and Decrees of the Carolingian Empire

The second half of the eighth century was to prove vital for the Frankish church, because a series of councils were held, and decrees issued, that had as their objective the implementation of far-reaching ecclesiastical reforms. In the 740s, Saint Boniface was requested by Pepin III, to begin reforming the Frankish church with a view to promulgate stricter organization, and the first of several assemblies were held in 742 under his presidency. Reflecting the relative independence of the spiritual sphere, later councils held between 755 and 767 encouraged the clergy themselves to organize and direct reforms in which standards in ecclesiastical practice were established and disputes settled. Pepin III attended some of these meetings in person and issued laws in order to ensure that their decisions were enforced.

Capitularies were royal ordinances that comprised a series of legislative or administrative acts emanating from the decisions of individual assemblies of secular and ecclesiastical officials. Several of these were issued with the aim of developing methods to improve Christian teaching and clerical standards. The Assembly of Herstal in 779, for example, issued two capitularies which elaborated some of the duties of bishops regarding the spiritual care of those in their diocese. However, some of these capitularies were particular in their application, such that they were promulgated in local assemblies comprising only the men of those provinces. Thus, it would appear that, despite the autocratic nature of Charlemagne's rule, he would oftentimes observe the maxim that laws should be made by those who have to obey them.[27] Other ecclesiastical capitularies, decided by councils of bishops would have applied to all Christians in the empire and yet others would have contained decrees which all subjects of the empire had to obey.

In one of his great edicts, Charlemagne, with Alcuin of York as his main consultant, carried out a major reform of the Frankish church in 789, the agenda for which was the *Admonitio Generalis*, addressed to all his subjects throughout the Frankish kingdom. Charlemagne was determined that the *Admonitio* should serve as the groundwork for the correct teachings of Christian doctrine, which referred back to the notion of *correctio*, mentioned earlier. It consisted of 82 chapters, clauses, or sections, many of which were devoted to instruction for the clergy and laity. The aim was to improve Christian learning and create a *societas christiana*, a Christian society, and to provide guidance in resolving all kinds of ecclesiastical disputes. One part consisted of rulings of past church councils, and others had their origin in papal decrees. Another was to make religious texts and books, corrected and standardized, accessible to the clergy. All of them were connected with the duties and responsibilities of the clergy, from the top down through the ecclesiastical hierarchy. Similar enactments continued to be issued for a considerable period during the Carolingian Renaissance.

A theological revival that long outlasted Charlemagne was triggered by the numerous synods that were conducted during his rule and by his own personal interest in theological issues.[28] One such synod, and an important one, was held at Frankfurt in 794, discussed below, in which it condemned various Spanish and Greek heresies. It also resulted in a number of canons which aimed at regulating the life and work of the bishop and his clergy, and to encourage and discipline the clergy to follow correct practices. It might seem strange that such measures as these were necessary, coming as it did soon after the *Admonitio Generalis*, but it reflected the need to combat constant relapses among Frankish clergy and monks. The canons concerned a range of topics, for example, the organization of secular clergy, popular observances, the demand that all Christians be taught the Lord's Prayer, the Creed, and the correct doctrines of the Catholic faith, and the requirement for monks and nuns to adhere to the Rule of Saint Benedict.[29] Charlemagne even conceived it his obligation to protect all defenceless Christians in any part of the world where they were exposed to violence from other peoples and governments, for example, to intercede, successfully, for Christians in the Middle East, and to found a hospital for Latin pilgrims in Jerusalem.[30]

## Defeat of the Beast and the false Prophet

From Revelation 19:17 onwards, John's apocalyptic narrative reveals the outcome of the battle that takes place with the Rider on the white horse. A complete victory is won over the two beasts of the Apocalypse and the kings of the earth together with their armies. Michael Wilcock held the opinion that this second beast should not be identified solely with religion but rather was to be understood as the ideology, which underpinned any form of human society that does not respect or obey God and so leaves Him out of account.[31] The Apocalypse then states in Revelation 19:20-21: "And the beast was captured, and with it the false prophet who in its presence had worked the signs by which he deceived those who had received the mark of the beast and those who worshipped its image. These two were thrown alive into the lake of fire that burns with brimstone. And the rest were slain by the sword of him who sits upon the horse, the sword that issues from his mouth." In these two verses John has in mind the very instant in which the powers of the beast and the false prophet, together with their armies, are defeated.[32] This could be interpreted as proclaiming the final overthrow of the pagan and polytheistic religions within Western Europe's borders, religions which had played such an important part in the Roman state and amongst the barbarian tribes. Nevertheless, pockets of pagan worship would still remain, for example, within the lands bordering the Baltic Sea. In Lithuania and Prussia there remained a hard core of pagan resistance, finally extinguished only in the fourteenth century. What is being symbolized here is the victory of the 'Word of God' over these hosts of wickedness and paganism, their conquest serving as the introduction to the thousand years.

The early church had fought without respite against traditional polytheist worship and pagan pantheism within the Roman Empire. One might well have inferred from the unexpected conversion of the Emperor Constantine in 312 that the recognition of Christianity as the newly favoured religion of the Empire, would have brought an end to the dominion of paganism, and would correspond to the defeat of the beast and the false prophet. In that instance, John's chronology would have seemed to have gone astray, and the passage from Revelation verses 19:17-21 should have been inserted earlier in John's narrative when he is describing the Empire's demise. But Christianity's historical victory over the pagan Empire was equivocal to the degree that demonstrated that this was not the case at all, for the beasts had constantly reappeared in deceitful ways, Christian or otherwise, and clearly the conversion of the Roman Empire did not usher in the long-awaited promised kingdom.[33]

By the end of the fifth century, the Christian church had become the only public religion of the Roman world and it was asserted that paganism had been eradicated, but remnants of the old beliefs would remain. It would be reasonable to assert that John's description of the beast could encompass any form of paganism, against which Alcuin of York continued vehemently to oppose. In this case the kings of the earth mentioned in Revelation 19:19 could well be represented by the leaders of pagan tribal groups, such as the Saxons in the eighth century, the Scandinavians in the ninth century, the principalities of eastern Europe in the tenth century, Wendish paganism in the twelfth century. It was not until the fourteenth century that the last piece of the Christian jigsaw was put into place in the West. Whilst the Slavs resisted Christian conversion in the seventh century, and the Danes in the eighth, both were readier to accept it later, at a time when paganism, now lacklustre and deficient in organization, encountered the Christian religion, now organized, resurgent and confident.[34] Not until the natural world had been demystified could it be repopulated, this time with Christian figures, more especially with the Christian saints. Once again, therefore, John's chronology concerning the defeat of the beast and the false prophet proves to be correct compared with actual historical events.

The date was 743, close to the countdown for the commencement of the thousand years and in that year the *Indiculus Superstitionum et Paganiarum* (*Index of Superstitions and Pagan Practices*) was composed. This document declared, in effect, that paganism had effectively been wiped out. At last, it seemed to the Carolingians that in the areas of Western Europe formerly within the Roman Empire, conversion to, and the practice of, the Christian faith, was no longer perceived as taking the form of a straightforward battle with the forces of evil. That had once been the principal factor in the saga of Christianity's triumph, but in the eighth century, victory over pagan gods could be taken for granted. The bishops' sole task henceforth was with survivals of pagan remnants, the persistent resurgence of which demonstrated the ignorance and obstinacy of those people who insisted in clinging to their old practices.[35]

One solution to the ongoing problem of pagan customs was to make religion an affair of state which entailed that only those who belonged to the Christian society could also belong to the public society, and excommunication was equivalent to being placed outside the law.[36] This principle could be traced back to Saint Augustine, who was the first Christian thinker to propose that everybody in a given society, with the exception of the Jews, should be a Christian. This was very different from proclaiming, as previous Christians had done, that Christianity was a universal religion in the sense that anyone could, in theory at least, become a Christian voluntarily. In this respect, Charlemagne's political thought was also derived from Saint Augustine. The latter commented that in this life nobody would be able to attain perfection in the situation where divine and satanic forces were embroiled in constant conflict. Church and state in the newly formed Western society responded, contrariwise, by confronting the forces of evil, and not by disengagement from the world.[37]

### The Schism between West and East

One last task remains before we enter the thousand years itself, and that concerns the schism between the Latin papacy and the Eastern Orthodox Church, centred in Constantinople. This did not occur only in the eighth century, for the two cultures had been gradually diverging from each other during the 'Dark Ages', but differences over doctrine or practice became more frequent and more acute as time passed. Between 726 and 843 the emperors in Constantinople enforced a policy of iconoclasm upon the Orthodox Church. All religious images, in painting, sculpture, metalwork, wood, plaster, glass, or any medium whatsoever were to be destroyed. It was an attempt to cleanse the church of any idolatry by abolishing images which focused on religious veneration. The iconoclast ruling was denounced in the strongest terms by the Western ecclesiastical authorities. Pope Gregory II summoned a council in 731, which rejected it. Charlemagne and his court also condemned the Orthodox decrees at the synod of Frankfurt in 794. This synod went well on the way to finalising what had been a long journey towards rupture or schism between the churches of East and West, and it had the effect of encouraging the West to be a separate and self-conscious unit.

Theodulf of Orleans was commissioned to prepare a memorandum on the cult of images which came to be known as the *Libri Carolini*, and in it no opportunity was lost to distinguish the Christian rule of Charlemagne from what the Franks considered as the essentially pagan government of Constantinople. Law was God's gift to mankind. When it came to visual symbols, God preferred to make himself known by His commands, namely by words, and not by images or comparable means. With the iconoclast controversy we meet a curious twist to the 'Word of God' theme. For the Carolingian leadership, Christian people needed the sharp words of the Law, and the Greeks, with proud insouciance, took the easy way out, since they used the medium of little pictures.[38] Words, not images, took precedence. Of much greater importance in the long term for the relationship between East and West was the doctrinal conflict, which concerned the alteration of the Christian creed by the addition of the *filioque* clause, which we shall meet in the next chapter.

Charlemagne's tactics towards Constantinople, whether political, ecclesiastical or religious, were in every way motivated by an attitude of rivalry rather than accord.[39] The Franks availed themselves of a number of spurious documents, the foremost called the *Donatio Constantini (Donation of Constantine)*, to assist in justifying a western imperial authority which was independent from the East. We see here an enduring divergence between East and West, two spiritual centres of very different characters. What the coronation ceremony in 800 symbolised was of enormous significance for it acknowledged, *inter alia*, the consolidation of the Latin Christian West as something distinct from the Greek Christian East. In Theodulf of Orleans' opinion, the Carolingian Empire was superior to Byzantium because, in the Latin West, the religious and the secular powers were considered distinct from each other.

\* \* \* \* \* \* \* \*

The claim has been made that the thousand years of the Apocalypse commenced around the year 800 at the time of the Carolingian Renaissance. Whilst no commentator other than Ernst Hengstenberg has ever before explicitly made such a statement, we must ascertain whether the writings of other historical and theological authorities lend support to the idea that this particular date assumed a very great importance in European history.

Charlemagne's professed restoration of the Western Empire was the first time that Western Europe had experienced some kind of unified state since the Roman Empire in its heyday. It could also be said that it was the starting point of Western culture, involving a great spiritual and intellectual upheaval. Now Western Europe, dominated by the church and the feudal system, adopted a new character, and its development was affirmed by the end of the eighth century with the constitution of the new empire. It set the seal on the break between the Christian East and the Christian West. The Middle Ages were beginning, and this new political order could with good reason be called the 'birth of Europe'.

An anonymous poet extolled Charlemagne, as the *Father of Europe* (*Europae Pater*). There are several theories regarding the origin of the name 'Europa'. One theory suggests that it came from Greek or Phoenician mythology, but it is significant that the term was employed for the first time around the turn of the eighth century for the territory over which Charlemagne had nominal control.[40] The political unity of the Carolingian state did not last long, but an international European unity of culture in its French, German, English and Italian modes, did survive. That culture became a fundamental part of the core concept of Europe.

The Mediterranean basin had served as the centre of the ancient Hellenic world. Now, as the Mediterranean was in part becoming an Arabian sea, the focal point of Charlemagne's empire shifted to the Rhine.[41] The German theologian, Hans von Schubert, in his book *Geschichte der christlichen Kirche im Frühmittelalter* (*History of the Christian Church in the early Middle Ages*) has described this reversal in the following terms: "The home of Western Christendom, the main theatre of its history, was thrust northwards. It was marked off by the line Rome-Metz-York. Rome, the mistress, lay no longer at the centre, but on the periphery. The unitary culture of the Mediterranean countries was shattered...a new age was beginning; the age of transition was over."[42]

For the historian Judith Herrin, the coronation of Charlemagne in 800 represented a watershed between the Dark Ages and the High Middle Ages.[43] The historian James Bryce expressed a somewhat similar view: "The coronation of Charles is not only the central event of the Middle Ages; it is also one of those very few events of which, taking them singly, it may be said that if they had not happened, the history of the world would have been different."[44] The successful development of this society was due to the efforts of three groups: Catholic missionaries, Roman popes and Frankish kings. The empire over which Charlemagne and his successors ruled would come to be called some centuries later the Holy Roman Empire, and its creation was a key step in the creation of the parallel concept of 'Christendom'.

Curiously, the date of Charlemagne's coronation also happened to be of enormous significance within a cosmic timetable. In Saint Augustine's time it had been calculated that six long millennia would pass, and that upon the 6,000th year of the world's existence, the time of the Antichrist would dawn, and the world brought to an end in the year 801. Alarm was raised that the end of the world was now imminent. The year passed by and the Antichrist did not appear. Did the leaders of the Christian West ever really believe that he would? Was there some connection between Charlemagne's coronation and this prediction, or did it represent a most curious coincidence? We may contend that what appeared instead was the start of the thousand years and Christ's millennial reign, not the Antichrist, but that this event would certainly not have been recognized at the time. A similar situation arose at the end of the tenth century, when claims were made resulting from a similar augury.

Until the middle of the eighth century, what legislation of a Christian nature there had been in the Western barbarian kingdoms were merely an adjunct to the existing barbarian tribal laws. In a discontinuity with the past, the Western church was able for the first time to strike out on its own, by making its own laws. The traditions of the Hellenic world had been transformed. Now a new civilization with a Romano-Germanic ethos was about to evolve.[45] The thousand years would bring cultural and intellectual progress in every field of endeavour: architecture, philosophy, art, science, mathematics, music, but the one theme that was given the chronological pride of place was the 'Word of God'.

CHAPTER FIVE

*Three Aspects of the Christian West I: The Faustian Society*

"Restlessness is discontent, and discontent is the first necessity of progress." *Thomas Edison*

WITH THE first verses of chapter 20 of the Apocalypse, we have arrived at the most controversial part of John's book. Unsurprisingly there have been endless disagreements as to how to understand it. Verses 1 to 3 describe the chaining of the dragon and no speculation would be necessary to ascertain what the dragon represents, for we are told this unhesitatingly in Revelation 20:2. "...that ancient serpent, who is the Devil and Satan." The events portrayed by John in this chapter introduce an event that is another subject of controversy, namely, the Devil's departure from the scene. The assumption has been made that it occurs solely within the context of John's apocalyptic prophecy. Viewed from a completely different perspective, intriguingly this is not the case. Arnold Toynbee set forth a similar idea when he was describing in his mythical scheme the genesis and chronology of civilizations, which has been described in chapter 3. After a new civilization had been created with the Devil's assistance, he stated that the Devil has shot his bolt, which is to say that he has completed his appointed task. This inferred that once the new society had entered the formative stage, the Devil was given no further role to play and departed the stage. In chapter 20 of the Apocalypse, John's narrative appears to pre-empt Toynbee's description, albeit in a different, prophetic, guise. The seer is giving an account of a situation which Toynbee maintained, mythically speaking, was common to all emergent civilizations.

For those who object that such comparison is unjustified, we can summarize the situation by stating that, in the first instance, a new set of circumstances was being created, namely, a society ruled by Christ and the saints. Secondly, we have seen that the Devil was employed as a kind of catalyst to begin this fresh act of creation, and thirdly once the new society was established, God's purpose would continue to be fulfilled without the Devil's further participation. That Satan was consigned to the abyss, and was of no importance in later proceedings, has been indicated by the fact that it was not God who dealt with him, nor Christ, but only an anonymous angel. In other words, the Devil's function was to recommence the creative process and so enable a new situation to emerge, and nothing more. The narratives of both John's Apocalypse and of Toynbee converge on this point.

The Apocalypse states in verses 20:2-3 that the angel held the key of the abyss, or bottomless pit, and a great chain, and bound Satan. The angel cast Satan into the abyss or pit, locked him up, and sealed it over his head. How can we reconcile this biblical statement with an actual historical event? The plain answer to this is that we cannot within the pictorial terms stated here. John's statements are clearly figurative or metaphorical, for there cannot be a key to the abyss nor can an angel lay hold of the Devil, an immaterial being, and bind him by physical means. The comment of the theologian John Walvoord is appropriate. He states that this passage describes the way in which the event appeared to the seer as part of his visionary experiences.[1] It does demonstrate, however, that the angel had authority over the abyss and that he could restrain Satan.

### The Millennium explained

Together with the destruction of evil at its most radical, in due course it would be the Devil's turn to suffer the same fate as had befallen the beast and the false prophet, but that event is delayed for a thousand years. What significance should we attribute to the fact that the precise phrase 'a thousand years' is nowhere else described in the New Testament, except in John's Apocalypse? John introduces it as a completely new term at this point. He places so much emphasis on the phrase, to denote that he has been made aware of such a period, that he repeats it, not once, but six times over, in each verse from Revelation 20:2 to 20:7. The millennium itself raises dilemmas. Does it refer to an actual period of history as many students of the Bible have understood it, and as the present narrative understands the matter? Or is it a symbolical representation of the eternal rule of Christ and the saints, as Saint Augustine and others have taken it to signify? The word 'thousand' as referring to a number of years was specified in the second book of Enoch or Slavonic Enoch, chapters 22-23, but only in John's Apocalypse is the millennium mentioned in the New Testament. Until about the year 150 B.C., the Jews thought that the Messiah would usher in a reign of eternal happiness on earth, and in the period just before Christ's advent and ministry, vestiges of that belief still remained. In some Jewish circles it was supposed that the Messiah would reign on earth for a limited time, the estimates of which varied.

The millennium gives John the opportunity to introduce something new into his narrative, but it is a matter of contention as to how this time period should be understood. Many exegetes would argue that a thousand years in biblical terms was meant to signify only a long time, and was not meant to represent an exact period. To maintain that this term can be mapped to an actual historical period of a thousand years would surely be a gross error. Not only the Apocalypse but the rest of the Bible is full of references to periods of time other than one thousand years, and in no case can the accuracy of these be accepted. For example, 'half an hour' in Revelation 8:1, 'three days and a half' in Revelation 11:9 and 11:11. 'five months' in Revelation 9:5; 'a thousand two hundred and threescore days' in Revelation 11:3 and 11:12; 'forty and two months' in Revelation 11:2 and 13:5 are time periods that John writes about, or infers from his visions, not periods that he witnesses. Other wording is employed, for example, 'forty days and forty nights'. The symbol of 'one thousand' is often used in the Bible to refer just to a large and complete set.

Some historians have maintained that all higher cultures pass through a life cycle analogous to that of an organic evolution, from birth to maturation to inevitable decline. Arnold Toynbee wrote of the genesis, growth, breakdown and disintegration of human societies. He outlined over twenty great cultures, and Oswald Spengler found eight, each of which were self-contained and had a distinctive soul or style. Furthermore, at the end of Toynbee's major work *A Study of History*, a table of chronologies is presented in which his civilizations are listed, and it is significant that thousand-year periods can be discerned, at least from the foundation of a society until the onset of a 'universal state', this latter being one of the important phases in a society's decline. Western society appears to be undergoing a pattern which is no different from any of these. Therefore, it might seem from our modern point of view that there should be nothing unusual for a prophecy to include a period of a thousand years. But John of Patmos would not have had any knowledge whatsoever of the kind of historical and cultural detail which has become available to modern historians, from which he might have grasped the significance of a period of one thousand years. Mention has previously been made that historical scholarship of the kind that we are discussing was unknown in the ancient world in which John lived. It is also noteworthy that a period of one thousand years is equivalent to forty generations, if it be accepted that the number of years that constitute a generation has consisted historically of around twenty-five years. The number forty appears in the Bible in many places to designate important time periods, and scholars understand it to represent symbolically a period of probation or testing. The very concept of discrete civilizations in history could well find its justification on such a basis, analogous to Arnold Toynbee's idea of challenge and response that we discussed earlier.

*In fine,* just as the Devil's departure from the scene is attested both in the Apocalypse and by Toynbee, so the concept of a thousand-year period appeared analogously in both Spengler's and Toynbee's works. It must be emphasized that there will not necessarily be any relationship between John's apocalyptic narrative and the accounts of these two modern historians, but the several correspondences in detail between them are beginning to seem intriguingly rather more than just a set of surprising coincidences.

Perhaps it was possible, some dared to maintain, as the first millennium of the Christian era drew to a close, that John really had intended that the number one thousand should be taken literally after all. We may ponder over this point anew, but for Christians in the early medieval period who were growing accustomed to dating years from *Anno Domini*, this question was far more urgent for them than it is for us moderns. At the start of the tenth century, for example, nine hundred years and more had passed since Christ's coming, and the thousandth was approaching. Christ might be expected to return somewhere around the year 1000. Similar to the year 801 mentioned previously, as the year 1001 dawned, the anticipation still lingered that an apocalypse was imminent, a feeling that had become deeply engrained in the Christian people of the West. Yet once again the Antichrist did not appear. Eventually, western Christians came to enjoy periods of peace and spiritual well-being, which persuaded many that the binding of Satan would now occur sometime in the future. Oswald Spengler maintained that the Faustian soul of Western man was born during this very same period when the idea of the impending end of the world spread over Western Europe.[2]

Christianity is a universal religion and Western Europe was now destined to be the bearer of that universality. This concept created the problem that such an attribute could not be reconciled with Western Europe's bound geography. As the Christian West came to feel encircled by a hostile and alien world, European self-awareness with a distinctive culture was bound to develop. Moreover, this Christian universality as it found expression in the West, was to provide an important impetus to European expansion in the centuries ahead.

### Three eschatological Schools of Thought concerning the Millennium

Many exegetes have treated Revelation 20:4, which deals with the thousand years, as a prophecy about the distant future, or, to put the matter in a different way, perhaps as an event that would occur eventually. This thousand-year period came to be interpreted in various ways and given a variety of labels, such as millenarian, millennial or chiliastic. Interpretations of the millennium in the Apocalypse have been influenced to a great extent by the connection which students and scholars have made between it and the second coming of Christ. Revelation 20:10 states that Satan will be bound for a thousand years, and at the end of this period, he will be released to wreak havoc for one last time, and will finally be banished to the lake of fire. In what way exegetes expounded this section of John's text in order to provide an explanation of it, gave rise to three eschatological schools. The main question for scholars was whether the second coming of Christ would take place before or after the millennium, and these two interpretations were called premillennialism and postmillennialism respectively. A third interpretation, which was entitled amillennialism, rejected the idea that there should be any actual millennium occurring in historical time at all.

**Premillennialism.** This interpretation emphasized the concept that Christ's second coming, which would inaugurate his kingdom on earth, would take place before the thousand years, and the period immediately preceding that return would usher in a plethora of earthly disasters. The transitional period prior to the millennial kingdom would involve a conflict between Christ and his enemies, and the reign of Christ and the saints would follow. According to some exegetes, this interpretation is in conformity with the progression of events as described in the apocalyptic narrative. Moreover, it is accredited to be that which the church Fathers held in the early years of the Christian faith. The premillennial interpretation is closely connected with eschatology, for the kingdom of God could not be accomplished apart from the personal and visible return of Christ. In modern times, this view has been commonly held by evangelical Christians. Supporters of premillennialism further divide into two groups, following either dispensational or historical premillennialism, which concerns the rapture of the faithful, the end-time ascension into heaven of all the faithful.

**Postmillennialism.** This view of the millennium normally expected the thousand years to begin in the future. The transition to the millennium would be viewed in terms of historical progress, a series of victories by which the world would finally enter into a state of spiritual fulfilment. It was depicted as a period of growth and prosperity for the church and without any spectacular supernatural events. The return of Christ would take place after the thousand years, and the resurrection before the millennium would be spiritual, not physical. This was the interpretation inspired by Joachim of Fiore. Although the postmillennialist interpretation became popular during the eighteenth century, examples of it occurred during the previous century in the writings of the theologian John Cotton of Boston, Massachusetts, the clergyman and commentator Thomas Brightman, and in a volume of annotations by members of the Westminster Assembly. The German Pietist and theologian, Philipp Jakob Spener, too, expected a thousand-year period of prosperity for the church, at the end of which Christ would visibly return to earth. Thus, postmillennialism tended to exalt the church rather than the manifestation of Christ. The liberal theologians of the nineteenth and early twentieth centuries also espoused this view, placing the emphasis, however, more on moral and social factors.

Supporters of one or the other interpretation disagree over the question whether God alone acts to establish the kingdom, the premillennial view, or accomplishes this through human agents, the postmillennial view. In addition, disagreement exists over the extent of the power of evil, with the premillennialists maintaining that their opposite number underestimates this factor, while the latter accuse the former of having an overly negative viewpoint.[3]

**Amillennialism.** In addition to premillennialism and postmillennialism, amillennialism was a third option. At the present time, this interpretation finds many supporters in the mainstream Christian denominations and also amongst many Messianic Jews. Following Christ's second coming, there would be no future administrative reign of Christ. Instead, His reign is being fulfilled during the present age. It implied a rejection of belief in an actual millennium. 'Spiritual' would be a more appropriate description than amillennial, or perhaps one could consider the millennium of chapter 20 to be symbolic only, since the negative prefix attached to the word amillennialism implied a denial of a literal kingdom of Christ. Amillennialists based their concepts from the work undertaken by Origen of Alexandria and Saint Augustine in which they transformed the apocalyptic texts into allegory. In this context, the expression 'a thousand years' represented ideas rather than arithmetical values or an actual period.

In any survey of Christian history, one of the three versions outlined above should be more appropriate than the others, but which one? Christ will come again, and at the Last Judgment Satan will be destroyed, or else forever cast into the abyss of hell. This last chronology, found in the apocalyptic narrative, indicated the changing faith of the church after the first century, when it had become clear that Christ's first coming had not removed evil from the world, and that, moreover, His second coming, or *parousia*, had failed to occur.

Saint Augustine's way of looking at this problem was equivocal. He opted for a literal view at first, and espoused the interpretation of chapter 20, in which the kingdom of God was to be a future literal reign of Christ undertaken with His saints on earth. Subsequently his views fundamentally changed. He was credited with having popularised the amillennial interpretation, but this was an inaccurate portrayal of his thought. He actually agreed with the millennial doctrine and taught that Christ's incarnation heralded the start of the millennium, but the time period could stand for the remainder of the sixth millennium of the world's history. His viewpoint may be described in some sense as veering towards the postmillennial. The term 'spiritual' might once again be a more appropriate description.

The Nicene creed states that Christ will come again to judge both the living and the dead, and the presumption has always been that the Last Judgment will take place at the end of history. The premillennialists held that Christ will return before the millennium. It must be presumed that in this case the Last Judgment for them will also occur before the millennium. There are some exegetes, however, who believe that a *parousia* will occur twice. One will occur before and one after the millennium. This is exemplified in the first instance by the passage describing the Rider on the white horse, already explained in the previous chapter, and in the second instance by the passage concerning the one who sits upon the great white throne as depicted in Revelation 20:11. What, then, is the point of the subsequent thousand years and the release of Satan at the end of this period? Surely the release of Satan to do his worst will be a testing-time for those of the Christian faith, and this in itself will necessitate a subsequent judgment of sorts. Furthermore, if the Last Judgment before the millennium will be followed by a multitude of events, this does not sound very much as if it signifies the end of history. Would not the thousand years and the release of Satan be themselves historical events of tremendous significance? The Apocalypse is quite clear on this point, however. For John, the opening of books and the judgment take place after the thousand years and after Satan has been released for the last time, and Revelation 20, verses 11 through to 13, bear witness to such chronology: "And the dead were judged by what was written in the books, by what they had done." Whilst this may not bring the controversy to a final close, in historical terms at least, we do seem to be looking at a postmillennial interpretation of both history and the apocalyptic text at this point.

### The Millennium was coterminous with the Christian West

The Devil, or Satan, is banished and locked up for a thousand years, but this takes place not as a punishment, but as Revelation 20:3 states, so "...that he should deceive the nations no more, till the thousand years were ended." The wording is significant, and will repay some attention. In Revelation 12:9, Satan is described as the deceiver of the whole world, and Revelation 20:7-8 states: "And when the thousand years are ended, Satan will be loosed from his prison and will come out to deceive the nations which are at the four quarters of the earth." In both cases, it appears from the wording that all humanity the world over will be involved. But why does John not say the same earlier in his narrative at Revelation 20:3, when detailing the thousand years, with such wording as: "that he should no more seduce the nations which are *in the four corners of the earth*"? But he does not insert the phrase italicized here. Are we to conclude that the omission of the words *in the four corners of the earth* is a mistake on John's part? If this is not the case, the difference in wording must be deliberate. Only the words 'the nations' on their own are stated at this point, and so it would appear that only a part of humanity is involved in the millennial scheme. We are not told in John's narrative exactly what constitutes this group of nations, but it must be contended that the phrase could just as well refer to, and be restricted to, the nations of Western Europe as to any other collection of nations. But the question remains, why should the whole world not be involved in this process?

Arnold Toynbee maintained that whenever new societies or civilizations have been formed, only a part of God's creation must be put at risk. In the course of human history many have indeed been found to fail during their initial stages, and all civilizations have been limited in both historical time and geographical space. Whatever else may be controversial about this section of the Apocalypse, it seems quite clear that a new, and different, society was being created over which Christ and the martyrs would reign for one thousand years, and Western civilization personifies this situation. Indeed, the writer Edward Edinger, in describing symbolically the concluding events of the Judeo-Christian myth, stated that John's apocalyptic narrative "has been the womb and the metaphysical container of Western civilization."[4]*

From what source or sources did the seer obtain the term 'nations'? It is an intriguing question. At the time when John wrote his Apocalypse in the 90s, the Roman Empire covered a large land mass in Europe, and parts of the Middle East and North Africa, with the Mediterranean Sea as the central geographical feature. In Toynbee's opinion, it had become a universal state comprising many peoples. Throughout the Empire any

---

\* © 1999 Dianne Cordic. Reproduced with permission of the publisher, Open Court Publishing Company.

of its citizens, who were not slaves, could travel without let or hindrance, and all of them could enjoy freedom under the *Pax Augusta* or *Pax Romana*. But the Empire was not a nation, nor was it a collection of nations. Neither did nations exist on its periphery. There were indeed empires, the Assyrian and Parthian, for example, and, in addition there were many Germanic barbarian tribes which in the future were to pose increasing, external threats to the Empire as we have noted in chapter 2. These in no manner whatsoever could be called nations. Neither would the seer have received his idea of nationhood from the Greeks, who had flourished earlier in the history of the Hellenic civilization under a collection of city-states. The ancient world had its republics and its municipal kingdoms, but these could not at all be considered as nations. Indeed, the French philosopher and historian Ernest Renan stated that nations are something rather new to history. There was nothing similar to them in antiquity.[5] There was only one nation which could have given John this idea. This was the Jewish nation, one bound by its religion and history as narrated in the Old Testament, but also bound partly by blood-ties, and partly by geography, at least until the diaspora. However, this Jewish nation would not have conformed to the modern idea of a nation, or indeed to any collection of them.

Moreover, it is quite strange that John did not say "that he may not deceive God's people until the thousand years were ended", 'God's people' being a phrase which he had employed earlier in Revelation 19:8, and reiterates later in Revelation 20:9. Is this difference of wording significant, or merely another potential slip in John's narrative? Why does John employ the phrase in other contexts, but not here? One would have thought that it would indeed be God's people who were being referred to during the thousand years as being kept immune from the Devil's wiles. In chapters 19 and 20 of the Apocalypse, it would appear, therefore, that what John was implicitly describing was the commencement of a new thousand-year society ruled by Christ and the martyrs, and a society that was comprised of nations. We can certainly associate this society with the Christian West, which had created a temporary political unity in Western Europe under the Carolingian Empire, but this unity proved to be transient. Once this empire had come to an end, the establishment of a new empire, even one resembling that of the Carolingian, had now become unfeasible. A single political community in Western Europe was not to be realized during the thousand years. Instead, the concept of the nation-state, was held to exist in an essentially religious, or spiritual, framework during the early centuries of the Christian West.

## The Emergence of Western Nations

We must conclude that the mention of the word 'nations' by John is deliberate, and indeed the new nation-states of the Christian West, which gradually emerged in the tenth century, fitted his description quite accurately. Originally, some of these new national kingdoms arose in part as a result of the failure of Charlemagne's empire, a failure which stemmed from that empire's inability to create institutions. But the movement also came into being as a need to organize resistance against yet another bout of heathen invaders, for the Norse, Viking and Magyar attacks on Western Europe began about 850 and continued into the tenth century. Leaders from these new nations were all engaged in successful military resistance against them. They not only assisted in nation-building but also served as a stimulus for the West, in a concept described by Arnold Toynbee, to be one of the challenges and responses necessary to carry the infant Western society over into the next phase of its development.[6]

As a result of 'shared suffering', to quote Ernest Renan, during these invasions, Western nations of Faustian characteristics started to emerge ever more distinctly from the time of Otto the Great, Holy Roman Emperor from 936 to 973. When peoples came together and at the same time possessed a common Christian ethos, nation-building became attainable. It so happened, therefore, during these early centuries that the Christian West began to develop as a plurality of separate nations. The primitive peoples of the Dark Ages – Saxons, Franks, Visigoths, Lombards, Norsemen to name the most notable – rapidly dissolved as a result, and national peoples akin to those that we recognize today – Germans, Frenchmen, Spaniards, Italians, English – took their place. After England, during the medieval period it was principally in France that the forces of nation-building were generated, and this process spread from there into other countries,[7] such as Burgundy, Lombardy and Portugal, and later Spain, the Netherlands and Switzerland, though it would take many centuries before the process and the adventure of nation-building in Western Europe would be fully completed.

The Western church too suffered a period of devastation at the hands of the Norsemen. The great monasteries, especially those of Southern

Germany, St. Gall, Reichenau and Tegernsee, were the only remaining islands of intellectual life left amidst this renewed tide of barbarism which threatened to submerge Western Europe. Though ill-equipped to withstand yet another bout of lawlessness and warfare, the monastic system managed to recover in an extraordinary way, and Christian belief was not obliterated. On the contrary, once the invaders had accepted the Christian faith from the moment of their settlement, Christian influences filtered back to their native countries. The conversions of the Scandinavian lands were a good example of this.

The subsequent revival of spiritual life in the monasteries in the tenth and eleventh centuries originated from the Burgundian abbey of Cluny, in which the rejuvenation of the Benedictine rule became the archetype of all subsequent Western social reforms that were to transform the medieval church and society. As a result, all over Western Europe monastic reforms took place, and these became an independent and important power in Western society. A similar challenge, albeit an internal one, confronted the papacy during the same period. The Church had declined once the papacy had become the preserve of Italian families. The situation was resolved by the Hildebrandine reforms of the papacy and its spiritual leadership in the eleventh century.

The idea of the divine right of monarchs, or a guarantee of particular rights conferred by God, was derived from the belief that these new Western nations derived their political sovereignty from a divine mandate.[8] Then at the end of the eleventh century royalty began to play its own part in laying firm foundations for these nations, just at the time that the European bourgeoisie began to emerge. The law school at Bologna, as part of the autonomous university, dedicated to the study of the *Corpus Iuris (Body of Law)* of Emperor Justinian, fostered the development of sovereign independent nations. At the Council of Constance, 1414-1418, for example, called by Sigismund of Luxembourg, who was to be crowned later as Holy Roman Emperor, significantly the voting was by nations, and it indicated the importance which nation-states were beginning to assume in the history of Europe,[9] fuelled by economic and population growth.

The cornerstone of the medieval political order was the alliance between church and state, a feature established during Otto the Great's reign.

Political philosophy from the Carolingian age through to the twelfth century, was not so much concerned with theories about the state itself, but rather with the relationship that should appertain between spiritual and temporal authority. The Holy Roman Empire, itself a major symbol of the Christian West, was reconstructed, and it was destined to last until terminated by Napoléon in 1806. Two hierarchies now coexisted in the West, the religious or spiritual represented by the papacy, and the secular or temporal represented by the Holy Roman Emperor. The separation between politics and religion, unique in history, and the resultant conflict between the two, was an important and significant hallmark of Faustian culture, which was to last until after the Reformation.

### A brief Note on the Devil or Satan

In this chapter we shall deal with the Faustian legend, and in a later chapter the demonic nature of modern society. Any treatise which deals with these subjects would be incomplete without a note on the Devil, however brief. Apart from the appearance of a devil in the Persian Achaemenid Empire from 550 B.C. onwards, little or no mention of such a being was to be found in the early period of man's spiritual development. The idea of the Devil originated from several elements, which included the Jewish Lucifer in the Old Testament, but in Judaism, the Devil received very little attention. He appeared to operate on many different levels, but most notably at the level of the individual. It was a controversial point as to whether he was indeed a person at all, or rather a force for evil in God's creation. Rudolf Steiner in his work *Luzifer und Ahriman in der Seele des Menschen (The Influences of Lucifer and Ahriman in the human Soul)* (1919) analysed the Christian Devil into different forces that constantly worked upon the individual human psyche, seeking to divert humanity away from right conduct.[10] The Devil was said to achieve this oftentimes by transforming himself into an angel of light, in the capacity of Lucifer, meaning the 'light-bringer', but was, however, unable to create anything new himself. He could only pervert the good that had already been created.

The other power was Ahriman, the dark and malevolent Earth spirit of the Zoroastrian faith, but also known as Satan, Mephistopheles or Moloch. In Dostoevsky's book Братья Карамазовы *(The Brothers Karamazov)* (1880), he wrote that God and the Devil were engaged in a struggle in which the battlefield was the heart of man. The scholar

Stephen Smalley suggested that, in contrast to his status as a person, Satan was referred to in the Apocalypse as the personification of evil.[11] It has also been said that the Devil was employed as a supernatural being by those who wished to create a convenient scapegoat by which they might attempt to absolve themselves of responsibility for their own wicked deeds.

We can survey only briefly what the Devil has come to mean specifically during the Christian era. The problem of evil has loomed large in Christian belief, and the development of Christian theology brought this question into the foreground in a more intense way than ever before. Christianity dealt with the problem by asserting that evil had substance and personality as the Devil, Satan or Lucifer. The Christian faith holds that the Devil was the first and chief among the angels that God created, but was also the first to disobey Him and as a consequence was expelled from heaven, and other angels were expelled with him. Having been often accredited this status of a rebellious angel, his function was regarded as the Lord of Hell, and a counter-principle to, or adversary of, Christ Himself. For the first time mankind was able to perceive the stark contrast between God's bright celestial kingdom and the dark pit of hell.[12] In contradistinction to some earlier religions, this did not by any means infer that Christianity was a dualistic religion. On the contrary, the opposition between good and evil must always remain asymmetrical, since the good must always prevail. Christian theologians were quick to point out that in this connection the Devil himself cannot acquire human nature.[13]

The diabology of the New Testament is almost the same as that of Hellenistic Judaism, which had separated the good from the evil aspects in its spirituality, the former appertaining to the Lord and the latter to the Devil. The latter tempted humans to sin, if not committing evil deeds himself, and the Apocalypse describes him as commanding a force of evil spirits, known as demons. Revelation 12:9 states: "And the great dragon was thrown down, that ancient serpent, who is called the Devil and Satan, the deceiver of the whole world – he was thrown down to the earth, and his angels were thrown down with him." Jesus considered him as an existent being and an enemy of God.

The New Testament authors, too, had an acute sense of the immediacy of evil, and the conflict between good and evil stood at the centre of their teaching. Throughout, there was an emphasis on conflict between God and Satan, and this battle was tantamount to an intense confrontation. The Devil is thus a central concept in Christian teaching, and as the ultimate principle of evil. Christ came at the critical moment in history to promise salvation from evil and the power of the Devil, or as the Orthodox version of the Lord's Prayer states, from the evil one, and this was the quintessential message of the New Testament. Never before in historical time had these themes been promoted in so forthright a manner. It would be impossible to compose any history of Christianity without the Devil, and next to God and Christ, he has played a significant part. For most of the Christian era, including the thousand years, the faithful were required to believe in the Devil just as much as they were required to believe in God.[14]

Christ's opponent could variously be considered as a force leading to deception, as an evil teacher, or as a particular facet of society. He has been described as a roaring lion who goes about seeking those whom he may devour. We can envisage evil on earth as emanating from an energetic Satan, but it is also true that we can never conceive the Devil as having a completely free hand. The essence of Christianity would be greatly impugned and compromised if the Devil was considered to be merely a marginal or insignificant concept, and if his power was ignored. In such a case, Christ's mission of salvation would be rendered meaningless. We shall see in chapter 9 that the advance of apostasy from the Christian faith, a movement which arose in the nineteenth century, could be considered in just this light.

At the end of time, it is the Antichrist that will become the final enemy in the main Christian tradition. Satan will inhabit and possess this Antichrist as fully as possible. The Russian theologian Vladimir Soloviov made this point clear. "Only a human being, not the Devil, can possess the ability both to command and perform or refuse to perform the good. There is no understanding of the real meaning of evil apart from the Antichrist."[15] So this aspect could adequately describe the work of Satan in the world. He may be a human or a spiritual adversary. The fact that the Devil may have no physical reality and is instead a symbol for evil within the human heart, or as Immanuel Kant would describe it, a principle of 'radical evil', does not mitigate such evil.

## The Devil and the thousand Years

John describes Satan as being bound for the thousand-years, and just as specifically he states that Satan was prevented from deceiving the nations. Does this phrase mean that he was completely neutralized during this period? The religious commentator Beatrice Neall maintained that the Devil was indeed prevented from performing all evil during the millennium, and that he was completely immobilized by being banished to the abyss and locked up there. Others differed from this interpretation in that they considered that the Devil was not altogether prevented from engaging in his nefarious activities. They interpreted the phrase to mean that although Satan was still busy, he was restrained from doing his worst. Many exegetes objected that Satan was so evidently active that it was nonsense to talk of him as bound during the present, or indeed any, age. We are reminded that John does stress his present activity in Revelation 12:12: "...the Devil has come down to you in great wrath, because he knows that his time is short!" Moreover, the end will be decided by God in His own time and in His own way.

Whilst the Devil was prevented from seducing the nations, he could still remain active in a personal manner to target, tempt and seduce each individual. Indeed, the people of the medieval period believed that they lived precariously on the edge of the abyss. It was quite apparent to many leaders of medieval society that the activity of the Devil was indeed manifest, and this led the church to declare that there was a conspiracy which was headed by Satan. Life in this world was a ceaseless and desperate struggle with the Devil, in which everyone in the Christian community was engaged as a member of the church militant. The churches employed the idea of the Devil as a big stick with which to chastise and control its Christian followers, by constructing a solid framework of ecclesiastical ways and means, and to threaten punishments which would be inflicted by Satan and his demons in the fires of hell for those who proved wayward.

In this situation, both a Mary-cult of prayer and a Devil-cult of exorcisms and spells were presented, and disbelief in either of them was a deadly sin. Mary was the protectress and comforter, a sentiment which found its expression in the figure of the Virgin and Mother Mary, representing the world of purity and light. However, inseparable from this realm was another lurking in the background that bred evil, schemed, seduced and destroyed, namely, the domain of the Devil.[16] The Dominicans played their part in this fight against the Devil by forming the Inquisition. Indeed, belief in the Devil's potency became more vivid than ever as the Christian society of the West progressed. A similar feeling existed among opinion makers in the early modern period, in which they depicted Satan as lurking beneath the most trivial, everyday choices, with the result that every infraction was stigmatized as, literally, devilish.

Curiously, though, the notion that the Devil was active to a greater or lesser extent during the medieval period did not seem to be shared by everyone. A contradictory source can be found in Hildegard of Bingen's allegorical morality play *Ordo Virtutem (Order of the Virtues)* (c1151). In Part II of her text, we encounter the words, "my colleagues and I well know that you are that ancient dragon who wished to fly higher than the greatest, but God Himself threw you into the abyss."[17] The Devil and his minions may have been imprisoned in hell, yet they seemed to remain present in the air, in time and in history. It was indeed a problem over which many found enigmatical, including the bishop of Paris, Peter Lombard, in the twelfth century. Lombard was less than certain whether Satan had been imprisoned in hell, or not. He recognized that there were authors, by employing the apocalyptic text, who maintained that Satan had been bound and he did not have access to tempt man. Moreover, in his *Summa Theologiae (Summary of Theology)* (1265-1274), arguably the greatest of all systematic Christian theologies, Saint Thomas Aquinas, was also unable to resolve this paradox. Was Satan bound in the bottomless pit and yet still active in Christian society? There was a further 'demonic' issue here. In so far as the Devil was God's servant and the enforcer of His will, God had to shoulder the responsibility for the evil that the Devil committed. This problem was also involved with the various theories concerning the millennium discussed above. It was not clear whether the binding of Satan had already occurred, or whether and when, it would happen in the future, or whether this event should be taken literally. It was also intertwined with the question as to how Christ's rule was to be construed during the thousand years.

The Protestant Reformation reinvigorated the idea of the Devil. Martin Luther accused the Devil of perverting the Word of God, and he thought that the Devil enticed the faithful to deviate from true doctrine. The idea was sufficiently real for him to be credited with throwing an inkpot at him. For Luther life was a desperate battle against the Devil, and he called upon everyone to fight against him. The Reformed churches continued to provide evidence of what they regarded as Antichrist and his practices, but this Antichrist was no longer a person for the most part, but rather a tyrannical or deceptive force. Ecclesiastical identification and vituperation with the concept of the Antichrist spread so widely that finally the term became virtually meaningless.[18]

The preoccupation with the Devil did not cease after the Reformation, quite the opposite. Europe was absorbed once again by a huge preoccupation with the diabolic mania. This was now spread by far and wide, for example, by preachers, popular stories, Protestant literature, and the Inquisition, and all sought to render the Devil more powerful than at any time since the early centuries of Christianity. It generated an entirely new genre of writing, for example, the popular *Teufelsbücher* or Devil's books in Germany. It became a Christian tradition, dramatized by Alighieri Dante and John Milton, to view Satan as the master of hell in which he tormented people there. Unlike his predecessors, Milton painted Satan as a heroic figure, only to show that this was a pretence, in order to make Christ's triumph all the more noble and magnificent. In his work *Paradise Lost* (1667), Milton addressed the Devil thus: "And thou, sly hypocrite, who now wouldst seem patron of liberty."[19]

The witch craze, which originated in the Middle Ages, also fuelled belief in the Devil. Christian people everywhere were now presumed to be threatened by witches, led by Satan, and it was claimed that they were all connected to one great conspiracy. Whilst there never was in point of fact such a conspiracy at all, this certainly did not deter unanimous declarations of its reality from myriad ecclesiastical institutions, both Catholic and Protestant, and even Orthodox, as well as from academics and secular organisations.[20] Indeed, witchcraft was now placed within a legal framework, and prosecutions for witchcraft reached a high point at the end of the sixteenth century. It was only later in the middle of the seventeenth century that scepticism would arise with respect to the Devil's powers, by which time the witch craze was on the decline. The notion began to circulate that demons might be nothing more than symbols of human evil. Around the same time, Sir Isaac Newton's system, together with the views of the English philosopher, John Locke, the French philosopher René Descartes, and the Portuguese-Jewish philosopher, Baruch de Spinoza now discouraged any belief in the Devil.

After John Milton's comprehensive and persuasive description of the traditional lord of evil, there would be no other that was comparable until that of the German literary genius Johann Wolfgang von Goethe, since the topic was brought into disrepute by the rationalism of the eighteenth-century Enlightenment, and afterwards somewhat perverted by the Romantics in the nineteenth century. Since diabology was always the most vulnerable part of traditional Christian belief, the *philosophes* of the Enlightenment, and in particular the philosopher David Hume, helped finally to destroy any belief in the Devil. They had little time for such ideas, oftentimes resorting to mockery. For Hume, the Devil appeared virtually beneath his notice, for François Voltaire evil was not connected with the Devil, who he considered to be a bizarre Christian superstition, and for Immanuel Kant statements about the Devil, and indeed about God, were deemed to be meaningless.

Others of atheist persuasion reacted in a similar way, with Denis Diderot and Baron Paul d'Holbach treating the subject with disdain. The result was that by the end of the thousand years, most educated people had abandoned such views. The *coup de grâce* was accomplished by Immanuel Kant in particular, in whose conceptual ethics any and every idea of the Devil assumed a final shape as the 'Radically Evil'.[21] Indeed, it was only those attached to the Pietist movement that continued to uphold belief in the Devil. That Satan had now been relegated to the margins of the European intellectual mind was boldly depicted by William Hogarth in his print *Credulity, Superstition and Fanaticism*, published in 1762. In this, he ridiculed religious gullibility, and this included the very idea of the Devil. Thus, by the end of the thousand years, Europe's intellectual elite had begun either to doubt the existence of the Devil or to repudiate altogether the idea that he could perform any significant role in the world. For them, he had become a fictional figure, who was considered never to have been involved in history in the first place, being a mere idea of the human imagination without any firm substance.

## The Faustian Legend

Every civilization creates its own distinctive myths, and in view of the prominent position which the Devil has held in Christian belief, the quintessential Western myth related to this very topic. There have been many tales about people who have made pacts with the Devil, and so we need to refer back to the origins of the legend that gave rise to what has come to be known in the Christian West as the Faustian one. The oldest known version of this story, and which was probably the inspiration for the later German version of the legend, concerned Saint Theophilus the Penitent, or Theophilus of Adana, a cleric in the sixth century Christian church. He was reputed to have made a pact with the Devil to secure ecclesiastical advancement. As an historical figure, this story gained an element of popularity during the Middle Ages, but it was reworked into a myth which was more suitable for the European mind at that time. It proceeded to serve as the main ingredient for the later, Faustian story, which in turn was based on a real magician, necromancer and alchemist known as Doctor Johann Georg Faust. He lived in the late fifteenth and early sixteenth centuries, and the Faustian legend probably had its origins in northern Germany, reaching a definitive form in 1587, with the *Historia von D. Johann Fausten* published by the printer Johann Spies. Given the West's preoccupation with the Devil, it was hardly surprising, therefore, that Faust now became a popular character in the history of Western culture.

The legend itself centred around the fate of Faust in his search for the true essence of life. Faust, or 'Faustus' was derived from Latin meaning 'lucky'. One version of the story ran as follows. Though a highly successful and eminent scholar, Faust was frustrated and bored with learning and no longer found enjoyment in life. This legendary Faust was guilty of a particular kind of hubris associated with a thirst for scientific knowledge. He decided to invite the Devil to provide him with still further knowledge and, in addition, with magic powers with a view to indulging in all knowledge and in every worldly pleasure. Faust succeeded in attracting the Devil's attention, represented by Mephistopheles, and made a bargain with him, by which he exchanged his soul for the attainment and satisfaction of his desires. Mephistopheles agreed to assist Faust with his magic powers for a term of years, but at the end of that term, the Devil would claim Faust's soul and Faust would be eternally damned. In the early tales, 24 years was often stipulated as the contractual term or alternatively the term would last until the moment when Faust attained the peak of contentment. Faust was pleased with the deal, as he believed that this happy moment would never arrive. When the agreed term eventually expired, however, the Devil carried him off to hell.

In another version of the legend, the Lord Himself recognized that Faust was in turmoil over his attempts to grasp the mysteries of the universe, and resolved to lead Faust to the place where there was heavenly light. Mephistopheles in his turn took that statement as a challenge and determined to turn Faust's will away from God, by providing him with the knowledge that he was seeking, and in so doing win over his soul for all eternity. It was a wager which the Lord agreed with Mephistopheles in heaven. Was this version of the story the basis of Arnold Toynbee's mythical interpretation that we met in chapter 3 for the genesis of civilizations? The Lord granted Mephistopheles permission to tempt Faust, and the wager involved the bet that all the Devil's delights, flatteries and lies would never lure Faust into satisfaction with a sensuous life only. Furthermore, even in his darkest moment, it was thought that Faust would still be aware of the path of righteousness. Mephistopheles then hurried Faust from one experience to another, all of which in the end proved to be unsatisfying for him. Faust began to gain the self-mastery necessary to rise above his passions, but at that moment died. In both these versions, Faust became utterly corrupted and realized that his sins could not be forgiven, but in the second version, Faust won his salvation with the help of the spiritual world.[22]

In medieval tales prior to the Reformation, most of what was called alternative religion had been implicitly integrated into popular Catholicism, and so medieval Faust figures were on the whole redeemed despite the pact with the Devil. The medieval concept depended upon the Devil as Christ's adversary, but in the later Faustian legend the story was human-centred.[23] In this case, the Devil upheld the importance of the ego, and persuaded people to reject any duties that the divine had placed upon them. This modern, homocentric version of the Faustian story had a close affinity with Protestant individualism, reinforcing the idea that each person must endure a lonely struggle in his or her combat with the spiritual powers, in theory at least.

The Faust of early books, ballads, dramas, and puppet-plays was irrevocably damned because he preferred human to divine knowledge: "He laid the Holy Scriptures behind the door and under the bench, refused to be called doctor of Theology, but preferred to be styled doctor of Medicine."[24] Plays and comic puppet theatre loosely based on this legend were popular throughout Germany in the sixteenth century, often reducing Faust and Mephistopheles to figures of vulgar fun. The story was popularised in England by Christopher Marlowe at the end of the sixteenth century in his play, *The Tragical History of Doctor Faustus*, and was continually revived many times afterwards in various forms. At the end of the eighteenth century, Johann Wolfgang von Goethe made Faust the central character in his great dramatic work. In this case the Devil allowed Faust to have energy, life and youth until he became so utterly carried away that he would wish that things would never change. At this point, his life and soul were forfeit to Mephistopheles. We shall encounter Goethe's work again later.

### Western Man and the Faustian Myth

The essential character or ethos of Western civilization has been the subject of several interpretations, and one of the most famous was that of Oswald Spengler. In his famous two-volume work, entitled *Der Untergang des Abendlandes (The Decline of the West)*, published in the early 1920s, Spengler drew attention to the similarities between the tragic figure of Faust in the legends of that name and the history of the West. Ever since, the adjective 'Faustian' has been employed as one epithet among several to describe Western society. To demonstrate more clearly what he was portraying, we can begin by noting Spengler's comparison with two other major world-cultures. These were, first of all, that of the Mediterranean civilizations epitomized by ancient Greece and Rome, which he called 'Apollonian', and secondly that of the middle-eastern culture exemplified by Islam, which he called 'Magian'. Each of the three civilizations had its own particular ethos, and that of the West was quite different from the other two. In the Magian world of the Middle East the separation of politics and religion was considered theoretically impossible and nonsensical, whereas in the West during the medieval era the conflict of church and state as separate entities was an inherent aspect of its culture. In classical culture, the intellect was the servant of the eye, but by contrast, in the Faustian West, its master. Consequently, from the earliest days of Western culture, Faustian man made the firm resolve to put nature on the rack in order to gain control over her, and idea that was attributed, probably falsely, to the philosopher Francis Bacon, an influential English essayist and statesman.

By maintaining that the course of Western society followed a trajectory similar to that of Faust in the medieval legends, Spengler likened the soul of Western Europe to the Faustian legend. The original, legendary notion of a wager between God and the Devil appeared to captivate the Western mind, and the Faustian bargain has had a long and abundant history as the pre-eminent Western myth. In a similar way to Faust selling his soul to the Devil to gain greater power, so Western man sold his soul to 'technics', for the same purpose. It was an implicit pact with the Devil by which Western man ventured forth on the pursuit of knowledge. The project was characterized by an exceptional dynamism, an 'endless aspiration', a restless thrust toward the infinite, a technical Will-to-power' *(ein technischer Wille zur Macht)*; these are the terms in which Spengler described it.[25] This Will carried with it an ambition for the boundless, whereby it strove to overcome all geographical-material barriers,[26] and this entailed that Western peoples have constantly striven for the unattainable, with turbulent, continual endeavour. The phrase 'to fly among the stars' reflected for Western peoples their dissatisfaction with the human condition as they found it, in a manner once again similar to the Faust of legend. It was to the utmost degree a culture of conquest, whether political, economic or spiritual, demanding activity, determination, self-control. To achieve its aims, Faustian society employed the powers of rationality, of logic, of science, of technology. Silent and irresistible, sacred causality was surrendered to man, and so the ambition to achieve omniscience was set in motion.

This 'Will-to-power', ensconced within Western man, caused him to strive in order to direct the world according to his will, and to force it upon humanity, by reinterpreting, overcoming, destroying. By so doing, his will, his visions, and his energy would have seemed incomprehensible to anyone from any other culture. As an example of this difference, in the Middle East, the centre of Magian culture, the shepherd leads his flock, whereas in the West the shepherd drives it forward, the epitome of the steely determination of a Faustian culture. Change has permeated the whole of Western culture to the degree that the two have become permanently entwined with each other. It pervaded even morality, for the Socratic formula 'Knowledge is Virtue', was replaced by the formula 'Knowledge is Power'.

The fate of Faust was linked to the fate of this culture, and so European peoples have been called Faustian because they were historical peoples, and they perceived themselves as bound together not by place or consensus but by history, epitomized by the ruling dynasty. The English and German languages emerged from the Teutonic languages of the Frankish period, and the French, Italian and Spanish languages emerged from the common language of the former Roman provinces.[27] This set them free to evolve further, as they rapidly escaped from the restraints of Latin, now considered to be an archaic language.

Spengler claimed that it was not early Christianity handed down from the church Fathers, that transformed Faustian man, and by implication Western man, but the very opposite. It was Faustian man who transformed western Christianity. We have seen how, in chapter 3, the West gave Christianity a new direction, as the result of several centuries of the Western church's dreadful experience during the Dark Ages, at a time when barbarian rule was transcendent. The Faustian soul as a consequence ultimately lost its connection with ancient Christianity, the faith which gave it birth. It was during the knightly, epic age of Teutonism (900-1200), that the great world-image of a new religion – should we prefer to call it an ethos? – came into being. What was born at this time was the Faustian mythology. It was in this age that the folklore of Western Europe blossomed. The quietist spiritual morale of Jesus, which had been recommended as necessary for salvation, and which had been bestowed as a special act of grace, was in course of time put into a new form as a morality of imperative command.[28] It was to assume its final shape in the idea of the categorical imperative stipulated by Immanuel Kant at the end of the thousand years.

Earlier we described how the practice of private penance and confession replaced the ancient canonical tradition of public penitence. An important and essential element in the Western tradition was the Faustian prime-sacrament of contrition, entailed by the sacrament of confession of the Western church, contrition and penitence being acts performed by oneself. Such conscientious examination of one's own past deeds represented the earliest evidence of the developing historical sense of Faustian man.

How did this situation come about? What was the origin of these distinguishing features of Western society? A unique combination of circumstances created the dynamism of its culture. During the 'Great Migrations' from the third to the fifth centuries, we have noted from chapter 2 that the majority of the invading tribes, with the exception of the Alans and the Huns, were composed of Germanic stock. This may have been one of the factors which prompted Ernst Hengstenberg to aver that the thousand years of Western civilization constituted the 'German ascendancy or millennium'.[29] We noted that whilst these peoples brought nothing of any value to a declining ancient world, nevertheless their insatiable energy may have been an important factor in Europe's subsequent development. They ever yearned for, and aspired to, change, and so the political, economic and social history of the Christian West has been replete with such change, and there were to be no limits to this enterprise.

The epithet 'Faust' and the adjective 'Faustian', have often been used to describe an arrangement in which an ambitious person surrenders moral integrity in order to achieve power and success, the proverbial 'deal with the Devil'.[30] Moreover, a work of fiction, or a fictional character, might be called Faustian if it involved a similar literal or proverbial deal, such as that portrayed above. Such narratives are often also referred to as 'Faustian bargains', and as such there was usually a short-term gain, for example fame, fortune or knowledge, that was exchanged for, and resulted in, pain in the longer term.

### Other Contributions to the Faustian Debate

Oswald Spengler's work was one possible explanation of Western history, but there were other persuasive interpretations. For Christopher Dawson, it was Augustinian theology and philosophy of history with its doctrine of original sin on the one hand, and concomitantly the idea of divine grace on the other, that generated a spiritual energy, which in turn made an unconscious, but definite impact on Western culture.[31] It contributed to producing the dynamic activity of the West, which was transmitted into secular channels in all directions, economic, political, cultural.

Arnold Toynbee's explanation of the genesis of civilizations was described in chapter 3, and he continued with the assertion that, once a civilization has 'taken off', the Promethean myth was the paradigm which was better suited to describe the subsequent growth of that civilization. In the legend of that name, Prometheus defied the gods with an insatiable creative spirit by stealing fire from them and giving it to humanity in the form of technology, knowledge, the useful arts and more generally, civilization. For such defiance the god Zeus, omniscient and omnipotent in Greek legend, sought to punish him. The philosopher Henri Bergson claimed that it was necessary for all successful young societies to generate a life-force, an *élan vital*, which represented the essence of growth. Europe seemed to fit this pattern as it has been constantly transformed by an energy that refused to be ruled by the restraints of social tradition. Moreover, the vibrant dissemination of ideas throughout Western society was facilitated by a series of movements which had the effect of creating a unified yet diverse culture. The importance of the discovery of the printing press in the fifteenth century cannot be over-emphasized as constituting a major contribution to this process.

Early Christian thinkers claimed that Christianity was the only true philosophy that could be accepted by human reason, as one of God's greatest gifts, and so could be employed to manipulate the world. Religion became intellectualised as a consequence of the idea that God can be known in this way. As a result, the Christian faith threatened to become the exclusive domain of the learned. The Carolingian principle that quasi-classical, not low, Latin should be used in church services, led to a uniformity of Christian worship, but it tended to be tailored to, and have an affinity with, the culture of the learned classes. The commentator Karen Armstrong has put the case in another way, by remarking that the abstruse speculations of philosophers such as William of Ockham and John Duns Scotus meant that theology and spirituality parted company.[32] The Christian West thrust its face determinedly outward towards the external world, for it never abandoned the hope that this world could be redeemed. This ideal has not been confined to the religious sphere alone, however, but has had far-reaching effects on every aspect of social and intellectual life, in an attempt to change the world.

Theologians of the Eastern Orthodox tradition have also made contributions. The Russian theologian, Nikolai Berdyaev, wrote a significant critique of Oswald Spengler's book in 1922, immediately after its publication. He commented that Spengler was not only himself non-religious but that he did not understand the religious life of mankind. On the contrary, he considered Spengler's work to be areligious. Traditional culture was religious by nature and was distinct from culture-turned-civilization, which is irreligious, and it cannot be denied that Spengler examined the role of Christianity only within the historical examination of culture. He did not contemplate Christianity within the context of European history, for example, nor did he see any religious meaning behind events.[33] For Berdyaev, therefore, Spengler's book was spiritually deformed.

Eastern Orthodox criticism, however, has concentrated for the most part on the controversy caused by the modification of Christian doctrine by the Western church, namely, the unilateral insertion into the Christian creed of the *filioque* clause. So far as the traditional creedal statement was concerned, the church considered that its wording was as perfect an expression as possible of Christian dogma. The later insertion of the *filioque* clause produces the statement that the Holy Spirit proceeds from the Son as well as from the Father. The Eastern Orthodox Churches have always opposed this addition, considering it, at the very least, to be in error, or even *a fortiori* to be heretical. They have always insisted that the Spirit proceeds from the Father alone, and to say otherwise is doctrinally false. The clause first appeared between 589 and 693 in the Councils of Toledo in Visigothic Spain to counter Arian heresies that were circulating there. According to the theologian Adam Zernikov, the word *filioque* then made its appearance in the creed at Charlemagne's court, and once the Roman Catholic Church had officially sanctioned its inclusion in 1054, the schism between the two churches was complete. The Orthodox claim that it has profoundly affected Western history, as the source of a certain 'westernization', the feeling of superiority with regard to other cultures, and we shall return to this point several times later. It is possible that it contributed to the Faustian ethos as it developed in the West. This change in mood, according to the Orthodox priest Andrew Phillips, led to Scholasticism, which generated an obsession with science and technology, the first stirrings of which can be witnessed in Gothic architecture.[34] The rift between the Eastern Orthodox Church and the Roman Catholic Church has remained to this day.

### Western Development in a Faustian Environment

In the ancient Hellenic world, physical labour had been considered vulgar and servile, but in the West the Rule of Saint Benedict completely reversed this conception, and this change encouraged a new foundation for Western economic life. As a consequence, Western society's success in the economic and technical fields evolved as a result of a belief in the dignity of physical labour, and led to the question as to how much the medieval period owed to the influence of the Fathers of the early church. It was to provide an impetus for the succeeding phase of economic growth which began in the tenth century.

The reawakening of culture in the Middle Ages was stimulated by the revival of the city. Ernst Troeltsch, for example, maintained that it was the medieval city which first provided the favourable conditions for a thorough-going christianization of social life. It was the city, in the same way as the monasteries in earlier times, which provided a haven of peace and security apart from a troubled world. This gave rise to the commune and the guild, which were associations to which the inhabitants of a town or city could belong, and it was in Lombardy where it attained its greatest development. As the European cities emerged, they became centres for progress in the sense that they provided most of the important and indispensable conditions for almost every advance in public life.[35] This dynamic movement grew throughout the succeeding ages in all spheres of activity, and it embraced science and metaphysics as well as the activities of commune and guild, and it continued to gain strength well after the Middle Ages.[36]

We should not overlook the importance of economic and financial matters. Capitalism was not invented amongst the Protestant businessmen of the seventeenth century, contrary to the famous thesis which was propounded by Richard H. Tawney and subsequently modified by Max Weber. During the ninth century, a nascent form of capitalism developed on the monastic estates, and out of this early phase, Christian doctrine was reformulated in order to render the monks' faith compatible with their economic progress. The actual term 'capital' was introduced in the fourteenth century denoting monies which were put to work for productive or investment purposes. In this respect, the symbol of Faustian money is indeed that of function, the importance of which lies in its effect and power and not in its mere existence as a measure of value. This novel way of thinking about economic matters surfaced when the Normans began to organize their spoils of land and people with a view to encouraging an improvement in trade and commerce. It sparked an economic boom in the tenth century. A few centuries later, the Italian Luca Pacioli introduced the double-entry book-keeping system as a means of keeping accounts. The foundations of the contemporary credit system were established from the very beginning of Western culture as a result of confidence in the strength and endurance of its economics.

In his writing, Spengler emphasized on numerous occasions that technology was a key Faustian element in Western history. For him, the whole European ethos reflected a discoverer's soul. Centuries before the rise in the nineteenth century of modern science and technology, a comprehensive plan was conceived to reorganize the sciences and to give man the mastery over nature. For Spengler, this spirit was from the very beginning, not the handmade of theology, but rather the servant of the technical 'Will-to-Power', and therefore directed to that end both mathematically and experimentally. It was the Faustian symbol of the machine that urged Western man to mechanical constructions from the very beginning. The working hypothesis assumed the greatest importance, the very kind of thought-product that was meaningless to other cultures. Within Baroque philosophy, for example, Western natural science was equally peerless, for no other culture possessed anything similar to it.

The monasteries of the West were important centres of technology. Thomas Hughes in his book *Human-built World* (2004) provided the example of the Benedictine order of monks which stressed the importance of manual landscape work.[37] Those subtly inquiring and meditative monks in their quest for individual perfection and salvation, in their desire to lay bare God's secrets, thought that they were serving God thereby. This reflected the truly Faustian conception of the machine which would transform the land with the intention of creating a Paradise on earth. Medieval Catholic and later Protestant theologians considered that they too were fulfilling the divine purpose as they mastered the earth. The deliberations of John Scotus Eriugena, who attended the Carolingian court, and Hugo, director of the Abbey of Saint Victor in Paris from 1120 to 1141, extolled machine technology and Hugo defined three types of philosophy, theological, practical and mechanical philosophy, the latter having a status which he considered to be the equal of the liberal arts. However, the origins of modern science as we know it, can be placed with the *Scientia Experimentalis (Experimental Science)* (thirteenth century) of the medieval philosopher Roger Bacon, the first pioneer scientist relentlessly to question Nature. The disciples of both Bacon and William of Ockham assumed that the ability to develop machines was God-given and that machines were wondrous means of satisfying the human longing to create. All the great inventions now slowly ripened in the background, destined to emerge at last in the light of day to begin a movement 'with levers and screws', wresting nature's secrets from her, to end finally with a countryside dotted with factory chimneys.[38]

This spirit of technological invention can be witnessed during the early medieval period. The list of technical improvements reflected an impressive Western achievement, for a good variety of works were created even by the year 1200, such as water- and wind-powered mills, mechanical clocks, dams, and new building techniques. It was the Cistercian order which became particularly renowned in the twelfth century for its development of these devices. Equally impressive was the mechanization of paper manufacture, advances in agriculture, and in cloth and clothing manufacture, as described by the sociologist Rodney Stark.[39] European merchant guilds, private benefactors, religious houses as well as rulers and municipal councils constructed roads and bridges for the purpose of long-distance overland transportation of heavy and bulky goods. In addition to the technology which was utilized specifically for production, medieval Europeans benefited from other diverse inventions of immense indirect importance, such as chimneys, eyeglasses, the compass, and improvements in ship-building. Book-printing appeared in the fifteenth century. On the heels of the polymath and astronomer Nicolaus Copernicus came the telescope, the microscope and the chemical elements. In handsomely illustrated sixteenth-century books describing machines, architects and engineers continued to celebrate the mechanical arts, arguing that, as with the monastic orders, they could be employed to recover a paradisiacal environment. The Protestant reformer John Calvin argued that Christians were completely free to work in secular occupations, and success in business and industry was a requirement for their faith, and as a means by which a person would achieve salvation.[40]

### Intellectual and artistic Perspectives of the Faustian Society

Art, mathematics, philosophy, sciences, music, drama, and poetry all came to reflect the ethos of Western culture. Even before the period known as the Renaissance at the end of the fifteenth century, there had been two great outbursts of Western culture that could also truly be called renaissances. The first was the Carolingian, described in the previous chapter, and the second occurred between 1050 and 1250, called the high medieval renaissance. At the end of the twelfth century a succession of famous teachers, beginning with Peter Comestor, started a movement to create schools of theology with Paris at its centre, culminating with Peter the Chanter and Stephen Langton. This led to the creation of European universities. The first was established in Bologna during the eleventh century, with Paris, Oxford and Cambridge and a host of other such institutions being founded later. The rise of these universities was the hallmark of this second renaissance. The teachers offered new learning and provided a meeting-place for students. The institution of the university was something completely novel, devoted as it was exclusively to higher learning, and it created an international European community of learning quite apart from the monasteries, whose monopoly over learning was now coming to an end.

The enthusiasm for dialectic and the spirit of philosophical speculating had already started to change the intellectual climate of Western culture with Peter Abelard and John of Salisbury.[41] The technique of logical discussion and disputation became the principal feature of these higher studies, with the result that the educated classes of Europe thereafter underwent a rigorous and elaborate training in the art of logical thinking, which left its mark on European culture. The foundations of science and technology similarly reflected the Faustian passion of discovery, and it was the universities that enabled Western culture to acquire the necessary intellectual discipline to impel it onwards. These establishments of higher learning provided the foundations for that later renaissance, in which new ideas emanated from, inter alia, the revival of Greek studies in the fifteenth century.

Cathedrals were built in the Gothic style of architecture with their tall steeples, and such architecture too reflected to a great degree the Faustian impulse with its constant thrust toward the infinite. The Romanesque and Gothic, together with the Renaissance, Baroque and Rococo were only stages of one and the same style. In art, the Franciscans transformed the whole meaning of painting in the West by the discovery of depth perspective in the early Renaissance period, with parallel lines meeting at infinity, once again symbolizing the impulse towards the infinite. Furthermore, when natural backgrounds in early Gothic, as opposed to the gold backgrounds of the East, appeared, with blue-green skies and far horizons, they seemed to those living at the time to adopt a profane and worldly appearance.[42]

The passion of discovery was manifest also throughout Western music. Medieval musicians invented polyphony and harmonies, the simultaneous sounding of two or more musical lines, and this occurred probably before 900, according to a description in a manual published at that time. Moreover, the instruments needed to exploit such harmonies were subsequently developed. Around the tenth century, an adequate system of musical notation was invented and popularised so that music could be accurately performed by musicians who had never heard it previously. The manuscripts of Western music were written down in the scriptoriums of monasteries, and from the tenth century onwards they were preserved in the cathedrals and music libraries of Europe. Much later, in post-medieval times, the preservation of musical manuscripts was assured by European and American institutions.

*  *  *  *  *  *  *  *

All these developments have given rise to the epithet 'Faustian' when referring to Western society. We have noted that during the thousand years, the West progressed in all fields of endeavour. The soul of the Christian period of history could indeed be called a Faustian one, and this soul was gradually corroded by the Mephistophelean principle. To what end did the endless strivings of this Faustian soul lead? They led to a material rearrangement over the world with the potential for mastery over it. It was the same spirit which encouraged the Portuguese explorers Prince Henry the Navigator, Vasco da Gama and Ferdinand Magellan in the fifteenth and early sixteenth centuries to embark upon voyages of discovery around the globe.

The Faust of legend consciously made a pact with the Devil as a result of his dissatisfaction with his endless strivings and studies. However, there never could be, and so there never was, a pact made with the Devil for the purpose of deliberately creating a Faustian society. Here we indeed encounter a mystery. Embedded within the Christian psyche was the capacity for continual change which may be called Faustian, and for Western innovators and discoverers there was the truly Faustian danger of the Devil being involved in the process. It carried with it the suspicion and the risk that he was leading them in spirit to that mountain on which he would promise all the power of the earth. In this way there was born the notion that the machine is a miniscule universe that obeys the will of man alone. This is the significance of the *perpetuum mobile* dreamed of by those Dominicans such as Petrus Peregrinus. The result has been one of restless striving, progress and change during the whole period of the thousand years and beyond it. However, the attempt to master nature would lead to human pride or hubris, in a world where human beings come to see themselves, rather than God, as the all-powerful creator. We shall have something more to say on this matter in a later chapter.

Unlike Christ on the mountain, however, those medieval Western monks were playing hostage to fortune, or perhaps Arnold Toynbee's simile of Prometheus playing with fire might be more apt. According to the legendary Faustian story, the Devil eventually came to claim his price as a fulfilment of his contract with Faust, and this entailed that the Devil would claim Faust's soul. In the same manner, it would not be outside the bounds of possibility to suggest that in the mythological scheme hinted at above, European culture and technology might ultimately suffer a similar fate. A price might have to be exacted for the Devil's participation. We may not be certain of what that price would be, but can only speculate in the light of later Western history.

Just as Faust was permitted a certain term of years, the West was to experience the loosening of Satan at the end of the thousand years in order to wreak havoc among the nations once again. The reader must await this scenario until a later chapter. Meanwhile, it is a point worth considering as to whether the Faustian legend could ever have been created in a society other than the Christian society of the West.

CHAPTER SIX

*Three Aspects of the Christian West II: The Cult of the Saints*

JOHN OF Patmos states in Revelation 20:6 that those who had suffered for their faith, and whom John of Patmos calls priests of God and of Christ, shall reign together with Christ for the thousand years. The second theme of our survey of the ethos of the Christian West during this period, therefore, concerns the veneration of these priests, or saints, who were considered to be the great heroes of the Christian faith. In Latin, this veneration was called *cultus*, or the cult of the saints, as it developed throughout late antiquity and the Middle Ages. Those who will reign during the thousand years are those whom the beast had put to death. It conforms to what the Roman Empire means for John in Revelation 17:6: "And I saw the woman, drunk with the blood of the saints and the blood of the martyrs of Jesus." In this passage, John is employing the term martyrs for the Christian saints. Later, in chapter 20, verses 4 to 6, although he does not employ these titles, it is clear that he is referring to the same group of people.

Persecutions of the Christian faithful and the veneration of martyrs' lives and their relics made enormous contributions to the faith from the time of the early church onwards. It could be contended that this aspect of the faith goes back further in Christian history than any other.[1] Indeed, whilst the Christian norm has been to live in the world with passive acceptance, Christianity's perspective towards martyrdom was the one exception to this, and its distinct character was moulded out of two traditions. First of all, in the Old Testament, the Maccabean wars of the second century B.C. were considered to act as the cleansing of the Jewish nation's sin, at the same time justifying that nation's cause against the oppression that the Jews had experienced.[2] According to the theologian Ethelbert Stauffer, in the period after the emergence of the Jewish canon, or list of Jewish writings, apocryphal literature developed the notion that historical events have their roots in martyrdom and in suffering for one's beliefs, and that conflict between the believer and the outside world was the clearest sign that the person was being true to his or her faith.³ The second tradition developed from the idea that the imitation of Christ was the fundamental purpose of Christian life, and this involved fellowship with Him.

During the period of the early church this tendency persisted even more, so that the cross not only became the hallmark of salvation but also served as a vindication of martyrdom itself. Both the conception and the traditions of martyrdom prevailed to such a degree that it became a source of inspiration for Christian people. The idea developed that discipleship would be virtually meaningless if it were not connected with earthly tribulations similar to those which the saints had endured. Persecution therefore became a predictable and integral element in the Christian experience. In order to have any impact on the world, the Christian must be willing to face the world by conflict, if necessary, by bearing witness to another, spiritual, reality, and if necessary, be willing to die for Christ.⁴ It was in such an environment that the cults of both the saints and their relics originated among Christian communities. A figure of speech eventually gained acceptance within the Christian community, namely, that the disciple must become a soldier of Christ, sometimes also called a knight, who fights the good fight to the end. To members of the faith, martyrdom became so important a topic that it covered every aspect of human life.

The cult also played an important role in spreading Christianity, and its popularity continued to be underpinned through what was thought at the time to be a steady flow of miracles. Furthermore, persecution was regarded by early Christians, and by later historians, as one of the crucial influences also on the development of the church and of Christian belief. The martyrs' deaths did not destroy Christianity, for the stories of their ordeals kept the faith alive, and the Christian martyrological heritage was to a certain extent interpreted in a mythical form. Chapter 1 has shown how the Christian faith developed a providential philosophy of history. Persecution formed an essential part of that process, reflected in the works of the author Lucius Lactantius and the theologian Paulus Orosius. The former's *De Mortibus Persecutorum* (*Of the Manner in which the Persecutors died*), written between 313 and 315, was a source for the political history of the years which had just experienced the great persecutions under the Roman emperor Diocletian, who reigned from 284 to 305. What was made manifest here through the written word of Lactantius was God's involvement in human history.

### Who were the Martyrs in John's Narrative?

Revelation 6:9 mentions those who had been slain or slaughtered for the Word of God and for the witness that they had borne, and could refer to those who had already been slain by the time that John wrote his narrative in the 90s, no doubt as the result of the persecutions carried out by the Emperors Nero in the year 64 and Domitian. Revelation 6:11 states that those who had been slain for the word of God were told to rest a little longer until the number of their fellow servants and brethren should be complete, and this refers to those who were to be killed in the future as they themselves had been. A precedent had been duly set after the execution of Christians by Nero, namely, that being a Christian became an actionable offence thereafter. John foresaw, correctly, that the future history of the church would involve yet further persecution and suffering, and this time the word 'martyrdom' would be appropriate.

John resumes his description of the saints in chapter 20:4: "Also I saw the souls of those who had been beheaded for their testimony to Jesus and for the word of God." Secondly, he describes those, "who had not worshipped the beast or his image and had not received its mark on their foreheads or their hands. They came to life and reigned with Christ a thousand years." They share in the first resurrection. Since Satan's banishment during the thousand years is stated earlier in the apocalyptic narrative at verse 20:2, John is implying that this first resurrection occurs at a later point than this event.

Certain it is, that in this passage John is describing Christian people, who remained loyal to their faith despite the ordeals that they would have experienced at the hands of their persecutors.[5] The word 'beheaded' would entail execution irrespective of the manner which was applied. John is not limiting the first resurrection and reign to those who were slain or beheaded, for it is important to note that throughout the Apocalypse the Greek word *martyria* refers to faithful testimony, not necessarily violent death. Christians were killed because they were already martyrs in the sense of bearing testimony to Christ. In John's visions all Christians who had remained faithful to the end have been 'killed'. By describing those who had not worshipped the beast or his image, John is stressing that such faithfulness may not necessarily involve martyrdom. They were not an elite group that was more spiritual than other believers. This passage must be interpreted therefore to include Christians who were not executed during a persecution but on whom a lesser penalty was imposed, for example, imprisonment.[6] John seems to be making a distinction between the martyrs who were slain, some exegetes call them the 'martyrs of the tribulation', and those who were faithful but had not suffered martyrdom, and it also indicates that he did not view all the saints as martyrs. The martyrs as such constitute a part, but not the whole, of those who reigned with Christ for the thousand years. In other words, John is describing in Revelation 20:6 two groups or classes of people who are the 'priests of God and of Christ'.

A question much debated by biblical scholars concerns the first resurrection stated in Revelation 20:5. Is it a literal resurrection of the body, or a spiritual one? John sees the 'souls of those who had been beheaded', and this must infer surely that the locale of John's vision has shifted to heaven. The first resurrection does not signify the martyrs' physical return to earth for the period of the thousand-year reign and so John is not referring to a literal resurrection. There would exist during the thousand years, a state of things 'as if', as if the martyrs were raised from the dead. In the next verse, we learn that death has no further power over them. The ideals and moral spirit which they represent would be invigorated in the hearts and minds of Christian people as if the martyrs themselves had indeed come back to earth. Archbishop Richard Whately wrote: "It may not signify the literal raising of dead men, but the raising up of an increased Christian zeal and holiness, the revival in the Christian church of the Spirit and energy of the noble martyrs of old."[7]

From the same passage we learn that those who share in the first resurrection are priests of God, who are to reign with Christ. They were 'God's own people'. Again, John says nothing about the location of their reign, but it appears to mean that the martyrs, despite their ignominious deaths, enjoyed a subsequent heavenly life with Christ. John's description of them as 'sitting on thrones' is a way of describing this, and heaven is the appropriate place for thrones in the Apocalypse, whether God's throne or those of the twenty-four elders, and we have discounted above the idea of an actual physical resurrection. Beatrice

Neill, for example, maintained that the reign of the saints had to be considered as a spiritual one during the Christian era.[8] Post-millennialists too considered that the martyrs' reign must be seen in the context of a purely spiritual kingdom for the thousand-year period. It would be incongruous for the saints with resurrected bodies to associate with ordinary mortals still living on earth during this period, and there is no support in the Bible for such a notion,[9] for the saints' state is one much superior to an earthly life.

In contradistinction to these views, the theologian R.J. McKelvey stated that the evidence in John's narrative points to an earthly reign. The souls mentioned by John in Revelation 6:9 are 'under the altar', therefore presumably on earth. The promise that was offered to the suffering saints was to share in the reign of Christ as priests.[10] Later in the chapter it will be ascertained how and to what extent the saints did in fact influence Christian life in Western society during the thousand years. A possible solution to these conflicting views would be to conclude that, during the thousand years the martyrs enjoyed a heavenly *existence* but with an earthly *activity*, freed from bodily limitations.

With regard to the phrase in Revelation 20:4 "those to whom judgment was committed," some exegetes maintain that the explanation for this phrase was not that the martyrs were endowed with divine authority to judge, nor that at some previous time they had been given such authority, but that a favourable verdict was bestowed on them. Whilst they are priests of God and of Christ, they do not act as judges, for that privilege is reserved for Christ alone.[11] Other writers took a somewhat opposing view, by maintaining that the original act by which the martyrs had been persecuted, judged and condemned is now completely reversed. The martyrs themselves become the judges, and their reign gives them the authority to participate in Christ's activity of judgment.

### Who were the Saints in Western History?

In the early church during the New Testament period, in theory, all Christian believers were called saints, no matter where they lived,[12] for example, in Acts 9:13 and 9:32. It had become customary over a long period for members of the early church to call one another in this way, and this is reflected in Saint Paul's numerous references. Whenever he writes to Christians, for example, he calls them saints, sons and heirs of God, and so forth. He commonly addresses people in the Christian communities as saints (Romans 1:7; Philippians 4:21 and 4:22; 1 Corinthians 1:2; 2 Corinthians 1:1), especially the community in Jerusalem (1 Corinthians 16:1). In 1 Timothy 5:10 he speaks of the widows who washed the feet of the saints. We can now comprehend the grounds for the continuing New Testament tradition that all Christians should be referred to as saints, a point which later became particularly relevant again in the post-Reformation period. However, in due course of time the cult of the saints came to differ somewhat from this, because in practice, the Christian church proceeded to grant the title of saint to a restricted number of people. Thus, whilst many Christians were considered holy, the word 'saint' came to be reserved mainly for the early martyrs, those whom the Christian communities first recognized as such and whose relics those communities first venerated. The word employed to designate a saint in Latin, *sanctus* or *sancta* had as its root meaning a holy person. Over time, the word slowly acquired the status of a title.

The first group of saints and martyrs epitomized the first age of the Christian church until Constantine's conversion, a period known as that of ancient Christianity. It was an age which became hailed as heroic, revered in legend, and practically unrepeatable as an historical phenomenon. The saints from this period were the only saints venerated by the new Christian church, apart from the Virgin Mary, John the Baptist and the Apostles. Their courage and blood were the foundation from which the new church sprang, or to quote a sentence attributed to Quintus Tertullian but also quoted by John Foxe in his book *The Acts and Monuments of the Christian Church* (1563), "the blood of the martyrs became the seed of the church."[13] In the book *On the Glory of Martyrdom*, Saint Cyprian wrote that "so great is the virtue of martyrdom, that by its means even he who has wished to slay you is constrained to believe."[14] Saint Gregory of Tours wrote of them as 'the snow-white number of the elect'. Martyrdom was claimed to be the indubitable proof of Christ's 'truly divine and ineffable powers'.[15] They were portrayed as men and women fortified by the same power, and it carried the implication that by their deeds others should be inspired to follow in their footsteps.

The first martyr was Stephen as early as the year 35. About 167, Saint Polycarp, bishop of Smyrna, was arrested for his Christian beliefs, refused to recant, and was put to death by burning. This event gave rise to the earliest surviving example of Christian hagiography, the *Martyrdom of St. Polycarp*. The author of this account wrote: "For him as Son of God we adore; the martyrs, as disciples and imitators of the Lord, we reverence as they deserve on account of their unsurpassable loyalty to their King and Teacher."[16] The congregation of Smyrna from that time onwards celebrated the date of his birthday as a feast-day.

However, even when the persecutions were at their height, martyrdom did not occur frequently. The true extent of persecution against Christians in these centuries may never be ascertained. It was in all probability unpredictable as a practice. The church and its Christian membership living within the Empire did endure periods of persecution at the hands of the authorities. However, annals which related these incidents generally concur that violence against Christians during the first three centuries of the faith was sporadic, and was to a large extent the result of local hostility towards the Christian faith, and implemented on an *ad hoc* basis.[17] In addition, there were several periods of empire-wide persecution which was directed from the central administration in Rome. Though Christianity was oftentimes considered a crime, suspects were generally pursued only when they were denounced by local populations.[18] When the Empire prospered, the Christian communities were reluctantly tolerated, but it was not necessary for martyrdom to occur often for it to make a tremendous impact when it did occur. Therefore, whilst the overall consensus of scholars was that relatively few Christians were actually executed, nevertheless, the experience of persecution and martyrdom served to advertise the martyrs' faith. Such suffering would be commemorated by successive generations of Christians, and would thereby become a central feature of their self-understanding.

People turned to the saints and their shrines for a variety of purposes, for example, to avert the power of evil, to promote healing, to bridge the great chasm between life and death.[19] When Christianity became the official religion of the Roman Empire and later on for the peoples in the new Western society, they recognized and honoured those who had suffered for their faith. However, a difference developed between the

Orthodox East and the Catholic West. In the East the saints were monks who had renounced the world, but in the West, great leaders and powerful men later came to be revered, and this movement was recorded in the hagiographical writings of men such as Saint Gregory of Tours: the four books on *The Miracles of Saint Martin*, *The Glory of the blessed Martyrs* and *The Glory of the Confessors* (588), *The Life of the Fathers*, which encompassed twenty lives of saints, the books of *The Suffering and Miracles of Saint Julian of Brioude*. The key concept in these cases was edification, which meant presenting the saint as a role model to the Christian faithful with the aim of inspiring them in their devotions.[20]

As time passed, the church began to recognize further models of Christian endeavour, especially but not exclusively from the monastic movements, which were experiencing phenomenal growth throughout the Mediterranean world in late Antiquity. Now the age of the martyrs was succeeded by an age in which a new type of saint was recognized, and these came to be known as 'confessors' or 'doctors'. As the host of the early martyrs was consigned to tapestries and liturgical homilies, the way was being prepared for the monks to take their place, and this began to be the case even during the early persecutions. As a result, the gradual ascent to holiness did not entail that one suffered martyrdom, for a development eventually took place in Christianity in which the term 'saint' was applied as a title for someone who had led an ascetic or exemplary life, in addition to those who had been slaughtered.

A remarkable diversity of human abilities and callings came to be included in this later sainthood. Ascetics, and later, bishops and teachers and even popes, amongst others, came to be considered as saints under this heading, which is to say that they preached, or were learned in, the faith. Alternatively, they had demonstrated conspicuous endeavour in missionary or pastoral work,[21] for example, men such as Saint Martin of Tours, Saint Porphyry of Gaza, and Saint Augustine. Additionally, some saints of the fifth and sixth centuries were bishops who protected the Roman population against their new Germanic masters, a situation in which divine power appeared to avail to a greater degree than the former secular powers of a now moribund Empire.[22]

### John's 'Martyrs' and the historical Saints compared

We have encountered a duality in the discussion of John's saints. He is careful to distinguish between two groups, on the one hand those who had been martyred for their testimony to Jesus, and on the other those who had remained faithful by not worshipping the beast or its image, but had not suffered martyrdom. He describes both groups in Revelation 20:4 as participants in the first resurrection. They taught the Christian community how to *die* for Christ. In exactly the same way, in historical Christianity the martyrs originated from two groups as well. During the first centuries of Christianity, the first people perceived as saints in the church were the early martyrs. After Christianity became the official religion of the Empire, Christians could finally fully participate in Roman society thanks to imperial tolerance, and by enjoying such favour the nature of sainthood changed. The age of the martyrs was succeeded by the age of the confessors. The new hagiography's main focus was a didactic one. The second group, those later saints from the monastic orders and the Western church, taught the Christian community how to *live* for Christ. In the estimation of this community, the saints were credited with possessing a power that was of divine origin.

In both theological and historical terms, therefore, it seems that we are speaking about the same two groups of people, whose status as saint included not only those who died for the faith in the early centuries but also those whom the church later recognized for outstanding Christian service and conduct. They would be those who presumably will share in the second resurrection. As Andri Vauchez has remarked, for both groups of saints the decisive factor was the profession of their faith, and this served to minimize any differences there may have been between them.[23]

The role of the martyrs holds a central position in John's account of the thousand years, and so we must ask whether the cult of the saints occupied a similar place in the life of the Christian West. Edward Gibbon stated the matter thus: "it was evident that the superior spirits of the saints and martyrs did not consume that portion of their existence in silent and inglorious sleep."[24] Gibbon's view was correct, and the cult of the saints did indeed play a part in the life of the medieval Western society, but it will be germane to discover how important was the cult's influence and what spheres of life the cult affected. In the following narrative, we can examine only a portion of the manifold ways in which the cult permeated the life of the Christian West, and as such we may ponder for ourselves whether, through its influence on the lives of the faithful, it became tantamount to a reign on earth during the thousand years, parallel with the apocalyptic narrative.

### The Cult during late Antiquity

The Edict of Milan in 313 officially recognized Christianity, and the cult thrived from that time onwards. By its encouragement of the cult, a suspicion developed that the church, despite its monotheistic beliefs, was implicitly making a concession to polytheism. Nevertheless, it continued to inspire priests, monks and the whole host of the faithful. During the fourth century large churches were built at the shrines of many martyrs, and these commemorated the martyrs and, even more the champions of asceticism, for example, Saint Martin of Tours, Saint Hilary of Poitiers and Saint Germanus of Auxerre. Later on, the faithful came in such numbers to these and similar shrines that bishops gave their approval for the recitation of prayers at these locations. In this way, the cult of the saints spread rapidly, especially after the Christian faith began to expand from the towns into the countryside. Interest in martyrdom and the lives of the saints did not diminish as the church became securely established. The saints, as patrons of towns or villages now served as special protectors, and it was commonly believed, and expected that, as a test of sanctity, they would be able to perform miracles in times of crisis, with divine assistance if need be. The faithful expected such miracles whenever they petitioned them. Throughout this period, little more than a list of marvels was known about the lives of the saints.

The age of martyrdom was also involved in the development of liturgical worship and in church architecture. Saints' cults edified the faithful with Christian ideals, but the holiness that had appertained exclusively to Christ, was now repeated in diverse ways that would foster the development of the different cultural characteristics of the various European peoples.[25] Christian sentiment towards the martyrs proceeded from love to reverence and then to veneration, but quite early on, such sentiments were increasingly combined with entreaty.[26]

To Saint Augustine and his contemporaries, the saints had their place in the first rank as *membra Christi,* for the exceptional favour which God had bestowed upon his Son was at the same time bestowed also upon his elect. They became much more than just examples of heroic virtue to be imitated. The martyrs, who had shown themselves to be true servants of God, and who had been of the same order as men, had the capacity to lead their fellow men closer to God than could the angels. The angels, as intermediaries between men and God, had tended to be a hindrance in this respect since they were of a different order from men themselves. Only the martyrs, replete with the humility which came with human death, could bridge that divide. To the extent that men would have perceived God as distant and unapproachable, the importance of the martyrs stemmed from their once having lived human lives, and so it was thought that they were able to understand, and have compassion for, human concerns. This intercessory role of the saints can be found in Christian writings dating from the third century. However, the historian Peter Brown suggested that there was ever the suspicion that many people would come to venerate the saints, and at the heavenly court offer devotion and prayers to them, merely as a bid to find an easier route to heaven than by living out an authentic Christian life.[27]

During the period of late antiquity, explicit procedures had not been determined for proclaiming saints, and ratification of sainthood often occurred as a result of local or public knowledge and recommendation. It had been considered unnecessary for the hierarchy of the church to intervene in this matter, but as the cult of the martyrs spread in the fourth and fifth centuries, bishops made it their task to secure at least a modicum of control over the cult. The principal way was to move saints' relics and shrines to specific churches in specific localities and as a result, pilgrims had now perforce to travel to these shrines in order to venerate the saints. Once the stories of the saints' sacrifices had become part of the epoch's culture, their tombs and relics were considered to be important links between heaven and earth. It came to be assumed that the saints acted as patrons to their 'client-devotees'. Whilst the main emphasis still lay with the traditional doctrines and ideals of Christ as stated in the Gospels, the cult encouraged and defined new forms of piety, and in so doing nourished Catholicism. Prophecy, visionary experience, mystical union and exorcism were an essential part of this *cultus*. Rather than praying directly to a saint, the practice developed whereby individuals would petition a particular saint to intercede with

God on their behalf, but the practice eventually emerged whereby prayers were offered to the saints themselves. From the sixth century onwards, mention of the saints now began to be made in the Roman Catholic mass.

## The Cult during the Middle Ages

A single canon of saints which could be universally observed did not exist in the Western church during the early Middle Ages. Canons differed widely between one region and another, and even from one period to another, although many feasts, such as that of the apostle Saint Peter or of the first martyr Saint Stephen, were extensively observed. Several martyrologies circulated, of which the most influential was the *Martyrologium Hieronymianum (Martyrology of Jerome)* attributed to Saint Jerome. Important saints were commemorated on their feast-days, and these celebrations would range from readings whose subject matter concerned their lives to public processions.[28]

The cult of the saints was greatly changed in character by reforms which were instituted by the Carolingian rulers and bishops at synods, such as the one held at Mainz in 813. This particular synod declared that a new saint would not be recognized without the prince's permission or a licence from a holy synod of bishops, and it had the effect of strengthening Episcopal control over the cult. Various capitularies were also issued to the same effect. Attempts to regulate liturgical practice resulted in the composition of many new martyrologies by such authors as Florus of Lyon, Ado of Vienne, Rabanus Maurus, and Notker the Stammerer. In the *Admonitio Generalis* of 789, Charlemagne made an order forbidding the veneration of any martyrs whose names were suspected as being fictitious or doubtful,[29] once again reinforcing the practice by which each bishop would be able to exert control within his own diocese. During the following two centuries many ancient monastic houses were reformed and in the process the cults of their traditional patron saints were renewed. The timing of these important consolidations cannot be over-emphasized, coming as they do significantly at the beginning of the thousand years.

The cult was profoundly modified in various ways around the year 1000 and again after the middle of the twelfth century, a period considered as the 'high Middle Ages'. For example, there was a large increase in the number of people recognized as saints by Christian communities. Additionally, in many areas, contemporary figures began to be acknowledged as saints, and, as an additional innovation, such recognition might occur only a short while after their death. These practices increased rapidly, and in the space of a few decades the new cults frequently attained a similar popularity and reverence as the earlier saints had enjoyed.[30] For example, the tombs of some new saints, such as Saint Bernard of Tiron (1117) and Prince Louis of Anjou (1297), enjoyed popularity for a brief period.

From the end of the tenth century onwards, the papacy gradually usurped more and more control over the official recognition of saints and the process which would lead to canonization. Finally, it was Pope Alexander III (1159-1181) who made the decision to reserve such cases to the Holy See, and ecclesiastical lawyers established thereafter a formal process, whereby new saints were canonized by the device of issuing a papal bull, and this process became standard procedure for centuries after. Now a person could not be made a saint in isolation. He or she had first to qualify as bearing an especial mark of holiness by a Christian community, and then had to be recognized as such by the church authorities.[31] This amounted virtually to a clericalization of the canon of the saints, although not for another 600 years was that control securely established. However, in contradistinction to this, the religious orders pursued an especially vigorous policy regarding the cult, and often paid little attention to the official rules.[32] The Franciscan order was highly organized in this respect.

Until the end of the Middle Ages, the majority of candidates for sainthood originated for the most part from the ruling classes, for example, members of the families of the counts of Andech, of the Arpad dynasty in Hungary, the Angevins of Naples or the Capetians in France. The reason for this derived from the conviction that these persons enjoyed a kind of stock of sanctity.[33] But the sanctification of bishops became increasingly preponderant with the passage of time thanks to the support of the cathedral clergy. Indeed, most of the saints recognized by the church between 1198 and 1431 were bishops. Though lay aristocrats were never wholly overlooked, high ecclesiastical dignitaries gradually replaced them. They could be assimilated to resemble the 'holy sufferers', which remained the primordial, and popular, model of sainthood. The clergy also later promoted to the cult lay people of popular or bourgeois origin.

The greatest popularity and expansion of the cult of the saints in the Christian West was attained between the thirteenth and the sixteenth centuries. The rapid growth of the cult during this period was caused by an increase in popular piety, and compensated for a faltering church leadership, with the result that private devotion to the saints now became increasingly noteworthy. There was an increasing emphasis on private devotions to the Virgin Mary, on saints venerated by the entire church and to Christ himself,[34] and the period manifested a steady growth in shrines dedicated to the former. For example, the new pilgrimage shrines of the late fourteenth and fifteenth centuries such as Wilsnack in Brandenburg were almost all dedicated to both Christ and Mary rather than to the saints. As a result, the great shrines declined somewhat in importance, as did traditional monastic shrines.

The Christian faith, which had been for a long time in the past the religion of the elite and the dominant classes, now began to penetrate the masses, with the laity becoming more devout. The people made the faith their own and moulded it to suit their own aspirations, and as a result the cult of the saints became even more popular, even if it often continued under the guidance of the clergy. This sentiment was particularly strong in Italy, but was also felt in many other countries of Western Europe. The later increase of baptismal Christian names reflected the need to conjoin the identity of an individual to a saint, and so local names gave way to the Christian names of apostles and evangelists, saints and martyrs. This custom would grow and eventually become universal throughout Catholic Europe. In late medieval Germany lay Christians were expected to choose an apostle to act as a personal patron and focus of devotion.

The number of Italian cults significantly increased throughout the thirteenth century, and this trend continued into the fourteenth and fifteenth centuries.[35] During the age of the Italian commune, all kinds of civic undertakings were made legitimate with the aid of the cult. In time, virtually every Italian commune had its own special saint whose holy life had been lived inside its walls within the preceding centuries. In France, just prior to the Reformation, the cult of the saints had the effect of strengthening the Catholic faith. An even greater emphasis was now given to the saints 2as having the power of intercession with God. The very success of the cult boosted the custom of developing specifically local attachments to a saint. This appetite of the faithful for their own *sanctus proprius*, or local saint, caused a huge increase of the cult in the later Middle Ages. However, in other parts of Europe, there was a decline in new saints' cults after the twelfth century, the degree often depending upon how important cultic veneration had been for popular piety.

**Teaching and Edification**

Sainthood was to become a powerful medium for teaching religious and moral values, one in which relics and images, pilgrimage and shrines, and the provision of various 'services' were all involved. Edification was an important concept here, in which the cult was a means by which the Christian ideals of faith and holiness could be promoted. The first route to edification was the preservation in writing of the miracles and similar holy works that had been performed by the saint. The clergy fed a popular appetite for miracles by regularly publicizing successful intercessions to the saints. Monks, too, compiled collections of miracles performed at the shrines of many saints, such as that of Saint Benedict of Nursia at the monastery of Fleury and that of Saint Philibert at the monastery of Noirmoutier.

In the later Middle Ages circumstances subtly changed. The idea began to be circulated that the principal role of the saints was to provide examples of virtues which the laity could attempt to emulate. This took place under the influence of the Mendicant orders, who tried to steer the faith of lay people in this direction. The saints were considered to possess more virtue than the laity of medieval society, and this would include such qualities as self-restraint, sobriety and charity, the latter to include concern for the poor and their needs. The church praised such virtues enthusiastically and encouraged them in the faithful. The means which the friars and the clergy employed was to demonstrate the life of the saints with vivid stories whose specific content and purpose was to edify. In these cases, not only the saints' virtues, but also their charity and their indefatigable pastoral fervour were stressed, in preference to their miracles or asceticism. This is reflected in Pope Innocent III's desire to scrutinize with much care all claims to sanctity. His bull of 1199 stated that two requirements are necessary before anyone may be regarded as a saint: theological and cardinal virtues such as faith, hope, and charity, justice, fortitude, and temperance, together with evidence of at least two miracles, but the latter aspect was now subordinated in favour of the former. The papacy itself assisted in the task of exalting virtue rather than miracles by canonizing the Saints Dominic de Guzmán, Francis of Assisi, Antony of Padua and Peter Martyr of Verona, between 1228 and 1253. That of Saint Dominic in 1233, for example, contained a list of at least twenty-five items concerning his holiness and virtues. Later on, evidence of other attributes such as visions assumed a new importance.

One means of preventing the memory of a saint from fading was by reciting a memoir describing the saint's life, and this would take place where the holy man or woman had lived.[36] Preachers employed exemplary stories taken from the lives of the saints to enliven their sermons and for edification. The walls of churches were often decorated with frescoes of the saints which could serve a didactic purpose. In lay people's homes, 'books of hours', a Christian devotional book, was read during saints' feasts, as well as to celebrate the cult of the Virgin Mary.[37] Martyrs were honoured by having their 'heavenly birthdays' celebrated annually, that is, on the anniversaries of their deaths, such celebration being held at the grave of the deceased with prayer, oblations, communion, and an account read of the martyr's history of suffering and death. By dedicating themselves to a servant of God, the Christian faithful considered themselves to be placed under saintly protection, and in return promised to perform a task which would be pleasing to him or her, and to perform charitable works. Oftentimes when petitioning a saint, the clergy endeavoured to make it a condition that the petitioner desist from behaviour that they considered to be morally repugnant.[38] Thus, the influence of the saints was derived from the moral and spiritual aspects of their sanctity as well, and this influence continued to evolve during the Middle Ages.

### Relics and Images, Pilgrimage and Shrines

The cult of relics became an important form which the veneration of saints assumed. The Ecumenical Council of Nicaea held in 787 stipulated that all new churches should possess a relic, and those churches which did not have them at the time should attempt to obtain them. The spiritual power of the saints came to be manifested in whatever was associated with their material remains, and to the faithful such objects would assist in seeking the assistance of the departed saints. The Latin word *reliquiae* from which the term 'relic' derives means items 'left behind' by the saint, and kept after his death as an object of reverence. Another perspective on sainthood which was applicable in all cases in the later Middle Ages was a force or energy, *virtus*, which remained active in the saints' remains after death, which served to express the sacred power of these people, and which was revealed by signs that they were incorruptible. The veneration of saints' relics assumed many forms. Since a saint, or member of the divine court, was able to convey supplications on the petitioner's behalf, to pray before a relic was considered the same as addressing the saint himself or herself. Legal documents specified Fleury, for example, as 'the place where Saint Benedict rests'. An alternative sense of the importance of relics can be gained from the Latin word *pignora*, or pledges of the intercessory power of a saint. Saints possessed such power because at death they had been judged worthy of admission to the divine court.

It would be evident that the relics which were most highly prized would be the saints' original corpses, as well as smaller parts of their physical bodies which had been separated purposefully for veneration, such as pieces of skin and bone or locks of hair. Since it was believed that the essence of a person could be transferred to another object, relics also included anything that had belonged to, or been used by the saint, and which could thereby contribute to the saints' spiritual aura, and this could include clothing, pieces of furniture, official insignia, or books. It could even include items which were not relics as such but had been brought into contact with them, such as pieces of cloth which had been in physical contact with a shrine, phials of water which had washed a corpse, or blood which had miraculously exuded from a long defunct corpse.

It was not known exactly at what date the honour paid to the martyred dead began to be transferred to their physical remains also, but the account of the martyrdom of Saint Polycarp, already mentioned, included a statement that the church of Smyrna counted the bones of the saint "more valuable than precious stones and finer than gold."[39] Christians in Antioch esteemed highly the remains of Saint Ignatius, while Saint Cyprian's blood and clothing became objects of veneration. Once the persecution of Christians within the Roman Empire had ceased, public veneration of the martyr's bones now became firmly established. As a fifth-century inscription at the tomb of Saint Martin of Tours read, "Here lies bishop Martin of holy memory, whose soul is in the hand of God, but who is completely present here, manifesting through the power of miracles his every grace."[40] Saint Gregory's work provided confirmation that the veneration of relics had become a central feature of Christian practice, and one of his aims was to furnish the cults of local saints with trustworthy histories. It led to the presence of relics in altars, and in the foundation stones of buildings built for worship.

The presumption that the relics of saints were more valuable than precious stones or metals stimulated the clergy to multiply the treasures of the church, though the claim started to gain ground that this was a superstitious practice. Certainly, the emphasis on procuring martyrs' relics produced many abuses but this did not diminish the church's desire to honour its faithful dead. The importance of relics had now grown to such an extent that the Lateran Council of 1215 decreed that relics must be placed in the altar of a new church before it could be consecrated. The same Council also ordered that relics should be displayed only in a reliquary or case, and many were so placed into ornate jewelled examples. Relics would also be placed beneath altars as predicted in the Apocalypse.

It was a common belief that saints' relics had miraculous powers. While it was thought that such power could be channelled through relics, miracles could not be performed by these objects themselves, but by the saints or rather, as the hagiographers themselves reminded the faithful, by God working through the saints.[41] It was their relics which purported to establish their credentials. Throughout the Middle Ages there was an extensive and profitable trade in relics as princes, clerics and churches competed for them. Fragmentary corporal relics were so eagerly sought, that the Lateran Council tried to eliminate the trade, but there was no stopping the pursuit and interest in them. Relics came to be displayed more prominently in the churches of the later Middle Ages than they had been in earlier periods, but they no longer carried the significance which would have been attached to them in earlier periods.

Finally, it was not only in their physical remains, real or spurious, that the saints of the Christian West lived on, but images also became an important appendage to the cult. During the later Middle Ages, from the twelfth to the fifteenth century, as a new feature, the faithful came increasingly to venerate images and statues of the saints alongside their relics. This was occasioned by paintings, especially in Mediterranean countries, and statues of stone or wood. The images were no longer the direct, physical relict of the saint, of course, but provided a representation of the saint's presence, or events from his or her life. They would often be displayed on an altarpiece or as frescoes on church walls. In the thirteenth century images of recent saints became common, for example, the effigy of Saint Thomas Becket was painted in a chapel in the cathedral at Anagni. As the Middle Ages progressed, the faithful increasingly dedicated themselves to a servant of God before a painting or statue which substituted for their tomb. Beginning in the fifteenth century, the faithful were able to obtain images of the saints and the Virgin Mary in a popular form which they were able to venerate in their own homes.[42]

The multiplication of relics encouraged the proliferation of shrines in which to house them. They were erected over the tombs of saints or in those places where the saintly bodies were finally laid to rest, many of them affording an impressive demonstration of the Christian faith. Europe was littered with these shrines which attracted pilgrims in numbers great or small. The most famous were those of Saint Peter at Rome, Saint Martin at Tours, Saint Cuthbert at Lindisfarne and Saint Boniface at Fulda. But Saint Augustine stressed, and the church taught, that, "When we make our offerings at shrines, it is to God. The martyrs have their place of honour...but they are not adored in the place of Christ,"[43] which meant that they were to be venerated but they were not to be worshipped.

The church had encouraged Christian pilgrimages to the Holy Land ever since the fourth century. It was during the early Middle-ages, that the practice and tradition of peregrination took on its modern meaning, namely, a journey, often lengthy, involving travel to a holy place and back again, though the word 'pilgrimage' originated only in the thirteenth century. The ecclesiastical establishment recommended these expeditions as a religious practice that the faithful should undertake. As a result, in the course of the eleventh century there appeared for the first time the phenomenon of the mass pilgrimage, which reflected the fact that by this time the cult had become irrepressible. Large parties of pilgrims were organized by local church leaders in such a way that those who could not otherwise have afforded it were able to participate.

Most of the thousands of traditional shrines that attracted the faithful in Europe were of local importance and quite small, appealing to people only from their own environs. However, these were to some degree replaced in the later Middle Ages by shrines of international significance, the most important being the holy places around Jerusalem, but also Saint James at Compostela, Mont Saint Michel in France, Faith at Conques, Becket at Canterbury, those of the martyrs in Rome. The European sites became more important on the religious landscape during the fifteenth century as a result of the collapse of the Byzantine Empire and the rise of Ottoman power in the eastern Mediterranean, events that effectively cut off the Holy Land as a destination for all but the most resourceful of European pilgrims.

### The Saints provided 'Services' and Assistance in communal Life

The veneration of the saints served a practical purpose as well in the ordinary life of the Christian believer, for it was considered that they performed social services that could not be dispensed with. Fortified by their aura of holiness and their examples of asceticism and miracles, the Christian faithful secured their protection by bringing them gifts, and in exchange the saint provided them with intercession in the divine court and protection against worldly suffering. Individual Christians and communities alike sought the aid of 'specialist' saints who they thought could be effective in dealing with particular problems in many areas of life: intellectual, manual, household, to counter famine, to quell fires, to defeat enemies, to mediate disputes, to dispense charity, to heal disease. If an epidemic raged, or if you were lost on a journey, or your house caught fire, you sought the aid of a saint.[44] In this respect, recognition of the saints' role as specialists was universal throughout medieval society. Furthermore, to most people, the saints were believed to possess power over nature, which could involve control over the clemency of the weather, to achieve good harvests or an increase in the available productive resources. Later in the Middle Ages, the saints were increasingly invoked to deal with all of life's difficulties, such as imprisonment, a sentence of hanging, threats by bandits or by one's enemies.

The intrinsic role of the saint was to heal, not to convert, and it was stressed that the miraculous power attributed to them was a gift from God. Much importance was attached to the belief that the saints were able to cure the sick, and all manner of ailments were the subject of their therapeutic function: contagious and organic illnesses, paralysis and motor problems, wounds and fractures, blindness and deafness, mental illnesses and sterility. It was supposed that the bones of the martyrs, their blood and their garments contained the power of healing.[45] One might call upon Saint Roch for the plague and Saint Margaret of Antioch for difficult childbirths, for example. Perhaps a lame person had become afflicted thus as a result of sin. A friend of God could plead that the limb be made whole. It was believed that such miracles were extensions of those which had been performed by the saints in their own lives.[46] Healing might also happen through accidental contact with objects or places associated with the saints. For example, it sufficed for a person to visit and come into contact with the tomb of a saint for a cure to be effective. Many recovered their health after visiting the place where the remains of a saint lay and was thought to be sleeping in the vicinity, for it was believed that the saint's therapeutic power was all the more effective during sleep. If a person had been possessed by a demon or evil spirits and wished to be cleansed from them, a saint had the power to drive away such spirits. Or perhaps a person simply feared being consigned to hell, in which case a holy person already living in heaven would serve as a valuable ally on the Day of Judgment.

Saints served not only individuals. The cult was also attached to whole communities, in which holy men and holy women were not considered to be remote figures but familiar members of the local community. They were invoked to fulfil the function of a patron, particularly of churches and guilds, in a more individual and less universal role than that of Christ. Such patronage of a dead saint could become, if anything, more noteworthy than the services they rendered. A patron saint would have a 'family' amongst which would include the monks or canons of the community, the serfs who worked locally, the nobles who donated land to a saint, or the pilgrims who brought offerings or just their prayers to a shrine. There were also many connections between sainthood and the hierarchy. The bishop made the saint accessible to the community, and this rendered the saint a community figure.[47]

In the medieval town, once economic activities developed, which potentially were thought to conflict with traditional values, this could lead in turn to a kind of insecurity and guilt.[48] Saints' cults provided the solution since the saint was seen to act as an intermediary in order to produce new expressions of piety. Thus, cults of holy men and women, which were predominantly urban, proliferated in the thirteenth century as never before and never since. Towns marshalled relics, and built shrines and chapels. With the increasing emphasis on devotions to Mary, Christ and the apostolic founders, Italian townspeople of the thirteenth century now added their own heroes and heroines to the saintly lists. Above all, religious confraternities or *charités*, with the patronage of a popular saint, encouraged the growth of communal life in the merchant and craft guilds.[49]

## Changes wrought by the Reformation

By the time of the Reformation in the sixteenth century, the amount of superstition surrounding the cult in the later Middle Ages led certain sects, such as the Bergomiles and the Waldensians, to criticize the practices. The Reformation itself now subjected the traditional structures of the church's organization to unprecedented attack, and this offensive affected first and foremost the veneration of the saints. Reform theologians and preachers often reacted radically against the cult and their relics. They condemned the cult because, in their view, veneration of the saints conflicted with their principal theological doctrine of justification by faith alone, and moreover distracted attention away from the worship of Christ. The rejection of the cult of the saints therefore was one of the more important of the Reformation's distinguishing features. With every man's salvation now a matter between himself or herself and God, many of the medieval devotional practices were eliminated from Protestantism. In its most extreme form, this change abolished the cult completely, and often forcibly. It was considered that dead Christians, those who are awaiting resurrection, were not able to succour the living.

The principle Lutheran doctrine of justification by faith alone entailed that the saints' attributes, such as asceticism and holiness, which had formerly assisted in earning divine grace, were now considered to be superfluous. Even some Catholics who remained loyal criticized some of the more extreme aspects of the cults. For example, the Dutch philosopher and Catholic theologian Desiderius Erasmus attacked the lax practices of the Catholic Church, many of which he considered to have descended into formalism, which had the result of merely going through the motions of tradition. He fiercely ridiculed the cult which included worship of saints, and in which veneration had turned into superstition. Even some of the Catholic faithful came to reject the notion that saints were able to intercede for the living, because Lutheran doctrine held that this constituted a reliance on works rather than on faith. John Calvin composed a systematic critique of the cult of relics in the vernacular *Traité des Reliques (Treatise on Relics)* (1547), in which he rejected the veneration of relics for theological reasons and took delight in denigrating what for him was a ridiculous practice, taking as an example the many heads of John the Baptist that had cropped up in various churches throughout Europe! Ulrich Zwingli in his articles accepted that prayers could be exchanged between the faithful, both living and dead, and therefore hesitated to condemn prayers for the dead, but all the same, following Protestant teaching, he rejected intercession to the saints as deflecting prayer and worship which would otherwise be devoted to Christ. The reformers, moreover, maintained that the practice of venerating the saints was not explicitly recorded in Scripture.

Notwithstanding the above, the role of the saints and their cults became a theological dilemma for scholars and laity alike throughout the Reformation era, and it has posed continuing problems for post-Reformation Protestant theologians. To a large extent they have viewed the cults as a form of idolatry which serves to distract the Christian believer away from studying directly the Word of God in Scripture.[50] As Protestants tried to remove themselves from the grip of the Catholic Church, the cult of the saints remained a formidable hurdle. From an analysis of 180 pamphlets by reformers in German-speaking Europe, for example, Carol Heming has demonstrated the Protestants' denunciation of the cults and the struggle that ensued to purge the cult from their faith.[51]

For the reformers, however, the Virgin Mary, unlike other saints, could never be completely eliminated from evangelical piety, since her veneration was closely linked to that of Christ. Apart from the emphasis on justification by faith, reliance on Scripture, and rejection of Rome's authority, little unanimity emerged among the reformers as to how to treat Mary. In the early modern period, she did not disappear from Protestant devotional life, although the Protestant church calendar tended to ignore her feasts.[52] Though there was no desire to dishonour Mary and she continued to play an important role in Protestant circles, her veneration had to be altered to accommodate the Protestant interpretation of Scripture. She was assimilated into Lutheran devotional life, but no longer as a divine intercessor. Such ambivalence facilitated the preservation of images of the Virgin, and devotion to her, in parts of Protestant Germany. For example, although Nuremberg became the first German city to adopt the Lutheran faith in 1525, the city's churches continued to display paintings and statues of Mary, of her assumption and coronation, and statues of the Madonna of the Rosary. Various Marian festivals continued to be celebrated. The strong support that Mary enjoyed in Bavaria, where the Wittelsbach court actively sponsored the Counter-Reformation, led to an intensification of her cult in Augsburg under the Jesuits, who sought unsuccessfully to impose their own form of the cult of the Virgin throughout Catholic Germany.

In some Protestant areas, people were more than willing to part with their saints, occasionally with animosity, and eagerly rejected shrines and images. For example, theological antagonism often turned to violent iconoclasm on the part of the Huguenots during the Wars of Religion in the seventeenth century. Relic collections were destroyed and the statues of the saints in many French churches still display the damage caused by these attacks.[53] In other places believers were more reluctant to give up their saintly intercessors by resisting their elimination even while their church publicly adopted the opposite policy. In northern Germany and in Scandinavia, where the various states supported Lutheranism, the cult was comprehensively overturned. Veneration of the saints had been less an integral part of religious practice there than in European lands further south, and the antipathy to the cults as a consequence of the Reformation may have reflected an existing predisposition. In England, it was easy to incite people against Romish popery and the monastic orders, more difficult to persuade them to abandon their traditional religious practices and the cult of the saints. This indeed did take place, but some saints, for example, Saints Edward the Confessor, and Thomas Becket, maintained their affection within Anglican church circles.[54]

As an integral part of Protestant doctrine, the conduct which would formerly have appertained to the saints, the individual believer was now beholden to follow for himself. For example, the 45th hymn of the *Ausbund*, the oldest hymnbook of the Swiss Brethren written by Anabaptists in the sixteenth century, had the characteristic title: 'A new hymn in which a disciple lamented because he met tribulations for the sake of God's Word; but the Lord answered kindly by telling him how he has fared in this world'. This hymn well reflected the mood and outlook of a typical Anabaptist believer. Following Revelation 13:10, he was supposed to have "the endurance and faith of the saints". It was inevitable that social changes were accompanied by changes in the structure of piety. As the domination by clerics and the nobility gradually faded away, the Protestant centuries that followed now experienced the spread of a piety that was reflected in personal commitment by lay people, which led eventually to Pietism, a movement to be described in the next chapter.

Who were the 'saints' in Protestantism? In many Protestant churches, the traditional New Testament meaning of the word was emphasised. The word 'saint' referred to any believer in conformity with the doctrine of the priesthood of all believers. Nor, according to Martin Luther, was this an innovation, since it had been the practice of the early church. Luther stated that "therefore saints are all those who believe in Christ, whether men or women, slaves or free."[55] In this sense, anyone who was within the Body of Christ, namely a professing Christian, was a saint on account of their relationship with Christ. As a result, many Protestants considered that prayers to the saints constituted idolatry or even necromancy. Within some Protestant traditions, the term 'saint' was also used to refer to any born-again Christian. For evangelicals who considered the New Testament to be an inerrant history of the early church, it was understood that to be a Christian, inevitably one would have to suffer persecution. Protestants could still follow the role models as exemplified by the Christian saints and martyrs.[56]

## Reformed Catholicism

The Catholic reformers of the sixteenth century drew a different conclusion from those of the Protestant faith. While the criticisms of the latter put an end to the veneration of relics, pilgrimage, and indeed most of the aspects of the cult of the saints in Protestant regions, the cult continued undiminished in Catholic regions. In reformed Catholicism, the concept of sainthood did undergo something of a revision in such a way that the best of the tradition was preserved. The Council of Trent, which was held between 1545 and 1563 in order to redefine Catholic doctrines and to reform abuses, undertook the task of reorganizing the practice of the cult and the ways in which saints were now to be canonized within early modern Catholicism. The register and list of saints was simplified and many names that were considered spurious or doubtful were removed. Saints' lives would still be held up as ideals to follow and saints could still provide intercession for spiritual needs. The Catholic Church assumed ever-increasing control over the cult in an effort to parry the mockery and disdain that arose from Protestant quarters. The canonization of saints now became a process even more discriminating and more judicial than had been the case in the Middle Ages. The decrees of Pope Urban VIII in 1625 and 1634 clarified papal requirements for canonization, by reserving the beatification of saints to the Holy See, thereby giving the papacy complete control in determining who qualified as a candidate. Popes and bishops took extra care to determine the spiritual qualities of candidates, and so they tended to be restricted to those where it could be demonstrated that they had displayed either outstanding missionary fervour, or pastoral care.[57] Evidence was required that the dead holy person was qualified to take his or her place in heaven as a member of the community of saints.

The Counter Reformation took advantage of cultic veneration by using it as a means for rallying the faithful to the Catholic Church, and the cult of the saints continued to play a vital role in the church's official life. It was not only in that part of Europe that became Protestant which experienced a great deal of variation but also that part which remained Catholic. The cults in France were divided into two different kinds, both expressing the changing needs of lay piety. On the one hand there were many national cults, and on the other there were many that could claim considerable local popularity but were of little importance nationally.

Although attempts were made by the Catholic Reformation to dissuade the faithful from displays of popular piety and religious enthusiasm which could be considered superstitious, in some places, both urban and rural, the veneration of saints and belief in miracles continued to be as strong as ever.[58] Local saints and relic cults survived, often thriving beside Marian shrines and the international saints of the Europe-wide church. In sixteenth-century Spain, for example, there were hundreds of shrines dedicated to the Virgin Mary and to local and international saints throughout the Iberian peninsula.[59] Later in the sixteenth and seventeenth centuries, the Catholic Church was well served by the militancy of saints such as Ignatius Loyola, Francis Xavier, Teresa of Avila and Philip Neri.

### The Protestant Churches' official Interpretations

Since one of the effects of the Reformation was to eradicate the abuses of the cult or to eliminate it altogether, it became a widely-held misconception that Lutherans did not have saints. The *Augsburg Confession* was one of the first expressions of the Protestant faith as held by the German reformers, and this was presented to Charles V, Holy Roman Emperor, at the Diet of Augsburg in 1530. It was the accepted statement of the creed of the Lutheran Church, and the confessional documents contained within it acclaimed both the general and particular use of the word 'saint'. Because the Lutheran Confessions based all Christian teaching on the Bible alone, it was not surprising that their teaching on the saints mirrored the Scriptures. Since they also considered themselves faithful Catholics, they were willing to retain all sound teaching about saints from the early church. Lutherans kept the saints, therefore, not as saviours or intercessors to God, but rather as exemplars and an inspiration for their own faith and life.

When the explicit question, "Who are the saints?" was asked with reference to the Lutheran Confessions, the answer was: "All believers in Jesus Christ, both those living on earth and those living in heaven." Both heavenly and earthly saints were therefore confessed. The Lutherans formally declared the belief that, according to the Scriptures, all earthly believers were saints, that is, holy in the sight of God. Consequently, in the *Augsburg Confession* the church, in its proper meaning, was the assembly of all believers and saints.[60] Again, in the *Large Catechism*, the statement ran: "I believe that there is upon earth a little holy body and congregation of saints, under one head, Christ, called together by the Holy Ghost in one faith, mind and understanding…I am also a part and member of the same, a sharer and joint owner of all the goods it possesses,"[61] a statement undoubtedly referring to earthly saints.

In addition, the Lutheran Church regarded Christians in heaven as saints and were even willing to honour those that the Catholic Church regarded as saints, but with qualifications. As the Lutheran Apology, which was drawn up by Philip Melanchthon, who replaced Martin Luther as chief Lutheran theologian at the diet of Augsburg in 1530, stated, "Our Confession approves honours to the saints. For here a threefold honour is to be approved" (Apology 21.4). Luther commended this 'threefold' way in which the saints were to be honoured, first of all, by thanking God for examples of His mercy and gifts which He manifested in the saints, secondly by using the saints as exemplars for strengthening the faith in which believers should be encouraged when they fell away from faith or lapsed, and thirdly by imitating their faith and their virtues.

Traditionally, Lutherans acknowledged that the saints prayed for the church in general, but did not serve as mediators of redemption. Another passage in the *Augsburg Confession*, entitled *Of the Worship of Saints*, stated that it was permitted for saints to be kept in remembrance, so that believers might emulate their faith, and this in order to strengthen their own faith, when they saw how they received and were sustained by grace. Moreover, their good works were to act as a model for each believer according to his or her own calling. However, the *Confession* rejected prayers to the saints, stating, "Scripture does not teach us to pray to the saints or to ask for help from them, but it sets before us Christ only as mediator, expiatory sacrifice, high priest, and intercessor."

The double and often conflicting influences of Martin Luther and John Calvin, with a still present memory of Catholic orthodoxy, was felt in the Anglican Confessions. On this point the Thirty-nine Articles were decidedly Lutheran, rejecting as they did the "worshipping and adoration as well of images as of relics, and also invocation of saints," because the Anglican Church saw in it "a fond thing, vainly invented, and grounded upon no warranty of Scripture, but rather repugnant to the Word of God."[62] The term 'hero' or 'heroine' was sometimes made to refer to those holy people whom the church synod or an individual church praised as having had special benevolence and who have lived and died since the church's schism with Rome. The Anglican Communion commemorated many of the saints in the General Roman Calendar, often on the same days, and it had special holy days in honour of Christ, the Blessed Virgin Mary and the Apostles, but English and local saints were often included, for example, those who were opposed to the Roman Catholic Church, such as John Wycliffe, William Tyndale, Thomas Cranmer, Nicholas Ridley, and Hugh Latimer.

The *Westminster Confession of Faith*, which was composed in 1646, was the document which had the most influence in the English-speaking world and was the last of the classic confessions of Protestant belief. The Westminster Assembly, summoned by the English Parliament in 1643, took as its mission to restructure the Church of England in a Puritan direction, although it regulated the Church of England only for a short time. Whilst differing views of church government were represented, Presbyterianism was the dominating factor. It became the subordinate standard of doctrine in the Church of Scotland, and has been influential within Presbyterian churches, such as the Congregationalists and Baptists, worldwide. Whilst this confession did not state explicitly that the living members of the church were saints, the text irrefutably led to that conclusion. For example, the passage entitled *Of the Communion of Saints*, stated that "saints are bound to maintain their holy fellowship and communion in the worship of God, and in...relieving each other in outward things, according to their several abilities and necessities." Another passage of this Confession taught that religious worship should not be given "to angels, saints or any other creature." This communion which the saints had with Christ did not allow them in any way to share in the substance of His Godhead, or to be equal with Christ in any respect, either of which would incur the charge of impiety and blasphemy.

While Methodists as a whole do not practice the patronage or veneration of saints, they do honour and admire them. In common with the Protestant tradition, Methodists believe that all Christians are saints, but mainly use the term to refer to biblical people, Christian leaders, and martyrs of the faith. Some Methodist congregations observe All Saints' Day and many churches were named after saints. John Wesley, the theological father of world Methodism, did not practice or permit Roman Catholic practices associated with the veneration of the

Virgin Mary or prayers to saints. Many encouraged the study of saints, that is, the biographies of holy people.[63]

\* \* \* \* \* \* \* \*

The saints were, both during their lives and after their deaths, vital participants not only of the Christian community, but of Western civilization itself. As a man of heroic virtue, the saint was considered to be a living power in Christian life, a power that was granted by God, and who was considered to take an active interest, and share, in human affairs. Moreover, after the Reformation, the Catholic Church continued to foster the cult but with changes. We could take the view that the resemblance between Revelation, chapter 20, and the cult ends with the Reformation in those areas of Europe where the Protestant tradition came to hold sway, but this would not be correct. Rather, the meaning of the term 'saint' changed. Martin Luther employed the word 'saints' freely with reference to all Christians in accordance with New Testament teaching.

John uses the word 'reign' to be synonymous with 'rule', and a rule can signify not only obedience but also admiration and respect, *a fortiori* something worthy of emulation by all Christians, as were the saints equally for post-Reformation as for medieval man. In manifold ways, therefore, the cult of the saints, howsoever interpreted, gave meaning to John's apocalyptic verses. The one difference between the two was that of historical timing. John's prophecy looked forward to the persecutions of future martyrs. The Western church looked backwards in remembrance of this same group of people. It would be reasonable therefore to maintain that the cult of the saints as it evolved in Western Christianity mirrored to a great extent John's description of the martyrs' reign as he describes it in chapter 20. Persecution and martyrdom for the faith was a central and integral feature of the Christian experience and both had important consequences as the culture of the Christian West evolved. The cult of the saints illustrated how piety itself consisted of three elements that would be pursued by the faithful: spiritual perfection, reverence, and divine help. As the second of the fundamental themes which moulded the Christian West during the thousand years, the cult assumed an importance as a major expression of Christian doctrine and of popular piety and worship throughout the Middle Ages.

During the Reformation, Luther completely liberated the Faustian personality, already alluded to in the previous chapter. The person of the priest as intermediary, formerly standing between man and God, was dispensed with. In earlier ages, opposition to the Devil had involved the whole Christian community, but now the individual stood alone, self-oriented, his own priest and his own judge, in the task of warding off the Devil and resisting his temptations. The whole panoply of Catholic devotion and sacraments and the cult of the saints, Luther replaced by the doctrine of salvation by faith alone. However, many people could only feel, but not understand, the element of liberation that had been generated by the Reformation movement. They welcomed, with enthusiasm indeed, the abandonment of the old visible duties, but it took some while for them to come to the realization that the new intellectual regimen of the Protestant Reformation was even stricter. The Protestant work ethic, particularly the Calvinist one, was to became an important force in the later years of the Christian West, and it influenced and encouraged large numbers of people to engage more fully in work in the secular world. This work ethic prompted people to become either passionate against the Church or at least indifferent to it.

The mindset promoted by the Protestant religion was responsible for the transition from feudalism to capitalism in Western Europe in the sixteenth century, and the cult of the saints was but one victim of this movement. Religious devotion, Max Weber argued, had been to a great extent accompanied by a rejection of worldly affairs, and so after the Reformation the focus of attention shifted away from the otherworldliness hitherto found in Catholicism. We shall learn in forthcoming chapters how the Faustian ethos was to come into its own, as the cult of the saints and the energy and devotion that had been paid to the saints were now diverted to other more worldly objectives.

CHAPTER SEVEN

*Three Aspects of the Christian West III: The millennial Reign of Christ*

"Religion is the key of history." *Lord Acton*

THE REIGN of Christ is mentioned twice in chapter 20 of the Apocalypse, at verses 20:4 and 20:6, and in these verses John states that throughout the thousand-year period the saints and martyrs reigned together with Christ. This concept may be interpreted and explained in different ways, and we shall investigate first of all several misconceptions concerning Christ's reign and also the concept of 'Christendom'. Then the role of the church will be investigated, as the intermediary between Christ and the Christian society of the West, and as the authority for disseminating the Christian message of redemption. We shall examine the idea that Christ reigns over the nations in accordance with the apocalyptic text, thereby fulfilling John's prophecy in verses 19:15-16: "...and he will rule them (the nations) with a rod of iron...On his robe and on his thigh he has a name inscribed, King of kings and Lord of Lords." An overview is also given of the secular rulers' responsibilities as Christian monarchs during the millennium. Christ's reign is examined in His role as a teacher through the mediatorial agencies of the monasteries, the Bible, education and preaching. Finally, we examine in a little further detail the post-Reformation period.

At the start of chapter 20, John had visions of the world continuing for a thousand and more years after the triumph of the Word of God. Yet he tells us very little as to what that world would resemble during this period. He states only that the Devil has been banished and locked up, and that Christ and the martyrs reign over the nations. This clearly implies that there will be a population which would otherwise be susceptible to Satan's attacks. One possible explanation for the paucity of description is that the millennium simply provides an interval between the demise of the Roman Empire, which threatened the

Christian church in John's own day, and the end of the world as an historical process. J. Ramsey Michaels called it a 'cushion of sorts' between the two.[1] Another exegete asked why it was necessary to interpose a time period of a thousand years at all and suggested only that it suited John's purpose to include this. These explanations demand further analysis, and we must therefore offer alternatives which better accommodate our historicist thesis.

Richard Bauckham maintained that the theological point of the millennium is to demonstrate the triumph of the martyrs.[2] George Caird considered the millennium to be an essential part of John's narrative, by maintaining, in the first place, that it was incorrect to treat the battle of chapter 19 as the end of world history, since it would be a pointless victory if Christ and the martyrs were to reign over a world which had been completely depopulated. Secondly, Satan was confined so that he would not be able to practise his arts of deception during the thousand years.[3] Certain it was that the Dark Ages in Western Europe came to an end, but a more cogent reason for the millennium was that it was to become a training ground in Christian 'life and rule', and as a 'Bride of Christ' described in chapter 3, the Christian church in the West was destined to play an all-important role.

### The Concept of 'Christendom'

In any historical narrative which deals with the Christian faith in Western society, inevitably the appellation 'Christendom' would be cited. The term has been employed quite sparingly, if at all, in earlier chapters, and this was a deliberate ploy. The concept was a vague one since commentators have oftentimes attached different meanings to it. It was recorded in the late ninth century in Anglo-Saxon England, but there was no completely equivalent word in Latin or Greek. The Middle Ages in European history came to be known as Christendom, and the term has been applied only to the Christian society of the West, dominated by the medieval Catholic Church. This appellation tended to overlook the fact that a Christian empire still existed in Eastern Europe, centred upon Constantinople. The title could, and probably should, in theory, have embraced the whole of the Christian world, which would also include the Orthodox East.

Whilst many historians would hold the view that Christendom itself was not to last the full thousand years, it would be reasonable to maintain that Christendom, the history and culture of the Christian West, became the history of Europe,[4] and this society was to develop to its maturity during a time-span identical to the thousand years of the Apocalypse. The adoption of Christianity by the Roman Empire in the fourth century was one of the accepted starting points for Christendom, but the unity of all Christians was eventually broken as a result of the schism between the Eastern Orthodox Church and the Western Catholic Church, which developed gradually by degrees from the sixth century onwards. Rather than constituting a geographical or political entity, Christendom was essentially a vision of a European society united by the Christian faith under the guidance and the leadership of the church.[5] Such a concept made European peoples conscious of their own culture, and it was tacitly understood that most Christians learnt and practised their faith in a society where it was believed that the laws were founded on Christian principles,[6] and it realized its culmination in the eleventh century.

The historian Mark Greengrass in his book *Christendom destroyed 1517-1648* (2014), argued that Christendom for the Western Christians was a self-created myth and that myth had helped to unite the Christian peoples of the West. We have seen that the Reformation had resulted in a second schism within Christendom, this time between the Roman Catholic and Protestant churches, and this division into two conflicting camps helped to generate the Thirty Years' War, from 1618 to 1648, also known as the 'Wars of Religion'. For Greengrass, the Reformation in general and that war in particular was instrumental in the disintegration of Western Christendom. Roland Bainton maintained that the war left Christendom only as a state of mind,[7] but in all probability that was only what it had always been anyway. Other historians have asserted that Christendom continued into the nineteenth century. Whilst the seven hundred years of the Middle Ages can be sustained as an integral whole, for which the appellation Western Christendom might be considered correct, it would be incorrect, therefore, to aver that Western Christendom was strictly coterminous with the thousand years of the Christian West.

### Misconceptions regarding the Reign of Christ

The concept of the reign of Christ during the thousand years has led to misconceptions, the first of which concerned the actual period of time during which Christ was considered to reign. John of Patmos states that the saints and martyrs reigned throughout the thousand years, but in contrast with this, nowhere in the Apocalypse does he state that Christ's reign itself lasts only for this same period. The opposite is the case since, after Jesus' ascension into heaven, Saint Paul, in 1 Corinthians 15:25, tells us that Jesus is currently reigning: "For he must reign, until he has put all his enemies under his feet." Indeed, according to Luke's gospel and the seventh angel of the Apocalypse, He shall reign for ever and ever. But what John asserts in chapter 20 is that, for the millennial period, both Christ and the saints reign together.

Secondly, many exegetes viewed this period as one in which Christ undertook to reign over the kingdoms of the whole world, and quoted Revelation 19:11-16 in support of this. It has already been stressed that Revelation 19:15 merely states 'the nations', and the reference to the whole world is not stated until Revelation 20:8 which follows Satan's release. It is in this latter verse that John states the words 'which are at the four corners of the earth'. Significantly the phrase is inserted by John at this point *only*, for he never mentions it previously. We must therefore conclude that for the thousand years, Christ and the saints reign over some, but not all, the peoples of the world, and the material in this chapter will be discussed making this assumption.

Thirdly, and most importantly, a further view of many exegetes must be challenged regarding the kind of society that has traditionally been associated with the millennium period. Nothing is said directly on the matter in the Apocalypse, nor is there described the kind of reign that Christ will enjoy, whether visible or spirutu`al. John merely makes the assertion, and does not further elaborate. Origen of Alexandria was quite firm on this, for he asserted that the promised kingdom was to be a purely spiritual one. If Christ's reign was to be construed as taking place on earth, some commentators considered that the beginning of the millennium and Satan's binding were to be future events. On the other hand, if His reign was to be a heavenly or spiritual one, the millennium could have already started.[8] In contrast to this view, we have asserted several times over that the millennium, or the thousand years, has now run its course.

The millennium has often been understood, in the first instance, as a utopia, a blessed time. This impression had its source in Jewish writings of the New Testament period. Those who held such a view alleged that the period would usher in a golden age, and the Christian community believed that it would be a glorious administrative reign of Christ preceding the final age to come. That Christ would return to earth in order to inaugurate a thousand-year era of blessedness has always had many supporters, even in modern times. In the second and third centuries, Chiliasts expected the thousand years to instigate an era of material prosperity and bliss. Saint Irenaeus, for example, depicted the joys of the millennium in terms of Isaiah 65. "People shall build houses…and they shall plant vineyards and themselves eat their fruits of them and drink the wine."[9] Indeed, in chapter 5 we alluded to the gradual but inexorable material progress of Western society during the thousand years. A reading of the Apocalypse itself seems to offer the promise of future happiness, and some, particularly members of the early church who were suffering injustice and persecution, have applied this promise to the thousand years itself.

However, it may come as a disappointment to many, but it is nowhere hinted in chapter 20 that Christ's reign will be anything as glorious and prosperous as has been traditionally supposed. Christ never misled us into thinking that his kingdom would compare with other secular kingdoms, in which he would sit on a throne in Jerusalem, with a host of administrative advisers and officials.[10] Furthermore, it would hardly make any sense to declare that European medieval society with its feudal structure, or even the post-Reformation period, manifested all the features of a perfect social, political and ethical system. The *philosophes* of the Enlightenment would certainly have not thought in this way. Whilst paganism in Western society as a whole had almost entirely been eliminated, nominal Christianity was the norm, at least in the early Middle Ages. Rather, such a society would experience struggle and travail in order to approach anything vaguely resembling the Christian utopia of the kind which most exegetes expected. The Augustinian tradition long exerted its influence over Christian belief, and we have seen in chapter 1 that the idea of a *civitas terrena* or city of Babylon had fostered a spirituality which was distrustful of the world. As pilgrims on this earth, human beings travelled over a confusing, chaotic and perilous landscape, and this would have applied to the thousand-year period also.

Saint Augustine inferred that during the millennium people would experience tears, grief, crying and death,[11] but nowhere in John's text is such a state of affairs so described during the thousand years. Where, then, did Saint Augustine obtain this idea from? It seemed that he was relying on Revelation 21:4. In this verse John states that these former things will pass away *after* the thousand years and the Judgment, and so John must be implying that people would still be experiencing suffering and tribulation during the thousand years itself which precede the Judgment, but he does not explicitly state this. In keeping with this idea, Karl Löwith maintained that one must comprehend the meaning of history as the explanation of human suffering,[12] and the cross is the symbol of that suffering. This would apply equally to the thousand years as to any other period of history, since the thousand years itself occurred within historical time. Christ Himself said in Matthew 10:34: "Do not think that I have come to bring peace on earth; I have not come to bring peace, but a sword." Origen of Alexandria too rebuked those who looked for bodily pleasure in the millennium. "The saints will eat, but it will be the bread of life which sustains the soul; they will drink, but it will be the cup of divine wisdom."[13] A treatise entitled *The Commentary on the Book of Revelation* (1658) by the seventeenth-century Scottish Calvinist divine, James Durham, stated that "seing clear Scripture promiseth no such earthly temporal Kingdom to Saints, but warneth them to be alway looking for the crosse and affliction."[14]

### Regarding the Reign of Christ generally

'Life and rule' was the issue on which the contests between the martyrs and the beast had focussed. Once the beast had been thrown into the lake of fire, and the Devil or Satan had been bound and consigned to the abyss, the earth was handed over to Christ to rule with the saints. Christ's rule could be described as evoking a response of Christian people to the Gospel, and it was the task of the Holy Spirit to generate that response within the hearts and minds of the Christian faithful. They were made thereby citizens of the kingdom that Christ ruled. As a result of its authority, pre-eminence and its moral convictions, the church insisted that there was a moral law that was superior to all purely human law. People were certainly not paragons of virtue in Western society during the thousand years, and religious observance may have oftentimes been perfunctory, but at the very least lip-service was paid, not only to a set of moral rules and principles, but also to a belief in the supernatural which could assist in dealing with life's troubles.[15]

We can consider two ideals of living as Christ did, one taken from the medieval period and the other written after the Reformation. The first is that of the devotional handbooks with the comprehensive title *The Imitation of Christ*, credited to have been written in the first instance in the fifteenth century by the Dutch humanist and mystic Geert Groote. However, it is generally acknowledged that Thomas à Kempis submitted second and third revisions of the text between 1418 and 1427. The impetus for it stemmed from the rediscovery of sincere pious practices and for the conversion and reconversion of lukewarm clergy. The books placed an emphasis on the interior life and withdrawal from the world. The first book was concerned almost entirely with the reformation of character, and with the admonition to establish Christ's reign in us, that is, the presence of Christ in the soul.[16] The ideal of the imitation of Christ has been an important element of Western Christian theology, ethics and spirituality, and references to this concept and its practice were found in the earliest Christian documents, such as the Pauline Epistles. Saint Augustine had viewed the imitation of Christ as the fundamental purpose of the Christian life, and as a remedy for Adam's sins. The authentic apostolic life was seen to be one that was modelled upon the earthly life of Jesus as it was revealed in the Gospels, a life which came to be increasingly understood as that of teacher, lawgiver, and example.[17]

This idea of Jesus as a role model also featured in William Law's concept of Christian perfection, which he developed in his book *A serious Call to a devout and holy Life* (1729). As an Anglican priest, he maintained that the truly religious man should strive to live a Christian life "as near it as a sincere intention and careful diligence can carry you".[18] Whereas the original Protestant reformers emphasized the enormous gulf between man and God, later writers in the Reformed tradition recognized the possibilities for human achievement, an idea which fitted well with the outlook of the eighteenth century. They acknowledged that optimism, and the pursuit of happiness, should not be conceived solely in secular terms. We return to this latter concept at the end of the chapter.

The postmillennialists interpret chapter 19 of Revelation as meaning simply the triumph of the testimony of Jesus in the world, not the advent of Jesus personally as we have already explained, so that the thousand years of chapter 20 would signify a time span in which the church considered its primary task to be the proclamation of the Christian Gospel. To repeat Saint Augustine's teachings on the millennium, it was not a visible reign of Christ, rather that he reigned in heaven. Johann Alsted, in one of the most influential millenarian treatises of the seventeenth century, wrote in a similar vein. Christ would reign during the millennium, but his presence would be invisible.[19]

Furthermore, François Guizot held the view that moral and intellectual developments during Europe's history have been essentially theological. After surveying European history from the fifth to the twelfth centuries he came to the conclusion that it was theology that took possession of, and directed, the human spirit. Philosophical, political and historical questions were all considered from a theological point of view, and all opinions were expressed in Christian, theological terms. Christian theology possessed such sovereignty in the intellectual order, that both the arts and the mathematical and physical sciences were held in submission to its doctrines.[20] Again, according to François Guizot, European civilization has come into an eternal truth since "it progresses according to God's intentions. This is the rational principle for its superiority."[21] Whilst this sentiment is perhaps justifiable, nevertheless it reflects a certain degree of hubris, a characteristic of the West we have already encountered in chapter 5 and which we shall encounter again later.

### The Role and Authority of the Church

Whilst John does not specifically declare a connection between the marriage of the Lamb and the Bride of Christ in Revelation 19:7 on the one hand, and the subsequent thousand-year reign of Christ on the other, we are able to infer from these statements considered alongside each other that Christ would reign with, and through, His church during the whole thousand-year period, and by establishing His sovereignty over the nations. Joachim of Fiore, writing in the thirteenth century, affirmed such a statement, and read the Apocalypse as a continuous story connected to Christ. This was aptly fulfilled by the ascendancy which the medieval church achieved over medieval society. The theologian, Karl Barth, argued that church government was indeed all about Christ, as a community of people which Christ rules,[22] and the saints reigned with Him. It was regarded as having been appointed by Christ in the capacity of a royal priesthood of believers, and Jude 1:3 states that it represented directly "the faith which was once for all delivered to the saints". Colossians 1:13 states: "He has delivered us from the dominion of darkness and transferred us to the kingdom of his beloved Son." The theologian John MacQuarrie stated that the church *is* the communion of saints.[23]

The Western Church, transformed and distinct from both the ancient Church and the Eastern Orthodox Church, guided and led the nascent Western society during the last centuries of the 'Dark Ages' and the first centuries of the thousand years. Such leadership gave it a vigour that reflected in a similar way the youthful society of the West. It played a major role in the progress of Western society, with, as we have previously surveyed, missionary work, teaching and a new penitential order by which it could transmit its values. For François Guizot, it alone possessed two great means of influence: first of all, movement and order, and secondly energy and regularity.[24] Postmillennialists expected the thousand years to be a period in which the church would enjoy spiritual growth. Moreover, the English martyrologist, John Foxe, interpreted the book of Revelation to mean that for about a thousand years the power and glory of the Gospel increased,[25] and that "it shoulde please the Lord to bridle the malice, and snaffle the power of the olde Serpent, and giue rest unto his church."[26]

The medieval church had a particular understanding of her vocation on earth, from which she gave the thousand years the specific form that it eventually assumed. It was regarded as a purely superhuman institution. Every facet of life was grounded in the salvation of the soul and the church was considered to be the only intermediary necessary to achieve it. Salvation could be attained only through a piety which consisted, above all, in obedience to the church, in respecting its feasts, and in complete submission to it. As a result, all agreed that the church had an authority which derived from a highly developed organization that was universal and powerful. Saint Gregory the Great's work *Liber Regulae pastoralis (Book of pastoral Rule)* already cited in chapter 3 was written with the intention of improving the quality of pastoral care and the 'government of souls', and it came to have great influence throughout the Middle Ages. It helped to end the dependence of the clergy and secular rulers of Western Europe on the Eastern Empire, for the book gave them clear and multifaceted rules and a code of conduct.

As a result of its major concern with eschatology, the Catholic Church achieved an ascendancy over men's souls which it had never previously enjoyed,[27] for it was able to maintain a virtual monopoly of authority over society during this period. It was the social identity of the West that engendered this religious monopoly, because all human society, not just the state, was subject to the reign of Christ, a refuge in a sea of physical and moral ruin.[28] That is to say, given the dysfunctional state that the West had endured during the Dark Ages, the church, as the only social and moral force, was bound to attain a monopolistic position over society in the course of time. The social theorist Peter Berger stated that religious establishments have indeed acted as monopolies in past societies in order to bring the secular under their control, and the medieval Western church with its religious institutions was no exception.[29] During the whole period from the seventh century onwards, and especially from the reign of Charlemagne from the ninth century onwards, only orthodox and obedient believers were eligible for full citizenship, apart from certain specified outsider groups such as the Jewish community, a doctrine that remained a practical reality almost to the end of the eighteenth century.

In accordance with Augustinian thought, the church considered itself to be an institution which was placed above, and in opposition to, the rest of society, the *civitas terrena*. With the aim of constructing a social and moral society that would be congruent with its unique vision, the medieval church developed a role and authority for itself such that it was able to influence and dominate all areas of social and cultural life. To all intents and purposes, the church did succeed in creating a European society that had Christian concepts and ideals woven into many of its most fundamental ways of operating. While many of these were distorted and in some cases corrupted over the medieval period, the decisions made by the church in the early medieval period had a significant impact on the development of Christian society in the West.[30]

After the demise of the Carolingian Empire, medieval Christian society came to possess a fresh unity in the eleventh century, but it was no longer derived from secular or political authority as it had been formerly. Such unity was now on a cultural and religious level, and it came to possess a supra-political or international character. Therefore, if one excluded the single exceptional case of Charlemagne's rule, there has never been any other unitary structure of Western civilization and its culture since the time of the Roman Empire which has succeeded in exerting and maintaining its influence upon society, apart from that of the Christian church, and this ensured a spiritual unity among the emerging, and competing, nation states of Europe. Despite this situation, or rather because of it, the young society of the West acquired the degree of liberty and flexibility which, so Arnold Toynbee maintained, were the necessary conditions for its subsequent growth.[31] The papacy continued to provide the vital ingredients of leadership, organization and vitality which succeeded in propelling the young society forward, a society which, as we have seen in chapter 5, continually strove to improve the quality of life of its peoples.

The church and the Holy Roman Empire, which represented on the one hand the spiritual power and on the other the temporal power, vied for supremacy throughout the medieval period. Both were regarded as integral components of Western society, in which their own characteristics, whether religious or secular, were taken for granted, even though there was little agreement with respect both to their relationship with each other, and to their respective duties and privileges.[32] It was bound to produce tension, but such tension became one of the fertile sources for criticism and change, encouraging thereby the dynamic activity of Western culture. One might come to the conclusion that the church's absolutism and the resulting closed intellectual environment of the Middle Ages would be a hindrance to what the German author Thomas Mann called 'boldness of thought', but paradoxically the people of the Middle Ages and after proved to be far more imaginative than many in a more individualist age.[33]

In order to fulfil its mission, the medieval church aimed to achieve a complete independence from temporal interests, and so it came to reject all tutelage and interference from the laity in its affairs. In this respect there was no question of collaboration of church and state, but only of subordination of man and society to the church in the spiritual realm, a church that considered itself to be the intermediary between man and God.[34] Pope Gregory VII, for example, attacked any conception which would have made the Holy Roman Emperor the equal of the pope. The monopoly attained by the church was not impaired by the ensuing struggle between Henry IV, Holy Roman Emperor 1056-1105, and the papacy. On the contrary, the relationship between the two powers resulted in the subordination of the temporal to the spiritual, and this emancipated the church from both feudal and imperial dependence on the secular power. With such an uncompromising situation, everyone, reformers and conservatives alike, was obliged to accept the supremacy of the spiritual power in the life of the Christian West.[35]

The papacy's successful struggle with the temporal power and its supremacy over it had two main results. It exercised many of the functions which are reckoned today to be essentially political. All social structures depended for their viability on the holy orders, since these were intimately involved in the community's affairs at every level.[36] The terms 'cleric' and 'scholar' became synonymous in a society where hardly anyone outside the church retained any knowledge of Latin. The church was therefore able for centuries to impose its language on the administration. With an organized bureaucracy and its own juridical system, the papacy implemented its own laws and upheld them in its own courts, thereby acting as if it were an independent sovereign state.[37] We can easily understand how this situation often presented a direct challenge to the European monarchies and the civil authorities. The most acute example of this can be evidenced by the Investiture Controversy of fifty years' duration which occurred during the eleventh century. This dispute revolved around the issue as to who possessed the authority to appoint and install church officials, which term would have included bishops, abbots of monasteries and even the pope. It ended in 1122 with the Concordat of Worms, which *inter alia* gave the church the authority which it had sought over such investitures.

Secondly, the essential nature of medieval society; the *Corpus Christi mysticum* (*The Mystical Body of Christ*), was one in which every member of it was part of one body, forming an indissoluble unity between the members and its head, that is, Christ. This followed the biblical concept which is laid down in 1 Corinthians 12:12. From the middle of the twelfth century popes began for the first time to take the specific title of 'Vicar of Christ', and to claim the new title for themselves alone. At this point, the ancient tradition in which the title of 'Vicar of Saint Peter' had been used, as the trustees of Saint Peter on earth, was discarded. The new title made the precise assertion that the pope was now the deputy of Christ in every respect. Since he was accepted as Christ's earthly vicar, he automatically assumed Christ's role as the bridegroom of the church. The loyalty to Christ which had inspired men's souls was no longer distinguishable from loyalty to his 'Vicar'. This development now rendered it feasible to apply any biblical text which referred to Christ to refer also to the pope. When he spoke, his words would be heard and revered to the ends of Catholic Christendom.[38]

Christian concepts and ideals certainly changed after the upheavals brought about by the Reformation, but these were generally concerned with church governance. The Christian churches continued to play an important role in public life. The Roman Catholic Church's administrative structure was overhauled as a result of the Counter-Reformation, with its moral prestige reinstated. The Reformation and Counter-Reformation fell somewhat short of what the reformers in both the Protestant and Catholic camps had expected and striven for, but they raised the standards of the Christian ministry in every sphere of activity. Whilst this was true for many Protestant areas, a similar situation obtained in those cities where the Catholic Church was dominant, and in particular where the Jesuits and Dominicans were influential.[39]

### Christ as Ruler of the Nations

It had been one of the original ideals of Christendom, that the church should serve as the unifying force to link the rulers and people of Europe, a Christendom which envisaged a divine society ruled by God's appointed sovereigns. The church began to consider itself as the supreme authority over and behind the new nation-states of Europe. During the whole thousand-year period, every secular ruler in the West was considered an earthly representative of God's order and was subject to Christ as the supreme ruler. In such circumstances Christianity acted as if it were a common language, which could be shared by the devout, the lukewarm or even the sceptical. Toleration was not usually conceded to dissenters, and anyone who openly disagreed with the church's teachings were denounced as heretical and thereby risked punishment.[40]

Throughout the thousand years, every dynastic ruler, whether Carolingian, Bourbon, Tudor or Habsburg, regarded themselves, and was regarded by their subjects, as enjoying a unique mandate from 'on high'. Their peoples were subordinated to their rulers because God by his grace had invested those rulers with the authority to govern. But in matters of faith the ruler was himself subordinate either to God's 'Vicar' on earth, or alternatively to his own conscience, a situation which once again reflected the separation of secular from church authority, the temporal differentiated from the spiritual. Although many rulers paid only lip-service to such an arrangement, it rested on something which had the original intention of fostering the common good, rather than encouraging autocracy. Strictly speaking, the king was regarded as a servant, a vessel, a vehicle, through which the divine will manifested itself. In the Europe of medieval Christendom, kings indeed had laid claim to rule by divine right, but this right had to be endorsed and legitimised by the church. In effect, the church was the guarantor of such an arrangement. All European rulers professed the Christian faith during the thousand years, and it was not until the French Revolution and afterwards, that any European government adopted a purely secular orientation, or became avowedly anti-Christian.

It was now understood that Western rulers shared in every respect the human condition and should not lead or rule by coercion or force. The vital role which medieval Christianity played in the medieval era was to ensure that the Western ruler's political power and authority should be limited in this way. This may be contrasted with the Roman concept of autocracy, whereby the emperor's rule had been viewed as an image of God's own sovereignty. Divine rule destroyed the legitimacy of such human autocracy, for it was considered that God was the only ultimate source of all power. This new *regnum Christi*, underpinned by the church, demanded that in place of force, its leaders should rule by counsel and moral guidance,[41] supported by the traditional affection of the governed.

Although it was common knowledge to everyone who read the Bible that a king ruled by divine right, he might lose the allegiance of his subjects by tyrannical rule. The king's secular power was granted to him by God, and such power was limited by a moral and religious restraint that the ruler was expected to uphold. A ruler had to observe a constant standard of virtue and a sense of moral responsibility, in the capacity of God's servant, the guardian of justice and the protector of the rights of the people. If the people were bound to obey the Christian ruler, the ruler himself was no less bound to keep his oath, for a religious ideal was set before him, in which there were limitations imposed on him by Christian morality.[42]

Another aspect which gave meaning and form to Christ's reign during the thousand years was what came to be known as the 'legitimisation of kingship'. From the eighth century onwards, the church reserved to itself the power to create kings. The Western church accomplished this by developing coronation rites in ways that were similar to Old Testament practice, and indeed its ultimate origin was to be found in the Old Testament where it embodied the theocratic principle that the secular power was dependent upon the spiritual. The origins of the Western ceremony are in some doubt, but in one form or another, would probably have existed since ancient times. There are references to it throughout the biblical texts. It was in use in the seventh century in Visigothic Spain, where the monarchy depended to a large degree on the support of the church. The ceremony of consecration included anointing with oil, and this ritual signified that the new king was such by the approval of the church, and therefore by the grace of God. The chrism or oil of consecration was held to confer a new, sacred character on the person of the ruler. The king himself derived from this ceremony a moral ascendancy, which made him a unique personage. The medieval monarchy possessed a theocratic character in a different sense from that which occurred in the Byzantine Empire. However, while it inspired in the ruler the obligation to reign in accordance with Christian morality, it did not confer upon him any formal title save that of the Defender of the Church, nor did it imply that he had been endowed with any clearly defined authority.

A momentous change in the idea of the state came into being after the Reformation, representing yet another new movement, in this case a legal change. It stemmed from the desire of European rulers, often dynastic absolute monarchies, to be free of the dominance of the Roman papacy and the Holy Roman Emperor. Protestantism represented, at least for some rulers, the opportunity to forge a legitimate break with Rome. Importantly, this resulted in many cases in the subordination of the clerical to the secular, a complete reversal of the medieval situation. Religious faith as such did not weaken, but many took the view that the pursuit of, and insistence upon, religious dogma might cultivate a desire to interfere with secular government.

The prince could still not be a completely secular ruler, for some political rulers acquired roles which entailed religious leadership as well. For example, from the sixteenth century onwards Henry VIII made the English monarch the leader of the Church of England, and in seventeenth-century France, Cardinals Armand Richelieu and Jules Mazarin became the king's chief ministers, thus blending secular and religious roles. The continued belief in divine right, however, allowed Protestant rulers to redefine their authority, and this included the right to intervene in the spiritual realm. In the post-Reformation period both devout and conventional believers alike continued to follow the Christian faith, for Christianity still provided a firm foundation of society. It followed that the consent of the governed was identical with the people's double loyalty to God and prince. Furthermore, in the seventeenth century no ruler could go without the support of the churches, Protestant or Catholic, since they both maintained a considerable membership, and church leaders were still held sufficiently in high regard to influence public opinion.

### Christ as Teacher – the Bible and the Monasteries

If it is true that the Bible was not only the word of God but also the record of God's deeds in history, it possessed a double significance. Besides the literal narrative or surface meaning, it was believed that its text concealed a deeper, hidden meaning that was indicative of a higher reality, and this could in principle be capable of detection. A system of interpretation developed that attempted to extricate these multiple levels of meaning in Scripture, broadly divided into the literal or historical level, the allegorical level, and finally, and perhaps most importantly, a moral application, which could be of service in daily life and teaching. Saint Thomas Aquinas' *Super Epistolam B. Pauli ad Galatas Lectura (Commentary on St. Paul's Epistle to the Galatians)*, and his *Summa Theologiae* (1265-1273) proceeded from the assumption that God had intended the Scriptures, as the supreme authority for Christian doctrine, to reveal all that was required for salvation.[43]

Direct access to the Bible for the layman was the exception rather than the rule in medieval Europe. Limitations were imposed by the cost of owning one. More importantly, the degree of literacy determined the layman's ability to consult the Scriptures, for few people could read or write at the start of the medieval period, but this situation gradually changed over the ensuing centuries. In any case, the clergy which had been trained in biblical exegesis actually discouraged the populace from reading the Bible. The Council of Toulouse (1229), imposed restrictions on reading vernacular translations of the Bible, and ruled that the laity should not even be permitted to own a Bible except the Psalter. At a time when the Bible was written in Latin and translations of it into the vernacular languages were frowned upon, the laity were able to understand the biblical texts only through the intermediary of the clergy's homilies and sermons. To this end, the papacy stressed that parish priests should be literate and be acquainted with the Scriptures.[44] Biblical texts were the foundation of all the sermons that were preached to the clergy and laity, and sermons were the most prominent of the ways that offered mediated access to the Bible. In the Middle Ages, all levels of education were provided for in this way. Preachers, while relying on biblical exegesis, simplified complex biblical texts, paraphrased their narratives, and interpreted archaic words. Priests aimed to make the biblical texts relevant for their listeners by interspersing their sermons with examples taken from contemporary life.

During this period, Western monasticism developed a strong sense of social responsibility. To achieve this aim, until the late eleventh century, monks 'embodied the Book'. This meant that the foundation of the monks' way of life, regulated and secluded as it was, was centred around the Bible, and their thoughts, words and actions were similarly entrenched in it. It was the Bible that was the monks' guidebook for living the most perfect life, while the monks in turn served as exemplars of perfect living for the benefit of society at large. The Bible became the main text of the medieval educational system, and it was the chief institution by which lay people were taught. As a result, the medieval monastery was no longer conceived, as it had been earlier, as an ascetic refuge for those who wished to live as though in a kind of wilderness away from the world, but was transformed into a school. Through numerous liturgical practices, the monks were able to act out, and in some instances even embody, the Bible in front of the populace throughout the year, by making use of biblical scenes, notably from the New Testament.

This pedagogic impetus led at a later date to reforms of the monastic movement, the importance of which should not be overestimated. From the middle of the tenth century, waves of such reforms swept over Europe, spreading through the whole of France, and into Italy, Flanders, and Lorraine, whence, at the beginning of the eleventh century, it overflowed into Germany. Wherever it made its way there was an increase of piety. The first and greatest of these reforms concerned the monastery at Cluny in eastern France. William the Pious, Duke of Aquitaine, founded a Benedictine abbey here in the early tenth century. Cluniacs were renowned for the spirituality that Rome lacked as well as for their rigid discipline, their hostility to simony and clerical marriage, and the beauty and solemnity of their architecture and worship. Eventually, there were hundreds of Cluniac sites spread across Western Europe, and by the middle of the eleventh century the movement had attained a Europe-wide influence on a spiritual, economic, social and political level and in the arts and architecture, led by the great abbots who were the leaders of the movement. Monasticism had ceased to be merely a spectator, but had become an important force in Western society.

The liturgy, or Mass in the Roman rite, was another important means by which biblical teaching could be delivered to lay people. The Bible was also employed for other aims, such as moral injunction and commentary on the liturgy. The fourteenth century philosopher John Wycliffe taught that the word of God was the greatest authority to which a Christian was bound, and he believed that all Christians should learn the faith for themselves, and to that end he encouraged the translation of the Bible into the vernacular languages. From his *Epistolae dominicales (Dominical Letters)* (1382) he stated: "...the truth of God standeth not in one language more than in another." Nevertheless, he considered that it was imperative that Scripture should be understood in the right way, and that therefore it had to be taught by the clergy.

From the end of the tenth century onwards after a period of decline, the production of Bibles resumed in the monasteries' scriptoria across Europe. Its resurgence was a result of the monastic reforms noted above,[45] and led to a revival in biblical studies in the late eleventh and twelfth centuries. In the thirteenth century for the first time, Bibles were copied in significant numbers, for example, the Paris Bible was copied and was widely circulated over Europe from about 1230. The chapter divisions used today in modern Bibles were oftentimes to be found for the first time in medieval Bibles dating from this period.

Reformation and post-Reformation Europe witnessed three important developments. The discovery of the printing press in the previous century, the translation of the Bible into vernacular languages, and the dissolution of the monasteries in many parts of Europe meant that teaching became more and more centred on the biblical texts, especially in the case of the New Testament. The reformers claimed to be restoring, or rediscovering, a form of teaching and a manner of worship that had been lost, and so, by studying the Scriptures in the correct way, it was thought that they would be able to recapture the vigour and enthusiasm of the apostolic era.[46] Once the Bible had been made available to everyone, it was also thought that it could be understood intuitively and its influence would be intensely felt. For Martin Luther, the Scriptures had to be understood in favour of Christ, not against Him. For John Calvin, what mattered was that people should have access to the saving truths of religion only insofar as God has revealed them in Scripture. In Calvin's case, this stance was indicative of his antagonism *vis-à-vis* the practices of the Roman Catholic Church.

The Bible, therefore, became of paramount importance in the Europe of the Protestant reformers. The slogan 'by Scripture alone', *sola Scriptora*, became a vital part of their programme, and this gave expression to their fundamental belief that the only infallible source of guidance for Christian faith and conduct was indeed the Bible. The family also discovered a more religious role for itself, since the Protestant churches encouraged family prayers, the regular reading of the Bible and other religious books, such as John Foxe's *Book of Martyrs*, and in Lutheran lands the singing of hymns within the family circle.

## Christ as Teacher – Evangelization and Education

Since the focus of Christ's earthly ministry had been concerned with teaching, surely His reign during the thousand years would in some way continue this. There are many references to the appellation of Christ as teacher in the New Testament, for example, there are more than ten citations in each of the four Gospels alone. In the society of the millennial period, no longer was education designed as a preparation for a life of civic duty as had been the case in the Roman Empire. It now laid an emphasis on the development of the moral life. Origen, for example, considered that Christ was teacher and master, for all those who are striving towards godliness,[47] the schoolmaster of the human race. A Catholic priest during the French Revolution expressed the sentiment that the preceding Christian centuries were indeed intended as a training ground in Christian morality and teaching. Furthermore, Desiderius Erasmus viewed the clergy as educators, whose function was to allow the laity to achieve the same level of understanding as themselves, and this idea reflected the important theme of Christ's role as teacher. Contemporaneous with Erasmus, the Renaissance humanist and reformer Juan de Valdés considered the death of Christ more as a means of instruction on the part of God, than for the purpose of redemption.[48] In Gotthold Lessing's work *On the Education of the human Race*, already cited, he stated that historic Christianity was one of several stages in the education of humanity. Such education targets the human race no less than the individual person.[49] Owen Chadwick remarked that it would be quite appropriate to think of the church as becoming more like a school,[50] in which the people of Western Europe were tutored in Christian ethics and religious practice. It is therefore appropriate that the history of the thousand years must be considered as an educative one for the European peoples.

The teaching office of the priesthood lay at the very heart of this concept and Christ himself instructed his disciples to spread the gospel. Theodulf of Orleans, during Charlemagne's reign, and with his consent, observed that the responsibility for teaching rested with the bishops, and he encouraged many of them to establish schools. Before the end of the eleventh century, new religious movements by way of the mendicant orders, notably the Dominicans and the Franciscans, sprang up in Italy and France which sought to realize this educational aim by combining poverty with itinerant preaching. They lived the monastic life but, unlike the monks, they were active in the world outside the monasteries. Their main task was the dissemination of biblical knowledge by preaching and ministering to the people. In the beginning they owned neither personal nor communal property, though this ideal was later to become compromised by the friars' very success. By opening their doors to outsiders, they made a significant contribution to raising the educational standards of the parish clergy. Pope Innocent III's preference for theologically instructed pastors was at least in part fulfilled. The people as well as the clergy were offered religious instruction, and the urban poor as well as the rural peasantry had the Gospel preached to them.

Education at a higher level was not neglected either. From the twelfth century onwards, reforms generated, and were themselves assisted by, an educational revolution. The enormous increase in intellectual and literary activity during the twelfth century onwards was also spurred on by youthful ambitions. As a method of critical thought, a new movement, led by the academics of medieval universities in Europe, dominated teaching until the eighteenth century. The theologians associated with it came to be known as 'schoolmen' because they lectured in the cloisters or cathedral schools that had been founded by Charlemagne and his immediate successors. These cathedral schools had been established to teach the liberal arts, and in the cities they became a force within the community. For this very good reason, the movement came to be known by the title 'scholasticism'. In the seventeenth century, the Jesuits established a large number of schools, in which promising young men of all classes were given the means to attend. The system proved itself on account of the number of brilliant minds that were produced by them. In short, the people of Western society were conditioned by the teaching of the church, which had the resources to be its educator. That society became the product of education, tradition and discipline during the thousand years.

### Renaissance and Reformation

During the course of the fifteenth century, the medieval synthesis, and the rigid scholastic system which was an integral part of it, began to break down. Accompanied by the decline of the papacy, this system was gradually replaced by a mental outlook that may generally be called 'modern', differing from that of the medieval period in many ways. The result was the rise of various movements within the Christian West, some more important and long-lasting than others, many of which reflected the diminishing authority of the church and the increasing authority of science. From the point of view of our millennial thesis, we must investigate how far these movements were Christian in nature and indeed whether the term 'the Christian West' could still be applied to Western Europe during the three hundred years until the end of the thousand-year period at the close of the eighteenth century.

The modern outlook began in Italy with the Renaissance, in all likelihood emanating from Florence at around 1400. The participants in the movement, by seeking knowledge of the ancient past, led to its being characterized primarily as a great revival of art and scholarship. It took advantage the fruits of Latin and Greek learning, for example in the study of Plato, and led to the revival of neoplatonism. Whilst it manifested itself in many ways, it became celebrated for engendering the intellectual movement known as humanism. From Italy this new humanist spirit slowly spread to all parts of Europe, aided by the invention of printing. The movement did not involve the mass of the population, but was composed of a small number of scholars and artists, encouraged by liberal patrons. As we shall see later with respect to both the Enlightenment and the French Revolution, the question arose as to whether the movement was fundamentally Christian or not. Certainly, Renaissance thinkers were ambivalent towards the church. Some aspects of the movement had a secular flavour, but its achievements were established against a religious background, and it relied upon the ideas and traditions of Christianity. Certain it was that the authority of the ancients was substituted for that of the church, but very few Italians of the fifteenth century would have dared to hold an opinion for which no authority could be found either in antiquity or in the church's teaching. Nobody involved in the movement seriously questioned Christianity. Its humanism was deeply religious, and the movement never completely abandoned faith in Christ. Many of its greatest works were devoted to the Christian faith, for the subject matter of its art was largely Christian, with much painting that depicted biblical scenes. Furthermore, by commissioning many works, the church became the patron of Renaissance art.

The Renaissance became more secular as it progressed. Typical men of the movement were Dante Alighieri, Francesco Petrarch and most importantly Desiderius Erasmus. The latter understood that the future vitality of Christianity would lay with the laity, not with the clergy, for there was no room any longer for superstitions which gave the clergy a permanent status superior to the layman. One example of this was the ethos of Swiss humanism, which possessed a strongly moralistic streak, and this led some to view the Bible as the blueprint for correct Christian moral conduct.[51] Desiderius Erasmus' strong emphasis upon 'inner religion' resulted in an understanding of Christianity which made no reference to the church, neither its rites, priests, or institutions. The rise of humanist biblical scholarship in the early sixteenth century discovered a series of translation errors in existing Latin versions of the Bible. As a result, pressure grew for the revision of some existing Christian doctrines, but the salient point was that there was no intention at that time to overthrow Christendom.

It was the Reformation which had several major repercussions so far as our historical analysis is concerned. The conviction which gave the movement its lifeblood, and what the church had always assumed, was that the 'Word of God' alone had brought the church into existence and nourished its daily life. It resulted in the afore-mentioned split of the Christian West between the Catholic and Protestant churches. Another result was a frontal attack by the Protestant churches on much of the medieval Catholic heritage, whose spell was now broken for many European peoples. A further major outcome of the Reformation was the gradual rise of a critique of existing Christian belief and practices, first of all by churchmen themselves and afterwards by a movement fuelled by a new European intelligentsia, whose writings came to be broadly categorized as the 'Enlightenment'. These two developments would fill out the remaining three centuries of Christian life until the year 1800.

The mainstream Reformation was concerned not with establishing a new Christian tradition, but, it was claimed, with the renewal and correction of an existing one. Adolf Harnack stated the matter thus: "The Reformation was the close of a long series of cognate but ineffectual attempts at reform in the Middle Ages. If the position which it thus holds in history proves its continuity with the past...it was not an innovation in regard to religion, but a restoration and renewal of it."[52] Western Christianity, and with it, the reign of Christ continued on its way, albeit in a Europe that had become religiously divided. However, it attempted to transform secular life itself in order to make it into a vocation of God. For many, it was a new beginning which was akin to a baptism of the secular world. With echoes of Oswald Spengler, one would be justified in saying that in place of the still and the contemplative ethos, Christian energy was turned towards the restless and the active. Those who formerly would have preferred to leave the world now became those who wanted to be involved in it, with the aim of changing it.

Martin Luther and John Calvin had not set out with the intention of destroying Christendom,[53] nor did the religious conflicts of the seventeenth century intend such a result either. Does this vitiate the thesis of the thousand years of Western Christianity that forms the mainstay of this book? Not in the least, for the events described did not entail the end of the Christian faith for the majority of the peoples of the West. Everyone assumed that Christian belief and culture would remain the cornerstone of society. They continued to accept the literal truth of the Bible and the existence of a Christian order until almost the end of the eighteenth century. The foundations of Christianity had not yet been harmed since the basic tenets of the faith had not been significantly challenged. Christianity was not replaced by another religion. The West continued to believe in the same revelation of the divine events described in the Scriptures. Men and women still believed that they were subject to a righteous, eternal Power, who governed every event. Those who were separated along religious lines nonetheless retained much of what they had in common. Shared churches even flourished for some Catholic and Protestant congregations in German-speaking lands. Protestantism, doubtless, renovated Christianity by a return to fundamentals, but importantly, at this stage there was no deliberate intention to secularize society.[54]

Conventional wisdom within historical circles declares that the division of Western Christianity resulted in the Thirty Years' War which lasted from 1618 to 1648, a period characterized by several individual conflicts. As such, these events would have to be judged as a serious stain on Western Christianity, but it is debatable whether the conflicts involved were entirely religious. They may have been nominally so, but they originated in the ambition of the Catholic Austrian Habsburgs to obtain political control of all Germany. In the course of the wars, which were largely fought by armies of mercenaries anyway, of which René Descartes was one participant, the French, a Catholic nation, intervened on the side of Protestant Germany to thwart Catholic Austria. The conflict ended with the Peace of Westphalia in 1648, which settlement established the principle of *cuius regio, eius religio*. This statement carried the meaning that each European ruler was henceforth allowed to choose the denomination that his subjects would take, the latter, of course, having no choice in the matter. As a result, in most of Europe rarely did membership of a denomination involve a conscious choice by the individual layperson. The norm was for whole communities to convert to a particular Christian denomination – or be told to convert by the ruler – and to stand by that decision thereafter. The conforming majority did not form a conscious membership of a church in any way distinct from their geographical community or neighbourhood. The outcome of this ruling created the confessional division of Germanic Christianity that exists to this day.

The medieval church had exercised a monopoly over Christendom, and another important result of the Reformation was that all three major Protestant branches, Lutheran, Anglican, and Calvinist, attempted to establish replicas of that erstwhile situation within the confines of their own territories. This was carried out with the intention of retaining their plausibility as thoroughgoing Christian communities. But they could not compare in any way with the universal Catholic medieval model simply because of their diminished size and the continual confrontation with situations which contradicted that model. We have, for example, mentioned already the fact that during the medieval period only orthodox and obedient believers could enjoy the full rights of citizenship. This monopoly was continued by the Protestant churches as strictly as the prevailing situation allowed, and they used methods that were as authoritarian as those used by the Catholic Church.[55] However, during the eighteenth century the European powers gradually became less resolute over religious uniformity, so that the viability of such uniformity was beginning to be questioned.[56]

Perhaps the m'ost important result of the Thirty Years' War was the widespread scepticism that ensued concerning church life, and the sense of weariness that accompanied it. Overall, the sceptics of the seventeenth century did not advocate abandoning Christianity in favour of atheism, but employed reason in an attempt to defend the Christian faith. The cultural horizon of most educated men and women in Western Europe during these centuries was still dominated by two sources of authority: Scripture and the classics. The European movements of the Renaissance and the Reformation reinforced this attitude.

During the final three centuries of the thousand-year period, science and religion did not stand in opposition to each other. Many Puritan clergymen not only gained membership of the Royal Society, but also were instrumental in founding it. For the seventeenth-century men of science, such as Nicolaus Copernicus, Johann Kepler, Galilei Galileo, René Descartes and Sir Isaac Newton who all affirmed Christianity, there was no antagonism between scientific discovery and religious belief.[57] Some have claimed René Descartes to be a sceptic, partly as a result of his reliance on human reason, but all these men were preoccupied with faith and had found Christian belief in God essential to their work, exemplifying the point that religious and scientific thought were closely intertwined. This ran counter to any incipient assumption that religion was inherently inimical to scientific progress. Francis Bacon articulated a philosophy of science and technology that drew upon earlier Christian thought and which considerably encouraged a work ethic. In his *The Advancement of Learning* (1605) he wrote that learning and knowledge had as its appropriate end "the glory of the Creator and the relief of man's estate."[58] The whole philosophy of Newton necessitated knowledge of a Supreme Being, who created everything and arranged all things of His own will. These pioneering scientists had no desire to eliminate religion. Instead, they developed a secular theology, written with the layman in mind. Many Protestants took the view that natural science afforded a rational and empirical way to improve men's earthly condition, or material circumstances. Even though the English revolution of the seventeenth century was a political one, it was firmly established in religion.

The last quarter of the seventeenth century and onwards into the eighteenth were the decades that witnessed the age of Gottfried Leibniz, Bernard le Bovier de Fontenelle, Baruch de Spinoza, John Locke, David Hume, Denis Diderot and François Voltaire, and were the seminal years of modern intellectual history. The difference between these new philosophers and scientists on the one hand, and the medieval scholastics on the other, was that the former shifted the weight of their faith far more towards reason than revelation to the extent that the Christian doctrine of salvation gradually receded into the background. Jeffrey Russell has put forward several logical stages that occurred in this process. Whereas all phenomena were originally thought to be explained by Christian theology, by a gradual process it was eventually science that became recognized as the only source of legitimate knowledge about the world.[59] René Descartes maintained belief in Christianity, claiming that the mathematical laws of nature had been laid down by God, but he engaged in a form of dualism that completely separated the material universe from the spiritual world.

### The Pietist Movement

Protestant orthodoxy experienced two severe shocks towards the end of the thousand years, the first of which was the impact of Pietism. The originator of the movement itself was Philipp Jakob Spener who was convinced that a moral and religious reformation within German Lutheranism had become necessary. He lamented the state of the German Lutheran Church in the aftermath of the Thirty Years' War, and laid out proposals which would serve to revitalize the church of his day. As a distinct movement, Pietism emerged in the German Lutheran Church about 1670. Through this movement, Christianity exerted a renewed resurgence of religious passion, and it took different forms in the three major Protestant groupings, namely, Pietism proper within Lutheranism, Methodism originating within the Church of England, and a variety of revivalist movements in Calvinism. North America, similar to England, witnessed it too with the movement known as the 'Great Awakening', which started in the 1730s.

Criticism had been raised against the shortcomings of the Protestant churches, with the charge that orthodoxy had become sterile. Without denying that priests were indispensable, lay people became increasingly impatient with, and critical of, the existing clerical leadership. A revival of practical and devout Christianity was therefore advocated, of which the most important forerunners of the movement were the Christian mystic Jakob Böhme, and the theologian Johann Arndt. The latter's *Wahres Christentum (True Christianity)* (1610) had a strong influence on the later leaders of Pietism. Arndt concentrated on its effect on the individual believer, foreshadowing the theological ideas of the romantic theologian Friedrich Schleiermacher, who was exposed to Pietism in his youth and whose theology we shall review in chapter 9.

The main difference between Lutheran Pietism's followers and orthodox Lutherans concerned the formers' conception of Christianity as chiefly consisting in a change of heart and consequent holiness of life. It emphasised the precedence of spiritual talents and insight over formal doctrine, and gave a new emphasis to personal Bible study and the role of the laity in the church. As we have already noted, sainthood came increasingly to mean a piety of personal commitment. The movement had a profound effect on Protestant orthodoxy. However, it provoked misunderstanding, scorn and severe criticism, especially from orthodox Lutherans, of which the theologian Valentin Ernst Löscher was one, because it tended to dissolve the church's dogmatic structures into various forms of emotionalism, treating systematic theology and philosophy as quite secondary. For example, in preaching against the prevalent laxity of morals, it relegated to the background the Lutheran dogma of justification by faith alone, and insisted on a life of active devotion, and the doctrines of repentance, conversion, and regeneration. Pietism attained its greatest following by the middle of the eighteenth century. Intense and diverse pietistic movements flourished during this period once its leaders started to encourage several forms of the movement.[60] For example, Count Nikolas von Zinzendorf organized refugees from Moravia into a kind of *collegia pietatis* within German Lutheranism.

We must enquire whether it would be correct to claim that this complex movement was a worthy participant in the life of European Christian society during the thousand-year reign of Christ. It represented a response by the Christian believer to the movement known as the 'discovery of the individual', in that it provided a Christian perspective on the individualism and practical-mindedness of a European civilization which was on the verge of the transition to modern times. In the context of Christian belief, Pietism represented a significant effort to reform the Protestant heritage. It was heavily dependent upon Scripture, and remained a source of distinctly Christian renewal, with the claim that it contributed to the revival of Biblical studies in Germany. It rejected the formality and dogmatism of the theological establishment and despised what it saw as its exhausted traditions, focusing instead on the individual's personal religious experience.[61] It shared something of the mysticism of the late Middle Ages, and the emphasis on lay Christianity which harked back to the early Reformation. However, the founders of Pietism had no idea of forsaking the underlying tenets of Lutheran dogma.

It is perhaps significant that Pietism made a late appearance within the thousand years of Western Christianity, and it is a moot point as to whether the movement presaged the end of the thousand years, by transforming Christian dogma into more emotional forms of Christian expression. Dietrich Bonhoeffer of the German Confessing Church voiced an appropriate sentiment when he described Pietism as the last attempt to save Christianity as a religion. Earlier, Rudolf Sohm had claimed that it was Christianity's last 'hurrah', the last great fling *(große Wellenschlag)* of the ecclesiastical movement which had been created by the Protestant Reformation. "Then came a time when another intellectual power henceforth took possession of the minds of men..."[62]

### The Enlightenment first considered in its Christian Outlook

We cannot leave our survey of the thousand years without considering the vitally important movement known as the 'Enlightenment', whose rationalism caused the second shock to Protestantism in the eighteenth century. In a similar way to Pietism, it intensely challenged not only the teaching and practice of the Protestant world, but also the Christian faith itself, and became the most powerful movement in European thought. Impressive indeed was the fact that several great Enlightenment and post-Enlightenment thinkers had been exposed to Pietism in their youth, for example, Immanuel Kant, Johann Wolfgang von Goethe, Friedrich Schleiermacher, as well as men such as Johann Georg Hamann, Johann Gottfried von Herder and Georg Hegel.

The Enlightenment has posed a dilemma for the historian, for it has been much debated as to whether this movement supported Christianity at least in its initial stages, or was opposed to it. It was a question similar to that which Jules Michelet dared to ask of the French Revolution in his book *Histoire de la Révolution (History of the Revolution)* (1847-1853), because he believed it to be a fundamental question in understanding history. This is not the place to settle the issue for either movement, but the Enlightenment did have a tremendous significance for the Christian faith. Certain it is, that the movement arose out of the centuries-old heritage of Western Christian civilization, but its philosophical polemic often resulted in conclusions that were far from Christian. In this chapter, we shall emphasize its pro-Christian aspects, in keeping with our thesis that the thousand years of the Christian West continued until the end of the eighteenth century and that some aspects of Enlightenment thinking supported Christian belief. In the next chapter, we shall discuss its anti-Christian sentiments, for what started out as a movement for religious toleration moved forward, passing through Deism, to display eventually a manifest hostility to Christianity and the Christian ecclesiastical establishment.

The origins of the Enlightenment can be traced back to the mercantile classes of the Netherlands.[63] In the middle of the seventeenth century, the Czech pedagogical reformer, Jan Comenius, was already predicting an 'age of light', promoted by the discoveries and developments of the previous centuries.[64] In a similar vein, it was John Locke who was responsible for launching the English Enlightenment at the end of the century. His philosophical work came to dominate thought to a considerable extent in the next century with its novel ideas, which also encompassed, *inter alia*, toleration, and its potentiality for equality and the moral improvement of man.[65]

The movement began by proposing a tolerant Christianity. As support for this idea gained ground, Locke could write: "A church, then, I take to be a voluntary society of men, joining themselves together of their own accord in order to the public worshipping of God."[66] John Tillotson argued that "all the duties of (the) Christian religion which respect God are no other but what natural light prompts men to."[67] Similar ideas were advanced by John Locke's *Reasonableness of Christianity* (1695) and John Toland's *Christianity not mysterious* (1696). From this, we can certainly appreciate that in the early part of the eighteenth century, compromise was already evident. Whilst religious toleration engendered stimulation for reform, it caused in its train a reaction which gave rise to fideism, an epistemological theory which held that since Christianity was unable to show evidence of its truths rationally, knowledge had to depend on faith or revelation. It involved the idea that faith is independent of reason, that reason and faith are hostile to each other, faith is superior at arriving at particular truths, and finally that the cosmos was wholly mysterious.

The Enlightenment, as an intellectual and forceful response to orthodox dogma, tended in its early stages to attack not religion itself but rather to scorn both the 'petulant capricious sects' and the disagreeable consequences caused by their militant dogmatism. Amongst the latter could be counted what David Hume in his work *Essays moral, political, and literary* (1758) called false religion, "...the pernicious effects of superstition and enthusiasm, the corruptions of true religion", as the result of unreasoning flights and fancies, a presumptuous pride and confidence and a "contempt for the common rules of reason, morality, and prudence."[68] A powerful challenge to traditional Christian beliefs about Christ was also a product of Enlightenment thought. Whereas Christ's death and resurrection had been considered more important than the quality of his moral teaching, the Enlightenment emphasized the latter, and in so doing succeeded in marginalizing his death and denying his resurrection, a stance taken especially amongst German thinkers and writers. Suffice it to say that for many in the eighteenth century, the New Testament's depiction of a supernatural Saviour of mankind was unacceptable to Enlightenment thinkers, but underneath lay concealed no more than a human being, an exalted moral teacher.[69] The latter portrait was acceptable to Enlightenment rationalism, but the former was not.

Similarly, the devout reading of Scripture had been an important feature which had resulted from the Reformation, but as the Enlightenment progressed, it distanced itself from this practice too, and replaced it with the idea that one should use one's own mind without guidance from another, and to use one's own reason in matters of conscience. It would be feasible to interpret the work of the *philosophes* in the beginning as condemning organized religion rather than the Christian faith, the practices and institutions of which in their view had strayed from Christ's authentic teaching, and evolved into an authoritarian, prejudiced, superstitious, ritualistic institution, apprehensive of scientific development and discovery, and mired in outdated conceptions.[70] Many *philosophes* appear to have dreamed of a purified, simplified, natural religion, shorn of all its supernatural, miraculous, or arbitrary elements. Their optimistic version of Christianity was defined by the ethical teachings of Christ, which would lead to the perfectibility of humanity, and \which entailed individual conscience and social justice. Liberal Protestantism, and to some extent liberal Catholicism, would inherit such ideas in the nineteenth century. Thomas Jefferson encapsulated this spirit by notoriously reworking the New Testament, in which he drew a distinction between Christ's words and teaching on the one hand, and all the miracle stories and mythical elements on the other, and by excluding the latter, he transformed it into a philosophical and ethical treatise.

Yet another movement emerged by the middle of the eighteenth century, when some thinkers within European intellectual circles, who became exhausted and disillusioned with both the Reformation's theological disputations and the violence of the Thirty Years' War, espoused Deism. Its followers retained a belief in God but limited His function to creation along rational lines with no further involvement on His part, for the world subsequently continued to operate by natural laws. They believed that God showed Himself in nature, and in the same way as the mainstream *philosophes*, they queried the existence of the supernatural and the miraculous. Some Deists, especially in England, preferred to retain the name 'Christian', but others, the French Deists for example, abandoned Christianity openly and their beliefs veered towards atheism and scepticism, discarding or minimizing everything in the Christian heritage: Scripture, tradition, miracles, revelation, and they did so oftentimes with an anger that contrasted with the English approach. The brief emergence of Deism does not really cohere with our millennium thesis, but it must be emphasized that this movement, and the Enlightenment movement which accompanied it, was the preserve of a small elite. Deism certainly did not occupy an intermediate position between the Christian faith and a complete denial of God, for the Deists were passionate about God, but they shared the belief with the *philosophes* that reason should be elevated over faith. In the same way as Sir Isaac Newton, they believed that they had discovered the primordial faith that underpinned the ancient biblical accounts. Deism was branded, as with the Enlightenment, by an anticlericalism, but it was by no means averse to religion itself. Deists needed God, recalling François Voltaire's famous remark, that if God did not exist, it would be necessary to invent Him.

It would be somewhat fallacious to consider the eighteenth century as the age of the Enlightenment only, since religion still exercised as great an influence over most sections of society as it had done throughout the thousand years. For example, there is the phenomenon of the first Great Awakening in North America. In addition, there is disagreement between historians over the strength of Catholicism in pre-revolutionary France. The church appeared to be still in a relatively healthy state during this period. Some commentators maintained that the Council of Trent had reformed and revitalised the church, and drew attention to its well-educated clergy, numerous and varied religious orders, and renewed forms of worship. Religious unity had been the hallmark of Western European states under the ancien régime, but religious minorities experienced civic disabilities, which were frequently severe, in those nations where they did have the freedom to practise their religion in public. Education and poor relief continued to be provided by the ecclesiastical parish as the responsibility of the churches' organizations, as was civil registration. The imposition of censorship, restrictions on unlicensed preaching and laws against blasphemy served to uphold the *status quo*.[71]

Other commentators have traced a small but noticeable decrease in religious observance after 1750 in the decades before the French Revolution, especially in the towns and among the middle class in both France and Germany. It would be incorrect to assert that God's authority was being rejected, rather the bonds of that authority were weakening. Many of the Enlightenment philosophes were themselves members of the privileged orders of church and nobility and their rational theology relied entirely on the belief that there was a God. It was out of the question intellectually to entertain the kind of atheism that became to be recognized in modern times. Indeed, François Voltaire considered it to be a monstrous evil, and it was not until the nineteenth century that the considerable growth of apostasy and unbelief occurred among the mass of European society.

Most of the intelligentsia in this period took the view that reason should be the final authority for belief and morality, and the sole way of obtaining truth. The Enlightenment philosophes would not have agreed that the seventeenth and eighteenth centuries could be viewed as a period of darkness rather than of light, merely because a few people abandoned the truths of the Gospel to follow a false idol of their own creation, namely, human reason. In their eyes, they were continuing the tradition of the eleventh century theologian Anselm of Canterbury, whose famous slogan was 'faith seeking understanding', *(fides quaerens intellectum)*. If faith must precede understanding, the phrase means that we should understand intellectually what we already believe.

A complex relationship, long studied by historians, existed between Pietism and the Enlightenment. They both attacked Protestant orthodoxy and doctrine, both asserted the rights of individuals, both strongly emphasized charity, compassion, and teaching, and both were concerned about practice more than theory or doctrine. Yet the essential nature of both movements with regard to religion could not have been more different. There were grounds for saying that the Pietists were always looking for biblically based enlightenment, centred around the Christian God, whereas some of the philosophes became obsessed with rationalism for its own sake. The crucial question was whether pietistic anti-traditionalism, its individualism and its practicality prepared the ground for a non-Christian expression of these very same traits amongst the Enlightenment philosophes. The rationalism of the Enlightenment sought to demystify, and ultimately to destroy, religion. Pietism, on the other hand, remained faithful to Scripture and emphasized an inward spirituality which was controlled by Christian beliefs. Whatever its relationship to the Enlightenment, it was not in reality the primary source of the latter's scepticism or rationalism.

The thrust of Enlightenment thought had only a limited effect on the polity and workings of the churches themselves. In most of Europe there was still an ecclesiastical establishment, whose doctrines the subjects of any given state were expected to follow. Whilst the role of the church did change in the later centuries of the thousand years, this did not mean that people were renouncing, or losing interest in, their religion.[72] Even if the intelligentsia were by the middle of the eighteenth century questioning every aspect of religious belief and observance, most people held to the Christian faith and worshipped as they had done throughout the thousand years. They continued to retain traditional Christian beliefs, and to obey what they alleged to be the determinative authority, be it the teaching of the Bible, the statements of the Christian creedal tradition, the decision of the churches or the witness of experience.

\*\*\*\*\*\*\*\*

The Christian faith during the eighteenth century was still influential, and, despite the Enlightenment, the period could not therefore be identified as an age of universal unbelief. There was as yet a very limited awareness in society at large, especially amongst ordinary people, of all the controversy and the intellectual criticism that was fermenting among the elites during this period. Once scepticism had become acceptable about religious dogma, it became feasible to write in a sceptical manner, but such practice was still confined to the intelligentsia and men of letters. Being an elite movement, it was the Parisian salons especially that provided a centre for discourse. Rather it was an age in which scepticism, which at its most extreme could indeed lead to unbelief, but the older world view, seeing God in all things, was still very powerful.

There was a continuity of Western culture from the Carolingian Renaissance until the French Revolution, a span of time which constituted the thousand years of our thesis. By looking back on this period, we can pose the question whether there were any characteristics of this period, that were common to all ten centuries and all places, despite the various historical events and political scenarios that occurred within it. One common thread that did weave its way throughout the thousand years, intimately linked to its culture and leaving its indelible mark was a sustained Christian belief amongst the majority of the ordinary people of Western Europe. The second thread was that of Christ's rule: as leader, as minister, as teacher, and this rule was reflected in the acceptance of Christian ideals by all the temporal rulers. Throughout the thousand years of Western Christianity, diverse Christian movements arose to challenge the existing ecclesiastical order, and each movement played its part in continuing to provide moral teaching. The 'life and rule' of the Christian faith during the thousand years was able to adapt and develop amid the changing circumstances of a progressive European culture, reflecting the fact that it was a living faith.

We have noted that the thousand-year period, education was an important element with respect to the reign of Christ. The banishment of Satan clearly did not entail the absence of all sin, nor that it would be free of moral lapses. Furthermore, it has been said that much of the clergy themselves and certainly the political leadership oftentimes accepted, but did not necessarily obey, Christian ideals and ethics. A culture that had lived in the light and teaching of the Christian faith eventually came to be replaced by the theological rationalism of the Enlightenment, and a civilization that was influenced by modern 'isms', which were political and social ideologies, namely, communism, fascism, nationalism, modernism, individualism, relativism, pluralism. These took the church and the Christian faith along an altogether different path, marking a fundamental difference between pre-1800 and post-1800 history. But this is to anticipate the chapters that follow.

CHAPTER EIGHT

*The End of the thousand Years: Satan let loose*

"Coming events cast their shadows before." *Thomas Campbell*

IN REVELATION 20:7, John continues with the words: "And when the thousand years are ended, Satan will be loosed from his prison." Previously we maintained that the period of one thousand years was coterminous with the culture and civilization of the Christian West, and according to Revelation 20:3 this period of years would be followed by Satan's release for a little while, or, as some biblical translations state, for a short season. This event brings down the curtain on the thousand years of Christian 'life and rule'. Satan is set free once more to resume his iniquitous activities and to deceive the nations. Unchanged, he emerges from the abyss still with his intrinsic antipathy towards God, for the thousand years of banishment had wrought no moral improvement in him. We might question why man's arch-enemy, the principle of evil, should be set at liberty after imprisonment during the thousand-year period. Henry Swete suggested that the reason for this particular event was that during a time when there was little or no opposition to the faith, people might come to treat their faith thoughtlessly and take it for granted. He stated: "It may be that the Christian nations which have long acquiesced in the faith without conviction will need to be sifted before the end."[1] We have attempted to show in the previous chapter that the thousand years of Western Christianity indeed provided a training ground or school for Western people, and the loosening of Satan could therefore be explained as a means whereby they were put to a final test in order to examine their faith and virtue.

The Devil, or Satan, is locked up for the thousand years, but the Bible makes no mention of an initial pact, or bargain, with him. However, we have described the Faustian myth as referring not only to an individual person but, as a theory, to Western civilization as well in the now famous exposition by Oswald Spengler. In the traditional Faustian legend, the Devil returned at the appointed time to exact his price, which, in the famous legend, was to claim Faust's soul. It would be ominous indeed for Western society if the Devil was to be released at the end of the thousand years for a kindred purpose.

The physical chain which bound the Devil, as depicted in the Apocalypse, is an allegorical image. In the same manner, we cannot conceive of a physical Devil who proceeded to stalk European society at the end of the eighteenth century, unless you agree with some commentators, both then and now, who would assign that role to Maximilien Robespierre or Napoléon Bonaparte. What can we deduce from the tumultuous events of this period? The apocalyptic narrative must be justified in historical terms in two ways. First of all, there must be evidence that the thousand years of Christian 'life and rule' were indeed coming to an end during the latter part of the eighteenth century, and that this came to pass by means of a concerted attack against the Christian religion, against the ecclesiastical establishment, and even against confessional orthodoxy. This onslaught, for that is what it truly became during the course of the eighteenth century, was carried out by the intelligentsia of Western Europe. Subtle and concealed at first, it gradually built to a crescendo, and must be interpreted as heralding the demise of Christianity's hegemony over the Western world. In the second case, and of particular note, we will record how the tumultuous events in France at the end of that century were seen in some quarters as acquiring a satanic and apocalyptic character. Following the evidence presented later, we shall draw the reasonable conclusion from this that the Devil was indeed released from the abyss and that his forces were now stalking the nations. We shall also have something to say about both the English industrial revolution, German developments in philosophical thought, and the change which took place in the piety of many European people.

### The eighteenth Century as a Turning-point

Earlier it was shown how important was the pivotal, or decisive, date of 800 with respect to the birth and subsequent development of Western Christian society, and it will take only the briefest of calculations to arrive at the year 1800 as the termination of a thousand-year period. Commentators of both Western history and religious belief have been particularly prone to ascribe the secularization and apostasy of the Western world in the modern period to a mysterious spiritual and intellectual fall from grace. In a comparable manner, others have stated that something odd happened in Western Europe during the approach to the modern period in the eighteenth century, which defies any historical explanation. Surely, it behoves the historian to seek an answer to this question. The so-called mystery is solved if one accepted the timetable prophesied in the Apocalypse, for these events could be said to have been pre-ordained in John's narrative. Satan has now returned and this event could be dated to a time-period centred around the year 1800. The modern world is still living with that inheritance.

The so-called 'Wars of Religion' had scarred a society which had grown weary of religious controversy, and so from the seventeenth century onwards the intellectual elite gradually became sceptical of, and disillusioned with, the Christian ecclesiastical establishment, and even in some quarters with the Christian faith itself. One result was the emergence of Deism, but eventually the main outcome led to radical criticism of the established order as well, both political and social, a movement which is known to historians as the 'Enlightenment' or 'Illumination'.

There has been virtually unanimous agreement amongst historians that the eighteenth-century represented an age of discontinuity, in which the secularization of European society had its immediate roots, even if it be accepted that earlier periods may also have played a part in this process. Historians of science, medicine, gender, race, ideas, society and culture, as well as politics and religion, saw the eighteenth century as the moment when the West shifted several gears upwards,[2] and the Enlightenment was the turning point. Something of great significance was happening. Hans Küng stated that the motivations and revolutionary stimulus generated by the French Revolution signalled a turn of the ages, an historic transformation which was to create modern Europe.[3] The remarks made earlier concerning decisive dates apply here with equal force, for important movements and events were happening around 1800 but they did not, of course, occur precisely in this year. The historian Lucian Hölscher viewed the eighteenth century as bringing, not a decline in Christianity, but a reinterpretation of it. In so far as the Christian world depended on conformism, the developments during the period were indeed challenging much of the faith, but neither the faith itself nor belief in the supernatural were instantly destroyed. We also need to survey the aftermath of these events which occurred in the following century, and these will be described in the next chapter.

The Enlightenment movement had taken many decades to develop. We have noted that sources of this movement, some distant, some nearer, specifically helped to encourage, if not an outright antipathy to established religion, at least to a reappraisal of it especially with regard to religious practice. The original world-view of the early medieval era, based upon Platonic-Aristotelian philosophy, was cast aside by the speculations of medieval philosophers, such as John Duns Scotus, Francis Bacon and William of Ockham, because such a perspective was considered pagan in origin. Ockham's theology proved to be the most subversive since it displaced the centre of meaning and truth from the divine to the human creator. Moreover, the relationship between reason and revelation, both considered as a distinct source of knowledge, became increasingly unstable over the ensuing centuries. Trust in the divine status of authoritative texts began to falter, leading to a rift between religious and secular reason, and between theology and spirituality, so that as time went on Western Christianity began to be viewed as a scholarly religion.[4] The quest became targeted on the search for a basis for rationality which was other than that of the doctrine of creation, and bit by bit confidence grew in intellectual methods based on pure reasoning.

As previously noted, the major Protestant churches sought to construct replicas of what they considered to be Christendom within their respective territories. The 'Wars of Religion' had inadvertently generated a pluralistic potential during the seventeenth century, with the effect that further fragmentation of this kind would follow all the more easily. By way of further explanation, once plurality had been conceded for Western Europe overall, it became difficult for the authorities of each nation or territory not to concede it for their own people as well. In due course of time, therefore, for practical rather than ideological reasons, an ever-widening religious toleration developed in both Protestant and Catholic territories. Secondly, the religious controversies resulting from the Reformation period were making people feel less confident in those authorities who were held responsible for making decisions on matters appertaining to Christian belief. Their apparent disability in this respect led some to investigate whether there were other, higher, authorities to which they could appeal in the quest for definitive answers, but the more perceptive recognized that in many cases no consensus could be achieved regardless of the approach employed.[5] But it took most of the three hundred years after the Reformation before the effects of all these situations began to be overly apparent, or even realised by churchmen themselves. Quite disconcerting too was the novel tendency to view European civilization in a world context. The age of discovery from the sixteenth century onwards, bringing in its train new knowledge about primitive religions, had raised disturbing questions which challenged the uniqueness of the Christian religion.[6]

Doubt began slowly to unravel the very fabric of Christianity. Controversially, philosophical or cosmological systems were created that had no need of Christian explanations. René Descartes, with his famous declaration, "I think, therefore I am," *(cogito, ergo sum)* was more than anyone else responsible for starting the 'Age of Reason' and establishing its place in history. He argued that all ideas that are 'clear and distinct' to him must be true, and claimed that the idea of God came into this category, thereby proving God's existence. God Himself was put on trial by Baruch de Spinoza. He attempted to construct his own system of metaphysics and ethics, consisting of a philosophy marked by natural science and incompatible with a literal belief in the Bible.

The churches were prepared to make concessions, and seemed encumbered rather than sustained by their dogma, and so educated men tended to drift step by step from Christianity to natural religion. Most sceptics of the period did not immediately envisage a shift away from Christianity, for the immediate response was to provide a rational defence of the Christian faith. For example, thinkers such as John Locke, Nicholas Malebranche, John Toland, Christian von Wolff and Gottfried Leibniz, proposed that religion and morality should be justified not by revelation but by reason based upon experience. Unlike David Hume, Gotthold Lessing thought that faith and reason were consistent and therefore religion supported the development of reason. John Locke's book *The Reasonableness of Christianity as delivered in the Scriptures* (1695) took a similar line. Locke's writing caused controversy in some quarters because he seemed to be advocating that human reason should serve as the arbiter of revelation, but the more perceptive realized that his arguments might ultimately undermine religion.⁷ From another perspective, however, it may well be that reason could serve to authenticate a genuine revelation as opposed to a spurious or dubious one which proved to be merely a figment of the imagination.

Efforts to reconcile rationalist views with Christianity were also made by deeply religious scientists such as Sir Isaac Newton, but his arguments subverted metaphysics even more than Locke had done, since he considered empirical observation rather than reasoning to be the foundation of knowledge.⁸ Whereas Saint Basil of Caesarea, Saint Augustine and Saint Thomas Aquinas had insisted that the natural world could tell us nothing about God, on the contrary, Sir Isaac Newton, the English scholar Richard Bentley and the English philosopher Samuel Clarke all argued in the opposite direction. The irony was that by seeking to set the principles of Christianity using rational arguments, the Christian advocates of such methods were unintentionally undermining the whole structure. Some more traditionally minded thinkers recognized this ploy for what it really was, namely, that these apologists were setting a future trap for themselves when beliefs came to be moulded by man-made opinions within an empirical framework. It would ultimately make the situation much more difficult, if not impossible, for the Christian faith.⁹ The philosopher, Blaise Pascal realized that Christianity was committing a blunder by admitting reason into the domain of religion. He was one of the first to predict that atheism would soon become a viable and seductive alternative.¹⁰ After the disaster of the Thirty Years' War, a rational theology that could control dangerous religious 'enthusiasms' seemed essential, but the newly emerging sciences were about to make the concept of God inconceivable. The scientists and theologians of the seventeenth century were starting to turn God into a mere human projection, a proposition which was to be actively pursued by nineteenth-century thinkers.

### The Enlightenment reconsidered in its anti-Christian Outlook

According to many historians the Enlightenment movement, now surveyed a second time but with especial regard to its anti-Christian sentiments, was the major turning point in modern Western history. From the very beginning its protagonists mounted the strongest challenge to the status of confessional Christianity since the commencement of the thousand years. The devastation caused by the Thirty Years' War had remained in the collective European memory and was a major factor in framing convictions that were inimical to religion. In eighteenth-century France, a new breed of philosopher or *philosophe* arrived on the scene, men of the world, united in their loathing of the prejudice and fanaticism which they observed in France's monarchy and in its church.

René Descartes had cherished the hope of turning his 'method of doubt' into a means for discovering metaphysical certainty, but others now perceived it to be a powerful weapon with which they could assail traditional theological beliefs. Descartes may have propounded his claims in a tentative manner, but this was followed in the eighteenth century by the radicals' much bolder assertions. They considered that every instance of belief deviated from the truth if it lacked a rational justification.[11] Christian apologists were now being caught in the trap that they had set themselves. What had started out as an enlightened, reasonable tolerance for the Christian faith, noted in the previous chapter, would give way in the course of several decades to an enlightened reasoned hostility against it. Or was it on the other hand an unreasonable process of transformation? Virtually without exception the *philosophes* unanimously repudiated traditional Christianity. Karl Marx claimed that the demolition of religion at a purely theoretical level had indeed begun with them.

Much of the responsibility for inaugurating the Enlightenment movement and its hostility to the Christian religion could be laid at the door of the philosopher Pierre Bayle, a refugee living in the Dutch Republic, with his consummate work, the *Dictionnaire historique et critique (Historical and critical Dictionary)* (1697). Jonathan Hill called it enlightened scepticism, and in the book Bayle described and questioned Christian revelation in an ironical way, stating that any and every religious claim was absurd.[12] For a Christian believer of the time, Bayle's controversial ideas were considered offensive and obscene. The Consistory of the Walloon Church in Rotterdam certainly thought so. In an attempt to avoid censorship, Bayle wrote the entries in such a way that they merely defined the subject in outline. Most of the material was hidden away in the copious supplementary notes, which were written in small print, with the aim of encouraging the censor to disregard them.[13] The movement proceeded a step further with the publication in 1721 of Charles Montesquieu's *Les Lettres persanes (Persian Letters)*. The style and content of this work epitomized the new spirit of the age: satirical, witty, urbane, with deeply held beliefs expressed in an irreverent, frivolous and flippant manner.

Decisive dates in history were often foreshadowed by events which took place during a prior interim period of some years' duration, and such a period would serve as a portent for the major changes which would occur later. When we consider the year 1800, true to form, from the middle of the eighteenth century onwards, a new atmosphere developed in Western Europe. The wars of 1740-1763 represented a landmark, of which the Seven Years' War was considered at the time to be particularly destructive. Much of Europe was henceforth affected by growing tensions and a feeling of instability, culminating in the upheaval of the French Revolution in 1789. The horrifying Lisbon earthquake, occurring in 1755, was also important, because belief in a beneficent Providence was now called into question amongst many notable writers and thinkers of the period, among them Alexander Pope, Johann Wolfgang von Goethe, Immanuel Kant and François Voltaire. The latter's *Poème sur le Désastre de Lisbonne (Poem on the Lisbon Disaster)* (1756) was the prime example.

Voltaire achieved notoriety for his animosity against Christianity and the church which reflected an unconcealed disdain for both. He attacked the doctrines of Christianity, and what he saw as the authoritarian and corrupt practices of the Catholic Church, and waged war against it mercilessly with much wit and irony. At first, he subscribed to the idea of a benevolent God, but later came to condemn God, and regarded morality as a purely social development in a scathing satirical novel, *Candide* (1759). By the 1760s, hatred of Christianity had moved to the forefront of his mind, and he began to end his letters with the famous phrase *'écrasez l'infâme'*. It was a duty to 'crush the loathsome thing', a phrase which was generally interpreted to be the church that was the intended object of his scorn. Christian people on the contrary misinterpreted *'infâme'* to mean Christ himself, with the result that many in Europe regarded Voltaire as the arch-enemy of Christianity.[14] As Voltaire wrote in *Le Dictionnaire philosophique (The philosophical Dictionary)* (1764), "The institution of religion exists only to keep mankind in order, and to make men merit the goodness of God by their virtue. Everything in a religion which does not tend towards this goal must be considered foreign or dangerous."[15]

A whole array of writers, critics and *philosophes* of the French Enlightenment followed Voltaire, virtually as vehement as he was in perceiving Christianity as both oppressive and irrelevant, and advocating its total rejection as an archaic and discredited belief system. Gradually in the course of time, it became acceptable to cease religious observance, to repudiate or deride religious belief, and to declare one's doubt, unbelief, or even atheism in public.[16] The Enlightenment *philosophes* such as Denis Diderot, Claude Helvétius and Paul d'Holbach not only abandoned Christianity for rationalist atheism, but strongly refuted arguments for the Deism of their time as well. Diderot's *Encyclopédie* (1751-1766) became the central text of the French Enlightenment. It was widely read by all levels of educated society, and played a major role in disseminating Enlightenment ideas and ideals around Europe.

Within orthodox Christianity, the Bible had still been widely regarded as a divinely inspired source of doctrine and morals, different from other types of literature. With the rise of a critical approach to literature, which term included Scripture, even this assumption was called into question. Rather than being treated as a unique document, the Christian Bible was now considered to be open to exactly the same method of analysis and interpretation as any other literary work, an outcome that led to disputes over its internal consistency, that is to say, contradictions in its narrative. For many *philosophes*, the Christian liturgy too was mere nonsense. Paul d'Holbach believed that the only possible basis for constructing an ethical system using reason was atheism. Sentiments which the Enlightenment thinkers were now uttering contrasted radically with those that Jacques Bossuet had made a century earlier, and reflect a complete bouleversement from endorsing, or at least tolerating, religion. Now, according to Alexis de Tocqueville, the *philosophes* "attacked the church with absolute fury. They assailed its clergy, its hierarchy, its institutions, its doctrines; to overthrow these, they tried to tear up Christianity by the roots."[17] Johann Herder, as a critic of the Enlightenment, sensed more than anyone else during this period, how the structure of the faith was being shaken as a result of these developments.

By the end of the eighteenth century, most of the European intelligentsia had abandoned the core Christian beliefs. For them, traditional Christianity had failed and was intellectually wrong and socially destructive. Something akin to an anti-Christian programme eventually became the single clearest identifying feature of the Enlightenment movement. A great deal had to be eliminated before the *philosophes* could achieve success in managing the world. Most aspects of Christianity had to be discarded, and all that would remain behind would be its moral teaching on universal brotherly love. No less important was the assumption that human reason could arrive at the truth without the aid of theology.

It was inevitable in this situation that the *philosophes* would challenge the arguments for God's existence that had been trusted for centuries. Pre-eminent among them was Immanuel Kant, whom we consider below, and David Hume. In his works *The Natural History of Religion* (1757) and *Dialogues Concerning Natural Religion* (1779), Hume assailed the main intellectual foundations of Christian thought. When theologians made claims that Christian beliefs were based on reason, he aimed to falsify them. Christianity was nothing more than superstition shored up with dubious reasoning, simply 'sick men's dreams'.[18] He claimed that Christians sought rationally to justify what was merely an opinion or belief, and that led them astray.[19] In other words, he was attacking the rational justification of religion and the arguments that had served this process. Hume's devastating attack against religion, which formed the philosophical basis of modern atheism, followed five main lines. The first and third were epistemological and historical. The second was psychological, in which Hume argued that religion was the projection of human attributes on to external objects. This was the stance taken later by the philosopher Ludwig Feuerbach. It was the fourth and fifth lines of attack, dealing with the concept of miracles and the existence of evil, which have been the most effective. His work *Essay on Miracles* (1748) was widely considered to have dismissed the existence of miracles, considering them as fiction, thereby impugning a religion based upon them, such as the incarnation and resurrection. In the fifth line of attack, David Hume argued that the existence of evil and suffering was incompatible with an all-loving God.

Much as philosophers had done earlier in proposing natural laws without any reference to God, scientific thought was becoming opposed to the concept of a universe created by God, and it had no need of divine intervention to keep it intact, thereby undermining belief in a God who was concerned with individuals. Pierre Simon, Marquis de Laplace, in framing his 'nebular hypothesis', from the *Traité de Mécanique celeste (Treatise on celestial Mechanics)* (1789) claimed that it would be easy to eliminate God from the whole process when one sought ultimately to explain the universe. He considered Him irrelevant to scientific discovery, and was reputed to have told Napoléon so.

The historians too were beginning to participate in the debate whilst exercising a little more subtlety. The Jesuit theologian Denis Pétau (Petavius) attracted criticism for giving the impression that the Church Fathers had entertained false notions of trinitarian doctrines that in later ages would be considered orthodox. Jacques Bossuet recognized that, if such a contention could be substantiated, it would completely refute Christian teaching.[20] In earlier ages, it had been assumed that Christianity's success was due to this very concept. Edward Gibbon's historical writing explained historical events, including the ascent of Christianity, in terms of other historical events in a chain of natural causation, that is to say, by means of cause and effect, thereby denying any supernatural involvement. His writing was littered with this idea.[21] All these claims, and the suppositions and insinuations which underlay them, contributed to endangering Christian faith and its doctrines, oftentimes disastrously.

Noted earlier was the decline in religious practice during the second half of the eighteenth century in France and Germany, but in a few large German towns the fall was dramatic. The ratio of communicants to the Protestant population, for example, fell from 115 per cent to 20 per cent in Hanover, from 150 per cent to 40 per cent in Berlin and from 100 per cent to 45 per cent in Hamburg. Often one of the first indications in this respect was a decline in recruitment to the priesthood and religious orders, and served to emphasize that change was brewing. Clearly, these trends began long before the onset of industrialization, and in some cases, such as that of Hanover, before the period of rapid urban growth or revolutionary activity. In Britain it was, however, evangelicalism together with mercantilism and the onset of the industrial revolution that brought to an end whatever remained of the *ancien régime*. One of the factors was undoubtedly Enlightenment reasoning, and in Britain's case studies have shown that evangelicalism became inherently linked to it, with religious experience now being derived from such reason.

The end of the century witnessed the transition from the Enlightenment to the Romantic movement, of which one of the earliest protagonists was Jean-Jacques Rousseau. He has been described as an undisciplined and obsessional personality, who suffered from a persecution mania later in life. He alienated the *philosophes* by affirming his faith in Christianity, but his repugnance for organized religion led eventually to his rejection of church traditions in favour of individual sentiment. With Rousseau's practical rationalism, reflected in his famous *Le Retour à l'État de Nature (Return to the State of Nature)* (1755), Oswald Spengler commented that Rousseau had completely abandoned the world-view of earlier centuries, which had been grounded on theology, and buried a thousand years (sic) of spiritual depth.[22]

### Denial of the Devil's Existence

There was an additional role for the Enlightenment movement to play in the prophetic timetable for the loosening of Satan. An important ploy which the Devil, that master of deception, was accustomed to employ in order to promote his nefarious aims was to disguise his presence by simulation. Did the Enlightenment *philosophes* fall for this bait? By attacking Christianity, they dismissed the likelihood of the Devil's existence. During the seventeenth century, the traditional world view, which supported belief in the Devil, was already being undermined. At the end of that century, the philosopher Balthasar Bekker wrote: "the empire of the Devil is but a chimera, and that he has neither such a power, nor such an administration as is ordinarily ascribed to him."[23] Bekker's publication caused enormous controversy, and David Hume continued in a similar vein with his philosophical scepticism, and the effective denial of belief in Satan had accompanied the end of the witch craze.

Atheists contemptuously dismissed the existence of the Devil, Paul d'Holbach observing that "aerial beings, of spirits, angels, demons, genii and other phantoms...are the object of the meditations of our most profound thinkers, and serve as the basis of metaphysics, an abstract and futile science." Again: "It is only by dispelling the clouds and phantoms of religion, that we shall discover the sources of truth, reason, and morality."[24] Showing his disdain, Denis Diderot's *Encyclopédie* limited the article on the Devil to just over one column, or less than one thousand words. François Voltaire, too, despised the Devil as a grotesque Christian superstition. In his view, the Devil had no connection with evil, whilst Immanuel Kant later claimed that the independent existence of the Devil could not be meaningfully demonstrated. The *philosophes'* attitude of mockery towards the Devil was epitomized in the group called Wharton's Hellfire Club, established in London towards the end of the eighteenth century.

Johann Wolfgang von Goethe's Mephistopheles was the most important Devil in literature since John Milton, but Goethe depicted his Devil in a mode which bore little comparison with the Christian one. He suggested that the religious sceptics felt ill at ease with symbols of evil and preferred the Devil respectably disguised as an urbane gentleman. Hence, he used the name Mephistopheles instead of Satan to stress the deception. The Enlightenment had progressed sufficiently by the middle of the eighteenth century for some among the intellectual elite either to deny the Devil's existence altogether, to question whether there was any historical role left for him to play, or whether he made any impact at all in the world.

Some commentators were able to see through these ideas about the Devil, recognizing the threat that they implied. They declared that belief in a demonology was not a mental aberration, for they were quick to perceive that any questioning on this subject would represent the thin end of a wedge that disbelief in the Devil would automatically lead to disbelief in the existence of God. However, by the end of the century, as an obsolete idea, Satan had become an embarrassment to the intellectual elite. Such a development would further undermine the entire religious structure. The idea of original sin, and therefore of redemption, would be discarded in due course of time, and the intelligentsia would be left without any defence to deal with the problem of evil. By rejecting these traditional arguments, the problem tended to be evaded. The traditional Devil of the medieval period had been condemned as a rebel. As a riposte to this, the churches took the view that by criticizing the eternal truths of the Christian faith, these critics might well suffer the same fate as the protagonists in the Faustian legend. In this statement we now have the very first indication of what might happen if, and when, a society based on Christian ideals was destroyed.

Left to itself, the Enlightenment movement may not have impacted so much on the beliefs and religious observances of the great mass of the European population. After all, it influenced only Europe's intellectuals at the time. But the movement is important for our apocalyptic thesis. It was an assault which presaged the end of the thousand years. The *philosophes'* devastating criticism struck at the heart of the Christian faith and, consequently at the very existence of the Christian faith itself. In his view of the Enlightenment, by noting the medieval elements which he saw in Martin Luther's writings, Ernst Troeltsch considered the Enlightenment rather than the Reformation as the watershed between a medieval culture pervaded by Christianity on the one hand, and the increasingly secularized, modern world of the nineteenth century on the other. With the loosening of Satan from his prison stated in Revelation 20:7, the apocalyptic text now brings the thousand years of the Christian West to an end.

### The French Revolution

In the course of the eighteenth-century, whilst many *philosophes* sought to reform rather than to destroy society, their comments encouraged a venomous anticlericalism that reflected the resentment of the wealth of the French church.[25] This was one cause of the French Revolution of 1789. Once the Revolution had erupted in France, a rebellion spread throughout the Austrian Habsburg monarchy as well, and in 1792 rebellion took place in the Netherlands. The revolutionary French government intended to create a new society based upon Enlightenment reason. A torrent of publications of ancient, medieval and more recent prophecies attempted to demonstrate that these world-changing events were in some way fulfilling a divine plan. For example, many religious people of the time considered the Revolution in its early days to be a blessing sent by God to free humanity, and they viewed it, not as the end, but rather as the actual commencement, of the thousand years and as heralding a new age. However, it ultimately detonated the most vivid expressions of apocalyptic feeling in modern times, and the chemist and theologian Joseph Priestley immediately interpreted the events in France in apocalyptic terms. He held a millenarian conception of a Providence that was leading the world inescapably toward a state of perfection, and concluded that the revolution was a harbinger of

Christ's return. The Revolution had no precedent in human history, according to Karl Jaspers.[26]

Verse 20:3 of the Apocalypse runs as follows: "...that he (that is, Satan) should deceive the nations no more, till the thousand years were ended." The French and German translations of the Bible follow the English narrative conventionally. An 1854 French translation by L. Moreau of this biblical verse is curious in that it refers to the 'revolution of one thousand years'. Undoubtedly the translator was thinking of the connotation of 'revolution' as a cyclic completion of time, or perhaps on the other hand it could be interpreted as a revolution in the progression of Western civilization from Dark Ages to Enlightenment, but it is curiously suggestive of its modern alternative denoting a political upheaval. Certainly, the Enlightenment's revolutionary ideology together with its political aftermath could justly be called a revolution.

Almost every revolution generates excesses, and the French Revolution was no exception. In conformity with every revolutionary regime, radicals took advantage of the resulting instability to create an ethos of fear, which was accompanied by numerous acts of violence.[27] As the Revolution proceeded at so swift a pace, with the monarchy outlawed in 1792 and King Louis XVI executed in 1793, apocalyptic predictions enjoyed a reputation that had rarely been bestowed on earlier ones. *A fortiori*, the French priest Henri Grégoire, often referred to as the Abbé Grégoire considered the possibility that this revolution should indeed be read in apocalyptic terms, and many thought that the last days had arrived. Within three or four years a liberal movement had turned itself into a totalitarian autocracy and the revolution entered a phase known as the 'Terror'. Enthusiasm for the revolution turned to horror in the minds of many at the time. In 1795, the French Directory attempted to stabilise the country with a new constitution, but four years later a *coup d'état* carried out by Napoléon and his cohorts led to the establishment of a modern type of dictatorship.

To repeat Jules Michelet's question which we posed earlier as to whether the French Revolution was Christian or not, it eventually transpired that a major part of the Revolution concerned itself with 'dechristianizing' France. The revolutionaries took the mocking scepticism of the *philosophes* as a precedent for turning against the church on a scale and with a speed that was horrifying. In retrospect, the Revolution seemed to stand for the complete demolition of the church of the *ancien régime*. It endeavoured to promote atheism and rationalism, which were identified with a new-found liberty, with opposition to Catholic thought the natural corollary. Revolutionary eschatology was hostile to Christianity, similar to the anti-Catholic sentiments of Protestants. The result was the greatest state persecution of Christianity in Europe since the Roman Empire. In the *Épître aux vrais Catholiques (Epistle to the true Catholics)*, written in 1791, the anonymous author gave vent to his feelings. He spoke of "...the beast of the Apocalypse which is unchained, and who exerts a deathly power which it has been given to make war on the saints. A deluge of evil descends which is inundating the clergy and the Church of France." There was no indication as to which of the three beasts of the Apocalypse was being referred to in this extract, but a sense of terror was being adequately conveyed here.

The Revolution attempted to destroy Christianity by striking devastating blows at the church's parochial machinery. During the few years after 1789, thousands of the Catholic faithful were killed resisting the Revolution in the name of their faith. 40,000 parishes had celebrated the mass prior to 1789, but there were only 150 remaining by 1794.[28] For a period of time starting in 1793 'dechristianization' as a policy was set in train, in which many priests were either put to death or abandoned the priesthood, and for several years the recruitment of new clergy ceased altogether. Those who remained religious during those years suddenly awakened to the fear that God might have abandoned humankind altogether. In October 1793 during the Terror, a decree was issued forbidding public worship. Over the next few months all visible signs of Christianity were destroyed as part of a state-sponsored campaign for the wholesale removal of religious symbols. Property such as crucifixes, relics, church bells and works of art were seized from churches and cemeteries, and occasionally destroyed.[29] France had been the leading Catholic nation in 1750, but Gérard Cholvy has described how the French church became a church in ruins; physical ruins first of all with the sale of church property, cultural items devastated, and convents turned into barracks, and spiritual ruin following, with divisions among the clergy, the ban on their recruitment, impiety dominant among the elites, and the onward march of dechristianization.[30]

The law entitled the *Constitution civile du Clergé (Civil Constitution of the Clergy)* (1790) subordinated the church to the state, thereby limiting the authority of the pope to spiritual affairs only, and reorganized and considerably reduced the number of dioceses. It also involved the popular election of both bishops and priests, but many French clergy saw this as the final raging of Satan. Alexis de Tocqueville commented that "even when the first enthusiasm for liberty had worn off, and peace had been purchased by the sacrifice of freedom, hostility to religion still survived."[31] In England the Revolution was seen as a countdown to the second coming. In Germany, the occupation of various areas by French armies from the 1790s onwards had especially dramatic effects in traditionally Catholic areas.

In summation, the French Revolution was the final event of the thousand years, and a major contributory factor in its demise. It represented a watershed in European history, for it unleashed the age of revolution and upheaval in Europe. It looked forwards rather than backwards, for its importance lay in what it promoted, namely, the movement towards apostasy that occurred in the nineteenth century. Some commentators may object that Napoléon, and indeed Robespierre, well understood the importance of religion, but it was quite a different matter to resume Christian 'life and rule' that had been the norm during the thousand years. The Revolution was not in any way a chance event, for it was the result of a long period of aspiration and endeavour, the outcome of a task that had been undertaken by several generations of men. Nonetheless, at the time it did take the world by surprise.

### Commentators on the Revolution

The French Revolution, as an example of historical change, aroused a great deal of apocalyptic expectation. However, a note of caution must be struck concerning the tendency of contemporary, or near-contemporary, commentators to judge unfavourably a revolution by its atrocities to the exclusion of all else, whilst those from succeeding generations always seem to err in the other direction.[32]

**Joseph de Maistre**, as a conservative Catholic supporter of the French monarchy, saw the Enlightenment as the direct parental precursor of the Revolution. He was very religious in his anti-revolutionary sentiment and denounced the Revolution and everything it stood for. He was disgusted by the events taking place in Revolutionary France, events which brought him profound spiritual anxiety. In *Considérations sur la France (Considerations on France)* (1796), he portrayed the French Revolution as a satanic experiment, an orgy of destruction, writing that "there was in the French Revolution a satanic character that distinguished it from everything we have seen, and perhaps from everything that we shall (ever) see."[33] Taking the *philosophes* as the root cause of the revolution, and the Jacobins the most radical of the political factions involved in it, he deemed them all virtually to be murderers.[34] He lamented Maximilien Robespierre's attack on the priesthood, the solemn apostasy of the priests themselves, the profanities against cultic objects, the inauguration of the goddess of Reason. All these went beyond the ordinary range of crimes, and seemed to belong to another world.

Maistre believed that without the foundation of Christianity any government would fail. It was an important aspect of the thousand years that we have noted previously, that all European rulers had formerly been Christian, but the revolutionaries removed God from government and pitched 'philosophism' against Christianity. 'Philosophism' was meant to represent the sum of Enlightenment ideas that seemed to propel the revolutionaries forward. Maistre argued that man could not, in such circumstances, produce anything that possessed any permanence, for in the works of man, everything is as contemptible as their author. Views are restricted, means rigid, motives inflexible, movements painful, results monotonous. This was why the Revolution continued long after its inception. The men who ran the government were never satisfied, and so they never stopped. "It has been quite justly remarked," he wrote, "that the French Revolution controlled men, rather than men controlling it."[35] In another striking passage in his work *De la Souveraineté du Peuple (On the Sovereignty of the People)* (1794), he wrote: "The need to act and an eternal restlessness are our two characteristic traits. The rage for undertakings, for discoveries, and for travel exists only in Europe. I do not know what indefinable force agitates us without relief. Movement is the moral life as much as the physical life for the European. For us, the greatest of evils is not poverty, nor enslavement, nor sickness, nor even death, it is tranquillity."[36] This exactly paralleled the idea of the restless dynamism which, according to Oswald Spengler, was the hallmark of the Faustian society.

**Alexis de Tocqueville**, in his book *L'ancien Régime et la Révolution (The old Regime and the Revolution)* (1856) expressed similar sentiments when he wrote that, "not till the strange and terrible physiognomy of the monster's head was visible; till it destroyed civil as well as political institutions, manners, customs, laws and even the mother tongue; till, having dashed in pieces the machinery of government, it shook the foundations of society, and seemed anxious to assail even God himself."[37] Some felt that this unknown power, which nothing seemed able to nourish or combat, which no-one knew how to stop, and which was unable to stop of its own accord, was going to push human society to its utter and final dissolution. Many considered it to be the all-too-visible behaviour of the Devil himself ranging over the earth.[38]

However, Tocqueville conceded that other commentators saw in the Revolution the benevolent workings of God, with the aim of reinvigorating the laws of France and creating a new type of humanity.[39] Thus, the Revolution was a political one which unfolded in the same way as previous religious revolutions had done. It assumed something of their character in the way that it resembled several of their features. Not only did it spread as they did but, similar to them, it advanced by means of preaching and propaganda. For him, the period's irreligion was perpetrating an immense public evil. In most of the world's great political revolutions which had appeared up until then, those who attacked the established legal system had respected religious beliefs, and in most religious revolutions those who attacked religion had not at the same time undertaken to change the nature and order of all power, nor to abolish completely the former government's constitution. After any great upheaval in any society there had always been one point of stability that remained over.[40]

**Edmund Burke**, statesman and author, came to acknowledge that by 1790 history had entered a critical phase, politically and socially. In his tract *Reflections on the Revolution in France* written during that year, he stated that the French Revolution represented "warfare between the ancient landed interest and the new monied interest (in which) the greatest, because the most applicable, strength was in the hands of the latter,"[41] adding that the spirit of ambition had taken possession of this (new monied) class as violently as ever it had done any other. Burke was fearsome of a coalition of those whom he labelled the middle classes, a coalition that would split apart the traditional union between the elites and the common people, and would put in its place a whole motley group of heterogeneous interests. This was for him an outrageous, but powerful outcome. Was this his way of warning against a drift towards a pluralist society? Would this situation, so vehemently described by Burke, become a fertile ground to promote Satan's activities in the approaching century? The swift emergence of the new monied interests, what he called unproductive parasites, appalled him. They were not a grand-bourgeoisie composed of entrepreneurs but a selfish, philistine, petit-bourgeoisie of lawyers, assignat- or bond-holders and brokers and bankers, or, as he put it, 'sophisters, oeconomists and calculators'.[42] Six years later in a letter to the British Parliament, he wrote: "out of the tomb of the murdered monarchy in France has arisen a vast, tremendous, unformed spectre, and this in a more terrifying appearance than anything previously known. France had been deprived of her former government, and now resembled an object of contempt and pity rather than the scourge and terror of the human race."[43] Many replies that followed were provoked by defenders of the Revolution, amongst which were Mary Wollstonecraft's *Vindication of the Rights of Men* (1790) and Tom Paine's *The Rights of Man* (1791).

**Thomas Carlyle** in his book *The French Revolution* (1836), called Paris a Pandemonium, or City of all the Devils, and stated: "France too is bescoured with a Devil's pack, the baying of which, at this distance of half a century, still sounds in the mind's ear."[44] **Hippolyte Taine**, a century after the Revolution, took a similar view. In the preface to his massive work *Origines de la France contemporaine (The Origins of contemporary France)*, composed between 1875 and 1893, he wrote of the god of Egypt, represented by the cult of a crocodile, indigenous serpent or some other dangerous animal, and likened this ancient worship to the situation found in France at the end of the eighteenth century. He was impelled to take a step further in order to comprehend the theology (sic) on which this cult was founded. It was composed, he said, of dogmas called the 'Principles of 1789'. This revolutionary crocodile or serpent became a destructive beast and man-eater, and in Taine's book there were laid bare all the details of this god, his habits, his way of life, his instincts, his faculties. Specimens of this brutish beast abounded, and he indirectly referred to the three most important of them, namely, Jean-Paul Marat, Georges Danton and Maximilien Robespierre.[45] When the Revolution increasingly descended into the reign of Terror, Taine could write that the body social had collapsed, and amongst the millions of disaffiliated atoms, there no longer remained a nucleus of voluntary cohesion and harmonious stability. It was impossible that civil France could be reconstructed. The ruling sects exposed their true character, akin to a group of pirates on a voyage, who, after ravaging their own coast, sailed off to pillage elsewhere. Having devoured France, the Parisian faction undertook the task of devouring all Europe, leaf by leaf, similar to the head of an artichoke.

As the Revolution progressed, some commentators remarked that its effects were similar to John's apocalyptic predictions of what life would turn out to be when, according to Revelation 15:7 "seven golden bowls full of the wrath of God" were poured out over the earth. The view had been that Satan had encouraged the Roman persecution of the Christians and acted through the Emperor Diocletian with his evil work, and so during the French Revolution in the same way he incited the terror and worked his will through Maximilien Robespierre and his associates. The men of the Enlightenment paid scant heed to the Devil, but churchmen living through the Revolution had no such mistaken illusions. In this case, the Revolution paralleled attitudes towards the Devil with respect to its protagonists. In their attacks upon Christianity, republicans and revolutionaries rallied to the side of those who opposed Christianity, amongst which, so it was believed, was indeed the Devil. Monarchists and traditional Catholics, on the other hand, took the view that the Revolution was the Devil's direct work. They looked forward to the restoration of the monarchy as the victory of Christ over the dark Lord.[46]

After such mayhem, into the role of 'saviour-emperor' stepped Napoléon by means of a military coup, but despite his religious leanings, some saw him as the Antichrist, the incarnation of political evil. There are certain similarities between Napoleon's situation and that of Charlemagne. For example, Charlemagne's reign, as we saw in chapter 4, heralded the start both of Western culture, and also of the thousand years, whereas Napoléon's reign marked their end. Napoléon crowned himself in front of the pope, rather than allowing the pope himself to perform this act, and consequently the wheel may be said to have come full circle since Christmas 800.[47] The infrastructure of both reigns was not to last. Charlemagne's empire dissolved when his empire was parcelled up between his successors, and Napoléon was defeated and his empire disappeared after the battle of Waterloo in 1815.

The end of the eighteenth century witnessed further important developments in the decline of Western Christianity. In 1791, the separation of church and state was written into the constitution of the United States by the First Amendment, and similar laws were enacted in the Netherlands in 1796 and in France in 1795, though this was later reversed in 1801. Hugh McLeod suggested that in Paris and the surrounding areas and many other parts of France, the turning-point occurred in these years when the Catholic Church was split in two by the Revolution, dividing into those clergy who accepted the new Constitution, the 'Constitutionals', and those who did not, the 'non-juring church'. In 1803 Napoléon imposed the Secularisation Law in Germany (*der Reichsdeputationshauptschluss*) by which all ecclesiastical estates were secularized and almost all church property confiscated. In 1806 the Holy Roman Emperor Francis II relinquished his title, and became instead Emperor Francis I of Austria. Thereafter the Holy Roman Empire, even as a concept, which had been fostered a thousand years before during the Carolingian era, came to an end.

### The English Industrial Revolution

The industrial revolution in England played its part in forging another important break with the past. The term itself was not coined until the 1820s, and as an economic phenomenon it would no doubt have been regarded at that time as an analogy with the French, political, revolution. After careful enquiry most historians are convinced that the 1780s was the decisive decade, for it was during that period that, so far as anyone can tell, all the relevant statistical and economic indices took a sudden, sharp, almost vertical turn upwards, and this has been called an initial 'take-off' in industrial activity.[48] A massive emigration of the population from the villages to the towns and cities took place from about 1800 onwards. James Watt's invention of the steam engine in 1782 preceded the French Revolution by only seven years, and it may not have happened by chance that the French Revolution reflected similar dynamics and underlying conditions that had impelled the English industrial revolution forward.[49] By 1809, part of the Ruhr Valley in Westphalia was called 'Miniature England' because of its similarities to the industrial areas of England.

Both the medieval European and the post-Reformation reformers had regarded the mechanical arts as providing a rational and practical way of improving man's earthly condition and they extolled technology by elevating the arts connected with the machine to an equal ranking with that of the liberal arts.[50] What was novel by the late eighteenth century was the idea that a different and very specific economic and physical environment was emerging. Industrialization and the growth of large cities appeared to lead to a decline in church-going, religious belief and morality. The churches in all historical ages have ever declared that the Christian order was being imperilled, a declaration which had the express purpose of warning against lapses in faith, but it was transformed into a perpetual and persistent theme in the special circumstances of the industrial revolution. The machines of the new industries were regarded as somehow ungodly. Furthermore, the nature of industrial employment was seen as a problem because it removed traditional ties of a paternalistic nature between social classes.

Oswald Spengler, in the same way as Johann Wolfgang von Goethe, characterized 'technics' as possessing a malign Mephistophelean characteristic, not something that is given by God, and this would inevitably lead to a kind of hubris. In chapter 5 we stated that the classical mind felt Prometheus' defiance of the gods to be similar in nature, and the description of technology as possessing a sinister side serves to remind us of this myth. So too did the baroque period feel the machine to be diabolical. Much later, Leo Tolstoy considered the railway an invention of the Devil. In the eighteenth century, European men's knowledge became Faustian power over the physical world. In the same way as Faust sold his soul to the Devil to gain greater power, one could say that Western man sold his soul to technology. "The spirit of hell betrayed to man the secret of mastering the world-mechanism, and even of himself playing the role of God. Ever and ever again, true belief has regarded the machine as of the Devil, and hence it is that all purely priestly natures, that live wholly in the world of the spirit, have for this world nothing but hostile silence for 'technics'."[51] By enacting the role of God, in the eyes of the faithful it signified that God had been dismissed. The relations between cause and effect, formerly sacred, were now surrendered to man with the result that a kind of omniscience was set in motion for the future.[52]

These sentiments were implicitly accepted even by the industrial innovators and inventors of the period. The inventor Richard Trevithick constructed a full-size steam road locomotive in 1801 and named his carriage the 'Puffing Devil' and in one of Richard Arkwright's factories, there was also a machine called 'The Devil', which opened and broke up raw bales of cotton. Moreover, William Blake has been credited in the popular mind as describing England's industrial scene when he referred to 'dark satanic mills', although this attribution was misdirected. The historian Eric Hobsbawm referred to the demonic element in capitalist accumulation, describing it as the limitless and irrational pursuit of luxury.[53] Unlike the French Revolution, the radical consequences of the British industrial revolution did not become evident at the end of the eighteenth century. Several commentators have remarked that its full effects became apparent only after 1830, and it is the latter part of the nineteenth century that will fully bear witness to the outcome of that revolution on religious belief.

### The Transformation of Piety

A further major change took place around the year 1800, all the more remarkable and mysterious on account of the claim by historians and sociologists of its apparent abruptness within European society. Recent research has revealed a crisis in, and redefinition of, masculinity around this time, particularly in England and Germany, but also to a certain extent in France.[54] The question mainly concerned the concept of piety. Once more we can question whether it was the rise of rationalism in the eighteenth century that led to attacks on its traditional formulations. In the Middle Ages and much of the early modern period, piety had been portrayed as appertaining to masculinity, whereas female piety had been considered religiously questionable, and this trait had been reflected in iconography which had depicted martyrs, saints and ascetics almost completely from a masculine aspect. Femininity, was perceived as endangering and contaminating piety. Continued recourse to folk religion or superstition aroused intensive condemnation, which resulted in the notorious witch-hunts of the seventeenth century.

However, according to the social historian Callum Brown, a change occurred in male-female piety in Britain, because at this time, almost precisely, gender polarities were greatly reversed. Women's religiosity became privileged rather than that of men, and it was evangelicalism that spearheaded this change.[55] Women were now credited to have special qualities which rendered them the guardians of Christian virtues. The feminisation of angels in the early eighteenth century was an important development in this process, but after 1800, the religiosity of women became the lynchpin for the evangelical scheme to establish a moral revolution. It was considered that the husband would be susceptible to masculine temptations and therefore a danger to piety within the home. It is difficult to define the pertinence for our thesis of this gender shift, other than to note its occurrence around the important date of 1800. However, the significance of this change may lie in the fact that the image of the old patriarch, who was placed at the centre of the extended family as a lord who ruled over the family in the name of God, and as the centre of the social community, was no longer destined to play these central and important roles. It must be asked whether this gender shift was another ploy undertaken by demonic forces in the task of undermining Christianity.

During the 1790s concerns about the relationship between religion and masculinity also reached a decisive point. As a result of Edward Gibbon's writings, critiques regarding the ways in which the Christian religion was considered to have undermined masculine vigour gained momentum during the French revolutionary wars.[56] Educators and intellectuals of the period made it clear that they were responding to a serious and urgent crisis that was eroding the existing social order. The problem spanned not only moral issues but physical appearance and cultural education. A new conception of masculinity was extensively explored and intensively debated during this period. This was to be an enduring and important shift which changed the concept of religiosity in the popular mind, and laid the foundations for a gradual transformation of the Christian religion in Western Europe and North America.

At the same time, a similar transformation occurred in the German states concerning the question of masculinity. The impetus emanated from what was considered at the time to be shortcomings in moral and physical qualities as well as in social effectiveness. Historians, however, have singled out once again the French Revolution as having some importance in this process, an event which made an influential impression not only on France but also on other parts of Europe. As a result, older social and cultural standards, including most importantly gender roles, were now acknowledged to be obsolescent. In the German states, changes began to emerge during the 1780s, especially in the field of education, yet it was only after the devastating Prussian defeat of 1806 at the battle of Jena-Auerstedt that the problem received official attention. A transition to a new model had taken place by the end of the Napoleonic era. Since prevailing ideas of masculinity were found to be deficient, a verdict which was attributed to all classes of the population within the German states, the task was to seek new concepts of virility throughout the social structure. A new type of masculinity was needed.

Faith was being privatised as an individual choice, but one which potentially was to privilege female piety and establish anxiety about masculinity. A certain amount of toleration came to be shown towards men's sexual activities, so long as they did not involve bestiality and sodomy. As in Britain, so in Germany, it was quite evident that the old patriarchal and pietistic order was disappearing simultaneously with the end of the thousand years. From the comments of historical and sociological commentators, it might be inferred that the concept of the male changed suddenly from being considered a patriarchal, and therefore a Christian figure, to become, if not a Devil, at least subject to the Devil's temptations.

### Important Writers of the Period

Four of the most important writers of the period around 1800 are considered from amongst the many who reflected and commented on the events of the time, but the philosopher who may justifiably be considered as the most important of these, namely, Immanuel Kant, follows in a separate section.

**Johann Wolfgang von Goethe (1749-1832).** It would seem of great significance and a curious coincidence that a major European author, perhaps the most celebrated of all, should rekindle an interest in the

Devil at the end of the eighteenth century. This refers to none other than the German author and poet, Goethe. First of all, he wrote his autobiography around the year 1775, and closed it with a discussion of the demonic as a natural force, which ran contrary to the moral order in nature. He described men who were possessed by such a force as having a remarkable power over others. "All the moral forces combined cannot prevail against them; in vain does the more enlightened part of mankind attempt to throw suspicion on them as dupes or deceivers; the masses are attracted by them."[57] This sounded as if Goethe was providing a strange portent of the furore that was to come in the form of the French Revolution. Later there emanated from his pen one of the greatest works of European literature, or indeed of all time, and this was also concerned with the Devil, namely, that masterpiece of German literature: *Faust: eine Tragödie (Faust: a Tragedy)*. That such a work emerged contemporaneously with the end of the thousand years of the Christian West is intriguing. It was a work that spanned both the Enlightenment and the Romantic movements, and according to Oswald Spengler, Goethe portended within it, psychologically, the whole future of the West. It is sometimes said of Goethe, that he represented the humanism of the eighteenth century.

Goethe completed a preliminary version of Faust between 1806 to 1808. It was followed by a revised edition in 1828-1829, which was the last to be edited by Goethe himself. In part one of this work, he depicted his literary Faust as gaining knowledge over many disciplines, for whom all his books came to represent dust, not life. However, his pact with the Devil allowed him to have energy, life and youth unless he became so entranced by the passing moment that he wished that things would never change. When Faust stumbled unthinkingly into that outlook, his world and his life were forfeit to Mephistopheles. Goethe's Devil became one of the most influential literary creations of all time, but was nevertheless a complex, cynical and witty exponent of materialism, scepticism and nihilism, an apt commentator on the society of his time, as well as a spokesman for secular, progressive humanism. He sometimes appeared to be Satan or Satan's equivalent and at other times only a minor demon. Mephistopheles represented the principle of matter opposing the principle of spirit; as evil opposing good; as chaos opposing order in the universe, or as we have seen in chapter 3 as a stimulus to further creativity. Goethe depicted him as possessing all the characteristics, which he ascribed to the academics whom Goethe despised, traits which were judgmental, censorious and aloof.

As a typical Enlightenment luminary, Goethe distanced himself both from Christianity and the church, but he drew upon Christian symbolism as a source. His intention was to express the complex and incongruous nature of his own culture, and of Western civilization as a whole. Goethe gladly used and developed the Faustian myth, but he always vehemently denied the literal existence of the Christian Devil and even Immanuel Kant's principle of radical evil. Notwithstanding this, one cannot but help harbouring a suspicion that Goethe may have implicitly been influenced by the current events of his time, and more especially the satanic nature of the French Revolution, and the Terror which ensued, since his work was written during or just after this period.

**Friedrich Daniel Schleiermacher** (1770-1831). The theology of Schleiermacher challenged traditional orthodoxy, and he came to be known as the father of nineteenth-century liberal theology. The main features of such theology can already be discerned in his thought. He provided one of the most significant responses to the challenge of Enlightenment rationalism because he eventually concluded that the Enlightenment had overlooked the core message of religion which is the realisation that we are always reliant on something outside of ourselves for our lives and fundamental existence. He considered that Christianity would be able to maintain its position in society only so long as it steered clear of current intellectual thought.[58] Religion should not be concerned with philosophical theses, but with an inward psychological state. His work *Über Religion: Reden an die Gebildeten unter ihren Verächten (On Religion: Speeches to its cultured Despisers)*, published anonymously in 1799, represented a defence of Christianity, which was based on a sense or awareness of a larger whole. It was not a hostile force but on the contrary, it was concerned with our most precious values.

His later, and major, work of systematic theology *Der Christliche Glaube (The Christian Faith)* (1821, revised 1830) was an attempt to show that the idea of God did not arise as a result of thought or will, but rather that the distinct identity of the Christian faith was analogous with a feeling of 'absolute dependence' on God, with the main emphasis on religious experience understood as a 'feeling for the infinite'. For Schleiermacher, therefore, religion had now to be justified by what Peter Berger called 'subjective emotionality', thereby replacing objective dogma as its main criterion. Furthermore, the essence of religious piety was not some rational or moral principle, but rather 'the autonomy of religious feeling'. Whilst this state relied totally upon the infinite, it was made known in and through the finite. Christ was the mediator of this experience, and the examples of Christian piety through the ages enabled us to trace it back to Him. The emphasis on the supernatural elements of the Christian tradition was now minimized in favour of a natural religion, to encompass both reason and the emotions. According to Ernst Troeltsch, Schleiermacher viewed religion as merely different ways of being conscious of one's immanence in God, thereby virtually dissolving religion itself.[59]

It must be explained how Schleiermacher's thought contributed to the changes around the year 1800. What was new and perilous here was a defensive attitude concerning the Christian religion over and against what were understood to be the definitive truths of philosophy and science, that is, of secular reason. He turned the whole Christian dialectic on its head by inaugurating what was later to become known as Christian apologetics. It entailed that theological debate must be undertaken henceforth with continuous recourse to the cultured despisers of religion to whom Schleiermacher had addressed his famous lectures in 1799, by attacking their ideas at the very root. It was this group, rather than the sources of the Christian tradition, which were to become the arbiters of what was considered acceptable in contemporary thought. All this gave the appearance of a new religious agenda, but the inspiration for this agenda now derived from modern, secular intellectuals rather than the Christian community of believers.

**Thomas Paine** (1737-1809) was the one man who, above all others, helped to form and then consolidate a radical critique of establishment politics and religion. He had originally made his revolutionary reputation in the United States with the publication in 1776 of *Common Sense*. During the 1790s he confirmed his position also in Britain as the principal enemy of revealed religion in two major works, *Rights of Man* (1791-1792) and *The Age of Reason* (published in three parts in 1794, 1795 and 1807). Paine may have intended the latter book to be a defence of Deism against atheism, nevertheless it completely rejected revealed religion and biblical Christianity with a scathing criticism of traditional religion. What was intended to be a Deist publication, nevertheless quickly acquired a pervasive and lasting notoriety, in the first instance in the United States and later in Britain, as a publication which promoted atheism. It not only praised the age in which Paine lived and which gave it the name of the book's title, but was the first assault on Christianity in Britain which attained a wide readership. In it, he wrote: "I totally disbelieve that the Almighty ever did communicate anything to man, by any mode of speech, in any language, or by any kind of vision, or appearance, or by any means which our senses are capable of receiving otherwise than by the universal display of himself in the works of creation..."[60] Most of the book was concerned with promoting the idea that "written or printed books, by whatever name they are called, are the works of man's hands, and carry no evidence in themselves that God is the author of any of them."[61] With this diatribe, Paine went too far for his erstwhile American admirers. Eventually, his writings were construed as atheism and his friends disowned him.[62] His chief significance is not that he added anything new to the arguments of his predecessors, but he said it in a way that the ordinary man could understand. Nourished on these works and on others such as the British political philosopher William Godwin's *Enquiry Concerning Political Justice* (1793) and French Enlightenment texts, an extreme form of radicalism emerged, rejecting conventional government, and by inference organized religion, and which closely resembled philosophical anarchism.

**Immanuel Kant's Philosophy heralded the End of the thousand Years**

More than any other thinker, the philosophical texts of Immanuel Kant, written at the end of the eighteenth century, are considered by many to have introduced a new direction in European thought. In his early writings, he had not yet broken away from his predecessors' rationalist metaphysical philosophy, which presupposed that all the theoretical arguments for the existence of God were still valid and adequate. Later on, however, in a celebrated section of the first of his two most important works, the *Kritik der reinen Vernunft (Critique of pure Reason)* (1781), Kant set out to refute all the purely intellectual proofs for the existence of God. According to Kant, there were three such proofs which had been established traditionally by pure reason: the ontological proof, the cosmological proof and the physico-theological proof. Kant demolished all three of them, and in so doing arrived at a universe which was completely devoid of God and his angels. It could be claimed that he exceeded even the Enlightenment *philosophes'* own criticisms. He believed that any and every statement that one could formulate was meaningful only when it referred to objects of possible sense perception. Therefore, metaphysical statements, about God and the Devil, for example, were meaningless because they were purely analytical and tautological. If our descriptions of the world encompassed only what we are able to discover from sense experience, much of traditional religious doctrine no longer made any sense. It is not difficult to understand how such conclusions would make a devastating impact upon the foundations of Christian belief.

More was to come from Kant's pen, however. As a sequel to the first critique, his *Kritik der praktischen Vernunft (Critique of practical Reason)*, completed in 1786, developed the practical use of reason as it applied to moral behaviour. Here Kant argued that the moral law demanded justice, that is, happiness commensurate with virtue. This could be guaranteed only by Providence, and because He has certainly not guaranteed it in this life, there must be a God and a future life where this could be ensured. There had to be freedom also, otherwise there could be no such thing as virtue, but Kant took care to insist that the affirmation of God and immortality that was being made on this basis did not in any way make them real, that is to say, objects of theoretical knowledge. For Kant, God, freedom and immortality may all be 'ideas of reason' but although pure reason may inspire us to frame these ideas, it cannot by itself establish their reality. The God that was derived from moral arguments such as this served only as a means to an end. As a consequence, the necessity to assume the existence of God was subjective, based on need. Therefore, for Kant, the conclusion must be that whatever it was that reason might conceive as the highest good took precedence over the divine will. The theologian Gordon Michalson came to the plausible conclusion that Kant's argument stipulated that it was a requirement for God to apportion happiness to virtue in an equitable manner, and this must lead to the suspicion that He was denied any freedom of decision in the matter.[63] Similar to Toynbee's idea of the wager with the Devil which we encountered in chapter 3, Kant's exposition is misguided.

God, therefore, was being degraded by Kant in ways that were just as detrimental as anything he had stated in his first critique. Not only was the list of divine attributes severely diminished by what he had stipulated, but it was beginning to look as if God's transcendence was being subordinated to, and significantly compromised by, the prerogatives of reason.[64] The traditional idea of the Christian God was now exchanged for a god who willed the good simply because it was good, and the good stood in some way independent of, and over and above, God's will. God's role became therefore subordinate, and very nearly an afterthought, in relation to the emphasis given to the free will. Kant postulated in this way a far more robust theory of autonomy than René Descartes had ever dreamed of. One can surely conclude that Kant's aggressive and original approach finally rendered God as little more than a kind of moral partner who must perforce perform a secondary role. Michaelson went on to suggest that Kant's stratagem in the second critique compared with his arguments in the first critique created the impression that he was virtually referring to two different gods.

In his work *Die Religion innerhalb der Grenzen der bloßen Vernunft (Religion within the Limits of Reason alone)* (1793), Kant effectively debunked Christian theories of the atonement. He argued that the idea of accepting the truth of an historical event, in this case the Christ event, as the highest condition of a universal faith which alone led to blessedness, was the most absurd thing that can be imagined.[65] Kant's rejection of Christ's vicarious atonement, namely, the idea that Christ stood as a substitute for us, by suffering the penalty for our sin, was replaced by an exemplary one.[66] His demythologizing programme sacrificed the uniqueness of the person of Christ, since Christ's erstwhile role was now assigned to each individual instead, leaving no significant role for Christ, not even an atoning one. Only Christ's virtuous life was left to serve as an example for humanity. As Christ conquered the power of the Devil, so for Kant each individual's conquest over evil takes place solely by means of an internal conflict.[67] With this substitution, Kant was effectively emphasizing the necessity for individuals to achieve their own salvation. Man's rational will was detached from all external constraints, leaving it to generate its own constraints. In Kant's schema, morality consequently did not need religion at all, whether objectively, as regards willing, or subjectively, as regards the ability to act. By virtue of pure practical reason, it was self-sufficient. Despite its finitude, human reason now took over the role of God as legislator for virtue. This critique of reason was for Kant a declaration of reason's independence.

Leaving aside Kant's own personal piety, his arguments about God, which encompassed both the absence of mystery and the supremacy of reason, led to the conclusion that any language about God would become either redundant or disguised language about ourselves. Iris Murdoch drew the conclusion from this that Kant had effectively abolished God and replaced Him by promoting man in His place.[68] This, too, is a forewarning of the stance taken later by Ludwig Feuerbach. Kant's philosophy in fact was to become a halfway house between Martin Luther on the one hand and Ludwig Feuerbach and Karl Marx on the other in the debates concerning otherworldliness. An impetus had now been given to the idea that theology may be translated into anthropology, and so lay the basis for humanistic atheism. Kant's theory of autonomy marked out fresh terms for the mainstream Enlightenment debate in ways that would permanently alter the course of European thought in the nineteenth century, and his philosophy would have to be viewed as a transitional phase which would lead to an entirely secular theory of ethics.[69] In short, Kant was proposing a moral reinterpretation of the Christian faith, and the role played by God would gradually become marginalized, eventually reaching vanishing point. In the struggle between the autonomy of reason and divine transcendence, for Kant God was on the losing side.

The poet Heinrich Heine impugned Kant's commitment to reason and called him the 'all-destroyer of metaphysics'. In his book *Zur Geschichte der Religion und Philosophie in Deutschland (On the History of Religion and Philosophy in Germany)* (1834), Heine characterized him as a worse terrorist than Robespierre. Maximilien Robespierre had murdered only a king, but Kant, with his relentless critique of Christian theology, had murdered God and acted, to quote the philosopher Moses Mendelssohn, as the 'world-crusher' *(der Alleszermalmer)*. Kant's philosophy, according to Heine, was a deliberate and ruthless attempt to hack away at any and all speculations that sought to understand the transcendent. In Kant's philosophy, there would be no quick or easy way to salvation through forgiveness offered by a personal God. Whether that was his intention or not, the importance for us is the effect it had on nineteenth century thought, for Kant went even further when he made the most radical assertion of all. Not only could the existence of God not be proved from the standpoint of theoretical reason, for Kant it would be considered illegitimate even to pose the question as to whether or not God exists.[70]

In retrospect, Immanuel Kant's writings may be said to have consummated the work of the Enlightenment *philosophes*. At the time, few people were acquainted with his philosophy with its impressive systemization of knowledge. Only occasionally were his ideas carried beyond the narrow circle of the intelligentsia to the wider world in which unbelief was beginning to flourish. Nevertheless, more than any other thinker it was his work that produced a radical, perhaps the most radical, attack on Christianity and its doctrines. Looking forwards, as the founder of German idealism, he rendered systematic philosophy in a form that would be the final outcome for Western man.[71] It would be reasonable to suggest that Kant's thought, as much as anything else, was instrumental in bringing the thousand years of the Christian West to an end.

\* \* \* \* \* \* \* \*

The year 1800 represented an important watershed in European history. Faith in the divine order had been challenged. The Renaissance, the Reformation, and the Enlightenment were stages in this process, in which the Christian tradition and its values were gradually destroyed or rendered contentious, and this gave rise to uncertainty about divine authority.[72] But we shall allow Oswald Spengler to have the last word here, because more than any other thinker he recognized and emphasized the discontinuity within Western society around this momentous period, and he accomplished this in stark and uncompromising terms. His main idea was concerned with the transition from 'culture' to 'civilization', the victory of the inorganic metropolis over the organic countryside, with the latter henceforward to be conceived in spiritual terms as 'the provinces'.[73] Culture and Civilization: the former term meant the living body of a soul and the latter term the mummy of it. Atheism came not with the evening of Culture but with the dawn of Civilization, and it belonged to the great city, to the educated man of the great city who acquired mechanistically what his forefathers, the creators of Western Culture, had begotten organically. For Spengler, all great cultures were town cultures, but that of a civilization was a city-based existence. Jean-Jacques Rousseau was a principal forerunner of this epoch, as the representative spokesman of these great cities. The Faust of the thousand years became the progenitor of Faust of the new century, the nineteenth. The French and English revolutions exemplified this historical shift, the former signalling the beginning of an age of revolution, whose impact we shall discuss in the next chapter, and the latter proving to be equally problematic. In this satanic epoch, the intellect of the modern world would represent the psychical petrifaction of the human soul.[74]

We have discussed in this chapter three main threads of discontinuity in Europe at the end of the eighteenth century, greater even than the Reformation: a political upheaval in France, the beginnings of industrial activity in England, and a philosophical development in Germany whose final and main representative was Immanuel Kant. These seemed at the time to be independent of each other, but they were to come together in various guises and combinations to form a heady brew in the ensuing century.

The cumulative knowledge of Western society henceforth began to attain a Faustian power over the physical world, with the result that a radical assault on the established order began. The Devil could now be said to be unbound. Johann von Goethe's magnum opus *Dr Faustus*, appeared at the very same time, the subject of which was indeed a pact with the Devil. It would not be an overstatement to say that the concurrence of all these events around the year 1800 had the potential to create an intriguing historical mystery. Previously we described how the years around 800 proved to be a decisive period in the early development of Western Christendom. Now the years around 1800, one thousand years after the coronation of Charlemagne, represented a watershed between the thousand years and modern secular civilization. Enlightenment had been for the few, but secularization was to be for the many, and the following two chapters will be dedicated to explaining how apostatic, secular movements gathered pace over the next two centuries after 1800.

CHAPTER NINE

*Strands of Apostasy in the nineteenth Century*

"New ideas are more potent than broken habits." *Louis Namier*

AFTER THE French Revolution, many people in Europe were becoming aware that significant changes were taking place in their society, but this awareness in the nineteenth century was to be split between those, on the one hand, who were filled with a foreboding of falling into the abyss, and on the other those with a faith in the expectation of a splendid dawn for mankind.[1] Or was it rather a twilight that was imminent? The century was to witness much complexity in its intellectual life, and a profound revolt developed against traditional systems of thought formerly regarded as sacrosanct and this served to continue the project that the Enlightenment had set in motion. That movement had demoted revelation in favour of reason, or rather had displaced revelation altogether, and appeared to be more critical than creative. The very foundations of Christianity were being questioned: historical, epistemological, doctrinal.

In the post-Napoleonic era after 1815, under the leadership of the Austrian chancellor Prince Klemens Metternich, a reactionary policy was imposed by the European powers, with the intention of suppressing democratic movements. Nevertheless, a genie had been let loose that was to cause further revolutionary activity throughout Europe in the following half-century. Eric Hobsbawm remarked that an age of revolution followed the French Revolution,[2] and where France led, other nations eventually followed. It has been said that whenever France 'sneezed' thereafter, other nations 'caught a cold'. Developments in the nineteenth century were to witness what for many Christians was the pernicious activity of Satan, who, to quote Revelation 20:8, "will come out to deceive the nations which are at the four corners of the earth." But the nagging question remained, whether Satan was in fact an actual person or being, since traditional belief held that the last times would witness the appearance of a real individual who would lead the armies of evil against God's people.

There were many in the nineteenth century who continued unashamedly to adopt an historicist view of the Apocalypse and at the start of that century they still retained a powerful influence. The most important of these was the English banker and writer Henry Drummond. He convened a series of six annual meetings in the 1820s, called the Albury Conferences, whose subject was the study of prophecy. In 1829 he summarized their conclusions, which stated, *inter alia*, that the decline in religion and culture was such that it had now reached a critical point, was now beyond recall, and would culminate in the final chapter of human history.[3] The Antichrist had always been considered a man of sin, but Drummond and his companions identified the Antichrist, not with any particular individual, but with a movement towards apostasy, which encompassed a theory of developing Antichrists. In this scenario, nations and peoples will be led astray by this great apostasy. Moreover, since the Antichrist was no longer depicted as a specific individual, any entity, whether ecclesiastical, social or political, that displayed deceit or similar characteristics could just as well be identified as such an Antichrist.[4] Cardinal John Henry Newman wrote in his work *Apologia pro Vita sua* (1865) that: "the more serious thinkers among us are used, as far as they dare form an opinion, to regard the spirit of Liberalism as the characteristic of the destined Antichrist."[5] Origen of Alexandria had stated that the Devil, as an angel, became an apostate, and induced as many of the angels as possible to fall away with himself.[6] This is almost a reflection of the nineteenth and twentieth century experience in Europe.

Other commentators were more socially orientated in their views but just as scathing about the new trends in European thought. In 1830 the historian Barthold Niebuhr, unnerved by the July revolution in France, wrote: "Now, unless God sends us some miraculous help, we have to look forward to a period of destruction similar to that which the Roman world experienced about the middle of the third century of our era, to the annihilation of prosperity, of freedom, of civility, of knowledge."[7] Alexis de Tocqueville and many others contemplated democracy as a kind of barbarian invasion. As the essence of every culture was religion, consequently the essence of every civilization must be irreligion. In a sermon of 1842, the Anglican, later Catholic, priest, Henry Manning, warned that the temper of the age was becoming increasingly irreligious with a tendency towards a more secular culture. Matthew Arnold in his 1851 poem *Dover Beach* wrote of the sea of faith that he hears now only as a 'melancholy, long, withdrawing roar'.

Apostasy can be observed in the decline of religious content in the arts, in philosophy, in literature and in the rise of science. It included especially the impact of new intellectual developments, of Darwinism, of biblical criticism, of industrialisation and urbanisation, and the associated process of modernisation, which led to an autonomous and thoroughly secular perspective on the world. The later years of the nineteenth century were to witness the start and then the intensification of a pluralistic environment, in which a vast range of leisure possibilities, as well as political movements and rival systems of belief, offered numerous alternatives to the church. We shall segregate the strands which encouraged apostasy by examining these various movements.

Was this apostatic process a brief one, or did it progress in gradual steps? Consider the verses of the Apocalypse in Revelation 20:8: "And they marched up over the broad earth and surrounded the camp of the saints and the beloved city." The biblical text seems to suggest that the advance of Satan and his hosts, Gog and Magog, would take place over a little while, and there is no suggestion of an abrupt transformation. In the same way, apostasy increased over time in Western Europe throughout the nineteenth, and continued into the twentieth century unabated. Callum Brown claimed that its true onset commenced in the 1960s, in Britain at any rate, rather than during the preceding 150 years. In opposition to this idea, other authors asserted that these developments were taking place throughout the nineteenth century, despite claims that Victorian Britain was labelled an age of faith. Peter Berger considered that the real crisis of Protestant orthodoxy occurred in this century. As apostasy gathered pace, so also did the process by which the secular European state evolved, resulting finally in an ethos radically different from that of the thousand years of the Christian West. In short, the comprehensive structure once provided by religion was being relentlessly dismantled.

Christianity began to face direct competition with a host of rival views, for example, the romantic, the rational, the scientific and the political, and the importance of these movements lay both in the fact that they were zealously propagated, and also that they attained an influence amongst considerable sections of the middle and working classes. According to Alan Gilbert, for the Victorian believer, loss of faith began to resemble a plague.[8] We can pinpoint a number of elements or what secularists may consider as their routes to salvation which were followed in this century, and this may justifiably be called a multi-stranded attack on the Christian faith.

### Philosophical Movements and Ideas

The previous chapter traced Immanuel Kant's destructive criticism of speculative metaphysics, and his work must bear much responsibility for the radical, secular nature of subsequent European thought. His philosophical writing could be construed as an agenda for the whole of the nineteenth century. Kant had maintained that a study of the moral law was essentially concerned with the will, and his work was followed by a philosophy that was practical, irreligious, socio-ethical. The philosopher, Arthur Schopenhauer, made the will the 'creative life-force' and the centre of his thought. In his principal work, *Die Welt als Wille und Vorstellung (The World as Will and Representation)* (1819), he adopted the idea of the 'cosmic will' and we might have expected that he would equate such a will with God. But Schopenhauer would have nothing to do with this statement, for his pessimism led him to a different conclusion. The will, as an irrational, relentless impulse was the origin of all of humanity's unending torment. Christianity taught that in knowledge of God stood our eternal life, but Schopenhauer utterly dismissed this as well. For him, what commonly passed for knowledge belonged to the veil of Maya, illusion, but when we pierced that veil, we beheld not God, but Satan, with his own insatiable, omnipotent will, perpetually busying himself in inflicting torture upon his creatures.[9]

The contribution of Georg Wilhelm Hegel as a post-Enlightenment figure is important, because he stood for the absolute supremacy of reason, apparently over and against revelation, and much of his philosophy derived from Immanuel Kant and the Enlightenment *philosophes*. Hegel's god had only a shadowy existence, and it has been described as the goal of his philosophy,[10] In discussing morality, Hegel combined, or rather inappropriately melded, transcendent concepts with the realities of political life. By this he meant that it was primarily the state which was 'the reality of the moral ideal', and the individual was therefore subordinate to the state, not to the church. One can deduce from this that morality was not an individual act but a social one, and the state was the culmination of moral action. The task for religion was no longer to turn moral ideals into practical behaviour, instead it was the state's task as having arrogated to itself the divine will. In its turn, there was no moral judge to which the law of the state had to bow, apart from the ultimate judgment of the historical process. The state's right, and indeed its highest duty, was to be selfish, and in the quest to pursue its own interests, Hegel maintained that it raised the ethical standards of its people. Hegel's thought had the potential to encourage atheistic thinking on account of a profound confusion over the exact relationship between transcendence and immanence, God and humanity. From this rather bewildering assortment of ideas, one can conclude that many of them ran counter to the traditional Christian concept of the importance of the individual. Hegel's analysis contained within it the seeds of the evil that became all too palpable in the twentieth century, namely, that of secular, and indeed satanic, totalitarianism.

Hegel's followers, the Young Hegelians, were quick to perceive that underneath their master's philosophy lurked a quite subversive system of belief, or rather of unbelief.[11] In the previous chapter we described how Friedrich Schleiermacher in his own way practically dissolved religion by considering it as merely individually different ways of being conscious of one's immanence in God.[12] It was in the aftermath of Schleiermacher and Hegel that the latter's pupil, Ludwig Feuerbach, published his work *Das Wesen des Christentums (The Essence of Christianity)* (1841), which became eagerly read, not just as a theological statement but understood also as a revolutionary tract. Feuerbach took Hegel's idea of God and this-worldly religion one step further. If the notion of a God external to man was so alienating, why not dispose of Him altogether? In constructing the notion of God, Feuerbach argued that mankind had projected its own human qualities on to a supernatural being, which was imaginary and oppressive, and merely a reflection of itself. In other words, "the divine being is nothing other than the human being, or rather, human nature purified, freed from the limits of the individual man, objectified."[13] His conclusion was that the problem of Christianity was really the problem of humanity. Such sentiments encouraged German intellectuals throughout the remaining years of the nineteenth century to engage in eager debate, and thereby challenge in diverse ways the familiar intellectual world of their day. Christianity was now being demonstrated to be untrue, or at least unstable, and this was to act as a catalyst in its future collapse in Germany.

It was but a short step to the next development, that of Karl Marx and his theories of society and economics, which became one of the most persuasive and original philosophies to encourage unbelief in the nineteenth century, and they came to stand at the very centre of the secular movement. He adopted from Hegel the idea of the historical process as a dialectical movement which ran with logical necessity through the opposites of thesis and antithesis. But the impulse according to him was not Mind but Matter in the sense of the innate forces that governed economic life. Thus, all historical phenomena had their origin in socio-economic conditions. He retained a progressive conception of history and human action, but with an unmitigated materialism bereft of all supernatural elements, resulting in a secular eschatology, in which he surpassed Ludwig Feuerbach. Marx thought that those who believed in religion were mistaken and illusional, referring back to men such as the Enlightenment *philosophes* by asserting that religion brought no benefits. On the contrary, it was harmful to human happiness. In an essay of 1844 entitled *Zur Kritik der Hegelschen Rechtsphilosophie (On the Critique of the Hegelian Philosophy of Law)* (1844), he stated, "The criticism of religion is at root...the criticism of this vale of tears of which religion is the halo."[14] Individuals such as Marx or August Bebel, the German socialist politician and one of the founders of the Social Democratic Workers' Party of Germany, maintained that to be a socialist entailed atheism. The German philosopher and businessman, Friedrich Engels, Karl Marx's colleague, became an atheist himself in 1842, and considered that the further quest for a true religion was doomed.

The detestation of Christianity similar to that of Marx was encountered in the works of the philosopher Friedrich Nietzsche, whose became famous for his declaration of the death of God. Similar to the thinkers before him, it too was akin to a proclamation that utterly denied that any spiritual realm existed.[15] For Marx, the death of God would be a future achievement, but for Nietzsche, it had already happened. It was only a matter of time before the idea of God would wither away completely in the Western mind. God had not died because thinkers such as Ludwig Feuerbach, Karl Marx, the German scientist and philosopher Karl Vogt and the German dramatist Karl Georg Büchner had voiced their critiques. It was rather the case that Victorian man's state of mind had changed.

Friedrich Nietzsche's philosophy had many similarities with Niccolò Machiavelli's, for both supported an ethic which aimed at power and was deliberately and defiantly anti-Christian. Nietzsche's objection to Christianity was that it gave rise to an acceptance of a slave morality. He considered Christianity to be degenerative, full of decaying and excremental elements, its driving force the revolt of the bungled and botched. He condemned Christian love and compassion as products of fear, and therefore a weakness which must be resisted. He was convinced that no religion was true, and that Christianity was nihilistic in the sense that it treated all men as equal, with no ultimate difference of value between one man and another. He claimed that he had discerned in the hearts and minds of his fellowmen that God had already died. "The death of God, the fact that the Christian God had ceased to be credible, was already beginning to cast its first shadows over Europe." The few who were able to understand the implications of this unprecedented event were already finding that "some sun seems to have set and profound trust has been turned to doubt."[16] From Oswald Spengler's writings, we can immediately recognize that which Nietzsche called the 'Coming of Nihilism', but it was the Danish philosopher, Søren Kierkegaard who was the first to confront man directly with Nothingness. He noted the advent of European nihilism, diagnosing its symptoms remorselessly. What is certainly true is that the prophecies of these thinkers as to the future were to prove nearly correct. Indeed, Nietzsche's philosophy has been claimed as a precursor to postmodernism, a movement which we will discuss in the next chapter.

A notable development which took place in nineteenth-century Western society was a social structure whose main preoccupation was with money and, to quote Pierre Teilhard de Chardin, the 'dynamization' of money'.[17] Marx could state that "money becomes the real community,"[18] and Alexis de Tocqueville wrote in a similar vein: "Men no longer are bound together by ideas, but by interests and it would seem as if human opinions were reduced to a sort of intellectual dust, scattered on every side, unable to collect, unable to cohere,"[19] by which he might have inferred financial interests. Later on, the economist John Maynard Keynes was to comment that love of money had become the prevailing sentiment.[20]

In such a context, Nietzsche's observation on the death of God was significant and apt, for it ran parallel with this growing influence of money, thereby confirming Christ's teaching in Matthew verse 5:24 that you cannot serve God and mammon. Indeed, the experience of the modern era would appear to make this biblical aphorism appropriate for whole societies as well as for individuals. If it is true that many individuals in a society might adopt a particular trait or traits, by extension it could also be said that their society would come to reflect a similar trait. When many people espouse a particular cause, their institutions will be influenced in the same manner. When Western society as a whole became obsessed with money and finance in the nineteenth century, following Matthew's Gospel so belief in God receded in equivalent stages.

### The Strand of Protestant theological Liberalism

Previously we described how Christian belief had been shaken as a result of Pietism, Deism and Enlightenment rationalism. To this, Peter Berger added Protestantism, for he made a comparison between it and the Catholic faith. In contrast with what he described as the completeness or plenitude of the Catholic universe with regard to its traditions, for example, ritual, sacraments and the cult of the saints, Protestantism adopted a radical abridgement, and minimized to the greatest possible extent two major aspects of the sacred, namely, mystery and miracle.[21] This process has been aptly described by the phrase 'disenchantment of the world'.

The main fruit of Protestant theology in the nineteenth century was the development of theological liberalism, also known as liberal Protestantism, which paradoxically had the effect of potentially endangering the Christian faith even more. The new liberal synthesis can be traced back to Friedrich Schleiermacher, for its main features could already be observed in his thought. The supernatural elements in the Christian faith were demoted and replaced by a natural religion in which reason and the emotions achieved prominence. It relativized dogma, and whilst this might not necessarily have led to apostasy or unbelief, it led, in the same way as Friedrich Schleiermacher's views, to a purely personal theology. It weakened faith, because it gave away too much by concessions to those whom Schleiermacher had called the 'cultured despisers'. The very foundations of Christian faith were being discarded in favour of these new ideas. The Protestant experience may prove to become the prototype for all other Christian traditions.

One of the most notable achievements of this Protestant movement, perhaps its crowning achievement, was the publication of a life of Jesus written by the German theologian David Friedrich Strauss, entitled *Das Leben Jesu, kritisch bearbeitet (The Life of Jesus, critically examined)* (1835). In this outspoken book, Strauss sought to establish Jesus as no more than a man, not the Son of God, thereby denying his divinity, and in the process robbing the Bible of much of its authority. The movement was fascinated with Jesus, but only in his capacity as a human being, a standpoint which had pietistic undertones.[22] This quest for the historical Jesus, in effect a biography and not a witness to faith, was a reaction to the new developments in historical studies, and may be considered to be another one of the causes leading to the crisis of Protestantism later in the century. However, Owen Chadwick considered that historians did not disconcert the faithful simply by portraying Jesus as a purely human figure. Rather it was the discovery that the evidence was not as reliable as had been anticipated. Indeed, the Swiss historian Jacob Burckhardt read Strauss's book, considered it to be simplistic, and became convinced that the degree of gravitas that Christianity had placed upon the New Testament texts, in order to nurture and sustain its faith, had been unwarranted.[23] Friedrich Engels, too, lost his faith in part as a result of reading this book.

Theologians were restating their beliefs alongside a developing secular culture that was deemed more attractive. Strauss as a Protestant theologian may have had no intention to weaken faith, but he had struck a mortal blow at the heart of Christianity. The movement has been said to be accommodation theology, since it sought for a theological happy medium between orthodoxy and liberalism, by attempting to save some of the elements of biblical religion, a posture which Thomas Mann considered to be excessive because it relied too much upon reason.[24] To put the matter in another way, it was considered appropriate to jettison certain aspects of the Christian tradition, but in the circumstances it might be more correct to say that the faith was destroying itself. However, this critical weakness did not end at this point. We shall see later that when the bourgeois world itself became threatened and faced with the shock of destruction, the whole Protestant liberal synthesis itself was faced with the same shock and became seriously challenged.

## Political and secular Strands

As an accompaniment to such philosophical and theological developments as we have outlined, new political developments would inevitably follow during the nineteenth century. The shift towards apostasy produced, amongst other things, a hunger for radical social and political change. In England, these could in one sense be said to have commenced with Tom Paine. Apart from Paine's writing, the social reformer Robert Owen generated the biggest influence for such change, for he came to be recognized as the main pioneer of socialism in Britain. Political radicals took the lead in criticism of the church. 'Blasphemous chapels' arose in London at the end of the 1810s, the members of which attacked Christianity with vulgar parody and vitriolic outbursts, accompanied by hints of satanic influence.

A significant resistance to the influence of Christianity began to flow from sections of the working and the lower middle classes. Liberal, radical, and later socialist political movements maintained a scathing antipathy against the established churches, which they viewed as upholding the unjust and tyrannical order. In their view, because the churches were intimately tied to the corrupt *ancient régime*, it was necessary for them to disappear, together with the God who had sustained the whole ecclesiastical structure. Often rejection of Christian belief followed rather than predated entry into radical politics. Supporters of all these movements often had a kind of religious faith themselves in the possibility that political action could achieve far-reaching and beneficial social reforms.

Anticlericalism was primarily political. It was originally a protest not so much against religious belief itself than against the political pretensions of the church. At the start of the 1848 revolutions in Europe, the churches co-operated with the revolutionaries, but it quickly abandoned the popular cause, and emerged on the winning, reactionary side. The struggle against the church and clericalism became a major open conflict of the nineteenth century, and one with many social ramifications. Right up to 1914, church and revolution shared an antipathy, because the word revolution stood for violence and illegality, but this word also stood, in the minds of many, for justice and freedom.

In 1865, the Irish historian William Lecky specifically referred to a 'secularization of politics'.[25] In places such as 'red' Saxony and the Thuringian states, the growth of socialism in this period was matched by a substantial decline in Protestant practice. A distinctive and novel *Weltanschauung* became the norm for Social Democratic activists in which the ideas of both Karl Marx and the English naturalist Charles Darwin became combined in a kind of synthesis which they considered could provide them with a sufficient explanation of the natural and social world. It was inevitable that, throughout the period from the 1860s to the First World War, the ethos of German Social Democracy should remain heavily secular. The leaders of the German socialist movement split. Those, such as the anarchist politician Johann Most in the 1870s and the socialist Karl Liebknecht later on prioritised attacks on religion and the churches, and supported movements of mass resignation from them. For them, religious prejudices were seen as a major obstacle to the socialist world-view. Others in the movement, however, maintained the view that religion was a personal matter. In his work *Aus meinem Leben (From my Life)* (1910) August Bebel was convinced that to encourage workers to support a socialist political system, this had to entail atheism.

The question whether the liberal movement of the nineteenth century on the one hand and Catholicism on the other could be reconciled had consequences which affected all Western Europe. It affected the relationship between Ireland and the British government, in the conflict between Poland and the Russian government, in the politics of education in Belgium, in Otto von Bismarck's *Kulturkampf* described below, and above all in the polemics of French political life after 1871. In 1874 Pope Pius IX gave some French pilgrims a special blessing for their efforts against the 'horrible plague which affected human society', namely, universal suffrage.

Because it tended to support political reaction and social conservatism after 1848, the French church destroyed the young movement of social Catholicism and created the final schism between itself, the urban artisan and working classes, and republican intellectuals. Anticlericalism in France primarily fulfilled a political need, and in this bipartisan climate, opinions polarised between those who supported and those who opposed the clergy. It was also, to a certain extent, France's alternative to England's Nonconformist movement. This conflict was a local problem for France which became more intense than elsewhere, but it stood for a religious predicament that spread across the whole of Europe. Established churches often formed alliances with conservative parties to protect themselves from attacks by anticlerical Liberal politicians, and this too helped to alienate many working-class people from the church.

In Germany, the Leipzig-based weekly magazine *Gartenlaube*, founded in 1853 by the journalist Ernst Keil, was one of the most widely-circulated periodicals. It eventually attained an estimated readership of at least two million. Apart from the aristocracy and the military, its targets included conservative forms of religion. Otto von Bismarck's government made the pope's decree of infallibility an opportunity to oppose the Roman Catholic Church, with attacks against it, instigated by Bismarck himself. The resulting conflict, known as the *Kulturkampf*, lasted throughout the 1870s. The German scientist and left liberal politician Rudolf Virchow, who coined the word, was himself a militant unbeliever, remarking that the movement should acquire the character of a great struggle against the Catholic Church. The attacks were master-minded by Peter Falk, the Minister of Public Worship and Education, and it had much in common with that in France. The religious orders were a special target. A law of 1872 expelled all foreign Jesuits, and placed such extensive restrictions on German Jesuits as to make most of the Society's work impossible, and in 1875 all members of Catholic orders that were not engaged in hospital work were expelled. Monety was used as a weapon, with many Catholic clergy being denied their salaries. By 1878 only three of the eight Prussian dioceses had bishops, nearly a quarter of 4,600 Catholic parishes were vacant, and Catholic and Protestant schools were forced to merge.

The use of Satan as a symbol, adopted at the end of the eighteenth century by the English Romanticists, was later employed in the nineteenth century by socialists, radicals and revolutionaries such as William Godwin, Pierre Proudhon, and the Russian revolutionary anarchist Mikhail Bakunin. In setting themselves in opposition to Christianity, they were apt to perceive Satan as a symbol of rebellion against the injustice and oppression of both the *ancient régime* and an oppressive religious establishment which bolstered it. Their view was that since God was on the side of the strong and the rich, Satan must be the champion of the poor.[26]

As a consequence, they demonized themselves as a way of rejecting the established system. It has been claimed by some commentators, most notably the Lutheran priest Richard Wurmbrand, in his book *Marx and Satan* (1986), that there is circumstantial evidence from Marx's writings that he adopted a satanic predilection.[27] In this respect, he would have held such views in common with many socialist followers. The Swedish scholar Per Faxneld in his article *The Devil is red: Socialist Satanism in the nineteenth Century* also maintained that a strong satanic influence pervaded socialist thinkers and activists during the late nineteenth century. He described how socialist satanism was prevalent among early Swedish social democrats, and their own publication which was started in 1891, was named 'Lucifer'.[28] Helena Blavatsky and her Theosophical Society published a journal controversially titling it with the same name from 1887 onwards, stating that this had no satanic or paranormal undertones, but her influential book *The secret Doctrine* (1888) at times reflected an explicit Satanism. Nineteenth-century politics therefore encouraged people increasingly to reject religion. Later in the century the rise of nationalism and imperialism and the emergence of organized political parties, whose tone was decidedly secular, also helped to diminish the importance of religion.

### Apostatic Strands from Science and scientific Discovery

The discoveries of modern science and science's own empirical methods generated the most widely debated question of all at the time, namely, the extent to which science was undermining Christian belief and was encouraging the rejection of the churches' teachings. From the French philosopher Pierre Gassendi's maxim stated in his book *Animadversiones (Observations)* (1649) "that there is nothing in the intellect which has not been in the senses", the zeal for measuring and observing nature had strengthened the protagonists of Deism and atheism in the previous century. By the middle of the nineteenth century, science was making ever new conquests and giving men a new conception of their powers over nature. Was this further proof of the West's Faustian ethos? Science became the symbol of irreversible progress, whereas religion and the established churches seemed part of a defunct world order that was doomed to die out.

By the early nineteenth century, scientific study had revealed at least two important facts. Much of the world's current state could be explained in terms of its own history, and secondly that the fossil record appeared to show that the earth had, in the past, been inhabited by creatures quite different from those that currently existed. In 1859 Charles Darwin published his work *On the Origin of Species by Means of natural Selection*, which effectively undermined William Paley's natural theology of the previous century, and the design-based theology that had become the mainstay of Christians. Darwin offered a religiously agnostic account of the development of species. He sought to explain his theories in terms of simple natural laws, namely, that over an incredibly long period of time the stronger species survived and gradually adapted to their surroundings, whilst the weaker species became extinct. It was his second major work, *The Descent of Man* (1871) that created the greater controversy, since it made a specific point of including mankind in his theory of evolution. It thereby raised manifold questions about the existence of the soul and its fate, and the unique relationship that was thought to exist between humanity and God.[29] For the first time, it became possible to deny God's existence without contradicting authoritative scientific evidence, and moreover to adopt unbelief as a viable intellectual option. It appeared to many to a greater degree than heretofore, that science and religion were travelling along different paths that could not be reconciled. Such a view was reflected in the book written by the historian Andrew White, entitled *A History of the Warfare of Science with Theology in Christendom* (1896), although its thesis and content is no longer accepted.

The attack on religion and the reality of any spiritual realm which followed Darwin's pioneering work can be attributed to the men of science who espoused the view that the concept of purpose could not avail with regard to the question of human evolutionary development.[30] God was no longer the only scientific explanation of the universe, if indeed such an explanation was any longer valid. Not only had Immanuel Kant shown that the existence of God could not be proved, Darwin's discoveries regarding natural selection accelerated the tendency to demonstrate that any attempt whatsoever at such proof was inconceivable. He had prepared the ground for a radically new way of looking at humanity according to which men and women could no longer be viewed as being made in the image of God, but must now be seen simply as a part of nature, subject to nature's laws. As a result, time-honoured religious and moral concepts such as the soul or free will were now designated to be meaningless, and conscience, if it did exist, had evolved from the evolutionary process.

Darwinism therefore came to symbolize the conflict between science and religion as the major threat to the theological claims of religion. Certain it was, therefore, that religious and clerical opinion at the time regarded Darwin's work as the culmination of a succession of attempts to discredit the whole religious structure, and these had a demonic aspect about them. Moreover, if Darwin's work were true, the dignity of man would have disappeared for ever, and the Christian scheme of salvation would collapse as if it had been built on quicksand.[31] Another important effect of science was its ever-expanding capacity to affect other areas of life, bringing apostasy in its train. Once the scientists had begun to undermine the Christian faith, men and women sought to organize their lives in different ways and the methods and results of science continued to strengthen the idea that God was less and less useful as a hypothesis, in the same way that Simon Marquis de Laplace had stated earlier. In short, science now provided an effective substitute for religion which was being cast aside.[32]

An aggressive anti-religious crusade emerged, fuelled mainly by Darwin's supporters. Darwin became the outstanding hero of those who championed a science that was becoming increasingly anti-religious, and that a new, and different, optimism was replacing traditional Christian apocalyptic hopes. As examples, one could quote the biologist Thomas Huxley in the natural sciences, and Herbert Spencer in philosophy and sociology. In 1862 the biologist Ernst Haeckel, impressed by Darwin's work, started the campaign to convert Germany to Darwinism. His book *Generelle Morphologie der*

*Organismen (General Morphology of Organisms)* (1866), was written in a form which exceeded even the claims that Darwin himself had made. Later in the century, in his book *Die Welträthsel (The Riddle of the Universe)* (1899), he asserted that science was solving all the mysteries of the universe, and he sought replace all religion with his own philosophy.

In 1860 it was Rudolf Virchow's turn to declare that the sciences had taken the place of the church. The European middle classes were being presented with the idea that there was an alternative explanation of the world, different from that which they had inherited. His campaign was strengthened with convincing arguments that the Bible was not what it was thought to be, and that miracles were of doubtful occurrence, if such doubt needed any reinforcement by this time. The concomitant loss of confidence over the precise expressions of religion caused uncertainty about the need for a creator, and whether the world could in any sense be ordered by a Providence. After the 1860s, many scientists were still Christians, but as scientists they no longer mentioned God. Some became captivated by the belief that the natural sciences could provide a panacea to solve all problems, and that men and society could be brought under scientific laws. This conflict could be characterized as a struggle between scientific and religious ideas for achieving cultural leadership.[33]

In 1874, John Draper, head of the Department of medicine at the University of New York, published his influential book *The History of the Conflict between Religion and Science*. In it, he stated that all revelation is a mere fiction, for God's mysteries, even when taught by such revelation, remain concealed by faith itself, as if by a veil, and thereby shrouded in darkness. Science, on the other hand, was forging ahead, giving the world modern inventions as well as canals, hospitals, sanitation, schools, firearms and warships. Karl Vogt was also an important contributor to this controversy. From his own physical investigations, he too maintained by inference that evolutionary theory destroyed traditional Christian theological doctrines. Ernst Troeltsch maintained that men were now eagerly pursuing the natural sciences with the intention of subjecting all life and reality to the laws of nature, with the sole intention of rendering spiritual values as fiction.[34] The neurologist Jean-Martin Charcot stated that humanity must abandon the expectation of illusory divine help, and liberate itself from the divine. For the philosophical writer Étienne Vacherot, in his work *La*

*Religion* (1869), science was the light, the authority, the religion of the nineteenth century, science founded upon experimental observation and not on the authority of revelation. He questioned whether Christianity or any religion was compatible with it. In France, the grievances were so great against the church that the cause of science was keenly seized upon by the anticlericals and opponents of Christianity. Positivism was one of the winners in this battle. Consequently, in France too all matters relating to religion and the belief in supernatural causation were now considered to be intrinsically incompatible with scientific rationalism and empiricism.

As scientific discovery progressed, the Christian churches felt themselves increasingly challenged by this rival protagonist which was making extensive claims for the authority and potential of its scientific enquiries. The situation caused more disquiet for Protestants than it did for Catholics, because the resulting discoveries eroded the chief support of Protestant authority, the Bible.[35] The most representative book to reflect the popular, rather than the real, antagonism between science and religion at this period, was *Kraft und Stoff (Force and Matter)* (1867), written by Karl Georg Büchner, one of the most uncompromising exponents of scientific materialism, and an international freethinker. During the last decades of the nineteenth century, Büchner, Karl Vogt and Ernst Haeckel amongst others, as the champions and advocates of Darwinism, toured Europe with an aggressive anti-religious campaign, and they lectured, moreover, to full houses.[36] Although the interests of Charles Darwin and Karl Marx were very different, their ideas, taken together, provided a matrix for succeeding generations to maintain that religion had been merely something that had been promoted for social purposes within a universe that was essentially materialist.[37]

## Strands of historical Relativism

Another road to apostasy was created by historical studies and the history of religion. Modern historical scholarship began in the early nineteenth century with Leopold von Ranke, whose contribution was discussed earlier. Georg Hegel, too, emphasized the importance of history and the historical process, and urged that it must be taken with much seriousness, but it was not until later in the century that the historicist view finally made its mark. An acknowledged authority on this movement was associated with Wilhelm Dilthey, who admitted that the strides taken by historical scholarship had actually led to an 'anarchy of values'.[38] One result of this new scholarship was to view Christianity as merely one religion amongst many. Ernst Troeltsch maintained that it was from such ideas that the crisis of belief had arisen, and asserted that the advent of the comparative history of religion, namely historical relativism, had done more to cultivate religious scepticism than anything else.[39] There was indeed a case for saying that it did as much or more even than scientific progress in this respect.[40] It raised the question as to whether history assisted the process of secularization by the emergence of new knowledge regarding ancient literature, and therefore of the Bible. Moreover, historical understanding came to make a significant impact upon religious faith, because of the way it affected ordinary non-academic minds.

Historical science cannot but be influenced by the intellectual and social environment of each historian's generation. French intellectuals of the 1870s were surrounded by positivist theory and this contributed to the advance of, and influenced, historical studies. Ernest Renan, whose priestly education prevented him from being a true positivist historian, maintained that intuition was one of the paths to truth and realized that historians could not do without it. He detested the idea that history could resemble geometry. In the article *Renan: the Man* (1924), Alfred Kaufmann remarked that Renan's own loss of the Christian faith, so he remarked, was due to biblical criticism,[41] the practice of critical analysis to explain the Bible, but Renan maintained that the acceptance of science did not imply the abandonment of all religion, taken in its broadest sense.

It has ever been a major feature of Protestantism that the Reformation predicated the sacred upon the Bible and only the Bible. We noted earlier that nineteenth-century developments in historical studies led to the quest for the historical Jesus. As a result, historical criticism of the nineteenth century succeeded in overthrowing the sacredness of the Bible, and such criticism was certain to come into conflict with Christian doctrine. We have noted earlier that God's revelation becomes known through the historical process and concerns the meaning of events that happened within historical time. Now the Christian believer was confronted with a dilemma, for it led to one of two stark choices. Either the Christian faith would have to be cast adrift from all its historical content or Christianity must comply with the principles by which all history, including the history of the Christian church and faith, is evaluated.[42] Wolfhart Pannenberg drew the logical conclusion from this that one could not simply discard ordinary history in order to construct a redemptive history of the faith. There is only a single history, and God's actions cannot be discerned beyond whatever is extant with respect to the historical record.

### The Industrial Revolution and the Growth of Towns

It has been claimed that the real origins of secularization were concerned with economics, and more particularly with those sectors of the economy that were being moulded by capitalism and industry. The Industrial Revolution in the nineteenth century and its concomitant movement, urbanisation, entailing the growth of large cities, have often been linked to the weakening of religious belief and practice, the decline of the churches and of Christian morality.

Industrialization, once it had taken off at various times in many of the countries of Western Europe, proceeded rapidly, and brought about an enormous shift of population from the countryside to the towns and cities. The emergent industrial working class found itself thereby in completely new surroundings. The traditional customs of the rural village were replaced by a friendless urban environment which were often accompanied by harsh working conditions. Many found themselves beyond the reach of the churches' parochial system when they migrated to the large towns. The Catholic Church in France failed to provide for this novel situation, and so the clergy were assigned to benefices in those areas where they were least needed.[43] The same could be said to be partly true for the Anglican Church, as the construction of new churches failed at first to keep pace with the growth in population. The large town of 1850 was not well prepared to receive large influxes from the countryside, for newcomers strained urban administrations and churches near to breaking-point. As a result, churchmen became convinced that urban growth was undermining religion. From the 1851 British census, an analysis was made which grouped towns according to the level of church attendance. It was concluded that attendance was to a certain extent inversely correlated with the size of an urban population, which led some commentators to state that bigger towns were one of the causes of the decline in church-going. The collapse in religious observance was in this view nothing but the consequence of the breakdown of the parochial system. It led to one theory that the process of secularization throughout the nineteenth century was but the nemesis of that situation. In Germany similarly, those classes in nineteenth-century society who were least affected by the developing industrial economy, in particular the aristocracy, the peasantry, craftsmen and small business owners, remained close to the church.[44]

As the new mode of work brought about social deprivation. Industrial townsfolk became lost in a crowd. They had little or no relationship with their neighbours. Furthermore, the customs of their former rural life became but a faded memory. They worked in a factory where they did not know the employer, and the new job was impersonal and monotonous. Therefore, working men's conceptions of religion changed. Social historians have concluded that the kind of work and the factory environment which the new machinery demanded, took men further from religion than the conditions which had existed previously in the traditional rural way of life. The gruesome industrial landscape was part and parcel of this environment. Arguing that the Christian religion had accrued excrescences and defects from its past, the political and economic theorist Claude Saint-Simon advocated a reformed Christianity. In his works *Du Système industriel (Of the industrial System)* (1821) and *Le nouveau Christianisme (The new Christianity)* (1825), he proposed a form of society that was to be ruled by technicians and industrialists.

The theologian David Hempton proposed another variation on the relationship between industrialization and religion, by arguing that in the short-term industrialization had the contrary effect of increasing the importance of religion, especially if one considers the massive growth in membership of the Nonconformist churches. The new urban working class, faced with perplexing social change, initially clung to religion as a form of security, thereby sustaining their faith.[45] However, later in the century, these same conditions actually reversed the process by helping to undermine the status of religion in English society, and this may be considered a form of latent, or delayed, apostasy. Similarly, in the United States, the Great Awakening, together with later revivals, had led to a revitalization of religion in the first half of the nineteenth century, but after that religious fervour began to ebb, with the gradual closing of the western frontier, and the development of industry after the Civil War of 1861-1865.⁴⁶ The conclusion would appear to be, as Owen Chadwick claimed, that industrial revolutions distanced, and then separated, men from God.⁴⁷

### The Contribution of sociological Thought

A similar process occurred in those disciplines now specifically called sociology and psychology. The new specialists in these fields, too, challenged the status of religion. Was it the case that social processes contributed to apostasy? Karl Marx asserted that the censure of religion had to be the point at which the criticism of society began, and so in the 1840s, criticism of the existing order was frequently couched in quasi-religious terms. A new school of sociology emerged which dealt with the status of religion in contemporary society. It originated from both Auguste Comte and the French sociologist Émile Durkheim. They brought new perspectives into the debate between the secular and the sacred, and as a result they too helped to revolutionize the mental habits of European people.

Comte championed the idea that science could acquire sufficient truths, and develop a positive knowledge of nature, as the foundation for pursuing purposeful social organization. Although he still believed that men expressed their highest needs in religion, he maintained that his doctrines could be developed by relying on scientific methods, and for him this entailed the observation of men and society. Catholicism, whilst it had the merit of seeing morality as the first of duties, had not succeeded in keeping pace with modern knowledge or scientific method because it was tied to a set of outmoded doctrines. Comte concluded that morality must be freed from religion, and this led him to the scientific study of the social world, a system which he called Positivism. It aimed at nothing less than the reorganization of society. Later in the century, Durkheim was to show how the religious ideas of a society were related to their ultimate social values, and in his construction of the sociology of religions concluded that religion and modernity were incompatible.⁴⁸

Positivism found adherents among a dedicated English group that lasted until the 1890s and included the philosopher John Stuart Mill and the author Harriet Martineau. As with Comte, the movement became in the hands of the Positivists a religion, the only religion for them which was real and complete, and it was to replace all systems that relied on a theology now deemed to be primitive. Félix-Antoine-Philibert Dupanloup Archbishop of Orléans warned against reading Hippolyte Taine because of his atheism and his mockery of theology, but the later Taine had no desire to abolish religion. For him religion was an eternal consolation, and an eternal lie. Revolution therefore had to oppose religion because religion was intimately involved in an outdated social structure which had to be overthrown.

### Aesthetic Strands

The arts, too, asserted their emancipation with the advance of apostasy. The general rule until the nineteenth century was that all art and poetry must be moral, but during this century, aesthetics proceeded to make a cult of itself, by replacing established religion with itself as the new religion, akin to a cultural secularization. This was exemplified by the adage *l'art pour l'art*, 'art for art's sake'. Substitute artistic creativity for the Christian liturgy and you had arrived at the new religion of the Romantic movement. Its understanding of Christianity would become noted for the subjectivism of all religious truths. The works of writers such as Klemens Brentano, John Keats, Percy Shelley, Alfred de Musset and Gustave Flaubert, reflected this, when they explicitly compared the artist to God. The Romantic movement had its origins in the northern countries of Europe, especially Germany, its dates being approximately 1770 to 1850, and its most famous proponent was Johann Wolfgang von Goethe. It swept across Europe, and eventually reached its fulfilment with Richard Wagner's productions of *Musikdrama* at Bayreuth, which themselves could be considered virtually as religious rituals. It reflected the sense of the self which assumed an increasing importance in nineteenth-century Europe.

Originally, with its tendency to put imagination before reason, the movement reacted against both the rationalism of the Enlightenment and orthodox dogma. Indeed, Romanticism took upon itself the task of correcting the mistakes of the Enlightenment, which it considered to have exaggerated and misrepresented the nature of reason. It later utilized Lucifer, as a symbol of liberty, in its literary works, and one characteristic of the Romantic movement was that it possessed a dark Dionysiac, even demonic, aspect.[49] The Romantics concluded that if the greatest foe of traditional Christianity was Satan, Satan must be good. Percy Shelley published a tract entitled *The Necessity of Atheism* in 1811, in which he denied the existence of God. A later work, the play

*Prometheus unbound*, would reveal his romantic satanism. Although romantic writers such as William Blake and Lord George Byron as well as Shelley showed ambiguity in their portrayals of Satan, such a stance provided an initial and important impetus to the movement for apostasy. It emphasized Satan in the role of God's adversary, and used him to make radical, political ideas easier to understand, thereby further antagonizing the church and the established order.

The French Romantic poets expressed an affinity with Satan, for example, Alfred de Vigny's poem *Éloa, ou la Sœur des Anges (Éloa, or the Sister of the Angels)* (1824). Christ was for Vigny, Gérard Nerval and Victor Hugo also a romantic hero. They rehabilitated religion, but not the union of God with men. Vigny in 1839 wrote: "Heaven is dark, and God does not reply."[50] Charles Baudelaire, who did not believe in progress, stated that it was "a big mistake of the time, (*une erreur fort à la mode*) of which I avoid like the Devil. The most wonderful of the Devil's deceptions is to persuade you that he does not exist."[51] The sixteenth-century Puritan Richard Greenham had already anticipated this famous epigram: "it is the policy of the Devil to persuade us that there is no Devil." The biblical text at 2 Corinthians, 11:14 is also apposite: "for even Satan disguises himself as an angel of light." Baudelaire juxtaposed Satan in opposition to God in his volume of poetry *Les Fleurs du Mal (The Flowers of Evil)* (1857), where the author expressed a sympathy with Satan and was accused of an insult to public decency. Jules Michelet, the historian and social agitator in his *La Sorcière (The Witch)* (1862), considered Satan, not as evil, but as the very embodiment of science and reason. Pierre-Joseph Proudhon attended Michelet's lectures in the 1830s and it may well be that he was influenced by his teacher's Satanism. In his book *De la Justice dans les Révolutions et dans l'Église (Justice in the Revolution and the Church)* (1858), he stated: "Freedom...is your Antichrist; freedom for you is the Devil. Come Satan, come, that I may embrace you."[52] Ever provocative, he complained about the tyranny and misery of God.

During the years 1860 to 1880, according to Gérard Cholvy, in the cultural field Romanticism was displaced by Positivism. Eventually as Romanticism declined, the romanticists' symbol of the literary Devil was brought to an end, and the concept of the Devil was given back to the theologians. Educated Europeans still looked heavenwards despite evolutionary theories, but they did so with hesitation. France, Germany and Britain had entered the Age of Doubt, and this change affected both the theologian, and the attitude of religious men.

### The Decline in Church Attendance

It seemed to some people in the later nineteenth century that increasing prosperity encouraged the idea that religion was no longer needed, and this led to indifference. The clearest evidence for this lay in the area of formal religious practices. In France, Germany and Britain, there was a move away from religious observance, although it must be admitted that the pattern was variable. The trend was probably a sign of incipient apostasy and religious doubt, and the period between the revolutions of 1848 and the outbreak of the First World War marked an important phase in the decline in church attendance in Europe.

One of the first to speak openly of the decline in religious observance was the Bishop of Limoges in 1875, but in France, this differed so greatly from region to region that it was virtually impossible to pinpoint the decline, or otherwise, of belief. In some regions of France, the church seemed never fully to have recovered from the French Revolution. During the July Monarchy of King Louis Philippe (1830-1848), a majority of infants were baptised in France within three days. By 1870, however, this had fallen considerably, and a further important fall occurred during the third republic after 1871.[53] Open rejection of the Catholic faith spread among convinced republicans in the 1850s, and this was indicated by the fact that civic, that is, secular funerals, first became common among French political exiles in Brussels during this decade.

By the middle of the nineteenth century, religious practice in France remained far stronger in rural areas, and much less noticeable in Paris and other cities. The *coup d'état* of 1851 was a notable date in the modern history of the French church, because, for almost two decades, as a consequence of the freedom given it by Emperor Napoléon III's government, known as the Second Empire, the church embarked on a policy in which it sought to persecute its enemies, and this policy destroyed most of the sympathy that liberals and republicans may have had for it. The figures for church attendance could be interpreted as showing a high point around 1860, followed by stabilisation and a steady decline in the period from 1879 onwards during the Third Republic. At the end of the nineteenth century there were many rural parishes where not a single man received communion. For the first time in 1868, those students who declared themselves to be Catholics at their entrance to the École Normale Supérieure in Paris were in a minority.[54] It was the Catholic sacrament of confession which elicited the most anticlerical hostility. The priestly confessor appeared to Jules Michelet to be the great enemy or rival of the husband.

In German towns, a large drop in church attendance occurred in the period before 1850, and it was in some cases dramatic. In the latter half of the eighteenth century the ratio of communicants to the Protestant population fell precipitously from 150 per cent to 20 per cent in Hanover. There was a similar story in other German towns, for example Dresden and Nuremberg, with the decline in attendance beginning in 1800, and by the 1840s it had dropped to low levels, although statistics were scanty. For Berlin, an estimate has put church attendance as low as ten per cent. Such decline was more likely caused by social, intellectual and cultural changes, rather than by industrialization which was still in its infancy in Germany. However, further declines in churchgoing in most parts of Protestant Germany occurred in the 1860s and 1870s when Germany did begin to industrialize on a large scale after unification. Until 1906, conversions roughly compensated for losses from the churches. Thereafter, this was no longer the case, especially in the big towns. Berlin and Hamburg were described by the historian Georges Goyau as 'spiritual cemeteries',[55] and Berlin achieved notoriety for its being dubbed the atheist capital of Europe.

The decline in church attendance in England occurred from at least the middle years of the century. There were occasional minor resurgences of support for Christianity, largely within the middle classes, but they were not sustained. Church attendance started declining substantially from the late 1880s until the First World War, and there was a smaller decline in church membership. The number of Anglican marriages declined from 91 per cent of all marriages in 1844 to 64 per cent in 1904, yet baptisms increased in the same period.

Two further influences were causing changes in religious practice. First of all, the state was extending its authority over several sectors such as education, and secondly there developed an increasing ascendancy of the towns over the countryside, for rural areas became increasingly susceptible to urban influences. Thus, in many parts of Western

Europe, the later nineteenth and early twentieth centuries saw a decline in the divergences between urban and rural areas by way of improvements in communications generally, and newspapers and political organizations in particular.

### Freethought, religious Diversity and moral Issues

When men and women no longer attended church, or were abandoning traditional religious beliefs, doubt or apathy were not the only causes. During the second half of the nineteenth century, a variety of rival views of the world emerged, especially among city dwellers, and often these other movements seemed to offer greater attractions. Alternative and wide-ranging forms of religion and belief-systems challenged, often with vehemence, the formerly dominant influence of the established churches, and directly competed with them. Rather than being the preserve of relatively small circles of intellectuals or political radicals, they became widely accessible to the mass of the population especially in the cities and large towns, places which had their newspapers, lectures, cafés and public houses, and many sub-cultures. However, the same was happening more gradually in small towns and rural areas too. The prevailing trend was not necessarily the rejection of traditional belief, but a tendency towards eclecticism, and to an accommodation between the traditional and the new. For example, the doubts about the Christian faith raised by Charles Darwin's publications caused the popularity of Spiritualism to develop from the 1840s onwards, as people sought for empirical evidence of the afterlife and the spiritual world. Such alternative paths to religious truth have often been cited as a major influence in encouraging apostasy.

As we have noted, French radical culture developed a tradition of outright anticlericalism, which often led to a complete rejection of religious faith, and this applied to most social classes in France. Freethought and humanist movements originated in France in the 1790s as alternatives to religion. After the return to peace in 1815, the ideas of the previous generation were revived by what was termed 'the blasphemous and seditious press'. In France during the Third Republic, organized freethought became a mass movement. The first societies were formed in Paris during 1848, but only after the Second Empire, when the republicans attained political power in the 1870s, were all restrictions lifted, and at this point the growth of the movement became very rapid. An almanac of 1894 listed 567 freethought societies which had been formed in the previous fifteen years. Freemasonry in France also played an important anticlerical role in the nineteenth century, as it did in Spain.

The freethought movement in England was led by George Holyoake and Richard Carlile, with the intention of spreading the twin doctrines of republicanism and materialistic atheism. Carlile republished Thomas Paine's *Age of Reason* in 1819, which led to his conviction for blasphemous libel and offensive language. By the early 1840s secularism had caught the public imagination and a national network was established. Probably only a minority of radicals at this time were outright atheists, but a common bond of anticlericalism brought atheists and others together to denounce 'priestcraft' in all its forms. By the end of the 1850s, huge rallies in the north of England were drawing thousands of supporters. The most popular organization opposed to religion in mid-century England was the National Secular Society formed in 1866. Secularist groups were to be found in almost all towns. The secularist George Foote in May 1881 began a new periodical, the *Freethinker*, an atheist, aggressively anti-religious, blasphemous and almost seditious monthly publication, which fiercely attacked Christianity. A tradition labelled 'infidel', distinct from parallel anti-Christian or sceptic movements, also mustered support amongst artisan and lower middle-class freethinkers.

In Germany an important role was played by the Free Parishes, originally established by Christian rationalists. After a brief surge in popularity in 1848-1849, and the repression of the 1850s, they gradually evolved towards a more thorough-going rationalism, minimising the importance of, or dropping altogether, all supernatural elements of the Christian faith and arriving in some cases at atheism. Those who thought that these groups were still too religious joined the German Freethinkers League, established in 1881 by the followers of Karl-Georg Büchner. The conception of religiosity now changed from outright submission to moral and ecclesiastical authority into a more contemporary understanding of religion as a matter of personal choice.

The view therefore developed that European freethinkers should set their face against authority, and concomitantly the traditional values that were associated with it. As an integral part of this process, one must discard God, not because the philosophers and thinkers had sought to disprove His existence, but because the very idea of God signified objectionable authority to freethinking minds.[56] Something very similar to this view was held by the anarchists in an extreme form, but it also might be faintly discerned within the ranks of more moderate and more conservative men.

If you equate religious beliefs with philosophical views which could be attained by reason and intellect without ritual, prayer or ethical commitment, religious sceptics have triumphed.[57] Ultimate and objective values would no longer be able to support morality. Ephemeral needs or whims would take their place. Indeed, one theory which circulated in the nineteenth century maintained that the demolition of an established consensus in moral authority was a fundamental factor in promoting apostasy. Furthermore, the expansion of the popular press during the century raised concerns that it contributed to weakening the established moral order of European and American society. At the same time as Auguste Comte was developing his ideas in the 1840s, a group in Germany known as 'Die Freien' asserted their freedom by declaring 'God is dead'. One of this group, the philosopher Max Stirner developed a system with the title *Der Einziger und sein Eigentum (The Ego and his Property)* (1844), which advocated an amoral egoism, and is deemed to have influenced the development of anarchism and also postmodernism, a movement which we shall examine in the next chapter.

In 1839 Jules Michelet, as a professor at the Collège de France, took it upon himself firmly to reject traditional Christianity. He lectured with an eloquence that displayed a fiercely partisan approach. For him, together with his artistic circle, everything that the churches represented was ill-conceived: the Christian ethic, celibacy, confession.[58] The advent of the kingdom of the Spirit was to supersede at last the dogmas, hierarchies and ecclesiastical structures of the past. We have already noted how European piety underwent a curious transposition at the end of the eighteenth century. Formerly, traditional society had privileged male piety, but now piety began to be conceived almost exclusively as a feminine trait. The cause was thought to be modern evangelicalism, whose agenda began to play an important role. Religion now faced the problem of men's exclusion from the domain of piety. Liberal, radical or socialist groups persuaded men to cease attending religious services altogether, and many did so in parts of France and

Germany.⁵⁹ The growing gap between more religious women and more secular men observed in Europe, affected all social classes and all the major religious confessions.

Auguste Comte thought that moral principles must be backed by religion. He was persuaded that how you act depended upon what you believed. For him, it would be futile to start by reforming institutions. You must start by reforming ideas and habits, and only then could you transform institutions. In this he disagreed with the Enlightenment *philosophes* who maintained that you improve men by altering their institutions first of all. In Comte's mind there was a close link between evolution of knowledge and moral progress. His proposals about ethics caused criticism, not least from moral philosophers, but they were the nearest to a popular theory of ethics the nineteenth century achieved. The writer Ferdinand Brunetière, although a positivist, attempted to show how much the positivism of Auguste Comte was akin to Catholicism.

### A Note on Secularization

Secularization is one of those movements, similar to the Renaissance, which is incapable of concise and precise definition by reason of its nature. To many historians, it is the one master narrative or paradigm which could provide a plausible explanation of modern history. We are speaking of the historical decline in the importance of religion, the supernatural and the sacred, a process by which religious institutions lose their former control or influence over certain sectors of society, its public institutions and culture. This would include, for example, the expropriation of church lands, or the severing of education, welfare, and hospital care from ecclesiastical authority. In anticlerical and progressive circles, the term has come to mean the liberation of modern man from the hold which religion maintained over men's lives, while in circles connected with the traditional churches it has been severely criticized with such epithets as dechristianization and, more popularly, as heathenism.⁶⁰

William Lecky appeared to be the first to refer to the secularization of politics and the declining influence of the church. The word 'secularism' appeared in the 1850s, though it was not a new movement, for it has been noted above that Henry Drummond's conclusions were obliquely pointing in the same direction in the 1820s. The word 'secularization' was not so far distant from the word 'anticlericalism'. Sometimes it meant a freeing of the sciences, of learning, of the arts, from their theological origins or theological bias, and sometimes it meant the declining influence of the churches, or of religion, in modern society. The sociologists demonstrated how deep-rooted religion was, both in mankind and in the consensus which constituted society. The word henceforth came to describe the changing relationship between religion and modern society, owing partly to the new conditions of urban and industrial life, and partly emanating from the enormous growth in new knowledge.

Secularization could be checked only as long as the churches were able to resist any concessions to this movement. Commentators were in agreement that it began in earnest in the eighteenth century, and continued to develop for various reasons and situations amongst the nations in Western Europe, and there was no common factor driving the change. The West did not move directly or immediately from a confessional state to one that was religiously neutral or militantly secular. Rather, the confessional state was dismantled piece by piece, first in France and afterwards in the other nations in Western Europe. Until the mid-nineteenth century the state was still considered to be Christian, and in various countries a privileged status continued to be accorded to some Christian confessions.

In France, Protestants secured equality with Catholics in 1815, although Baptists were still liable to harassment from the police. In Britain, the Emancipation Act of 1829 granted Catholics equality in law, and the abolition of the Test Acts in 1839 achieved the same for dissenters, although the Jews achieved full emancipation only in 1858. In Scandinavia legal moves from the 1840s onwards, Norway in 1845 and Denmark in 1849, accommodated non-Lutherans by relaxing the strict laws which had tied religious confession to citizenship.[61] From 1870, the pace of secularization moved up a notch as the state made inroads into areas previously considered to be the churches' domain, for example, in the provision of welfare. In England, the free churches were involved in pushing for this change. In France, civil registration had been removed from ecclesiastical control in 1792 during the Revolution. Its introduction in the 1870s in Germany, with the civil marriage ceremony being made legally valid, brought Germany into line with French practice. Civil registration in Britain, formerly the responsibility of the Anglican Church, was introduced in Britain in 1837. In the Netherlands, this took place between 1795 and 1811.

Some high points in the conflicts between church and state in France occurred during the Third Republic. A wide-ranging programme of secularization was implemented in many fields, both by French republican governments and by numerous local authorities. The Paris city council carried through a programme of secularization of schools and hospitals. Some councils ordered the removal of all religious artefacts, for example, crosses and statues of saints, from public places or prohibited religious processions through the streets. However, the main battleground was in education. The radicals passed laws which the minister of education Jules Ferry proposed in order to diminish the church's control of this sector, the main policy being the secularization of the state school system. A bill of 1879 prohibited unauthorized religious people from teaching, and ministers of religion were excluded from national and departmental education committees. By 1910, this had the inevitable result of virtually eliminating teachers in state primary schools who were members of religious orders.

The trend in Britain during the later nineteenth and early twentieth centuries was also towards a largely planned, institutional secularization. Moreover, the leaders, both in society and in the intellectual world, were increasingly disposed to deprecate religion, or at least to give little weight to it.[62] In England and Wales, with William Forster's education Act of 1870, the state now became the principal provider of finance for schools. In Germany during the *Kulturkampf* campaign pursued by the government, clerical school inspectors were replaced by professional educators. In north German Protestant cities such as Berlin and Hamburg, already in the 1830s and 1840s attitudes of this kind were having considerable influence not only on the intellectual avant-garde and on political radicals, but on wider sections of the educated middle-class, especially where religious participation was already low.

According to the sociologist David Martin, the process of secularization developed in two phases, and both adversely affected religious belief and observance. The first phase affected society's infrastructure, such as government and heavy industry, but many sectors of middle-class life, such as personal service, self-employment, family firms and the family itself were resistant to change.[63] It was the second phase, of more recent occurrence, which assailed precisely these sectors, and this stage tended to be the more corrosive. Wherever apostasy had developed earlier, religious belief and practice were subject to a redoubled attack later. Increasing centralization and large-scale bureaucracy produced a core sector that was liberated territory as far as religion was concerned. Peter Berger is broadly in agreement with this thesis. Secularization, by moving outwards into most areas of society, created what may be called a 'cultural lag' between the secularization of the economy in the first instance, then that of the state, and finally that of the family.[64] The Christian churches were eased out of the structure, gradually becoming more marginalized, and leaving Christian commitment as merely one leisure activity amongst many others. Those who have been more affected are still men rather than women, still people living in the cities rather than in the country, and still those directly connected with modern industrial production, particularly the working class. It seemed that the revolutions in Europe during the nineteenth century completed the process begun in 1789 and finally dismembered the ancient partnership of Christianity and the state that had been such a predominant feature of the thousand years of Western Christianity.

\* \* \* \* \* \* \* \*

Apostasy advanced by multifarious routes in the nineteenth century, and these to a greater or lesser extent contributed to the secularization of European society. We could pose the question as to whether apostasy and secularization were closely linked as part and parcel of the same development. We might justifiably apply the term secularization to institutions and the term apostasy to individuals, so that the two represented opposite sides of the same coin. This may have been so for Western Europe, but the situation was somewhat different in the United States. There, the constitution set up by the founding fathers in the late eighteenth century explicitly excluded favouring any one religion or Christian denomination, effectively creating an early example of a pluralist secular state. The American population retained their religious allegiances to a greater extent, but from the beginning these were voluntary and remained so, resulting in competition for membership amongst the various denominations, and in effect religion had to be marketed. The result has made the churches highly commercialised and it has been remarked that religion became internally secularized and therefore hardly religious in any real sense at all.

Towards the end of the nineteenth century, apostasy was beginning to have a distinct effect on the people of the West. Society was now witness to a wide spectrum of beliefs, ranging from those adherents who remained loyal to traditional Christianity, through those who chose half-belief and agnosticism, and finally to those who rejected all religious faith. A fair conclusion would be that the multi-pronged assault on the Christian faith in the nineteenth century was carried out on a scale and with a ferocity unprecedented in Western history. We shall see in the next chapter how this trend developed even further during the next century.

CHAPTER TEN

*The Hosts of Gog and Magog are as the Sand of the Sea*

"All we like sheep have gone astray; we have turned every one to his own way." *Isaiah, verse 53:6*

THE TITLE of this chapter is derived from chapter 20 of the Apocalypse. Its relevance will be explained as we continue to sketch the diminishing importance of Christian belief and practice for the majority of people in the Western world during the twentieth century. Just as modern society, its culture and its institutions have become secularized, so has it produced an increasing number of people who view the world and their own lives objectively without the need for any religious involvement or explanation. We described in the previous chapter how a whole host of attempts were made during the nineteenth century to discard the West's Christian faith. As that century drew to a close, science and scientific methods dominated European thought to such an extent that some Christians in the West were becoming convinced that, since the existence of the Christian God could not, or never could be, capable of being proved empirically in the same way as scientific proofs, the Christian religion had become incredulous. The classicist and philologist Frederic Myers asserted that "the most effective assailants of Christianity...strike at the root, and begin by denying...that a spiritual world, a world beyond the conceivable reach of mathematical formulae, exists for us at all."[1]

In the United States direct Christian influence on culture also began to wane, a consequence of the growth of liberal Protestantism, and a process that was to be nearly completed by the 1920s. Whilst some churchmen now had a respect for science, they did not yet completely comprehend the extent to which Darwinism had destroyed the theology that served as the foundation of their belief.[2] Besides, increasing numbers of people were turning to liberal or modernist versions of Christianity in order to salvage whatever they could from their Christian heritage. It was not religious people who were fuelling the dispute between the two disciplines, but the advocates of science. It led many commentators to aver what Nietzsche had already proclaimed, that a crisis had indeed occurred in the religious consciousness of the West. The diplomat and literary critic Eugène-Melchior de Vogüé was the prime example of a state of mind which faced Europe during the 1890s, that saw the physical sciences withdraw into their own proper fields. The immense reputation of science as the quest for truth remained, but also the sadness that science was not suited to offer truths about the moral being, and must surrender such claims, but uncertain that the churches could offer anything to compensate for this state of affairs.

**The Decade of the 1890s was an important historical 'Moment'**

The period around the year 1800 had been decisive for European history, because it came to be acknowledged as the gateway to the modern world. During the last decade of the nineteenth century, radical changes occurred to such an extent within European society that the years around 1890 must also be considered another important historical 'moment', a view supported by Jacques Barzun. A decadent trend, which earned the title of *fin de siècle*, emerged amongst the intelligentsia, and it witnessed the end of a cultural age. Stéphane Mallarmé expressed the feeling in his poem *Brise Marine (Sea-Wind)* (1865), echoing Goethe's Faust: "The flesh is sorrowful, alas! And I have read all the books."

Literature was foremost in highlighting the new cultural movements emerging in Western society. The distinguishing feature of the literary works of the period was both mounting religious doubt and the strained relationships between believers and sceptics. Such themes were not expressed in subtle undertones, rather they were now central to the whole structure of these works. Henrik Ibsen, whose plays finally came to be accepted, wrote that the virtues and institutions which had been formerly regarded as sacred and central to the European Christian tradition, such as marriage, being truthful, respecting authority, observing propriety, obstructed the pursuit of the good life. For him, all such ideals, abstractly considered, were calamitous for individuals and in the long run for society also.[3] Ibsen was only one writer amongst many in the drama which was unravelling the Victorian ethos. Other examples were Dostoevsky's *Братья Карамазовы (The Brothers Karamazov)*, Émile Zola's *Les trois Villes (The three Cities)* (1894-

1898), Thomas Hardy's *Jude the Obscure* (1895), Samuel Butler's *The Way of all Flesh* (published in 1903, but much of it written in the 1870s and 1880s). Mark Twain's *Mysterious Stranger* (1897-1908) has been designated as satanic existentialism and nihilism, and indeed its aura of pure pessimism could aptly form the Devil's prolegomenon for the new century.[4] Gerhard Hauptmann's work *Einsame Menschen (Lonely People)* (1894), depicted the tension created by the generational divide between parents who adhered to the traditional faith, and the child who has apostatised. In *Tess of the d'Urbervilles* (1891), Thomas Hardy referred to 'the chronic melancholy that was taking hold of the civilized races with the decline of belief in a beneficent power'. Alfred Tennyson, with the success of *In Memoriam* published in 1890, noted the implicit anxiety that was eroding the faith of his contemporaries. The historian Carl Schroske remarked that, in Vienna, not only the producers of culture, but its analysts and critics also, fell victim to a kind of fragmentation. The city's Secession movement, reflected, for example, in the work of Gustav Klimt, rejected a past which it saw as dull and conservative. Anatole France summed up the mood in 1895: "We have eaten an apple from the tree of knowledge, and the apple has turned to ashes in our mouths…It was sweet to believe, even in hell."[5]

From Beethoven onwards, musical composers had occasionally introduced disharmony into their compositions for effect. Composers, such as Claude Debussy and Arnold Schoenberg, were now beginning to introduce discords deliberately into their work, but music of this nature reflected a feeling of chaos, angst and seemed as if God's orderly plan was being shattered. Significantly, Jacques Barzun considered that disharmony suggested something of the demonic.

The men of the 1890s delighted in demonstrating that the old ideals were false and that one might well turn them on their heads. The Cambridge philosopher, Alfred Sidgwick, aimed to substitute a secular for a theocentric philosophy as the foundation of all social and individual conduct. In some quarters it was considered that such an attempt was bound to end in failure. John Maynard Keynes and his friends at Cambridge, in repudiating the doctrine of original sin, believed that human beings were now sufficiently rational to be freed from rigid rules of conduct, and could be left henceforth to follow their own intuitions as to what constituted the good.[6]

There were other ways in which the period around 1890 could be regarded as a turning point. Gérard Cholvy noted that scientific thought had profoundly permeated the intelligentsia at this time,[7] and the positivist attitudes of science became the model for all branches of knowledge. Upheavals in the physical sciences, with the new physics of Ernest Rutherford and Albert Einstein, redefined the nature of scientific laws. Training in advanced mathematics, hitherto unnecessary for the layman, was now required in order to understand the fundamental theories of science.[8] The chemist Alfred Mond recommended to businessmen the advantages of what is now known as 'R. & D.', in which a part of industry's profits should be set aside for research and development. By hiring pure scientists, industry might find processes that engineers could design and implement. In commerce, advertising had long existed as simple publicity, but this period witnessed the emergence of the advertising craft as we know it, with arresting displays that employed repetitious slogans, and boastful and extravagant claims, euphemistically termed 'puffery'. Employers had in the past often been able to maintain some influence on the political and religious behaviour of their workforce but by the 1890s this aspect too was beginning to wither, for the working class of the early twentieth century proved to be less willing to respond to such paternalistic leadership. It was in 1890 too, that the United States Census Bureau announced that the Western frontier was closed, entailing the end of the frontier era.

The approach to the First World War was also crucial in the evolution of modernist thinking. Consider novelists such as Marcel Proust: *Du Côté de chez Swann (Swann's Way)* (1913), Virginia Woolf: *Voyage out* (1915), D.H. Lawrence: *Sons and Lovers* (1913), Thomas Mann: *Der Tod in Venedig (Death in Venice)* (1913) and James Joyce: *Dubliners* (1914). C.S. Lewis's *God in the Dock* was a collection of essays on Christian themes and described the way in which Western culture increasingly put the Christian God on trial. Poets such as Ezra Pound and T.S. Eliot were developing new poetic forms. In art, a host of different movements from Cubism through Primitivism to Surrealism established new and challenging rules about what constituted or should constitute a work of art.[9] Composers carried the trend towards dissonance still further, and some such as Arnold Schoenberg abandoned traditional tonality altogether. Igor Stravinsky with his ballet *Le Sacre du Printemps (The Rite of Spring)* (1913) caused an uproar at its first performance in Paris, with one commentator suggesting that it changed the course of musical history.

Psychoanalysis was considered to play its part in bringing the whole of reality under the control of reason. Sigmund Freud, the father of modern psychoanalysis, has been called the last of the *philosophes*, and for him the idea of God was insupportable. His theories, fashionable for the time, stimulated atheism, and described religion in a paper of 1907 as the 'universal, obsessional neurosis of humanity',[10] and later repeated this view in his book *Die Zukunft einer Illusion (The Future of an Illusion)* (1927). After reading Ludwig Feuerbach's works, he expounded the idea of a conflict in which religion must inevitably be eliminated. He stated that if religious views are based on the assertion of a higher being, whose qualities are indeterminable and whose intentions are unknowable, people will lose interest in them.[11] For the religious believer, Freud's influence must be construed as malignant.[12] Interestingly, Freud developed a demonology whose central point maintained that the Devil is nothing other than a psychological reality emanating from repressed, unconscious drives.

In France, the Socialists were in the vanguard of the movement for secular legislation. Laws requiring Sunday rest were repealed, and restrictions imposed on the free, that is, Catholic, universities (1880); abolition of the confessional character of cemeteries (1881); legislation for divorce, and a ban on prayers during the meetings of public bodies (1884). Seminarists lost exemption from military service (1899); the use of religious symbols was prohibited in 1903, extended to courts of law in 1904. The final straw came in 1905 with the separation of church and state. Municipalities assumed ownership of most churches and presbyteries, and the state ceased responsibility for paying the clergy's salaries. The confrontations encouraged Pope Pius X in his resolve to be as unconciliatory as possible, and in 1907 he issued his decree entitled *Lamentabili*, berating modernism.[13] The French government's actions confirmed the French Catholics' image of themselves as a minority, fighting a desperate engagement against the forces of evil, together with a sense of being under siege as exiles in their own country. The ensuing decline in churchgoing was rapid and dramatic. Ordinations to the Catholic priesthood fell from 1,500 in 1904 to 800 in 1913, and during the same period, the number of students studying Protestant theology diminished by the same proportion.[14]

In Germany, the level of church attendance between about 1880 and 1895 stabilised, before going into another period of decline between 1895 and 1913. Studies undertaken in the period concluded that nearly all rural areas had succumbed to extensive influences from the towns and cities, and that these were generally associated with a further decline of Protestant religious practice. In the 1890s some rural Catholics left the Centre Party and joined the Bavarian Peasants' League. Apart from supporting measures to improve the economic status of the peasantry, the League strongly attacked the clergy by claiming that the latter was getting richer while the peasants were getting poorer. Those Catholics who joined the Social Democrats rejected the Christian faith altogether. Moreover, the emergence of nationalism and imperialism by the 1890s tended to overshadow religious or confessional factors. Those who advocated nationalist sentiments in the name of *völkisch* ideas could at the same time consciously reject Christianity as a phase of German history that had now long passed.

In England also, in the 1890s a substantial decline in church attendance occurred. A religious census carried out in London in 1903 showed that membership of the Church of England had fallen by a quarter between 1886 and 1901. Marriages in church also showed signs of decline. Far fewer people in the working class than in the middle classes had been associated with the Anglican church, and so this decline seemingly occurred among the latter classes.[15] Terms of abuse were now applied to religious belief and practice, such as puritanism, cant or Victorianism. Religious observance was to become almost totally eclipsed by the leisure revolution, in which sport became religion's major rival, together with popular culture. But were modern leisure activities the cause of religious indifference and the decline of church attendance, or were they rushing in to fill the vacuum that had already been created by advancing apostasy? Increasing working-class militancy often accompanied conversion to some form of socialism, reflected in the miners' strike of 1898. English Nonconformity was severely affected by these further shifts towards apostasy, and contributed to the chapels' decline. ranging over theological, political and cultural issues.

In 1905, Rosa Luxemburg, the one major rival in competition with Vladimir Lenin for the leadership of European Communism, published at Cracow a treatise on religion, under the pseudonym Jósef Chmura, entitled *Kościól a Socjalizm (Socialism and the Churches)*. She wrote with a zeal and with moral passion, which recalled that of the nineteenth century political worker. However much Christian teaching was good, and should be followed, having many affinities with socialism, yet the churches could play no part in any future enterprise because they had betrayed the spirit of early Christianity and were now one of the pillars of an establishment which had to be eliminated.[16] French Socialists, including the most celebrated, Jean Jaurès, adopted a similar attitude, together with many French Protestants.

By the eve of the First World War, Western society found itself in circumstances which it had never experienced before in its history. For more than a thousand years, it had professed a faith which had been unerring and absolute with no place for alternative belief-systems, but now there existed a whole host of such systems, conflicting and irreconcilable, each of which claimed to hold the answers to all the most important questions of the time. Encouraged by the progressive conclusions of the Enlightenment, by scientific, technical and manufacturing achievements, and by rising standards of living, optimism had grown among the elites during most of the previous century. These years witnessed an exuberance and complacency that transcended virtually all other periods of Western history. New fields of knowledge seemed unequivocally to portend a bright future, and which would bring, if pursued vigorously enough, enormous benefits to mankind. It would be reasonable to maintain that progress and civilization became in this period, a form of religion in themselves. Ernst Troeltsch noted somewhat hubristically in 1907 in his work *Das Wesen des modernen Geistes (The Essence of the modern Spirit)* that crisis or collapse was far distant, as were also any new religious ideas that were truly original.[17] For working-class people throughout Western society, a new era seemed to be dawning, bringing with it radical change. They considered that the religion and the churches of their forefathers were at best irrelevant, at worst a hindrance to the realization of their hopes. In Vladimir Soloviov's final work devoted to the problem of evil, *Три разговора (The three Dialogues)* (1900), whilst describing main trends of modern society as economic materialism, abstract moralism, hubris and greed, he foresaw that the twentieth century would be the epoch of great wars, internal civil strife and revolutions..."[18]

## The Great War and its Aftermath

...and he was right. His prophetic insight has been entirely justified. The dreadful experience of the First World War and its suffering came as the first great shock to the world of nineteenth-century bourgeois dominance and complacency. It could be described not only as a slaughter in God's name but as Europe's collective self-destruction, and for many the moral credibility of Christianity vanished. For a whole generation, it ended the optimism that had pervaded European life throughout the nineteenth century. Many believed that the horrific military encounters at the Somme and Passchendaele with their unspeakable suffering were battles which resembled Armageddon. Significantly, many Christians were now convinced that they were in the vanguard of a war that had apocalyptic undertones. In this connection, we must note the French television programme created by Isabelle Clarke and Daniel Costelle in 2014, entitled *Apocalypse, la première Guerre mondiale (Apocalypse, the First World War)*. With this war, an element of terror now entered conservative Protestantism in the United States. The monstrous events accompanying this and the Second World War seemed to confirm that the world and its sufferings were now meaningless as well as wretched, and the advances in technology had far surpassed mankind's psychological and moral development.[19] A crisis was looming within science itself, especially in mathematics, but between the profane sciences and faith, a truce was still barely detectible.[20] For many, Friedrich Nietzsche's analysis that self-destructive nihilism lurked at the heart of modern society, had been confirmed. Modern secular ideologies were proving to be as lethal as any religious bigotry.

The conflict made such a deep impact upon Western theological thought that inevitably there followed in the 1920s a serious reaction against Protestant liberalism, and the liberal, optimistic bourgeois way of life, which had been dominant during the previous century, and which had been assumed to be necessarily true. First on mainland Europe and later in Britain, such ideas were now considered to be fatally compromised by their over-optimistic views of human nature. The process of separation between the religious and the secular in the United States was virtually complete. Next, a series of shocks arose during the inter-war period which to some commentators were the source of moral paralysis, and profound and bitter disillusion. Also brought to light was the extent to which the churches were declining in importance. Two decades witnessed the growth of revolutionary movements on both extremes of the political spectrum, and which, inexorably, led to Nazi and Fascist parties and governments.

Knowledge splintered into increasingly specialized fields, each making mutually exclusive claims on its own behalf, with society incapable of choosing between them. The philosopher Martin Heidegger indicated that the relation between religion, morality and philosophy became the great intellectual problem of the age. The disciplines of sociology and psychology became progressively more separated from the religious context from which they had sprung. They staked their claims by challenging the erstwhile supreme status of religion, and proclaimed different and often conflicting values with the intention of eventually displacing religion altogether. But the trauma of both World Wars led to the understandable conclusion of many that, having once been betrayed, no field of knowledge could be respected or trusted any longer.[21]

The philosopher Julien Benda, in his work *La Trahison des Clercs (The Treason of the Intellectuals)* (1928), criticised modern intellectuals. An influential revolution had occurred in which the men of letters, or the 'clercs', promoted political and social ideologies which were often in defiance of reason. In the past, standards of truth, beauty and goodness, and the principles of humanity and of justice derived from them, had been on the whole observed and upheld. Such standards were opposed to the prevailing mood, which was based solely on the dictates of men's passions. As an example, Henri Bergson's philosophy had no sympathy with contemplative insight. In contrast, Benda defended the measured and dispassionate outlook of classical civilization, and the internationalism of traditional Christianity. For him, thanks to the traditional 'clercs', humanity may have done evil for two thousand years, but it honoured the good. The modern 'clercs' were now the advocates of realism.

The changing relationship between politics and morality reinforced Benda's conclusions. Plato had maintained that 'morality decided politics', and for Niccolò Machiavelli 'politics had nothing to do with morality'. Reversing Plato and disregarding Machiavelli, a third way now emerged: 'politics decide morality'. This was pure pragmatism, the preaching of nearly all the modern, influential European moralists. In twentieth-century Russia, Vladimir Lenin, the ultimate political manipulator, was to become a master of such pragmatism. The evil which served politics ceased to be evil and was now considered good. The practical in politics was the moral, and if what everyone else called 'moral' was opposed to the practical, it was immoral. With echoes of Henri Bergson, it seemed as if nothing more than an *élan vital* existed in the midst of men's tribulations.[22]

The Second World War has come to be regarded as linked to the Great War, in such a way that the two wars constituted one thirty-year conflict, separated only by a truce, the 1918 armistice. It could be maintained that together they represented to a large degree a European civil war, in which the protagonists were engaged in an orgy of self-destruction. The point, however, is to discover the real significance of this event. The wars certainly could be construed to be the result of Western hubris, which was exemplified by the writings of Ernst Troeltsch, François Guizot and Vladimir Soloviov that we examined earlier. Their effect, however, was to demote the West from its position of supremacy and dominance *vis-à-vis* the rest of the world, a stance which it had assumed in the nineteenth century. After 1945, the West's status now became one of *primus inter pares*. In the ensuing crises, the whole world would become increasingly inter-connected as the Apocalypse predicts, 'the four quarters of the earth' to quote Revelation 20:8.

The authority of the clergy declined, together with a diminishing knowledge of the Christian faith amongst Western people. Both Paul Tillich's theology with his 'anxiety of doubt', and philosophical existentialism were expressions of mourning for the death of the God of Western Christian civilization. After the Second World War, the very concept of God was problematic for philosophers and theologians alike. For Harvey Cox, however, the 'wake' has ended, and all that remains of the notion of God in the modern mind is a tepid inquisitiveness.[23]

The separation of church and state in 1905 presented the French church with major financial problems, but the challenge also had a revitalising effect. In the Netherlands, especially after 1917, and the Irish Free State after 1921, church and state were legally separated as much as they had been in France, but a mainly church-going electorate was able to vote into power political parties sympathetic to ecclesiastical interests. In the former country, education and a variety of social and cultural services were mainly provided by the churches or by other groups which had a distinct ideological basis, each of which received state funding. In England Christianity was still in the 1920s contested territory. The major changes around 1890 and ensuing developments up to the 1960s had virtually completed the process of secularization in the public sphere.

### The 1960s marked another historical 'Moment'

If the two periods around the years 1800 and 1890 had an important impact on the decline of the Christian faith, the years immediately after 1960 were also just as notable for representing another milestone. Callum Brown described the circumstances of the 1960s which were profound enough to change the character of the British people,[24] but, as we have seen, this decade was just the culmination of a process that had long been in the making. In a similar vein, some commentators alleged that the social position of the churches began to crumble only from the later 1950s, with the development of a rebellious and hedonistic youth culture, and a revolution in women's self-understanding. Whatever may be the case, since the 1960s the churches in most parts of Western Europe have suffered severe and continuing declines, and have increasingly lacked relevance to modern society. We have described how the movement towards the secularization of society had long been developing, but from this period onwards, the complete rejection of the Christian faith and its traditions quickly captured popular appeal. The most important theme in this decade concerned the relationship between Christianity and the laws relating to sex, marriage and the family. Britain was in the forefront of this movement with the laws on obscenity (1959), abortion (1967), and divorce (1969), legalisation of homosexual acts between consenting adults (1967), abolition of theatre censorship (1968), and the provision of contraceptives to unmarried couples through Britain's health service (1967). All these enactments were tantamount to a revolution. People turned their back on the churches' teaching that sex was morally right only within heterosexual marriage. There were similar moves to legalise divorce in Italy and Ireland, and abortion in France, Belgium and Italy.

The trend continued so that by the end of the twentieth century it became debatable whether Western society could any longer be considered Christian at all. There is no dearth of statistical evidence which portrays the story of this decline. Figures are readily available, and a whole litany of such would not be necessary in a book such as this. Whilst many Europeans, perhaps over half in some countries, still profess to be Christian, statistics in this instance are really too amorphous to be of any value. It might be more meaningful to separate out those who have disengaged completely from the Christian churches, whether they still profess Christianity or some belief in God or not. Further descriptions of this group are considered later. Amongst the group who still retain some relationship with the churches, statistics have been collated that report some kind of affiliation, namely entry on the church rolls, church attendance either regularly or occasionally, ordinations to the priesthood, percentage of Christian baptisms, confirmations and marriages in church. Statistics for all these areas have shown disastrous falls since the 1960s.

Figures for church attendance are notoriously unreliable, and the more so where self-reporting surveys are conducted. In most countries of Western Europe, regular church attendance was reported to be less than 10 per cent of the population, with a few exceptions such as Poland, Portugal, Malta and the republic of Ireland. In the Scandinavian countries, Russia and the Netherlands, the figure may be even lower than five per cent. In the United States, the figures may approach 20 to 30 per cent, whereas in the Africa and Latin American countries, the rate is much higher, and in China there is reported to be a growing number of people embracing the Christian faith. However, these figures may mask the fact that a substantial proportion of attendees or believers would be women, with the very rich and the very poor staying away. There would also be wide variations from region to region within each country. France would be a good example if one compares church attendance in the industrial areas and Paris, with the south west. In all these countries, Catholicism as much as Protestantism was affected. Even in the United States where church membership has been strong in the past – in the 1930s it was over 70 per cent – it is now reputed to have dropped to under 40 per cent. The decline in both religiosity and church attendance still continues. It would be reasonable to state from the evidence that people in the West had largely forsaken organized Christianity. For the first time since the conversion of the Roman Empire, the majority of people were growing up in almost complete ignorance of Christianity's basic doctrines.

In some Western European countries, links of one kind or another have been retained between church and state. In England and Sweden there were still state churches and in Belgium the state paid the salaries of the clergy. In English state schools, religious instruction is a legal requirement, and faith-based organisations are provided with funding to provide public services. In Italy the church-state treaty of 1984 contained very favourable terms for the Catholic Church.[25]

### Modernity, Modernism and Postmodernism

Almost impossible to describe, the movements known as modernity, modernism and postmodernism appear to many to be interchangeable, and a number of ways to describe them have been attempted. The situation is made more difficult on account of the wealth of textual and statistical data available, a host of commentators and commentaries, the complexity of the subject, its fragmentary nature, the difficulty in discovering a single principle which defines them, and the fact that these are uncompleted movements. This is not the place to attempt a thoroughgoing critique or explanation of them, but merely a brief summary of what they represent.

Modernity may be said to refer to the social order that emerged in the nineteenth century. As we have seen in chapter 5, the modern world is marked by its dynamism and restlessness, by its global ramifications, and by its scant regard for, or denial of, tradition, often made in contemptuous tones, a situation virtually unprecedented in history. For Max Weber, rationalization was the key factor, by which he meant that one can, in principle, master all things by technical means and calculation,[26] and this attitude would gradually prevail over more and more aspects of modern life. He feared that these features would eventually subdue the human spirit, enclosing it inside a bureaucratic iron cage.[27] The concept 'modernity' finally found its consummation after the Second World War when enormous scientific and technological developments were accompanied by a consumer boom. Secularization was indissolubly linked to this concept, and the word 'modern' itself took on a new meaning, with science and engineering leading the way.

The Enlightenment movement had encouraged European man to emancipate himself from the traditions of the Middle Ages, an era which had set limits to his freedom. Man, rather than God, became the focus around which everything else revolved. As a result, reason was promoted to a primacy above both tradition and revelation as the sole authority for thought and action, but reason, being only a means, was left without any spiritual or moral purpose. Ironically, the next step in this process has been the promotion of the self above reason, and such rebellion against rational thought is calling rationality itself into question. A new hedonism is emerging as part and parcel of this situation. Relativism flourishes in such a godless and disenchanted world where only subjective values are left. It could well transpire that rationalism will ultimately destroy itself or be destroyed, passing from the unlimited optimism of the Enlightenment to the unqualified scepticism of the present age. Max Weber in his book *Die Protestantische Ethik und der Geist des Kapitalismus (The Protestant Ethic and the Spirit of Capitalism)* (1904) argued that the Protestant work ethic was an important factor behind the emergence of modern capitalism, and that Puritan ethics and ideas influenced its development. Although the thesis has been modified several times since, the sociologist Daniel Bell nevertheless made the insightful comment that by jettisoning this ethic and its relation, Puritanism, and replacing it with a materialistic hedonism, the moral basis that underpinned capitalism has been destroyed.[28]

It is one of the features of modernity that it produces a multitude of diverse intellectual movements, a situation in which the intelligentsia formulate their own specialist languages. Jürgen Habermas and Seyla Ben-Habib, stated a similar case when they wrote that everyday life has effectively been split off, or divorced, from these movements, and laypeople are no longer able to understand or participate in areas of expertise that have a crucial effect on their lives.[29] George Steiner in the same vein stated that until about a century and a half ago, even the most radical of sceptics remained committed to a language which could be intelligible to most of the population, and this represented a kind of covenant between word and world, which was, however, broken from the late nineteenth century onwards. For him this development became one of defining hallmarks of modernity.[30] The story of the tower of Babel is duplicated perfectly in this situation, because each person speaks a language unrelated to that of any other person, and the only outcome must be a fragmented society.

The widely-heralded information revolution, which began in the 1960s, is considered to have given modernity a new lease of life. It was ever the belief of the supporters of modernism that ultimately knowledge would change the world completely and for the better, but this position has been abandoned in favour of a postmodern society. Its protagonists, the deconstructionists, go so far as to denounce modernity itself.[31] Some of the attributes which are claimed to lurk at the heart of modern life include futility, desperation, ephemerality. They all lead to a nihilism, which was presaged by Friedrich Nietzche so aptly and tragically decades earlier, and this proposition is restated by Daniel Bell to be the culmination of rationalism.[32]

What bearing does all the foregoing analysis have on the title to this chapter? The reader must be patient, whilst we cross just one further frontier. The longing for freedom, for example, has led to, and heightened, the conflict between the permissive society and Christian ethics. Modern social theorists have coined a name for this movement: they call it 'pluralism', reflected in the extreme diversity of belief and opinion in postmodern society.

### Pluralism best describes the Ethos of Western Society

If we had to describe the ethos of Western society in the twenty-first century in one word, the term 'pluralism' would be an even more appropriate epithet. As with modernism or postmodernism, pluralism is difficult to describe with any clarity. It has been said that it is the child of secularization. A pluralist society is one where a confusing host of differing life-styles, belief systems, and values are adopted and become acceptable. Consequently, the options within the private sphere expand, particularly but not exclusively so far as belief and ideology are concerned. Such freedom entails that religious choices, for example, can be configured to suit individual tastes. Unrestricted freedom of choice develops into a mentality as much as a situation,[33] and the result is often just change for its own sake. Since choice reigns supreme, hesitation, anxiety and doubt seem to be the price paid for that freedom. Jean-Paul Sartre believed that in every decision a person stands alone. Because there are no moral absolutes, there are no value-associated reasons to make one decision over another. Rules are no longer laid down by usage, custom or authority, and this reflects society's unwillingness to enforce any particular world-view on its citizens. Not only does it lead to extreme diversity but all tradition dissolves into a melting-pot, in which only functional relationships flourish, and consensual agreement vanishes.[34]

It could be claimed that this movement originated in Cartesian philosophical reasoning, for René Descartes' famous postulate, *cogito ergo sum*, led to a complete transformation in philosophic thought. If what each person claims to 'know' differs or even contradicts what other people claim to 'know', sooner or later inevitably the objectivity of knowledge becomes questionable. Descartes himself did not realize that such an outcome would occur, but that is exactly what has happened.[35] Jean-Jacques Rousseau and John Stuart Mill, the latter in his work *On Liberty* (1859) argued for the right of every man to freedom of expression with the aim of achieving liberation from the yoke of traditional authority. Historians have always maintained that the Wars of Religion in the seventeenth century released just this potential for pluralism. The practical situation was such that with the passing of time it resulted in an acceptance of religious diversity,[36] and this was one of the most significant turning-points in Europe's religious history. Modern pluralism, however, really had its origins in the religious situation at the end of the nineteenth century, another aspect of the 1890 'divide'. As the pressures towards religious conformity weakened, an increasing number and variety of worldviews emerged, so that personal choice now prevailed. Early in the twentieth century, Ernst Troeltsch was already recognizing this development in the feeling and thinking of modern man, a situation which was now concentrated on the individual, not the collectivity.[37]

Pluralism considered philosophically not only deprecates all objective truths but casts doubt on the possibility of ascertaining any objective truths whatsoever. Having disallowed all truth-claims, it locates meaning in the person who interprets, not in the text or object being interpreted.[38] The number of possible meanings therefore equates to the number of interpreters. For example, if someone claimed the authority to define how a work of literature ought to be understood, this would be viewed with suspicion, because such a claim denies the opportunity for others to exercise their own creativity.[39] Such an idea contains within it the potential to invalidate any attempt at interpreting biblical texts, for example, even by church authorities or the academic community. The diversity which results is pluralism's hallmark and is intrinsically intertwined with postmodernism.

In art, the prevailing tendency for Western societies to abandon their traditions is not the result of technical incompetence; it is a deliberate decision by the modern generation. As Arnold Toynbee stated, the abandonment of the West's traditional artistic technique is manifestly the consequence of some kind of spiritual breakdown in Western civilization.[40] If the most urgent task for historians is not for more detailed research but for a new master narrative to replace secularization, in the twenty-first century, it might seem that pluralism could provide it.

Pluralism is inimical to religion not solely by virtue of its link with secularization, but also, more importantly, because it is yet one more instrument in helping to destroy the monopoly and hegemony which the Christian religion enjoyed in past centuries. Since Western society has now turned its back on any or all absolute claims to truth, Christian belief and dogma are especially affected. Christianity is now experiencing a phenomenon which it has not encountered for over a thousand years, namely, the almost irreversible and significant proliferation of a variety of alternative belief systems, religious and non-religious, all of which are in competition with each other. Religion is now only one facet of life amongst many others, and for many it is of minimal or no importance. Any notion that a particular ideological or religious claim is superior to any other is considered to be misplaced. Once again, Ernst Troeltsch drew attention to the endless fragmentation of religious individuality leading to what he called the volatilization *(die Verflüchtigung)* or evaporation of any common cultus.[41] All absolutes, religious, moral or otherwise, have come to be distrusted, a legacy of the totalitarian regimes of the 1930s.

Religion has increasingly withdrawn into the private dimensions of personal life, and has become more a matter of free personal choice, thereby relegating religion to the realm of individual psychology. In the private world of the family, religious observance nevertheless has remained stubbornly beyond the secular net. Religion is therefore to be found only within the consciousness of the individual rather than being a part of the external, social world. Religion has lost its public, inter-subjective character in the process. Peter Berger commented that insofar as religion is a shared phenomenon it has no substance. It acts merely as a veneer for the body politic and public. On the occasions that it does have substance, it lacks the attribute of such sharing.[42] In this latter instance, religious beliefs remain confined within the mind of the believer, and any common intercourse is excluded. This runs counter to the traditional task of religion which was to serve as a standard universe of meaning. As the plausibility of the faith disintegrates, religious content can be maintained only in consciousness as opinions or feelings, and this recalls the thought of Friedrich Schleiermacher. Pluralism is a worldview that claims that the individual is its own god, a theme reminiscent of Kant's 'god-man', a stance which is not only non-Christian, but it engenders a relativism and worldliness, in which disbelief becomes engrained in society. Conspiracy theories abound as people become suspicious of authority and institutions. What results is the lack of any force or set of beliefs that can hold society together.

Pluralism does not entail the absence of all religious belief or the complete elimination of Christianity. Despite predictions to the contrary, Western society has fallen short of turning into a completely secularized one.[43] Rather, in a pluralistic situation Christian belief is still able to maintain a presence, but as only one amongst many aspects of belief, of half-belief, of agnosticism, or of unbelief. In the face of the many commentators who predicted the gradual disappearance of religion from the public domain, religious faith has persisted in many forms, for the Christian churches did not sit idly by when faced with this situation. They responded to the challenge, sometimes successfully, so that the religious and the secular co-existed side by side, thereby paradoxically strengthening the pluralistic situation. As religious controls were gradually lifted, an increasingly wide range of possibilities revealed themselves, including many alternative varieties of Christianity itself. Worldwide, Christianity has changed beyond recognition. Many thousands of separate denominations have been recorded, 34,000 being one figure that has been quoted. That phenomenon is in itself a reflection of modern pluralistic tendencies.

It has been said that truth is the first casualty of war, and in like manner ethics is the first casualty of pluralism, being sacrificed on the altar of an individualism which is entailed by pluralism. The triumphs of reason and science have destroyed not only religion but morality, not only tradition but human bonds. Post-Enlightenment attempts to reconstruct morality have led also to multifarious attempts to achieve compromises between traditional Christian morality and new conditions and values, but there is now very little consensus left in

Western countries over the proper basis of moral behaviour. Once again, there have been countless innovations, which often lead to moral scepticism.[44] We can trace the downward trend of Christian ethics through successive generations, and two very different theologians, Hans Küng and William Barclay, have made similar comments. In the immediate post-Enlightenment society, the doctrines of Christianity were still accepted by many people, but later in the nineteenth century, they were told that these doctrines were false, and so they abandoned them. However, they continued to believe in the traditional faith out of personal conviction. The succeeding generation rejected, or more probably ignored the faith and let it wither, but they continued to uphold Christian moral principles. After another couple of generations, these principles too fell by the wayside, leaving the moral vacuum that we are experiencing today. The modern world makes it difficult to transmit Christian faith successfully from generation to generation, and so in a word, not only has the theology been abandoned, but the ethic also.[45]

Ironically while it was claimed that modern society liberates individuals to pursue more diverse ends, individuals have become enslaved instead to technique and technology, a situation that recalls Max Weber's perceptive predictions. The novelty of the situation consists not only in the fact that the precepts of Christian morality are being widely ignored, but even more that alternative principles are being openly advocated. We have come a long way from Immanuel Kant's dictum that the free will was endowed with universal rational certainty and spiritual authority. The ensuing moral crisis may indeed be creating the very conditions which would assist in leading to modernity's and postmodernity's own demise. The biblical scholar Donald Carson wondered how long the pluralistic culture can survive.[46] Moreover, it is doubtful whether the protagonists of these movements themselves have any aims in mind except to deprecate objective truth itself.

### Alternatives to traditional Christian Belief

Alternatives to the Christian faith have accompanied these generational shifts in the form of apathy, agnosticism, or opposition to religion, and would even include wide variations in Christian belief itself. Social-survey data seem to confirm not only a decline in personal piety, private and daily prayer for instance, but also a fall in the proportion of those who believe in the basic tenets of Christianity, such as the existence of

God, and of heaven and hell. A majority of respondents in a Swedish survey, for example, chose to describe themselves as 'Christians in their own personal way'.[47] The understanding of the Christian religion now corresponds with everyone's own individualized version of it. Even as early as the commencement of the twentieth century, Ernst Troeltsch took note of this trend, by asking: "What is this religion that is dissimilar to the churches, but maintains itself outside, alongside and above them? Such does indeed exist, but there is in it absolutely nothing that has originality for religion, no new religious idea to inspire or launch a new movement. In it the most motley tendencies and inclinations meet with one another. Sometimes it is merely an internalised Christianity, somehow linked with the modern world of ideas, which cannot any longer join company with the historic churches."[48] From Matthew 24:11 we learn that Christ Himself had warned his disciples "And many false prophets will arise and lead many astray."

Any alternative to belief in God and the traditional Christian faith does not necessarily entail a belief in a rationalism based upon science. There are many who reject this as well as orthodox Christianity, and are searching for a view of the world which would be spiritual but without submission to any formal creed. The origins of this viewpoint lay in the compulsion for many to privatize their religion so that belief systems are fabricated to suit their own particular requirements. As a consequence, religion for them consists of an eclectic mixture of old and new ideas, often randomly fused together, or an attempt to reconcile various religious elements from all over the world, perhaps inspired by studies in comparative religion. The syncretism that results reflects a pluralistic outlook, and secular ideas and parallel beliefs might also participate in these selections. In Protestant thinking, it was never envisaged that the individual would determine Christian truth in this way. It brings to mind Thomas Paine's view that: "My own mind is my own church," or Thomas Jefferson's: "I am of a sect by myself, as far as I know."[49] There is not an absence of religion but, rather, the triumph of the religion of relativity.

The world may equally be interpreted by means of astrology, magic, occultism, demonology, spiritualism, telepathy, near death experiences or simply luck and so on, and attitudes may even revive primitive religion, but all kinds of proverbial wisdom can serve the same end, and have experienced a worldwide success. For others, a kind of religion based upon art may suffice.[50] Yet another element is a hedonic consumerism, entailing a crude search for self-realization through private possessions and sensationalism.[51] The notion of what constitutes truth may have little or nothing to do with this hotchpotch of ideas, but it is highly likely that there will be contempt for the churches if they do not share, or approve of, these private interpretations. It seems as if John's countless hosts have their parallel in the modern variations of all these particular themes. Jean-Paul Sartre, as the modern exponent of Friedrich Nietzsche's, 'will-to-power', has described the human project as a matter of self-reflection and choice, for which the individual must be responsible, and as a consequence must fathom his own ultimate solutions, but the price that has to be paid is the abandonment of what rendered traditional religion indispensable. This results in what Donald Carson has called 'triumphant secularism'.[52]

Once scientists were able to furnish explanations about the universe that implied that the concept of God was unnecessary, atheism was able to flourish in western intellectual circles. If all knowledge was made known by empirical means which had to be based upon observation, it implied that any ideas of God were superfluous. We have seen in chapter 8 that this growth of atheism was a logical extension of Enlightenment ideas which proceeded from rationalism through naturalism to materialism. As Friedrich Nietzsche had predicted, the idea of God simply withered away for many people. A form of secular fundamentalism has recently developed in the West that in style and strategy bears similarities to atheism, but these later 'new atheists' abandoned the agnostic restraint of Charles Darwin and Thomas Huxley and preached a more militant form. They are extreme exponents of the scientific naturalism, originally formulated by Paul d'Holbach, and it has now become a major world-view among intellectuals. In 1970, the French biochemist, Jacques Monod, in his work *Hasard et la Nécessité (Chance and Necessity)*, argued for the absolute incompatibility of theism and revolutionary theory. For these commentators, especially Richard Dawkins, humanity would be better off without religion or belief in God for such are the root of all evil.

In a society when the doubting attitude of modern man even turns against reason itself, we have reached the point where we live in a vacuum, the state of nothingness or nihilism, predicted so starkly in

Friedrich Nietzsche's writings. According to Karl Jaspers this is the result of a development which has led to a disenchanted world.[53] Marquis de Sade's philosophy was the legitimate outcome of such nihilism, with the denial of any ground of ultimate being. Jürgen Habermas put the matter another way. He stated that the Enlightenment movement by attacking religion, together with the advance of science with its critical methods, has resulted in indifference.[54] This movement, once claimed as a liberating force, contributes to the slide downwards towards the abyss. Modern writers have recognized that the only secure thing about modernity is its insecurity, its penchant, even, for creating chaos.

### The demonic Nature of modern Society

The expulsion of God from public consciousness and debate did not result in freedom, but led to something that many commentators have labelled demonic. For example, Daniel Bell, in describing the postmodern antipathy to rationalism, maintained that, whereas in the past religion had attempted to control the demonic aspect of man's existence, modern creativity, as a facet of secular culture, is often fuelled by an investigation, an acceptance and even an indulgence, of the demonic.[55] Furthermore, nihilism itself may entail a demonic rebellion against everything which God would forbid.[56] In a pluralist society, the assertion of the rights of the many has actually achieved the opposite, the subversion of the many by alternative means, in which the powers of evil become transformations of the good. Commentators have alluded to the demonic nature of modernity and postmodernity, in which modern conventional wisdom, the powers of modern political ideologies, the market, and so on, come to be accepted as the truth. But as travesties of the truth, the next step onwards from postmodernity may prove to be calamitous.[57] By casting out what many considered to be the 'devil' of traditional religion to promote secularism, this may well invite in a host of new demons worse than the first.[58] The absence of good creates a vacuum which evil likes nothing better. Since the French Revolution, it would seem that Satan and his cohorts have made great progress.

The reader may still be wondering how this description of the forces of Satan might fit the modern and postmodern situation. At the very least, we can infer that Satan's stratagem entailed a challenge to the truth of the Christian Gospel and so destroy, or at least neutralize, its influence in people's hearts and minds. As we have witnessed in the previous chapter, the encouragement of apostasy from the faith led to the denial of a divinely ordained spiritual realm. The pluralist situation prevailing in the West, therefore, could have been impelled, or at least encouraged, by demonic forces.

The hosts of Satan might well prove to be invincible, for deviation from, or denial of, the Christian faith takes many forms. The modern world possesses a consistent aversion to the Christian consciousness of sin. For this reason, perhaps, Carl Jung considered that modern society's readiness to dismiss the Devil was evidence of modern society's superficiality and how unwilling it was to confront the realities of evil.[59] In the interwar years, the growth of materialism, economic greed, war and weapons technology seemed to some of the participants of the Catholic renaissance in France, such as Georges Bernanos, Paul Claudel, François Mauriac and Charles Péguy, to believe that power was becoming increasingly concentrated in evil hands. All those subscribing to the postmodernist agenda have made it clear that their prime enemy is the Judaeo-Christian tradition of metaphysics, which must be destroyed once and for all.

Most social scientists do not think of secularization as necessarily contributing towards the abolition of religion, but in many instances the introduction of legislation, both statute law and case law, issuing from secular governments, and dealing with equality and diversity, are being used as a weapon to attack those of the Christian faith rather than a means to protect them.[60] Legal rulings reflect this state of affairs, for they often show a trend of increasing intolerance of Christian moral values. In short, those people who hold the Christians faith and its morality are being increasingly silenced. As an additional taunt, satire becomes the Devil's tool to construct an irreverent pastiche towards cultural traditions, in which Christianity itself is ridiculed and derided. It was François Voltaire who, by employing irony, exaggeration, and ridicule, could be said to have set this process in motion. In his work *Candide*, he depicted organized religion, and its protagonists, the clergy, as corrupt, fanatical and intolerant, and by so doing, he undermined and trivialized the vitality of the Christian faith, Christian values and devotion.

We have arrived at a pluralistic situation that is characteristic of postmodernity by way of apostasy, secularization, modernism and relativism, all of which are related, and all eventually seem to reduce to the same end result. We are now able to understand how the foregoing relates to the topic of this chapter. What is the importance of pluralism for our understanding of John of Patmos' prophecy for the modern era?

### The Significance of Gog and Magog

'Gog' and 'Magog' refer to names which occur in chapters 38 and 39 of the Old Testament book of Ezekiel, the former referring to a prince who opposed Israel's God, and the latter to the land in which he lived. Ezekiel was instructed by God himself to denounce these enemies and to forecast their overthrow. In later Jewish apocalyptic writings, Gog and Magog were portrayed as two leaders who often symbolized the forces of evil. The two names occur once again in John's narrative at Revelation 20:8. Many exegetes agree that, whilst the citations in both the Old Testament and in the Apocalypse bear the same nomenclature, they do not refer to the same people and events. It is simply the case that for his own narrative John has borrowed this appellation from the Old Testament. His intention no doubt was to create imagery in which many people in the course of time would come to rebel against God in a similar manner to those prophecies in Ezekiel which tell of a final assault against truth. Many scholars believe that this situation might occur at some point before the Day of Judgment, and in close proximity to it. Those who do disobey God and apostatize from the faith when the thousand years have come to an end, will be numbered amongst the hosts called Gog and Magog.

A possible misconception may arise in connection with the name 'Gog', namely that it alludes to Satan himself, but Revelation 20:8 is quite clear on this point. The name cannot refer to Satan since Satan can hardly mislead Gog if he himself is Gog.[61] Revelation 20:8 states that Satan "will be loosed from his prison and will come out to deceive the nations which are at the four quarters of the earth, that is, Gog and Magog, to gather them for battle; their number is like the sand of the sea." Significantly for the present thesis, this expression as mentioned in John's narrative, seems to imply that the armies of the evil one will be so very large that it will be fatuous and impossible to count them. Here is a situation where the final deception will be implemented by Satan with the assistance of his various agents, who have the collective names of

Gog and Magog, who become the instruments of Satan's will, and who will be divinely allowed to be at Satan's disposal for this task. Leon Morris stated that John is depicting the last great attack of evil on the things of God. Satan will assemble the greatest possible force to oppose God.[62] In John's vision, therefore, he has borrowed the names Gog and Magog in order to describe the hosts of the wicked, the evil enemies, which will assail and lay siege to the people of God in the last times. It would, however, be quite wrong to infer that modern men and women are the embodiment of Satan himself. It is rather the case, as countless as the grains of sand of the sea, they are the personification of Gog and Magog, who would seem to be impelled or influenced by forces that are either evil or have been distanced from God.

Vladimir Soloviov and Carl Jung were perhaps the last major thinkers who were convinced that the problem of evil necessarily involved the figure of the Antichrist. For Soloviov in his later years, in a world in which a religious culture was vanishing, there was an anguished sense of the onset of the kingdom of the Antichrist.[63] He painted a vision of a great crisis that would strike Christianity at the end of the twentieth century, and once again his accuracy was astonishing. For Jung, Antichrist was more than just a prophecy, it was 'an inexorable psychological law'.[64] We may perhaps compare this statement with Kant's idea of the 'Radical Evil'. Tyranny is only one aspect of this situation, for the most notable feature of evil has been one of deception, of falsehoods that pervert the good. Indeed, in the modern era, deceit or disinformation has reached greater and more sophisticated levels assisted by modern methods of communication.[65]

Some commentators think that the modern refusal to accept the reality of the Devil is a cause as well as a symptom of impending destruction. With the enormous collective forces of modern societies, where responsibility has become trapped in bureaucratic systems, a lack of any individual responsibility whatsoever prevails. In such circumstances, any trace of conscience has vanished. God, or the Christian element of Grace, has been entirely expunged from the equation, whether political, social or administrative. The Devil rather than God becomes the major element in the process, and so we are being led towards the abyss. It would be apposite to recall at this point Friedrich Nietzsche's analysis from his work *Der Wille zur Macht (The Will to Power)* (1888), "What is coming over the next two centuries, what can no longer come otherwise is *the advent of nihilism* (Nietzsche's italics)…the whole of our European culture has long been moving as if heading for a catastrophe: restless, violent, impetuous: akin to a river that no longer contemplates…that is afraid to contemplate."[66]

John's narrative continues in Revelation 20:9: "And they marched up over the broad earth and surrounded the camp of the saints and the beloved city'" in order to lay siege to God's people. This siege mentality, or something akin to it, has already been mentioned at several places. We encountered earlier the French Catholics' reaction against the incursions of the French state at the turn of the twentieth century as a minority group with a sense of being under siege. There were some areas where churchgoers were subjected to ridicule. For Elaine Graham, evangelicalism has pursued a discourse of traditional values under siege.[67] For Charles Colson and Ellen Santilli Vaughn, postmodernity represents a 'new barbarism' and is a clear indication of a culture, or indeed a society, undergoing a siege.[68] It is possible that the churches might become camps of believers in an unbelieving world from which they have become isolated, closed siege-societies, relying on the authority of Scripture, a prospect which would seem more likely to occur in the multifarious Protestant churches than in the Roman Catholic Church. Those who persist in viewing the world through the prism of their religious beliefs eventually find themselves in a minority.[69] Owen Chadwick, too, put into words this somewhat siege-like feeling, when he stated that the defenders of Christian orthodoxy tended to withdraw behind their ramparts. Intelligent people felt repelled by this devotional siege which served only to widen the sense of breach.[70]

Some exegetes have remarked that the phrase 'nations which are at the four quarters of the earth' is an intriguing one. From what has been said in earlier chapters, there should be no problem in providing an explanation. As to the mention of nations, John seems to be making an implied, but definite, contrast between this phrase and Revelation 20:3, which states that Satan shall deceive the nations no more during the thousand years. In that instance, he is referring just to nations, *some* nations, not *all* nations. But now the assault on the people of God will be global.

\* \* \* \* \* \* \* \*

A severe decline in church-going was bound to have an effect on religious belief, but it raised the question as to whether absence from church attendance was indeed the cause of unbelief, or did the opposite apply? Whichever is the case, since the 1960s, the churches have become increasingly irrelevant as a social force and it poses the question, therefore, what is left of Christian faith and ethics in Western Europe in the twenty-first century. Daily life in western societies is typically unaffected and unconcerned by any connection with religion, for contemporary culture treats Christianity as a phenomenon of the past. Yet other commentators have suggested that, if events continue in the same way as they have over the past two centuries, the status of the Christian church in relation to modern society could eventually resemble that of the early church in the Roman Empire during the first century.

The situation is a little different in the United States, where the churches still occupy a more central position, but it may be argued that they have succeeded in keeping this position only by becoming highly secularized,[71] whereas in Europe the demarcation between the secular and the religious is inclined to be better defined. The writer Will Herberg commented that the paradox in America's case is that she appears to be the most religious and yet the most secular of societies. He added that the distinction between religion and secularism in American society has become so blurred because religion itself has become expurgated of any dogmatic content, with the result that a person's religious commitment hardly matters.[72]

As a result of its struggle with the church, the secular modern state became fully cognizant of its authority which gave it sovereign power. From the standpoint of its legislative and administrative functions this may be correct. However, from another angle this is not so, for it cannot promote, recommend or intrude into, spiritual, religious or supernatural matters, and Edward Norman is of the opinion that the authority of the state appears to promote, in effect, a kind of undefined humanism.[73] Those who seek a Christian brotherhood of humanity and of a world-church, would consider this mind-set to cloak a new heathenism.[74]

Modern man participates in a society and a period in history, which can be referred to as Faustian because of his quest for power, as a wish to organize the world and recast it in form and substance to suit his own spirit. At its core, the new Faustian age believes in the self and the self's right and ability to control the conditions of its own existence. This unconditioned life was something different from enjoying rights and decent treatment from one's fellow citizens. It is to act as if nothing must stand in the way of every wish. Such an attitude expects and tolerates no rebuffs. The Faustian mind-set exalts reason, but it is practical or instrumental reason, which is seen as a tool that humanity can employ to manipulate the world. The creations of popular entertainment have foreseen the emergence of Faustian societies, for they continually portray humanity as gaining power over both the material world and the world of appearances. Materialism has increasingly taken the place of Christianity as the underlying world view of the peoples of Western society. For Oswald Spengler, the blame must lie with finance, which had shed every trace of feeling for earth-bound immovable values, with scientific criticism for omitting every residue of piety,[75] and with Immanuel Kant, as Jean-Jacques Rousseau's pupil, for shutting out every scrap of compassion from his ethic. Iris Murdoch, in her book *The Sovereignty of Good* (1970), offered a vigorous indictment of the modern conception of autonomy, and the contrast between such autonomy and reason. Copyright restrictions prevent her text from being quoted, but in a word, she attributed it to Kant, comparing Kant's own portrayal of the human condition to the unfettered, self-reliant modern character which had already been portrayed earlier so deftly by John Milton and which so resembles modern man. That character is called by the appropriate name of Lucifer.[76] The Faustian centuries-old folk legend still resonates in times of crisis, and it continues to haunt the Western imagination.

# EPILOGUE

## Prophecies fulfilled

"Those who cannot remember the past are condemned to repeat it."
*George Santayana*

OUR SURVEY of the Apocalypse or Book of Revelation, from chapter 17 through to chapter 20, has attempted to demonstrate that the prophecies that derived from the dreams and visions of its author, John of Patmos, have been substantially fulfilled during the course of Western history. In so doing, we have remarked upon the significance of the teaching, praxis and culture of Christian 'life and rule' which underlay this history. The Christian epoch had wrought a transformation in Western man from the Dark Ages until the Enlightenment, or has the 'revolution' or the wheel of history turned full circle, and are we now heading for another Dark Age?

At the end of the thousand years, around the year 1800, a significant and important shift or discontinuity, occurred in Western history. From that time onwards, the emergent metropolises of the modern world dispensed with the erstwhile traditions of the West. Giambattista Vico could depict the life of the metropolis as producing men who are unbelievers, who regard money as the measure of all things, and who lack moral qualities. It betokened the reappearance of the Roman world's *panem et circenses*, the obsession with economics and sport. The opening of a new phase, or it could be considered a reprise, of human existence pointed to the decline of Western culture. The theologian William Barclay also noted the similarity with ancient Rome, a world in which abject poverty and the grossest kind of wealth existed side by side.[1] The ideas of the eighteenth-century *philosophes* had proved fruitless because the toleration achieved by the Enlightenment was one which was not based upon Christian virtues. Many have ventured the question whether we might now indeed be encountering the dissolution of Western society comparable to that which ushered in the downfall of the ancient Hellenic world.

In his thought-provoking work, Oswald Spengler announced the end of European culture around the year 1800 at the point when he considered that it had crossed over into civilization. This signified for him the beginning of the death process and the plunge into the abyss, the fate of the Western Faustian soul in the legend of that name. As an alternative, or rather as a correction to Spengler, we have described a somewhat different interpretation, namely, the way in which the Christian West declined as a result of apostasy after the thousand years had passed, an apostasy which spread in gradual and multifarious steps amongst Western peoples, leading to a through-going secularization of society. If men such as Henry Drummond are to be believed, this apostatic movement and its consequences were the work of satanic forces. The claim is made that this represented precisely the prophecy contained in chapter 20 of John's Apocalypse. Such a breach in European history was a great deal more fundamental than just failing churches, for we are still experiencing the subordination of religion to politics which was the error of our sixteenth- and seventeenth-century forbears. Max Weber stated that officials have distrusted the competing priestly corporation of grace and, above all, have despised that quest for impractical values which lay beyond utilitarian and worldly ends. Political bureaucracies have regarded what remains of religious duties as merely social and peripheral obligations.[2] What emerges is a story not just of church decline, but of the potential end of Christianity itself as a means by which men and women, as individuals, construct their identities and their sense of self.

Questions will undoubtedly form in the reader's mind. In the first instance we must ask whether the narrative from the foregoing chapters has succeeded in proving that John's prophecies and the events in the history of the West bear any resemblance to each other. In a provocative and intriguing encounter with John's text, many of his passages appear to substantiate the theory, but in our critical age there will be those who remain sceptical, and the evidence presented here would still be insufficient to convince them that these prophecies do relate to actual historical events. They will reject the similarities, in which case no further comment will be necessary. However, to such sceptics and doubters, we must assign them the task of rewriting the history of the West in conformity with their own individual inclinations, that is to say, to examine the curriculum of Western European history in some other way that makes sense. For everyone else, one can only settle these matters by asking the reader, as Blaise Pascal once asked, to ponder over them for himself or herself.

A second question concerns the idea of Providence in history. Leopold von Ranke and Johann Gottfried von Herder called attention to something in history which they said remained over, when all was said and done, as subtle, unexplained, mysterious. To them, it felt as though a super-sensible power manifested itself through the deeds and lives of men in the midst of the flow of events. Was Providence the 'something' of which Ranke and Herder were vaguely conscious? Both Giambattista Vico and François Guizot believed that history has been guided by divine Providence, and still others hold the belief or suspicion that God does intervene in history, at least in some way, to achieve His purposes. The historians' arguments can be reworked to show that God intervenes in history, so that attitudes, purposes and forces are never completely man-made, and events are often not the result of men's conscious intentions.[3] Immanuel Kant used the term 'Providence' to mean the trajectory of mankind towards its moral destiny, but, as we have noted, we cannot be sure that he believed in the existence of a divine providential order which was guiding human moral efforts towards an harmonious final outcome. Was there, for him, only an imminent, impersonal dynamic of history?[4] By means of philosophical reasoning, he demolished the three traditional proofs for the existence of God, but he did not avail himself of philosophical reasoning positively to *disprove* His existence, leaving the matter open in the future to prove via a different route that there is indeed a God. If it is indeed divine Providence that governs history, when historians attempt to describe the process by which man has developed through the ages, they were discerning to a certain extent the plan which God has for mankind.

A philosophy of history became possible only with the advent of Christianity and it revealed a culture which implied an historical fate determined by God himself. Until the eighteenth century, it had been assumed that Christianity had succeeded because it was the one true religion. It would not therefore be at all surprising that the only apocalypse to be incorporated in the Christian canon should eventually prove to be one that concerns history.

If there is a lingering feeling that John's prophecies and Western history do proceed in some way in parallel alongside each other, the reader will be confronted with the next important questions. Whence did John of Patmos obtain his prophecies, and how do we explain this convergence between his prophecy and subsequent historical events? In seeking an answer, it would be utterly foolish and unreasonable to aver that an unknown, itinerant, Christian preacher, living in the first century, plucked his predictions out of thin air *ex nihilo* and, without aid, was able to foresee events that were to take place up to two thousand years into the future. For the sceptics and the unbelievers, we must challenge them for an appropriate answer. If they still arrive at the conclusion that John's book contains nothing of any value, then they should treat this present book according to David Hume's famous exhortation: "Commit it then to the flames: for it can contain nothing but sophistry and illusion."[5]

The word 'apocalypse' means uncovering or disclosure, but in modern parlance it has also acquired a meaning resembling catastrophe, an event or events involving destruction or damage on a disastrous scale. The results which will accompany these events might just be comparable to the decline and fall of the ancient world.[6] After the decline, or rather dismemberment, of the Roman Empire, its Western portion moved into the winter of the so-called 'Dark Ages', in which barbarism triumphed, with the barbarians' successor kingdoms positioned between the ancient, classical world of Rome and its successor, the Christian kingdom of the Franks. During this stage of history, barbarism was neither pleasant nor picturesque. It has been remarked that the next 'Dark Age' which will follow the demise of Western civilization could be worse than the one that preceded it. The predominant features of contemporary life that we call science and technology, with its immense benefits and threats, and the rise of those aspects of culture which set themselves in direct opposition to revealed Christianity, underlie the apparent fragmentation, even dissolution, that threatens late modern society. It is the weakening of the feeling of awe, of piety, of religious authority that spells the doom of the entire social texture which could well lead to a second barbarism.

If it be accepted that John's prophecies appear to have been justified by the history which followed, it would not be surprising that for many, the most urgent question would be, what will happen next both for ourselves and for our planet. We cannot and should not predict the future outcome of the secular West, the more so as we may be approaching the end of history as we know it. This is a view similar to that adopted by the French-American philosopher René Girard who contended that it is modernity that marks the end of history. To prophesy in these circumstances would be *de trop*. We can speak only in general terms, but it does seem that some kind of discontinuity, even metamorphosis, is possible, though historians would not accept its inevitability.

To elaborate further, a final cataclysm may not occur, but rather a continuous series of catastrophes, leading to a profound sense of attrition, and attrition is a movement that has many historical antecedents. Modern commentators have obliged by attempting forecasts, and many of these, pessimistic as they are, emanate from various official or private planning organizations, or from journalists. They are in reality apocalypses themselves, albeit of a secularized nature. Sometimes it is only by violent upheavals that man can extricate himself from the pernicious situation which is of his own making and which he has taken so much effort to construct.[7]

In the eighteenth century our knowledge was translated into a kind of Faustian power over the physical world. The rejection both of God, of the supernatural, and of objective morality has culminated in the curtailment or denial of human dignity. In the resolute pursuit of reason, it appears paradoxically to lead to the victory of the irrational. If Friedrich Nietzsche is right, the overthrow of the old religious and moral standards and limitations would leave nothing remaining over to replace them.

Johann Wolfgang von Goethe wrote: "Mankind will become cleverer and more percipient, but not better or happier nor more energetic. I foresee the day when God will no longer take delight in his creatures, and will once again have to annihilate the world and make a fresh start." In a similar vein, the German author Thomas Mann, depressed by the decline of European civilization and its cultural crisis, came to condemn not only what he saw as the Faustian drive of twentieth-century Western society, but also Nazi Germany's arrogance, barbarism and destruction, witnessed prior to and during the Second World War. He too likened this situation to a pact with the Devil. His book *Doktor*

*Faustus*, written between 1943 and 1947, represented a modern reworking of the Faustian legend. In it, he reiterated the original myth's pessimism, wherein Faust was finally damned. He sensed the satanic character of all ideology, and this is reflected in a force which exerted an influence over the events which were occurring contemporaneously as he wrote.

A society that is held together solely by the compliance with regulation is inherently fragile. The process will lend itself to further abuses which will be met by a yet further expansion of regulation. This situation reflects a deeper crisis; one that is moral.[8] The politician Philip Noel-Baker once remarked that one could not continue adding to the statute book *ad infinitum* by legislating for every possible moral circumstance. According to Carl Jung, it is of the greatest importance as to whether man can climb up to a higher moral level and a higher plane of consciousness.

If we take our own perspective as people living through collapse, we may see a major crisis point approaching, an event or trial that we will no doubt experience as something very similar to an apocalypse. How mankind is to accommodate itself in that instance is one of the most vital questions of the current times. The reader could with advantage turn his or her attention to John's text from the end of chapter 20 onwards for further illumination. Our task has been not to attempt clairvoyance, but to tell a history, albeit one that many would consider eccentric. At the end of his book in Revelation 22:10, John issues a warning, "Do not seal up the words of the prophecy of this book, for the time is near."

If the past were utterly irrelevant to the present, should we take any interest in it at all? But if it is agreed that such an interest is important, it may be the case that a study of the history of a nation or a movement would put us in a better position to forecast its future. Historians may not be prophets but they are often able to assess current events and the 'signs of the times' and to put these in their proper perspective. Nikolai Berdyaev stated that it is possible to foresee that mankind henceforth will be concerned not so much with problems of the philosophy of knowledge as rather by problems of the philosophy of history.[9] Ernst Troeltsch would agree, for he considered that the historian will become the philosopher and the philosopher an historian. Both Reinhold

Niebuhr and Wolfhart Pannenberg stated that it would be only when one stands at the end of history and can view history in its entirety that it could be expected at last to make sense.[10]

The mystery of John's Apocalypse concerning the final chapters of his book and his eschatological visions have been examined, explanations offered, and comparisons made, with respect to Western history. By so doing, many would question such an enterprise, and make the claim that surely the mystery that lies within John's narrative has been destroyed. This is not the case by any means, for the greatest mystery of all concerns the way in which God works *through* the process of human history to fulfil his purposes for mankind. But the time is approaching when we must await His judgment *upon* such history.[11]

# References

## CHAPTER ONE

1. Bury, John Bagnell, 1903, inaugural lecture given at the University of Cambridge.,
2. Collingwood, 1946: 249.
3. Niebuhr, 1949: 20.
4. Augustine, Saint, *Confessions*, book xi, chapter xx.
5. Augustine, Saint, *Confessions*, book xi, chapter xxviii.
6. Löwith, 1949: 4.
7. Barzun, 2000: ix.
8. Troeltsch, Ernst, 1913, *Gesammelte Schriften*, volume II, *Moderne Geschichtsphilsophie*: 691.
9. Bultmann, 1957: 138.
10. Butterfield, 1949: 9.
11. Löwith, 1949: 6.
12. Bultmann, 1957: 21.
13. Halbwachs, Maurice, *Les Cadres sociaux de la Mémoire* (Paris: Félix Alcan, 1925): 138.
14. Collingwood, 1946: 46.
15. Krüger, Gustav, *Hippolytus*, Encyclopædia Britannica (Cambridge University Press, 1911), volume 13: 520.
16. Collingwood, 1946: 5.
17. Lévy-Bruhl, Lucien, *The Philosophy of Auguste Comte* (London: Swan Sonnenschein, 1903): 336.
18. Teilhard de Chardin, 1959: 305.
19. Löwith, 1949: 1.
20. Frank, Erich, *Philosophical Understanding and Religious Truth* (Oxford University Press, 1945): 137
21. Niebuhr, 1949: 64.
22. Berlin, 2000: 218.
23. Mosheim, Johann Lorenz von, translated by Robert Studley Vidal, *De Rebus christianorum ante Constantinum Commentarii (The Commentaries on the Affairs of the Christians before the Time of Constantine the Great)*, (New York: S. Converse, 1753/1854): 105.
24. Thompson, 1990: 26.
25. Berger, 1967: 39.

26  Warfield, Benjamin B., *The Millennium and the Apocalypse*, The Princeton theological Review, 1904, volume 3.1: 599-617.
27  Frend, 1984: 110.
28  See Revelation 1:3, 22:7 and 9:18-19.
29  Luther, Martin, Preface to the Revelation of Saint John (I) and (II), 1522/1530.
30  Wainwright, 1993: 11.
31  Bale, John, *The Image of both Churches* (London: Thomas East, 1570): preface.
32  Luther, Martin, *Preface to the Revelation of Saint John (I) and (II)*, 1522/1530.
33  Taylor, David G. K., *Christian regional Diversity* from Esler, Philip F., *The early Christian World* (London & New York: Routledge, 2002): 338.
34  Edinger, 2002: 10.
35  Bauckham, 1999: 148.
36  McKelvey, 1999: 45.
37  Harnack, 1902: 14.
38  Bauckham, 1999: 148.
39  Bauckham, 1999: 1.
40  Thompson, 1990: 177.
41  Edlin, Handley H., *Commentary on the Revelation of Jesus Christ* (Maitland, Florida: Xulon Press, 2007): title page.
42  Yahuda collection of Sir Isaac Newton's manuscripts: MS 1.1, folio 16 recto.
43  Collingwood, 1946: 50.
44  Collingwood, 1946: 5.
45  Valliere, 2000: 82.
46  Edinger, 2002: xix.
47  Origen, *De Principiis*, book II.11: 2-5.
48  Marsden, Richard, 2012, *Introduction* from Marsden/Matter: 9.
49  Almond, 2014: 180.
50  Wainwright, 1993: 53.
51  Luther, Martin, *Preface to the Revelation of Saint John (I) and (II)*, 1522/1530.
52  Almond, 2014: 184.
53  Manuel, 1974: 88.
54  L'Abbé Guillaume, *Oeuvres complètes de Bossuet (Complete Works of Bossuet)* (Paris: Berche et Tralin, 1887), volume I: 188.
55  Luther, Martin, *Preface to the Revelation of Saint John (I) and (II)*, 1522/1530.
56  Dent, Arthur, *The Ruin of Rome* (Glasgow: Samuel Gardner, 1798): 370
57  Foxe, John, *The Acts and Monuments of the Christian Church*, (London: John Day, 1583): book V.

[58] Newton, Isaac, *Observations upon the Prophecies of Daniel and the Apocalypse of St. John in two Parts* (London: Darby and Browne, 1733): 251.
[59] Hengstenberg, 1852, volume II: 274.
[60] Manuel, 1974: 88.
[61] Wainwright, 1993: 81.
[62] Valliere, 2000: 82.
[63] Neall, Beatrice S., *The Concept of Character in the Apocalypse with Implications for Character Education* (Washington D.C.: University Press of America, 1983): 10-15.
[64] Edinger, 2002: 7.
[65] Wainwright, 1993: 154.

CHAPTER TWO

[1] Bauckham, 1993: 443.
[2] Toynbee/Somervell, 1946/1957: 12.
[3] Toynbee/Somervell, 1946/1957: 244.
[4] See Daniel, chapter 7.
[5] Wilcock, 1975: 161.
[6] Wallace-Hadrill, 1967/1985: 21.
[7] Todd, 1992/2004: 29.
[8] Howorth, Henry Hoyle, *The Ethnology of Germany – Part VI, The Varini, Varangians and Franks*, Journal of the Royal Anthropological Institute of Great Britain and Ireland (London: Trübner & Co., 1884): 213-237.
[9] Hengstenberg, 1852, volume II: 212.
[10] Todd, 1992/2004: 19.
[11] Sheldon, 1895, volume II: 7.
[12] Howorth, Henry Hoyle, *The Ethnology of Germany – Part VI, The Varini, Varangians and Franks*, Journal of the Royal Anthropological Institute (New York: Trübner & Co., 1884): 215-216.
[13] Hodges/Whitehouse, 1983: 20.
[14] Beck, Frederick G. M., *Alemanni*, Encyclopædia Britannica, 11th edition (New York: Cambridge University Press, 1910): volume 1, 468.
[15] Kulikowski, Michael, *Rome's Gothic Wars: From the third Century to Alaric* (Cambridge University Press, 2006): 123ff.
[16] Sinor, Denis, editor, *The Cambridge History of early inner Asia* (Cambridge University Press, 1990): 177-203.
[17] Beck, 1911, *Alemanni*: volume 1fs, 468.
[18] Anonymous, but attributed to Prosper of Aquitaine, 452, *Chronica Gallica*.
[19] Waldman/Mason, 2006, *Encyclopedia of European Peoples*: 821-825.

20. Paul the Deacon, translated by William Dudley Foulke, *Historia Langobardorum (History of the Lombards)* (Philadelphia: University of Pennsylvania Press, 806-810/1907), book 1, chapter xxiii.
21. Chadwick, 1995: 92.
22. Latourette, 1953/1975: 272.
23. Sheldon, 1895, volume II: 10.
24. Todd, 1992/2004: 119.
25. Chadwick, 1995: 82.
26. Green, 1996: 50.
27. Fletcher, 1998: 106.
28. Barrs, Ian, 2001, *Constantine to Charlemagne: The Medieval Church creates Christendom*, lecture given at Liss for the Katallassein Project, accessed September 2015 <http:// www.christianheritage.org.uk /..../Constantine_to_Charlemagne.aspx>.
29. Padberg, Lutz E. von, *Die Christianisierung Europas im Mittelalter (The Christianization of Europe in the Middle Ages)* (Leipzig: Reclam Verlag, 1998): 48.
30. Halle, Johann Jacob Gebauer, 1787, *Algemeinen Welthistorie durch eine Gesellschaft von Gelehrten in Deutschland und Engeland ausgefertiget (Global world History prepared by a Society of Scholars in Germany and England)*: volume 53.
31. Sheldon, 1895, volume II: 33.
32. Heather, 2006: 436.
33. Wallace-Hadrill, 1967: 115.
34. Waldman/Mason, 2006, *Encyclopedia of European Peoples*: 665.
35. Heather, 2006: 436.
36. Orientius, *Commonitorium*, c430: 2. 184. "Uno fumavit Gallia tota rogo."
37. Hengstenberg, 1852, volume II: 227.
38. Sheldon, 1895, volume II: 19.
39. Frend, 1984: 828.
40. Mann, Horace K., *The Lives of the Popes in the Early Middle Ages,* volume I *The Popes under the Lombard Rule,* part I (London: Kegan Paul, Trench, Trübner & Co., 1915): 105.
41. Sheldon, 1895, volume II: 18.
42. Pirenne, 1937: 49.
43. McNeill William H., *Plagues and Peoples* (New York: Anchor Press/Doubleday, 1976): 272.
44. Sheldon, 1895, volume II: 14.
45. Tainter, Joseph, *The Collapse of complex Societies* (Cambridge University Press, 1988): 150.
46. Cantor, 1895, Vol. I: 243.
47. See, for example, Gibbon, 1782/1845: book vi, chapter lxxi.
48. Frend, 1994: 701.
49. Moynahan, 2002: 150.

50. Hengstemberg, 1852, volume II: 244.
51. Piganiol, André, *L'Empire chrétien (325-395)* (Paris: Presses Universitaires de France, 1947): 422.
52. Dawson, 1951: 23.
53. Brown, Peter, 1995: 10.

CHAPTER THREE

1. Gibbon, 1782/1845: book xii, chapter lxxi.
2. Bauckham, 1993: 347.
3. Strabo, *Geographica*: book xvii, 1: 9-10.
4. Charlesworth, 1924: 58/63.
5. Strabo, *Geographica*: book vii, 34 fragments.
6. Pliny the Elder, Gaius, *Naturalis Historiae*, 78-79: book xxxiii:xxi / book xxxxiv:xxxi, xlvii and xlix.
7. Charlesworth, 1924: 69.
8. Pausanias, *Greciae Descriptio (A Description of Greece)*: book vii: 21.14/Pliny the Elder, *Naturalis Historia*, 78-79: book xix.xx.
9. Pliny the Elder, Gaius, *Naturalis Historiae*, 78-79: book xix:x.
10. Charlesworth, 1924: 64.
11. Charlesworth, 1924: 123.
12. Pliny the Elder, Gaius, *Naturalis Historiae*, 78-79: book xxxiv:xli.
13. Pliny the Elder, Gaius, *Naturalis Historiae*, 78-79: book xxxiv:xlix.
14. Charlesworth, 1924: 123.
15. Charlesworth, 1924: 65.
16. Charlesworth, 1924: 26.
17. Bauckham, 1993: 370.
18. Charlesworth, 1924: 240.
19. Pirenne, 1937: 82.
20. Gibbon, 1782/1845: book iii, chapter xxxvi.
21. Pirenne, 1937: 146.
22. Pirenne, 1936: 59.
23. Toynbee/Somervell, 1946/1957: 12.
24. Gibbon, 1782/1845: book xii, chapter lxxi.
25. Pirenne, 1937: 83.
26. Mommsen, Theodor, *Petrarch's Conception of the Dark Ages*, Medieval Academy of America (University of Chicago Press/Speculum, 1942), volume 17, no.2: 226-242.
27. Bishop, Edmund, *Liturgica Historia*, (Oxford: Clarendon Press, 1918): 179.
28. Dawson, 1951: 16.
29. Toynbee/Somervell, 1946/1957: 12.
30. Pirenne, 1936: 55.
31. Harnack, 1902: 228.
32. Pirenne, 1936: 121/394.

[33] Pirenne, 1936: 220.
[34] Pirenne, 1937: 101.
[35] Barrs, Ian, 2001, *Constantine to Charlemagne: The Medieval Church creates Christendom*.
[36] Saint Augustine, *Letter to Marcellinus, no. 138*.
[37] Barrs, Ian, 2001, *Constantine to Charlemagne: The Medieval Church creates Christendom*.
[38] Tertullian, *Apologeticum*, 197, chapter 39: 7. "Vide, ut invicem se diligent."
[39] Barrs, Ian, 2001, *Constantine to Charlemagne: The Medieval Church creates Christendom*.
[40] Hawes, Adeline Belle, *Charities and Philanthropies in the Roman Empire*, Meeting held at Boston University, The Classical Weekly (Baltimore: Johns Hopkins University Press, 1913), volume. 6, no. 23: 178.
[41] Herrin, 1987: 142.
[42] Flick, 1909: 365.
[43] Flick, 1909: 190.
[44] Flick, 1909: 222.
[45] Toynbee 1946/1957: 12.
[46] Toynbee, 1972/1988: 101.
[47] Teilhard de Chardin, 1959: 164.
[48] Toynbee, 1972/1988: 101.
[49] Saint Augustine. *De Civitate Dei*: book xi: chapter xviii.
[50] See Immanuel Kant, 1784, *Idee zu einer allgemeinen Geschichte in weltbürgliche Absicht (Idea for a universal History on a cosmopolitical Plan)* (Berlin: Berlinische Monatsschrift, 1784).
[51] Herrin, 1987: 6.
[52] Pirenne, 1937: 146.
[53] Sohm, 1888: 74.

## CHAPTER FOUR

[1] Hoekema, Anthony A., edited by Robert G Clouse, *Amillennianism, the Meaning of the Millennium, four Views* (Westmont, Illinois: Inter Varsity Press, 1977): 161.
[2] Campbell, Donald & Townsend, Jeffrey, *Evidence from Revelation 20, a Case for Premillennialism: a new Consensus* (Chicago: Moody Press, 1992): 247.
[3] Irenaeus Saint, 180, *Adversus Haereses*, book iv, chapter xxi.
[4] Rissi, 1972: 19.
[5] Warfield, Benjamin Breckenridge, *The Millennium and the Apocalypse*, The Princeton Theological Review (Princeton, New Jersey: Princeton Theological Seminary, 1904): volume 2, 599-617.
[6] Hills, Aaron Merritt, *Fundamental Christian Theology*, volume. II, part VI, *Eschatology* (Pasadena: C.J. Kinne, 1931): chapter 1, section XI.

7. Neall, Beatrice S., *Amillennialism reconsidered* (Lincoln, Nebraska: Union College, 2005): 191.
8. Pirenne, 1936: 45.
9. Dawson, 1951: 90.
10. Davis, H.W. Carless, 1906, *Charlemagne, the Hero of two Nations*: 218.
11. Wilson, 2006: 7.
12. Guizot, 1838: 82.
13. Brown, Peter, 1995: 435.
14. Davis, H.W. Carless, 1906: *Charlemagne, the Hero of two Nations*: 185.
15. Isidore of Seville, Saint. *Episcopi Sententiae, Liber tertius*, book iii, section xlii.
16. Davis, H.W. Carless, 1906: 234.
17. Herrin, 1987: 134.
18. Pirenne, 1937: 175.
19. Norman, Jeremy, *"Mass Production" of Bibles at Tours*, accessed March 2023 <https://www.historyofinformation.com/detail.php?id=4171>.
20. Contreni, John. J., 2012, *The patristic Legacy* from Marsden/Matter: 526
21. Liere, Frans von, 2011, *Biblical Exegesis through the twelfth Century* from Boynton/Reilly: 164.
22. Steinmeyer E. editor, *Die kleineren althochdeutschen Sprachdenkmäler* (Berlin: Weidmann, 1916), no.6: 29-38.
23. Dawson, 1951: 11.
24. Fletcher, 1998: 229.
25. Brown, Peter, 1995: 426.
26. Pirenne, 1937: 212.
27. Davis, H.W. Carless, 1906, *Charlemagne, the Hero of two Nations*: 259.
28. Winston, 1956: 319.
29. Herrin, 1987: 441.
30. Davis, H.W. Carless, 1906, *Charlemagne, the Hero of two Nations*: 230.
31. Wilcock, 1975: 127.
32. Swete, Henry B., *The Apocalypse of Saint John*, (London: MacMillan, 1911): 266.
33. Bauckham, 1999: 149.
34. Fletcher, 1998: 519.
35. Brown, Peter, 1995: 426.
36. Pirenne, 1936: 45.
37. Wilson, 2006: 121.
38. Brown, Peter, 1995: 449.
39. Herrin, 1987: 456.
40. Herrin, 1987: 295.
41. Wilson, 2006: 1.

42. Schubert, Hans von, *Geschichte der christlichen Kirche im Frühmittelalter (History of the Christian Church in the Early Middle Ages)* (Tübingen: J.C.B. Mohr, 1921): 287.
43. Herrin, 1987: 295.
44. Bryce, James, *The Holy Roman Empire* (London: MacMillan, 1920): 50.
45. Pirenne, 1937: 176.

CHAPTER FIVE

1. Walvoord. J., 1966, *The Reign of Christ*, article 20, accessed May 2014 <https://walvoord.com/ search/node?keys=reign+of+christ>.
2. Spengler, 1920, volume I: 231.
3. McKelvey, 1999: 9.
4. Edinger, 2002: 8.
5. Renan, Ernest, 1882, *Qu'est qu'une nation? (What is a nation?)* Conference held at the Sorbonne, Paris.
6. Toynbee/Somervell, 1946/1957: 548.
7. Pirenne, 1936: 182.
8. Bagent/Leigh/Lincoln, 1996: 176.
9. Latourette, 1953/1975: 630.
10. See lecture I of Rudolf Steiner's work *Luzifer und Ahriman in der Seele des Menschen* (*The Influences of Lucifer and Ahriman*) (New York: SteinerBooks, 1919/1995).
11. Smalley, 2005: 501.
12. Jung, 1958/1988: 64 & 70.
13. McGinn, 1994: 49.
14. Almond, 2014: xiv.
15. Solovyov, Vladimir, *Three Dialogues on War: Progress and the End of History: A short Story of the Anti-Christ* (London: Hodder & Stoughton, 1915): 180.
16. Spengler, 1922, volume II: 354.
17. Hildegard of Bingen, *Ordo Virtutum*, c1151: part II.
18. McGinn, 1994: 248.
19. Milton, John, *Paradise lost* (London: Peter Parker, 1667), book IV, line 957.
20. Russell, Jeffrey B., 1986:26.
21. Spengler, 1922, volume II: 372.
22. Buxton, 1945: 91.
23. Russell, Jeffrey B., 1986: 58.
24. Phillips, Walter Alison, Encyclopædia Britannica, 11th edition (New York: Cambridge University Press, 1910): volume 10, 211.
25. Spengler, 1922, volume I: 126 and volume II: 369.
26. Spengler, 1920, volume I: 463.
27. Spengler, 1920, volume I: 408.
28. Spengler, 1920, volume I: 468.

29 Hengstenberg, 1852, volume II, 292.
30 Phillips, Walter Alison, 1910: volume 10, 211.
31 Dawson, 1951: 144.
32 Armstrong, 2010: 149.
33 Berdyaev, Nikolai, 1922 <http:// berdyaev.com/berdiaev/berd_lib/1922_059>.
34 Phillips, Andrew, 1995: 63.
35 Pirenne, 1936: 180.
36 Dawson, 1951: 12.
37 Hughes, Thomas, 2004: 21.
38 Spengler, 1922, volume II: 627.
39 Stark, 2006: 42-44.
40 Hughes, Thomas, 2004: 21.
41 Dawson, 1951: 227.
42 Spengler, 1920, volume I: 341.

## CHAPTER SIX

1 encyclopaedia.com, 2016
    <https://encyclopedia.com/history/encyclopedias-almanacs-transcripts-and-maps/religious-piety>.
2 Frend, 1984: 133.
3 Stauffer, Ethelbert, *Täufertum und Märtyrertheologie (The Anabaptist Theology of Martyrdom)*, Zeitschrift für Kirchengeschichte, 1933: volume XLII, 545-598.
4 Frend, 1984: 133.
5 Hamilton, Jeffrey W, *The Thousand Year Reign,* The Expository Files, 2003 <http://bible.ca/expository-revelation-20-4-6.html>.
6 Morris, 1987: 237.
7 Whately, Richard, *A View of the Scripture Revelations concerning a future State* (London: B. Fellowes, 1832): 181.
8 Neall, Beatrice S., *Amillennialism reconsidered,* Andrews University Seminary Studies (Berrien Springs, Michigan: Andrews University Press, 2005), volume. 43, no. 1: 207.
9 Boettner, Loraine, 1977, *A postmillennial Response (to historic Pre-millennialism)* from Clouse: 49-50.
10 McKelvey, 1999: 81.
11 Michaels, 1997: 223.
12 Macquarrie, 1977: 399.
13 Foxe, John, 1583, *The Acts and Monuments of the Christian Church*, book I.
14 Cyprian, Saint of Carthage, translated by Alexander Robertson & James Donaldson, *The Writings of Cyprian* (Edinburgh: T. & T. Clark, 1869), volume 2: 241.

[15] Eusebius Pamphilus of Caesarea, 312-324, *Historia ecclesiastica*: book 8, chapter 12.
[16] Letter from the Church of Smyrna to the Church at Philomelion in Phrygia, translated by Kirsopp Lake, *The apostolic Fathers*, volume 2, *The Martyrdom of Polycarp* (London: Heinemann, 1913), chapter 17: 3.
[17] Castelli, 2004: 37.
[18] Bainton, 1964: 67.
[19] Kelly Joseph F., *Review of the Cult of the Saints by P. Brown, International Journal of comparative Sociology* (Thousand Oaks, California, Sage Publishing, 1983): XXIV, 1 – 2.
[20] Fletcher, 1998: 10.
[21] Cameron, 2005: 85.
[22] Noble/Head, 1995: xxvii.
[23] Vauchez, 1988/1997: 15.
[24] Gibbon, 1782/1845: book iii chapter xxviii: 3.
[25] Cameron, 2005: 85.
[26] Weinstein/Bell, 1982: 239.
[27] Brown, Peter, 1981: 67.
[28] Head, Thomas, 1995, *The Cult of the Saints and their Relics*, On-line Reference Book for medieval Studies, accessed June 2018 <https://the-orb.arlima.net/encyclop/religion/hagiography/cult.htm>.
[29] Head, Thomas, *The Cult of the Saints and their Relics*.
[30] Vauchez, 1988/1997: 105.
[31] Head, Thomas, *The Cult of the Saints and their Relics*.
[32] Vauchez, 1988/1997: 94.
[33] Vauchez, 1988/1997: 179.
[34] Head, Thomas, *The Cult of the Saints and their Relics*.
[35] Weinstein/Bell, 1982: 178.
[36] Fletcher, 1998: 10.
[37] Head, Thomas, *The Cult of the Saints and their Relics*.
[38] Vauchez, 1988/1997: 472.
[39] Lake, Kirsopp, *The Apostolic Fathers: Letter from the Church of Smyrna to the Church at Philomelion in Phrygia* (London: Heinemann, 1913), chapter 18: 2.
[40] Blant Edmond le, *Les Inscriptions chrétiennes de la Gaule, Antérieures au viii$^{me}$ Siècle* (Paris: L'Imprimerie impériale, 1856), volume I, *Provinces gallicanes*: 240.
[41] Head, Thomas, *The Cult of the Saints and their Relics*.
[42] Vauchez, 1988/1997: 450.
[43] Augustine, Saint of Hippo, *Sermons*, 273: 7.
[44] Vauchez, 1988/1997: 470.
[45] Gibbon, 1782/1845: book iii chapter xxvii, part iii.
[46] Head, Thomas, *The Cult of the Saints and their Relics*.

47 International Journal of Comparative Sociology, 1983: XXIV, 1-2.
48 Weinstein/Bell, 1982: 170.
49 Dawson, 1951: 202.
50 International Journal of Comparative Sociology, 1983, *Cult of the saints*. XXIV: 1-2.
51 Heming, Carol Piper, *Protestants and the Cult of the Saints in German-Speaking Europe, 1517-1531*, Sixteenth Century Essays and Studies (Kirksville, Missouri: Truman State University Press, 2003): volume 65.
52 Bainton, 1964: 367.
53 Kibler, William W. and Zinn, Grover A. *Medieval France: An Encyclopedia*, Head, Thomas, *Saints, Cult of* (New York: Garland Publishing, 1995): 854.
54 Weinstein/Bell, 1982: 186.
55 Luther, Martin, *Luthers Werke: In Epistolam S. Pauli ad Galatas Commentarius* (Weimar, Hermann Böhlaus Nachfolger, 1535/1914), volume 40/2: 103.
56 Dawsonweinstein, Jane E.A., 1994, *The Apocalyptic Thinking of the Marian Exiles* from Wilks: 80.
57 Cameron, 2005: 85.
58 Green, 1996: 188.
59 Soergel, Philip M., *Europe, 1450 to 1789: Encyclopedia of the Early Modern World*, (Farmington Hills, Michigan: The Gale Group, 2004): volume 5.
60 Melancthon, Philip, 1530, *Das Augsburger Bekenntnis,* article VII, *Von der Kirche.*
61 Luther, Martin and Georg Rhaw, 1531, *Der große Katechismus*, article III.
62 Cranmer, Thomas, 1563, *The thirty-nine Articles*, article XXII.
63 Hendrix, Scott from Carol Piper Heming, *Protestants and the Cult of the Saints in German-Speaking Europe, 1517-1531*, Sixteenth Century Essays and Studies, (Kirksville, Missouri: Truman State University Press, 2003), volume 65.

## CHAPTER SEVEN

1 Michaels, 1997: 228.
2 Bauckham, 1999: 106.
3 Caird, 1984: 251.
4 Schubert, Hans von, 1921, *Geschichte der christlichen Kirche im Frühmittelalter*: 231.
5 Barrs, Ian, 2001, *Constantine to Charlemagne: The Medieval Church creates Christendom.*
6 McLeod, Hugh from McLeod/Ustorf, 2003: 1.
7 Bainton, 1964: 320.

8. Almond, 2014: 170.
9. Irenaeus Saint, *Adversus Haereses*: book v, chapter xxxiv.
10. Hills, Aaron Merritt, 1931, *Fundamental Christian Theology*: volume. II, part VI, chapter 1, section XI.
11. Saint Augustine, *De Civitate Dei*: book xx, chapter xvii.
12. Löwith, 1949: 3.
13. Origen. *De Principiis*. Book II: 11:3.
14. Durham, James, *A Commentarie upon the Book of the Revelation* (Glasgow: Robert Sanders, 1680): 607.
15. Gilbert, Alan, 1994, *Secularization and the Future* from Gilley/Sheils: 515.
16. Knox, Ronald A., *The Imitation of Christ* (London: Burns and Oates, 1959): preface.
17. Bultmann, 1995: 53.
18. Law, William, *A serious Call to a devout and holy Life* (London: William Innys, 1729): 30.
19. Alsted, Johann, *Diatribe de mille Annis Apocalypticis* (Frankfurt: Conrad Eifrid, 1627): 37.
20. Guizot, 1838: 159.
21. Guizot, 1838: 38.
22. See Barth, Karl, translated by G. T. Thomson & Harold Knight, *Kirchliche Dogmati, (Church Dogmatics)*, volume I, *The Doctrine of the Word of God* (Edinburgh: T. & T. Clark, 1970): part 2, paragraphs 20/21.
23. MacQuarrie, 1977: 406.
24. Guizot, 1838: 118.
25. Foxe, John, 1583, *The Acts and Monuments of the Christian Church*, book I.
26. Foxe, John, 1583, *The Acts and Monuments of the Christian Church*, book V.
27. Pirenne, 1936: 123.
28. Southern, 1970: 23.
29. Berger, 1969: 132.
30. Barrs, Ian, 2001, *Constantine to Charlemagne: The Medieval Church creates Christendom*.
31. Toynbee/Somervell, 1946/1957: 350.
32. Dawson, 1951: 92.
33. Mann, 1947/1974: 355.
34. Pirenne, 1936: 120/123.
35. Pirenne, 1936: 154.
36. Martin, 1978: 281.
37. Dawson, 1951: 159.
38. Pirenne, 1936: 130.
39. Chadwick, 1964: 406.

40. Bovey, Alixe, 2015, *The medieval Church: from dedication to dissent*, British Library <https://bl.uk/the-middle-ages/articles/church-in-the-middle-ages-from-dedication-to-dissent>.
41. Herrin, 1987: 237.
42. Pirenne, 1937: 203.
43. Roest, Bert, 2011, *Mendican School Exegesis* from Boynton/Reilly: 186.
44. Cochelin, Isabelle, 2011, *The Bible and Monasticism (6th – 11th Centuries)* from Boynton/Reilly: 73.
45. Reilly, Diane J., 2011, *Lectern Bibles and liturgical Reform in the central Middle Ages* from Boynton/Reilly: 111.
46. McGrath, 1998: 148.
47. Origen: *Commentary on the Gospel of John*, Book I, Section 31.
48. Bainton, 1964:268.
49. Lessing, 1780: paragraph 82.
50. Chadwick, 1964: 42
51. McGrath, 1998: 109.
52. Harnack, 1902: 288
53. Greengrass, 2015: 6.
54. Jaspers, 1931: 9.
55. Berger, 1969: 154.
56. Southern, 1970: 16.
57. Neil W., 1963, *The Criticism and theological Use of the Bible 1700-1950* from Greenslade: 255.
58. Bacon, Francis, *The Advancement of Learning* (Oxford: Leon Lichfield, 1605): book I, V: 11.
59. Russell, Jeffrey B., 1986: 77.
60. Armstrong, 2010: 208.
61. Noll, Mark A., edited by Walter Elwell, *Evangelical Dictionary of Theology* (Grand Rapids, Michigan: Baker Academic, 1984/2007), 926.
62. Sohm, 1888: 166. translated by May Sinclair in the 1909 edition, 166.
63. Hill, 2004: 26.
64. Hotson, Howard, 2018, *Comenius as Prophet of the Age of Light* from Matysin/Edelstein: 23.
65. Hampson, 1968: 35.
66. Locke, John, *A Letter concerning Toleration* (London, Awnsham Churchill, 1689)
67. Tillotson, John. *The Works of Dr. John Tillotson* (Edinburgh: G. Hamilton and J. Balfour, 1820), volume I, 101.
68. Hume, David, *Essays Moral, Political, and Literary* (London: Grant Richards, 1758/1903): 75 & 78.
69. McGrath, 1998: 225.
70. Russell, Jeffrey B., 1986: 128.
71. McLeod, 2000: 52.

72  Armstrong, 2010: 164.

CHAPTER EIGHT

1  Swete, Henry B., *The Apocalypse of St. John*: 261.
2  Shaw, Jane, 2001, *The late seventeenth and eighteenth Centuries* from Harries/Meyr-Harting: 163.
3  Küng, 2002: 151.
4  Vauchez, 1988/1997: 138.
5  Pailin, David, 1994, *Rational religion from Herbert of Cherbury to William Paley* from Gilley/Sheils: 211.
6  Hampson, 1968: 19.
7  Hill, 2004: 115.
8  Russell, Jeffrey B., 1986: 84.
9  Armstrong, 2010: 183.
10  Armstrong, 2009: 194
11  Berlin, 2000: 93.
12  Hill, 2004: 134.
13  Barzun, 2000: 359.
14  Chadwick, 1995: 235.
15  Voltaire, François, translated by H.I. Woolf, *Le Dictionnaire philosophique (The philosophical Dictionary)* (New York: Knopf, 1764/1924): 103.
16  Cameron, 2005: 38.
17  Tocqueville/Bonner, 1856: 19.
18  Hume, David, 1757, *Natural History of Religion* (London: A. & H. Bradlaugh Bonner, 1757): 75.
19  Hill, 2004: 171.
20  Hill, 2004: 142.
21  See, for example, Gibbon, 1782/1845: book I, chapter ii part ii, or book iv chapter xlviii part i. or book vi chapter lxxi: part ii.
22  Spengler, 1920, volume I: 486.
23  Bekker, Balthasar, *The World bewitch'd, or, an Examination of the common Opinions concerning Spirits* (London, R. Baldwin, 1695): volume 2
24  Holbach, Paul Henri, revised H.D. Robinson, 1772/1836, *Le bon Sens*: section cxcix and ccvi.
25  Betros, Gemma, 2010, *The French Revolution and the Catholic Church*, History Review, (London: History Today, 2010): issue 68.
26  Jaspers, 1931: 9.
27  Martin, 1978: 16.
28  MacCulloch, Diarmid, 2010, *A History of Christianity*. BBC Television programme.
29  Betros, Gemma, 2010, *The French Revolution and the Catholic Church*.
30  Cholvy, 2014: 339.
31  Tocqueville/Bonner, 1856: 18.

# REFERENCES 337

32  Butterfield, 1949: 186.
33  Maistre, Joseph de, 1796/1797, *Considérations sur la France*: 76.
34  Hulme/Jordanova, 1990: 213.
35  Maistre, Joseph de, 1796/179, *Considérations sur la France*: 6.
36  Maistre, Joseph de, *Oeuvres completes*, volume I, *De la Souveraineté du Peuple* (Lyons, Vitte et Perrussel, 1884): 442.
37  Tocqueville/Bonner, 1856: 16.
38  Tocqueville, 1856: 27. (French edition)
39  Tocqueville/Bonner, 1856: 36.
40  Tocqueville, 1856: 157.(French edition)
41  Burke, 1790: 92.
42  Burke, 1790: 63.
43  Burke, Edmund, 1796, Two Letters addressed to a Member of the present Parliament on the Proposals for Peace with the regicide Directory of France. Letter I, *On the Overtures of Peace* (London: F. and C. Rivington): 6.
44  Carlyle, 1837: chapters 2.6.VI and 3.5.IV.
45  Taine, 1884, volume IV, book V, chapter 1: preface.
46  Russell, Jeffrey B., 1986: 168.
47  Spengler, 1920, volume I: 4.
48  Hobsbawm, 1962: 28.
49  Pinchbeck, 2006: 212.
50  Hughes, Thomas, 2004: 21.
51  Spengler, 1922, volume II: 371.
52  Spengler, 1922, volume II: 630.
53  Hobsbawm, 1962/1996: 259.
54  Hohendahl, Peter Uwe, 2008, *The new Man: Theories of Masculinity around 1800*, Project MUSE <https:// muse.jhu.edu. article232834>.
55  Brown, Callum, 2001: 58.
56  Gregory, Jeremy, 1999, *Homo religiosus: Masculinity and Religion in the long 18th Century* from Hitchcock/Cohen: 85.
57  Goethe, Wolfgang von, 1775, *Wahrheit und Dichtung*: 20th book.
58  Russell, Jeffrey B., 1986: 151.
59  Troeltsch, 1897/1913, *Die Absolutheit des Christentums und die Religionsgeschichte (The Absoluteness of Christianity and the History of Religion)* from *Gesaamelte Schriften*, volume 2: 359.
60  Paine, 1807/1880: 142.
61  Paine, Thomas, 1798, *A Discourse delivered at the Society of Theophilanthropists,* Paris.
62  Moynahan, 2002: 591.
63  Michalson, 1999: 21.
64  Michalson, 1999: 28.
65  Kant, 1793/1922: 212.

[66] Stanford Encyclopædia of Philosophy, 2004, *Kant's Philosophy of Religion* <http://plato.stanford.edu /entries/Kant-religion>.
[67] Benner, Drayton C, *Immanuel Kant's Demythologization of Christian Theories of Atonement in Religion within the Limits of Reason Alone*, Evangelical Quarterly: An International Review of Bible and Theology (Milton Keynes: Paternoster Press, 2007): 79(2),
[68] Murdoch, 1970: 79.
[69] Michalson, 1999: 49
[70] Michalson, 1999: 13.
[71] Spengler, 1920, volume I: 63.
[72] Bultmann, 1955: 7.
[73] Spengler, 1920, volume I: 203.
[74] Spengler, 1920, volume I: 490.

CHAPTER NINE

[1] Jaspers, 1930:10.
[2] Hobsbawm, 1962: 2.
[3] Sandeen, 1970: 22.
[4] McGinn, 1994: 248.
[5] Newman, John Henry, *Apologia pro Vita sua* (London: George Routledge & Sons, 1865): 207.
[6] Origen. *De Principiis*. Book I, Preface: 6.
[7] Bunsen. Chevalier and Professors Brandis & Lorbell, *The Life and Letters of Barthold George Niebuhr* (New York: Harper & Brothers, 1854): 523, Letter of 7 October, 1830.
[8] Gilbert, Alan, 1994. *Secularization and the Future* from Gilley/Sheils: 505.
[9] Russell, Bertrand, 1946: 724-726.
[10] Leihton, J.A., *Hegel's Conception of God*, The Philosophical Review, 1896, Vol. 5, No. 6 (Durham, North Carolina: Duke University Press, 1896)): 601.
[11] Reardon, 1985: 60.
[12] Troeltsch, 1897/1913, *Christentum und Religionsgeschichte* from *Gesammelte Schriften*, volume 2: 359.
[13] Feuerbach, Ludwig, *Das Wesen des Christentums (The Essence of Christianity)* (Leipzig: Otto Wigand, 1841): 38.
[14] Marx, Karl, *Zur Kritik der Hegelschen Rechtsphilosophie: Einleitung* from Deutsch-Französische Jahrbücher (Paris, Bureau der Jahrbücher, 1844): paragraph 379.
[15] Ward, 1992: 10.
[16] Nietzsche, 1887, *Fröhliche Wissenschaft*, verse 343.
[17] Teilhard de Chardin, 1959: 213.

18 Marx, Karl, 1857/1858, *Grundrisse der Kritik der Politischen Ökonomie (Foundations of the Critique of Political Economy)* (unfinished manuscript): Notebook II.
19 Tocqueville, Alexis de, *De la Démocratie en Amérique*, volume III, part I (Paris: Imprimerie Claye et Taillefer, 1848): 9.
20 Skidelsky, 2003: 456.
21 Berger, 1969: 107.
22 Berger, 1969: 155.
23 Chadwick, 1975: 223.
24 Mann, 1947: 142.
25 Lecky, W.E.H.,*History of the Rise and Influence of the Spirit of Rationalism in Europe* (London: Longman, Green & Co., 1865), chapter I: *On the declining Sense of the Miraculous*.
26 Faxneld, Per, *The Devil is red: Socialist Satanism in the nineteenth Century* (Leiden: Brill Publishers, 2013), Numen 60: 533.
27 Wurmbrand, Richard, *Marx and Satan* (Bartlesville, Oklahoma: Living Sacrifice Book Company, 1986)
28 Faxneld, Per, *The Devil is red: Socialist Satanism in the nineteenth Century*: 540.
29 Knight, 2008: 156.
30 Ward, 1992: 10.
31 Neil, W., 1963, *The Criticism and theological Use of the Bible 1700 – 1950* from Greenslade: 260.
32 Turner, Frank Miller, 1980, *Victorian scientific Naturalism* from Chant/Fauvel: 50.
33 Mandelbaum Maurice, 1980, *Philosophic Movements in the nineteenth Century* from Chant/Fauvel: 45.
34 Troeltsch, 1897/1913, *Christianity and the History of Religion* from *Gesammelte Schriften*, volume 2: 361.
35 Bainton, 1964: 394.
36 Armstrong, 2010: 244.
37 Knight, 2008: 157.
38 Troeltsch, 1904/1913, *Moderne Geschichtsphilosophie* from *Gesammelte Schriften*, volume 2: 678.
39 Troeltsch, 1904/1913, *Moderne Geschichtsphilosophie* from *Gesammelte Schriften*, volume 2: 3.
40 Norman, 1991: 62.
41 Kaufmann, Alfred, *Renan: the Man*, The Catholic Historical Review, (Washington D.C., Catholic University of America Press, 1924), volume 10, no.3|: 390.
42 Chadwick, 1975: 223.
43 Zeldin, 1973: 995.
44 McLeod, 2000: 132.

⁴⁵ Hempton, David, 1994, *Religious Life in industrial Britain 1830-1914* from Gilley/Sheils: 321.
⁴⁶ Herberg, 1955/1983: 109.
⁴⁷ Chadwick, 1975: 94.
⁴⁸ Cholvy, 2014: 37.
⁴⁹ Reardon, 1985: 14.
⁵⁰ Vigny, Alfred de, *Le Mont des Oliviers* (Paris: La Revue des deux Mondes, 1843).
⁵¹ Baudelaire, Charles, *Le Joueur généreux* (Paris: Michel Lévy Frères, 1869).
⁵² Proudhon, Pierre-Josephe, *De la Justice dans la Révolution et dans l'Eglise* (Paris: Librairie de Garnier Frères, 1858), volume 2: 540.
⁵³ Zeldin, 1973: 985.
⁵⁴ Cholvy, 2014: 106.
⁵⁵ Cholvy, 2014: 159.
⁵⁶ Chadwick, 1975: 86.
⁵⁷ Chadwick, 1975: 39.
⁵⁸ Chadwick, 1975: 152.
⁵⁹ McLeod, 2000: 136.
⁶⁰ Berger, 1969: 106.
⁶¹ Knight, 2008: 33.
⁶² Russell, Jeffrey B., 1986: 168.
⁶³ Martin. 1978: 85.
⁶⁴ Berger. 1969: 128.

## CHAPTER TEN

¹ Myers, Frederic W.H., *Science and a future life : with other essays* (London: Macmillan, 1893): 131.
² Armstrong, 2010: 244.
³ Barzun, 2000: 615.
⁴ Russell, Jeffrey B., 1986: 229
⁵ France, Anatole, *Pourquoi sommes-nous tristes?* from *La Vie littéraire*, 1895.
⁶ Skidelsky, 2003: 91, based on a speech entitled *My early beliefs* by John Maynard Keynes given in 1938.
⁷ Cholvy, 2014: 107.
⁸ Turner, Frank Miller, 1980, *Victorian scientific Naturalism* from Chant/Fauvel: 49.
⁹ Malpas, 2003: 8.
¹⁰ Freud 1907: 139. "...als eine universelle Zwangsneurose."
¹¹ Freud, 1928: 88.
¹² Lyon, 1999: 33.
¹³ Knight, 2008: 72.
¹⁴ Cholvy, 2014: 353.
¹⁵ Green, 1996: 299.

16. Luxemburg, Rosa, 1905, translated by Juan Pinto, *Kościół a Socjalizm (Socialism and the Churches)* Luxemburg Archive <https://marxists.org/archive/ luxemburg/1905/misc/ socialism-churches.htm>. The information is protected under the full terms of the GNU FDL
17. Troeltsch, 1907/1925, *Das Wesen des modernen Geistes* from *Gesammelte Christen*, volume 4: 337.
18. Soloviov, Vladimir, translated by Alexander Bakshy, *Three Discussions* (University of London Press, 1900/1915): 180.
19. Bagent/Leigh/Lincoln, 1996: 176.
20. Cholvy, 2014: 351.
21. Bagent/Leigh/Lincoln, 1996: 178.
22. Harvey, 1989: 15.
23. Cox, 1965: 80.
24. Brown, Callum, 2001: 1.
25. McLeod, Hugh from McLeod/Ustorf, 2003: 4.
26. Weber, Max, *Wissenschaft als Beruf* (Leipzig, Verlag von Duncker und Humblot, 1917): 16.
27. Weber, Max, *Die protestantische Ethik und der Geist des Kapitalismus, (The Protestant Ethic and the Spirit of Capitalism)*, Archiv für Sozialwissenschaft und Sozialpolitik, volume XXI (Tübingen: J.C.B. Mohr, 1905): 108.
28. Bell, 1976: 71.
29. Habermas, Jürgen, 1981, translated by Sevla Ben-Habi, 2016, *Modernity versus Postmodernity*, New German Critique, no. 22, Special Issue on Modernism, 1981, accessed January 2023 <http://jstor.org/stable/ 487859>.
30. Steiner, 2010: 93.
31. Carson, 1996: 21.
32. Bell, 1976: 4.
33. Guinness, Os, *The Gravedigger File* (Westmont, Illinois: Inter Varsity Press, 1983): 92.
34. Cox, 1965: 4.
35. Carson, 1996: 59.
36. Berger, 1969: 132.
37. Troeltsch, 1907/1925, *Das Wesen des modernen Geistes*: from *Gesammelte Schriften*, volume 4: 306.
38. Carson, 1996: 52.
39. McGrath, 1998: 245.
40. Toynbee, 1946/1957: 259.
41. Troeltsch, 1910/1913, *Die Zukunftsmöglichkeiten des Christentums im Verhältnis zur modernen Philosophie (The future Possibilities of Christianity in relation to modern Philosophy)* from *Gesammelte Schriften*, volume 2: 842.

42. Berger, 1969: 132.
43. Knight, 2008: 150.
44. Troeltsch, 1907/1925m *Das Wesen des modernen Geistes* from *Gesammelte Schriften*, volume 4: 325.
45. Barclay, 1971: 13.
46. Carson, 1996: 41.
47. Hamberg, Eva M., 2003, *Christendom in Decline: the Swedish Case* from McLeod/Ustorf: 49.
48. Troeltsch, 1907/1925, *Das Wesen des modernen Geistes* from *Gesammelte Schriften*, volume 4: 328.
49. Jefferson, Thomas, 1819, *Letter to Ezra Stiles Ely*.
50. Troeltsch, 1907/1925, *Das Wesen des modernen Geistes* from *Gesammelte Schriften*, volume 4: 328.
51. Martin, 1978: 92.
52. Carson, 1996: 391.
53. Jaspers, 1931: 25.
54. Habermas, 1968: 292.
55. Bell, 1976, 19.
56. Cox, 1965: 34.
57. Carson, 1996: 52.
58. Neuhaus, 1984: 86.
59. Russell, Jeffrey B., 1986: 228.
60. Graham, 2013: 150.
61. Jackson, Wayne, 2023, *Gog and Magog – What Is the Meaning of Revelation 20:8?* Fortify Your Faith Foundation, accessed January2023 <https://christiancourier.com/ articles/986-gog-and-magog-what-is-the-meaning-of-revelation-20-8>.
62. Morris, 1987: 239.
63. Berdyaev, Nikolai, 1922 <http://berdiaev.com/berdiaev/berd_lib/1922_059.html>.
64. Jung, Carl Gustav, translated by Richard F.C. Hull, *Gesammelte Werke, The collected works of C.G. Jung*, volume 9, part II, *Aion, Researches into the Phenomenology of the Self* (Princeton, New Jersey: Princeton University Press, 1959), paragraph 77.
65. McGinn, 1994: 276.
66. Nietzsche, Friedrich, *Gesammelte Werke, Der Wille zur Macht (Collected Works, The Will to Power)* (Munich: Musarian Verlag. 1888/1926): 3.
67. Graham, 2013: 164.
68. Colson/Vaughn, 1989/1999: 9.
69. Berger, 1969: 150.
70. Chadwick, 1975: 250.
71. Berger, 1969: 107.

72 Herberg, 1955/1983: 270.
73 Norman, 2002: 35.
74 Troeltsch, 1907/1925, *Das Wesen des modernen Geistes* from *Gesammelte Schriften*, volume 4: 302.
75 Spengler, 1922, volume II: 443.
76 Murdoch, 1970: 79.

EPILOGUE

1 Barclay, 1971: 188.
2 Gerth/Wright, 1948/1991: 283.
3 Berlin, 2000: 93.
4 Kleingeld, Pauline, 2004, *Kant's Philosophy of Religion*, Stanford Encyclopaedia of Philosophy <http://www.plato.stanford.edu/entries/kant-religion>.
5 Hume, David, 1748, *Enquiry Concerning Human Understanding*: Section 12, part 3.
6 Troeltsch, 1907/1925, *Das Wesen des modernen Geistes* from *Gesammelte Schriften*, volume 4: 334.
7 Butterfield, 1949: 61.
8 Graham, 2013: 79 &121.
9 Berdyaev, Nikolai, 1922, <http://berdiaev.com/berdiaev/berd_lib>.
10 Pannenberg, editor, 1969: 142.
11 Morris, 1980: 240.

## Bibliography

Almond, Philip C. *The Devil* (London: I.B. Tauris, 2014).

Armstrong, Karen. *The Case for God* (London: Vintage Books/Bodley Head, 2010).

Bagent, Michael, Leigh, Richard and Lincoln, Henry. *The Messianic Legacy* (London: Arrow Books, 1996).

Bainton, Roland H. *The History of Christianity* (London: Thomas Nelson, 1964).

Barclay, William *The Daily Study Bible – The Revelation of John* (Edinburgh: Saint Andrew Press, 1959).

——— . *Ethics in a permissive Society* (London: Fontana Books, 1971).

Barzun, Jacques. *From Dawn to Decadence* (London: Harper Collins, 2000).

Bauckham, Richard. *The Climax of Prophecy* (Edinburgh: T. & T. Clark, 1993).

——— . *The Theology of the Book of Revelation* (Cambridge University Press, 1999).

Bell, Daniel. *The Cultural Contradictions of Capitalism* (New York: Basic Books, 1976).

Benda, Julien. *The Great Betrayal* (Abingdon: Routledge, 1928).

Berger, Peter L. *The Sacred Canopy – Elements of a sociological Theory of Religion* (New York: Doubleday, 1967).

——— . *The Social Reality of Religion* (Faber & Faber, 1969).

Berlin, Isaiah, Henry Hardy, editor. *Three Critics of the Enlightenment* (London: Pimlico, 2000).

Beyer, Edvard. *Ibsen: The Man and his Work* (London: Souvenir Press, 1978).

Boynton, Susan and Reilly, Diane J., editors. *The Practice of the Bible in the Middle Ages* (New York: Columbia University Press, 2011).

Braaten, Carl E. *Principles of Lutheran Theology* (Philadelphia: Fortress Press, 1983).

Brown, Callum G. *The Death of Christian Britain – Understanding Secularization 1800-2000* (Abingdon: Routledge, 2001).

Brown, Peter. *The World of late Antiquity* (London: Thames & Hudson, 1971).

———. *The Cult of the Saints – Its Rise and Function in Latin Christianity* (University of Chicago Press, 1981).

———. *The Rise of Western Christendom – Triumph and Diversity 200-1000* (Oxford: Blackwell, 1995).

Bultmann, Rudolf. *History and Eschatology* (New York: Harper & Row, 1957).

Burke, Edmund. *Reflections on the Revolution in France* (London: Dodsley, 1790).

Butterfield, Herbert. *Christianity and History* (London: G. Bell/Fontana, 1949/1960).

Buxton, Charles Roden. *Prophets of Heaven and Hell – Virgil, Dante, Milton, Goethe* (London: Cambridge University Press, 1945).

Caird, George B. *A Commentary on the Revelation of St. John the Divine.* (London: A. & C Black, 1984).

Cameron, Euan. *Interpreting Christian History - The Challenge of the Churches' Past* (Oxford: Blackwell, 2005).

Cantor, Norman F. *Western Civilization: its Genesis and Destiny* (Glenview, Illinois: Scott, Foreman, 1969).

Carey, Frances, editor. *The Apocalypse* (London: British Museum Press, 1999)

Carlyle, Thomas. *The French Revolution: a History* (London: Chapman & Hall, 1837/1999).

Carson, D. A. *The Gagging of God* (Leicester: Apollo/IVP, 1996).

Castelli, Elizabeth A. *Martyrdom and Memory – Early Christian Culture Making* (New York: Columbia University Press, 2004).

Chadwick, Owen. *The Penguin History of the Church: The Reformation* (London: Penguin, 1964).

———. *The Secularization of the European Mind in the nineteenth Century* (Cambridge University Press, 1975).

———. *A History of Christianity* (Sheffield: Phoenix, 1995).

Chant, Colin and Fauvel, John, editors. *Darwin to Einstein: Historical Studies on Science and Belief* (Oxford: Longmans/Open University Press, 1980).

Charlesworth, Martin P. *Trade Routes and Commerce of the Roman Empire* (Cambridge University Press, 1924).

Cholvy, Gérard. *Les Religions et les Cultures dans l'Occident européen au XIXe Siècle* (Paris: Éditions Karthala, 2014). Translations from the French text by Thomas R. Sharp.

Clouse, Robert G., editor. *The Meaning of the Millennium* (Westmont, Illinois, Inter Varsity Press, 1977).

Collingwood, R.G. *The Idea of History* (Oxford: Clarendon Press, 1946).

Colson, Charles and Vaughn, Ellen Santilli. *Against the Night – Living in the new dark Ages* (Ann Arbor, Michigan: Servant Publications, 1989).

Court, John M. *Approaching the Apocalypse* (London: I.B. Tauris, 2008)

Cox, Harvey. *The secular City* (New York: MacMillan, 1966).

Cranston, Maurice. *Philosophers and Pamphleteers – political Theories of the Enlightenment* (Oxford University Press, 1986).

Dawson, Christopher (The Gifford Lectures of 1948). *Religion and the Rise of Western Culture* (London: Sheed & Ward, 1951).

Edinger, Edward F. *Archetype of the Apocalypse* (Chicago: Open Court, 2002).

Eliot, Simon and Stern, Beverly, editors. *The Age of Enlightenment: an Anthology of eighteenth Century Texts Volume I* (London: Ward Lock/Open University Press, 1979).

Fletcher, Richard. *The Conversion of Europe from Paganism to Christianity 371-1386* (Oxford: Fontana Press, 1998).

Flick, Alexander. *The Rise of the Medieval Church and its Influence on the Civilisation of Western Europe from the first to the thirteenth Century* (New York: G. P. Putnam, 1909).

Fordham, Frieda. *An Introduction to Jung's Psychology* (Harmondsworth: Penguin, 1953/1985).

Frend, W.H.C. *Martyrdom and Persecution in the early Church – A Study of a Conflict from the Maccabees to Donatus* (Oxford: Blackwell, 1965).

——— . *The Rise of Christianity* (London: Darton, Longman & Todd, 1984).

Freud, Sigmund. *Zwangshandlungen Und Religionsübungen (Obsessive Actions and religious Practices)* from *Gesammelte Werke Volume VII: Werke aus den Jahre 1906-1909* (London: Imago Publishing/Frankfurt am Main: S. Fischer Verlag, 1941).

——— . *Die Zukunft einer Illusion (The Future of an Illusion)* (Leipzig, Internationale Psychoanalytischer Verlag, 1928).

Funkenstein, Amos. *Theology and the Scientific Imagination* (Princeton: Princeton University Press, 1986).

Gellner, Ernest. *Postmodernism, Reason and Religion* (Abingdon: Routledge, 1992).

Gerth, H.H. and Mills, C. Wright, editors. *From Max Weber – Essays in Sociology* (London: Routledge, 1948/1991).

Gibbon, Edward. *The History of the Decline and Fall of the Roman Empire* London: Strahan & Cadell, 1782/1845).

Gilley, Sheridan and Sheils, W.J., editors. *A History of Religion in Britain:* (Oxford: Blackwell, 1994).

Graham, Elain. *Between a Rock and a hard Place* (London: SCM Press, 2013).

Green, Vivian. *A new History of Christianity* (Sutton Publishing, 1996).

Greengrass, Mark. *Christendom destroyed 1517-1648* (New York: Penguin Random House, 2014).

Greenslade, S.L. *The Cambridge History of the Bible – the West from the Reformation to the present Day* (Cambridge University Press, 1963).

Guizot, François. *Histoire de la Civilisation en Europe (History of Civilization in Europe)* (Brussels: Langlet et Compagnie, 1838).

Gunton, Colin E. *A brief Theology of Revelation* (Edinburgh, T.& T. Clark,. 1993).

——— . *The one, the three and the many* (Cambridge University Press, 1993).

Habermas, Jürgen, translated by Jeremy J. Shapiro. *Knowledge and human Interests* (London: Heinemann, 1968).

Hampson, Norman. *The Enlightenment* (London: Penguin, 1968/1990).

Harnack, Adolf, translated by Thomas Bailey Saunders. *Das Wesen des Christentums (The Essence of Christianity)*, (New York: Putnam's Sons, 1902).

Harries, Jill. *Sidonius Appollinaris and the Fall of Rome* (Oxford: Clarendon Press, 1994).

Harries, Richard and Mayr-Harting, Henry. *Christianity – Two Thousand Years* (Oxford University Press, 2001).

Harrisville Roy A. and Sundberg, Walter. *The Bible in modern Culture* (Grand Rapids, Michigan: Eerdmans, 2002).

Harvey, David. *The Condition of Postmodernity* (Oxford: Blackwell, 1989).

Hazard, Paul, translated by J. Lewis May. *The European Mind 1680-1715.* (London: Penguin, 1935/1964).

Heather, Peter. *The Fall of the Roman Empire – A New History of Rome and the Barbarians* (Oxford University Press/Pan Books, 2006).

Hengstenberg, Ernst, W. translated by Rev. Patrick Fairbairn, *The Revelation of St John, expounded for those who search the Scriptures.* (Edinburgh: T. & T. Clark, 1852).

Herberg, Will. *Protestant – Catholic – Jew* (Chicago: University of Chicago Press/Doubleday, 1955/1983).

Herrin, Judith. *The Formation of Christendom* (Sheffield: Phoenix Press, 1987).

Hibbert, Christopher. *The French Revolution* {London: Allen Lane, 1980).

Hill, Jonathan. *Faith in the Age of Reason* (Oxford: Lion Hudson, 2004).

Hitchcock, Tim and Cohen, Michèle, editors. *English Masculinities 1660-1800* (New York: Longmans, 1999).

Hobsbawm, Eric J. *The Age of Revolution* (New York: Vintage Books, 1962/1996).

Hodges, Richard and Whitehouse, David. *Mohammed, Charlemagne and the Origins of Europe* (London: Duckworth, 1983).

Holland, Tom. *Millennium: The End of the World and the Forging of Christendom* (London: Little, Brown, 2008).

Hughes, Philip. *A History of the Church, 2: The Church in the World the Church created – Augustine to Aquinas* (London: Sheed & Ward, 1935/1979).

Hughes, Thomas P. *Human-built World* (Chicago: University of Chicago Press, 2004).

Hulme, Peter and Jordanova, Ludmilla, editors. *The Enlightenment and its Shadows* (Abingdon: Routledge, 1990).

International Journal of Comparative Sociology. *Cult of the Saints* (1983): volume XXIV, 1 – 2.

Jaspers, Karl. *Die geistige Situation der Zeit (Man in the modern Age)* (Berlin: Walter de Gruyter & Co., 1931/1960); translations from the German text by Thomas R. Sharp.

────, translated by E. B. Ashton. *Der philosophische Glaube (Philosophical Faith and Revelation)* (London: Collins, 1967).

Jung, Carl Gustav. *Psychology and Western Religion* (London: ARK Paperbacks, 1958/1988).

Kant, Immanuel. *Die Religion innerhalb der Grenzen der bloßen Vernunft (Religion within the Bounds of Reason alone)*, (Leipzig: Verlag Felix Meiner, 1793/1922).

Katz, David S. and Popkin, Richard H. *Messianic Revolution* (New York: Hill & Wang, 1959).

Knight, Frances. *The Church in the nineteenth Century* (London: I.B. Tauris, 2008).

Küng, Hans, translated by John Bowden. *Christianity – The religious Situation of our Time* (Munich: SCM Press/Piper, 1994).

────. *The Catholic Church* (Sheffield: Phoenix Press/Weidenfeld & Nicolson, 2002).

Latourette Kenneth S. *A History of Christianity: Beginnings to 1500* (London: Harper Collins, 1953/1975).

Lawrence, C.H. *Medieval Monasticism* (Longmans, 1984).

────, editor. *The Impact of the mendicant Orders on Medieval Society* (London: I.B. Tauris, 1994/2013).

Lessing, Gottfried E. *Die Erziehung des Menschengeschlechts (The Education of the human Race)*, (Berlin: De Gruyter, 1780).
Löwith, Karl. *Meaning in History* (Chicago: University of Chicago Press, 1949).
Lyon, David. *Postmodernity* (Buckingham: Open University Press, 1999).
MacIntyre, Alasdair. *After Virtue* (London: Duckworth, 1981).
MacQuarrie, John. *Principles of Christian Theology* (London: SCM Press, 1977).
Mann, Thomas. *Doktor Faustus* (Stockholm: Bermann-Fischer Verlag, 1947).
Manuel, Frank E. *The Religion of Isaac Newton* (Oxford: Clarendon Press, 1974).
Marcuse, Herbert. *One-dimensional Man* (London: Routledge & Kegan Paul, 1964).
Marsden, Richard and Matter, E. Ann. *The New Cambridge History of the Bible* (Cambridge University Press, 2012).
Martin, David. *A general Theory of Secularization* (Oxford: Blackwell, 1978).
Marx, Karl, translated by Rodney Livingstone and Gregor Benton. *Early Writings:- Appendix A. Concerning Feuerbach* (London: Penguin/New Left Review, 1975).
Matytsin, Anton and Edelstein, Dan, editors. *Let there be Enlightenment* (Baltimore: Johns Hopkins University Press, 2018).
McGinn, Bernard. *Antichrist* (San Francisco: Harper, 1994).
McGrath, Alister. *Historical Theology* (Oxford: Blackwell, 1998).
McKelvey, R.J. *The Millennium and the Book of Revelation* (Cambridge: Lutterworth Press, 1999).
McLeod, Hugh. *Secularisation in Western Europe 1848-1914* (London: Palgrave, 2000).
McLeod, Hugh and Ustorf, Werner, editors. *The Decline of Christendom in Western Europe 1750-2000* (Cambridge University Press, 2003).
Michaels, J. Ramsey. *Revelation* (Leicester: IVP, 1997).
Michalson, Gordon E. Jnr. *Kant and the Problem of God* (Oxford: Blackwell,.1999).
Morris, Leon. *Tyndale New Testament Commentaries: The Revelation of St. John* (Grand Rapids, Michigan: Eerdmans, 1980).
Moynahan, Brian. *The Faith – A History of Christianity* (London: Pimlico, 2002).
Murdoch, Iris. *The Sovereignty of Good* (London: Routledge 1970).
——— . *Metaphysics as a Guide to Morals* (London: Chatto & Windus, 1992).

Nelson, Craig. *Thomas Paine* (London: Profile Books, 2006).
Neuhaus, Richard John. *The naked public Square* (Grand Rapids, Michigan: Eerdmans, 1984).
Niebuhr, Reinhold. *Faith and History* (New York: Nisbet, 1949).
Noble, Thomas F.X. and Head, Thomas. *Soldiers of Christ – Saints and Saints' Lives from late Antiquity and the early Middle Ages* (London: Sheed & Ward, 1995).
Norman, Edward. *Entering the Darkness – Christianity and its modern Substitutes* (London: SPCK, 1991).
——— . *Secularization* (London & New York: Continuum, 2002).
Pagden, Anthony (editor). *The Idea of Europe* (Washington D.C.: CUP, 2002).
Paine, Thomas. *The Age of Reason* (London: Freethought Publishing, 1794/1880)
Pannenberg, Wolfhart, editor. *Revelation as History* (London: Sheed & Ward, 1969).
Partner, Peter. *Two Thousand Years* (London: Granada Media, 1999).
Phillips, Fr. Andrew. *Orthodox Christianity and the English Tradition* (Colchester: The English Orthodox Trust, 1995).
Pinchbeck, Daniel. *2012 – The Year of the Mayan Prophecy* (London: Piatkus, 2006).
Pirenne, Henri. *Histoire de l'Europe: des Invasions au XVI$^e$ Siècle (History of Europe: from the Invasions until the sixteenth Century)* (Paris: Librairie Félix Alcan / Brussels: Nouvelle Société d'Éditions, 1936); translations from the French text by Thomas R. Sharp.
——— . *Mahomet et Charlemagne* (Librairie Félix Alcan / Brussels: Nouvelle Société d'Éditions, 1937); translations from the French text by Thomas R. Sharp.
Plested, Marcus. *Orthodox Readings of Aquinas* (Oxford University Press, 2012).
Reardon, Bernard M.G. *Religion in the Age of Romanticism* (Cambridge University Press, 1985).
Reeves, Marjorie. *Joachim of Fiore and the prophetic Future* (London: Sutton Publishing, 1976/1999).
Rissi, Mathias. *Time and History: A Study on the Revelation* (Louisville, Kentucky: John Knox Press, 1965).
——— . *The Future of the World* (London: SCM. Press, 1972).
Russell, Bertrand. *History of Western Philosophy* (London: Allen & Unwin, 1946).
Russell, Jeffrey Burton. *The Devil – Perceptions of Evil from Antiquity to primitive Christianity* (New York: Cornell University Press, 1977).

———. *Mephistopheles – The Devil in the modern World* (New York: Cornell University Press, 1986).

Sandeen, Ernest R. *Roots of Fundamentalism* (Chicago: University of Chicago Press, 1970).

Schama, Simon. *Citizens: A Chronicle of the French Revolution* (London: Penguin, 1989).

Schneewind, J.B., editor. *Moral Philosophy from Montaigne to Kant* (Cambridge University Press, 1990).

Schwarz, Hans. *The Search for God* (London: SPCK, 1975).

Sheldon, Henry C. *The History of the Christian Church* (New York: Crowell, 1895).

Skidelsky, Robert. *John Maynard Keynes* (Basingstoke: Pan MacMillan, 2003).

Smalley, Stephen. *The Revelation to John* (London: SPCK, 2005.

Sohm, Rudolf. *Kirchengeschichte im Grundriss.* (Leipzig: Verlag von E. Ungleich, 1888).

Southern, R.W. *Western Society and the Church in the Middle Ages* (Harmondsworth, London: Penguin, 1970).

Spengler, Oswald. *Der Untergang des Abendlandes, Volume I: Gestalt und Wirklichkeit (The Decline of the West, Volume I: Form and Actuality)* (Munich: Beck'sche Verlagsbuchhandlung, 1920); translations from the German text by Thomas R. Sharp.

———. *Der Untergang des Abendlandes Volume II*: *Welthistorische Perspektiven (The Decline of the West, Volume II: Perspectives of world History)* (Munich: Beck'sche Verlagsbuchhandlung, 1922); translations from the German text by Thomas R. Sharp.

Stark, Rodney. *The Victory of Reason* (New York: Random House, 2005).

Steiner, Rudolph. *Real Presences* (London: Faber & Faber, 1991).

Taine, Hippolyte. *Origines de la France contemporaine (Origins of contemporary France)*, (Paris: Hachette, 1893/1902).

Taylor, Charles. *Hegel* (Cambridge University Press, 1975).

Teilhard de Chardin, Pierre. *The Phenomenon of Man* (London: Collins, 1959).

———. *Activation of Energy* (London: Collins, 1970).

Thompson, Leonard L. *The Book of Revelation – Apocalypse and Empire* (Oxford University Press, 1990).

Tocqueville, Alexis de. *L'ancient Régime et la Révolution* (Paris: Michel Lévy Frères, 1856).

———, translated by John Bonner. *The old Regime and the Revolution* (New York: Harper & Brothers 1856).

Todd, Malcolm. *The early Germans* (Oxford: Blackwell, 1992/2004).

Toulmin, Stephen. *Cosmopolis: The hidden Agenda of Modernity* (Chicago: University of Chicago Press, 1990).
Toynbee, Arnold J. (abridgement D.C. Somervell), *A Study of History* (Oxford University Press, 1946/1957).
——. *A Study of History* (London: Oxford University Press/Thames & Hudson, 1972/1988).
Trigg, Roger. *Religion in public Life* (Oxford University Press, 2008).
Troeltsch, Ernst. *Gesammelte Schriften Volume II: Aufsätze zur Geistesgeschichte und Religionssoziologie (Collected Works Volume II: Essays on intellectual History and Sociology of Religion)* (Tübingen: J.C B. Mohr, 1913), translations from the German text by Thomas R. Sharp.
——. *Gesammelte Lage, Religionsphilosophie Schriften Volume IV: Zur religiösen und Ethik (Collected Works, Writings on the Philosophy of Religion Volume IV: On Religion and Ethics)*, (Tübingen: J.C B. Mohr, 1925), translations from the German text by Thomas R. Sharp.
——, translated and edited by Robert Morgan and Michael Pye. *Writings on Theology and Religion* (Atlanta: Duckworth/John Knox Press, 1977).
——, translated by James Luther Adams and Walter Bense. *Religion in History* (Edinburgh: T. & T. Clark, 1991).
Valliere, Paul. *Modern Russian Theology – Bukharev, Soloviev, Bulgakov* (Edinburgh: T. & T. Clark, 2000).
Vauchez, Andri. translated by Jean Birrell, *Sainthood in the later Middle Ages* (Cambridge University Press, 1988/1997).
Wainwright, Arthur W. *Mysterious Apocalypse – Interpreting the Book of Revelation* (Nashville: Abingdon Press, 1993).
Wallace-Hadrill J.M. *The barbarian West 400-1000* (Malden, U.S.A., Blackwell, 1967/1985).
Walsh, Katherine and Wood, Diana, editors. *The Bible in the medieval World* (Oxford: Blackwell, 1985).
Walsh, W.H. *Kant's Criticism of Metaphysics* (Edinburgh University Press, 1957/1975).
——. *An Introduction to the Philosophy of History* (London: Hutchinson University Library, 1967).
Ward, Keith. *In Defence of the Soul* (London: Oneworld, 1992).
Ward-Perkins, Bryan. *The Fall of Rome and the End of Civilization* (Oxford University Press, 2005).
Weinstein, Donald and Bell, Rudolph M. *Saints and Society* (University of Chicago Press, 1982).

Wilcock, Michael. *The Message of Revelation* (Nottingham: Inter Varsity Press, 1975).

Wilks, Michael, editor. *Studies in Church History: Prophecy and Eschatology* (Oxford: Blackwell/Ecclesiastical History Society, 1994).

Wilson, Derek. *Charlemagne, Barbarian and Emperor* (London: Pimlico, 2006)

———. *Out of the Storm: the Life and Legacy of Martin Luther* (London: Hutchinson, 2007).

Winston, Richard. *Charlemagne: from the Hammer to the Cross* (London: Eyre & Spottiswoode, 1956).

Witherington, Ben III. *Revelation* (Cambridge University Press, 2003).

Zeldin, Theodore. *A History of French Passions, Volume 2 Intellect, Taste and Anxiety. Chapter 20 – Religion and Anticlericalism* (Oxford: Clarendon Press, 1973).

———, editor. *Conflicts in French Society – Anticlericalism, Education and Morals in the nineteenth Century* (London: Allen & Unwin, 1979).

## Index of personal Names

Abelard, Peter, 151
Acton, John Emerich Lord, 185
Ado of Vienne, 165
Adrian I, Pope, 103
Adso of Montier-en-Der, 24
Aëtius, Flavius, 42, 45, 54
Africanus, Sextus Julius, 7
Agathias of Myrina, 47
Agobard of Orleans, 100
Aidan, Saint, 107
Ajax, Missionary, 50
Alaric the Goth, King, 41, 45, 56
Alboin, King, 54
Alcuin of York, 100, 104, 105, 116
Alexander III, Pope, 166
Alexander the Minorite, 25
Alexander, Severus, Emperor, 85
Alighieri, Dante, 207
Alsted, Johann, 27, 192
Amandus, Saint, 108
Ambrose of Milan, Saint, 82
Ammianus Marcellinus, 44
Angilbert, Saint, 100
Angilramnus of Metz, 104, 112
Anselm of Canterbury, 217
Antony of Padua, Saint, 169
Aquinas, Saint Thomas, 137, 201, 225
Arbogastes, 44, 46
Arcadius, Flavius, Emperor, 45
Arkwright, Richard, 243
Armstrong, Karen, 146
Arndt, Johann, 211
Arnold, Matthew, 257
Athaulf King, 46
Attila the Hun, 42, 54
Audoin, King, 43

Augustine of Hippo, Saint, 1, 24, 26, 49, 53, 59, 82–84, 88, 100, 105, 111, 117, 120, 122, 127, 161, 172, 190–192, 225
Augustus, Caesar, Emperor, 5, 14
Aureolus, Peter, 25
Bacon, Francis, 143, 210, 223
Bacon, Roger, 150
Bainton, Roland, 187
Bakunin, Mikhail, 267
Bale, John, 17
Barclay, William, 316
Barth, Karl, 193
Barzun, Jacques, 2, 289, 290
Basil of Caesarea, Saint, 225
Bauckham, Richard, 19, 20, 32, 63, 186
Baudelaire, Charles, 277
Baugulf of Fulda, 112
Bauto, Flavius, 46
Bayle, Pierre, 226
Bebel, August, 260, 265
Becket, Saint Thomas, 172, 178
Bede, The Venerable, 24, 111
Bekker, Balthasar, 231
Bell, Daniel, 301, 309
Benda, Julien, 296, 297
Benedict of Nursia, Saint, 82, 83, 105, 114, 168, 170
Bengel, Johann Albrecht, 27
Ben-Habib, Seyla, 301
Bentley, Richard, 225
Berdyaev, Nikolai, 147, 321
Berengaud, 24
Berger, Peter, 194, 248, 257, 262, 286, 305
Bergson, Henri, 146, 296, 297
Bernanos, Georges, 310
Bernard of Tiron, Saint, 166
Bertha of Kent, Queen, 49

## INDEX OF PERSONAL NAMES

Bickersteth, Edward, 26
Birks, Thomas, 26
Bishop, Edmund, 78
Bismarck, Otto Eduard von, 265, 266
Blake, William, 243, 277
Blavatsky, Helena, 267
Bleda the Hun, 42, 54
Böhme, Jakob, 211
Bonhoeffer, Dietrich, 213
Boniface, Saint, 107, 108, 110, 113, 172
Bonifatius, Comes, 42
Bossuet, Jacques Benigne, 11, 26, 228, 230
Brentano, Klemens, 276
Brightman, Thomas, 27, 126
Brown, Callum, 244, 257, 298
Brown, Peter, 61, 164
Brunetière, Ferdinand, 283
Bryce, James, 119
Büchner, Karl Georg, 261, 271, 281
Buckhardt, Carl Jacob, 263
Bukharev, Alexander, 28, 29
Bultmann, Rudolf, 3, 11
Burke, Edmund, 238, 239
Bury, John Bagnell, 1
Butler, Samuel, 290
Caesar, Augustus, Emperor, 67, 68, 71
Caesar, Julius, 37, 38
Caesarius of Arles, Saint, 23, 111, 112
Caird, George, 186
Calvin, John, 151, 176, 181, 203, 208
Campbell, Thomas, 220
Carlile, Richard, 281
Carloman, King, 99
Carlyle, Thomas, 239
Carson, Donald, 307, 308
Cassiodorus, Flavius, 78, 80, 105, 106
Cathaulf, 99
Chadwick, Owen, 204, 263, 275, 313

Charcot, Jean-Martin,, 270
Charlemagne, Emperor, 97, 98–107, 109–120, 147, 165, 194, 204, 205, 254
Charles V, Emperor, 180
Charles, Robert H., 18
Charlesworth, Martin P., 72, 73
Cholvy, Gérard, 235, 278, 291
Clarke, Isabelle, 295
Clarke, Samuel, 225
Claudel, Paul, 310
Clotilde, Queen, 50
Clovis I, King, 39, 50, 54
Collingwood, R.G., 22
Colson, Charles, 313
Columba, Saint, 107
Columbanus, Saint, 50, 107
Comenius, Jan, 214
Comestor, Peter, 151
Comte, Auguste, 10, 275, 276, 282, 283
Constantine the Great, Emperor, 23, 26, 34, 36, 41, 47, 115, 159
Constantius Gallus, 44
Cooper, Robert, 38
Copernicus, Nicolaus, 150, 210
Corbinian, Saint, 108
Costelle, Daniel, 295
Cotton, John, 126
Cox, Harvey, 297
Cranmer, Thomas, 182
Croce, Benedetto, 10
Cuthbert, Saint, 172
Cyprian, Saint, 159, 170
Dante, Alighieri, 138
Danton, Georges, 240
Darwin, Charles, 265, 271, 280, 309
Dawkins, Richard, 309
Dawson, Christopher, 60, 145
Debussy, Claude, 290
Dent, Arthur, 26
Descartes, René, 8, 139, 209–211, 224, 226, 251, 303
Diderot, Denis, 139, 210, 228, 231
Didier of Cahors, Saint, 76
Dilthey, Wilhelm, 3, 10, 272

Diocletian, Emperor, 14, 155, 240
Dominic de Guzmán, Saint, 169
Domitian, Emperor, 14, 16, 156
Dostoevsky, Fyodor, 133, 289
Draper, John William, 270
Drummond, Henry, 256, 284, 317
Duns Scotus, John, 146, 223
Dupanloup, Félix-Antoine-Philibert of Orléans, 276
Dürer, Albrecht, 26
Durham, James, 190
Durkheim, Émile, 275
Edinger, Edward, 29, 129
Edison, Thomas, 121
Edlin, Handley H., 21
Edward the Confessor Saint, 178
Edwin of Northumbria, King, 51
Einhard, 100
Einstein, Albert, 291
Eliland, Abbot, 108
Eliot, T.S., 291
Emmeram of Regensburg, Saint, 108
Engels, Friedrich, 260, 263
Erasmus, Desiderius, 176, 204, 207
Ethelbert, King, 51
Eusebius, of Caesarea, 7
Falk, Peter, 266
Faust, Johann Georg, 140
Ferry, Jules, 285
Feuerbach, Ludwig, 252, 259–261, 292
Fichte, Johann, 9
Flaubert, Gustave, 276
Fletcher, Richard, 60
Florus of Lyon, 165
Fontenelle, Bernard le Bovier de, 210
Foote, George, 281
Foxe, John, 26, 193, 203
France, Anatole, 290
Francis II, Emperor, 241
Francis of Assisi, Saint, 169
Freud, Sigmund, 292
Fritigern, King, 40, 48
Fursey, Saint, 107
Gaiso, 46

Galileo, Galilei, 210
Gall, Saint, 50
Gama, Vasco da, 152
Gassendi, Pierre, 268
Geiseric, King, 53
Germanus of Auxerre, Saint, 163
Gibbon, Edward, 9, 59, 62, 74, 77, 162, 230, 244
Gibuld, King, 50
Girard, René, 320
Goar, King, 42
Godwin, William, 249, 267
Goethe, Johann Wolfgang von, 87, 139, 142, 213, 227, 232, 242, 245–247, 254, 276, 320
Goyau, Georges, 279
Graham, Elaine, 313
Greengrass, Mark, 187
Greenham, Richard, 277
Grégoire, Henri, Abbé, 234
Gregory II, Pope, 117
Gregory of Tours, Saint, 35, 37, 50, 56, 57, 60, 78, 97, 159, 161
Gregory the Great, Saint, 51, 52, 82, 84, 85, 105, 108, 171
Gregory VII, Pope, 26, 196
Groote, Geert, 191
Guizot, François, 100, 192, 193, 297, 318
Gundahar, King, 42
Habermas, Jürgen, 301, 309
Haeckel, Ernst, 270, 271
Halbwachs, Maurice, 6
Hamann, Johann Georg, 12, 213
Hardy, Thomas, 290
Hariulf, 46
Harnack, Adolf, 19, 80, 207
Hauptmann, Gerhard, 290
Hegel, Georg Wilhelm, 9, 213, 258–260, 271
Heidegger, Martin, 296
Heine, Heinrich, 252
Helvétius, Claude, 228
Heming, Carol, 176
Hempton, David, 274

Hengstenberg, Ernst, 28, 92, 118, 145
Henry IV, Emperor, 196
Henry the Navigator, Prince, 152
Henry VIII, King, 200
Herberg, Will, 314
Herder, Johann Gottfried von, 213, 228, 318
Hermeric, King, 53
Herod Antipas, King, 5
Herrin, Judith, 119
Hilary of Poitiers, Saint, 163
Hildegard of Bingen, 137
Hill, Jonathan, 226
Hills, Aaron M., 96
Hinemar of Rheims, 112
Hippolytus of Rome, 7, 23
Hobsbawm, Eric, 243, 255
Hogarth, William, 139
Holbach, Paul d', 139, 228, 231, 309
Hölscher, Lucien, 222
Holyoake, George, 281
Honorius, Emperor, 41, 42, 46
Hughes, Thomas, 149
Hugo, of Saint Victor, 150
Hugo, Victor, 277
Hume, David, 139, 210, 224, 229–231, 319
Huss, Jan, 26
Huxley, Thomas, 269, 309
Hydatius, 56
Ibsen, Henrik, 289
Innocent III, Pope, 168, 205
Irenaeus, Saint, 23, 189
Isidore of Seville, Saint, 51, 101, 111
Jaspers, Karl, 233, 309
Jaurès, Jean, 294
Jefferson, Thomas, 215, 308
Jerome, Eusebius, Saint, 17, 23, 37, 104, 165
Joachim of Fiore, 8, 20, 24, 25, 126, 193
John Chrysostom, Saint, 106
John the Divine, Saint, 15
Joyce, James, 291
Julian the Apostate, Emperor, 39, 40, 44, 46

Jung, Carl, 29, 310, 312, 321
Junius the Elder, Franciscus, 26
Justin Martyr, 23
Justinian the Great, Emperor, 43, 51, 54, 132
Kant, Immanuel, 4, 9, 31, 88, 135, 139, 213, 227, 229, 232, 247, 249–254, 258, 269, 306, 315, 318
Kaufmann, Alfred, 272
Keats, John, 276
Keil, Ernst, 266
Kempis Thomas à, 191
Kepler, Johann, 210
Keynes, John Maynard, 262, 290
Kierkegaard, Søren, 261
Klimt, Gustav, 290
Küng, Hans, 222
Lactantius, Lucius, 155
Lampadius, Johannes, 27
Langton, Stephen, 151
Lantfrid, Duke of Alemannia, 108
Latimer, Hugh, 182
Law, William, 191
Lawrence, D.H., 291
Lecky, William, 265, 284
Leibniz, Gottfried, 210, 224
Leidrade, 100
Lenin, Vladimir Ilyich, 297
Leo III, Pope, 100
Leo the Great, Saint, 82
Leo XIII, Pope, 29
Lessing, Gotthold, 12, 92
Lessing, Gotthold Ephraim, 204, 224
Lewis, C.S., 291
Liebknecht, Karl, 265
Locke, John, 139, 210, 214, 224
Lombard, Peter, 137
Löscher, Valentin Ernst, 212
Louis of Anjou, Prince, 166
Louis Philippe, King, 278
Louis XVI, King, 234
Löwith, Karl, 10, 190
Lowman, Moses, 27
Loyola, Saint Ignatius, 180
Lull, Saint, 109

Luther, Martin, 17, 25, 26, 138, 178, 181, 183, 203, 208, 233, 252
Luxemburg, Rosa (Jósef Chmura), 294
Machiavelli, Niccolò, 261, 297
MacQuarrie, John, 193
Magellan, Ferdinand, 153
Maistre, Joseph de, 236, 237
Malebranche, Nicolas, 224
Mallarmé, Stéphane, 289
Mamertinus, Claudius, 40
Mann, Thomas, 195, 264, 291, 320
Marat, Jean-Paul, 240
Marcus Aurelius, Emperor, 32, 66, 75
Margaret of Antioch, Saint, 174
Marlowe, Christopher, 142
Martin of Braga, Saint, 51, 110
Martin of Tours, Saint, 161, 163, 171, 172
Martin, David, 286
Martineau, Harriet, 276
Marx, Karl, 9, 226, 252, 260, 265, 271, 275
Mauriac, François, 310
Maurus, Rabanus, 100, 106, 112, 165
Maximian, Emperor, 39, 40
Mazarin, Cardinal Jules, 200
McKelvey, Robert J., 158
McLeod, Hugh, 241
Melanchthon, Philip, 181
Mellobaudes, King, 46
Mendelssohn, Moses, 252
Merobaudes, Flavius, 46
Metternich, Prince Klaus, 255
Michaels, J. Ramsey, 186
Michalson, Gordon, 250, 251
Michelet, Jules, 213, 234, 277, 279
Mill, John Stuart, 275, 303
Milton, John, 138, 139, 232, 315
Mond, Alfred, 291
Monod, Jacques, 309
Montesquieu, Charles, 226
Morand, Paul, 1
Morris, Leon, 312

Mosheim, Johann Lorenz von, 12
Most, Johann, 265
Murdoch, Iris, 252, 315
Musset, Alfred de, 276
Myers, Frederic W.H., 288
Namier, Lewis, 255
Napier, John, 27
Napoléon Bonaparte, Emperor, 101, 133, 221, 230, 240, 241
Napoléon III, Emperor, 278
Naulobatus, 44
Neall, Beatrice S., 29, 136, 158
Neri, Philip, 180
Nero, Emperor, 14, 15, 156
Nerval, Gérard, 277
Newton, Sir Isaac, 21, 22, 27, 139, 210, 216, 225
Nicholas of Lyra, 25
Niebuhr, Barthold, 256
Niebuhr, Reinhold, 1, 322
Nietzsche, Friedrich, 260, 261, 295, 302, 308, 309, 313, 320
Noel-Baker, Philip, 321
Notker the Stammerer, 165
O'Regan, Emmett, 29
Ockham, William of, 146, 150, 223
Odoacer, King, 53
Orientius, Saint, 55
Origen of Alexandria, 24, 106, 127, 188, 190, 256
Orosius, Paulus, 155
Owen, Robert, 264
Pacioli, Luca, 149
Paine, Thomas, 239, 248, 249, 264, 281, 308
Paley, William, 268
Pannenberg, Wolfhart, 6, 12, 273, 322
Papias of Hieropolis, 23
Pascal, Blaise, 225, 318
Patrick, Saint, 107
Paul of Tarsus, Saint, 6, 17, 158, 188
Paul the Deacon, 37
Paulinus of Aquileia, 100
Paulinus of York, 51
Péguy, Charles, 310

Pepin III, King, 98, 113
Peregrinus, Petrus, 153
Pétau, Denis (Petavius), 230
Peter of Pisa, 100
Peter of Verona, Martyr, Saint, 169
Peter the Apostle, Saint, 165, 172
Peter the Chanter, 151
Petrarca Francesco (Petrarch), 78, 207
Philibert, Saint, 168
Phillips, Andrew, 148
Piganiol, André, 61
Pilate, Pontius, 6
Pirenne, Henri, 72–74, 77, 81, 89, 101, 103
Pirmin, Saint, 108, 110
Pius IX, Pope, 265
Pius X, Pope, 292
Plato, 297
Pliny the Elder, 37, 66–70, 73
Pliny the Younger, 14, 15, 85
Polycarp, Saint, 160, 170
Pope, Alexander, 227
Porphyry of Gaza, 161
Pound, Ezra, 291
Priestley, Joseph, 11, 26, 233
Primasius of Hadrumetum, 23
Proudhon, Pierre-Joseph, 9, 267, 277
Proust, Marcel, 291
Prudentius, Clemens, 107
Ptolemy, Claudius, 37
Quirinius, Publius, 6
Radagaisus, King, 45
Radbertus, Paschasius, Saint, 100
Ranke, Leopold von, 9, 271, 318
Rechiarius, King, 50
Redwald, King, 51
Remegius of Rheims, Bishop, 50
Remigius of Auxerre, 112
Renan, Ernest, 130, 131, 272
Ribera, Juan de Saint, 28
Richelieu, Cardinal Armand, 200
Richomer, Flavius, 46
Ricimer, Flavius, 46
Ridley, Nicholas, 182
Rissi, Mathias, 95
Robespierre, Maximilien, 221, 237, 240, 252
Roch, Saint, 174
Romulus Augustulus, Emperor, 60
Rousseau, Jean-Jacques, 231, 254, 303, 315
Rupert of Salzburg, 108
Russell, Jeffrey Burton, 210
Rutherford, Ernest, 291
Sade, Marquis de, 309
Saint Clement (Willibrod), 107
Saint-Simon, Claude, 274
Salia, Flavius, 44
Salisbury, John of, 151
Santayana, George, 316
Sartre, Jean-Paul, 303, 308
Schelling Friedrich, 12
Schleiermacher, Friedrich, 211, 213, 247–248, 259, 263, 305
Schoenberg, Arnold, 290, 292
Schopenhauer, Arthur, 258
Schroske, Carl, 290
Schubert, Hans von, 119
Scotus Erigena Hincmar, John, 100, 150
Sheldon, Henry, 39, 56, 57
Shelley, Percy Bysshe, 276, 277
Sidgwick, Alfred, 290
Sigismund of Luxemburg, Emperor, 132
Silvanus, 46
Simon, Pierre, Marquis de Laplace, 229, 269
Smalley, Stephen, 133
Sohm, Rudolf, 90, 213
Soloviov, Vladimir, 135, 295, 297, 312
Sozomen, 48
Spencer, Herbert, 269
Spener, Philipp Jakob, 126, 211
Spengler, Oswald, 10, 21, 123, 124, 142–145, 147, 208, 220, 231, 238, 242, 246, 253, 261, 315, 317
Spies, Johann, 140
Spinoza, Baruch de, 139, 210, 224

Stark, Rodney, 157
Stauffer, Ethelbert, 154
Steiner, George, 301
Steiner, Rudolf, 29, 133, 133
Stephen, Saint, 160, 165
Stilicho, Flavius, 41, 46
Stirner, Max, 282
Strauss, David Friedrich, 263
Stravinsky, Igor, 292
Suetonius, Gaius, 15
Swete, Henry, 220
Syagrius, 54
Tacitus, Publius, 15, 37
Taine, Hippolyte, 239, 240, 276
Tainter, Joseph, 59
Tawney, Richard. H., 148
Teilhard de Chardin, Pierre, 87, 261
Tennyson, Alfred, 290
Teresa of Avila, Saint, 180
Tertullian, Quintus, 23, 85, 159
Theodelinda, Queen, 51
Theoderic the Great, King, 42, 46, 53
Theodosius, Emperor, 46
Theodulf of Orleans, 100, 104, 112, 117, 118, 204
Theophilus the Penitent of Antioch Saint, 7, 140
Theucydides, 4
Tiberius, Emperor, 85
Tillich, Paul, 297
Tillotson, John, 214
Tocqueville, Alexis de, 228, 236, 238, 256, 262
Toland, John, 214, 224
Tolstoy, Leo, 242
Toynbee, Arnold, 10, 21, 32, 33, 86–89, 121–124, 129, 131, 141, 146, 153, 195, 250, 304
Trajan, Emperor, 32
Trevithick, Richard, 243
Troeltsch, Ernst, 2, 148, 233, 248, 270, 272, 294, 297, 303, 304, 307, 321
Turgot, Robert, 9
Twain, Mark, 290

Tyconius, 23, 24
Tyndale, William, 182
Uldin, 41, 45
Ulfilas, Salminius, 48
Urban VIII, Pope, 179
Ussher, James, 27
Vacherot, Étienne, 271
Valdés, Juan de, 204
Valens, Emperor, 40, 41, 48, 55
Valentinian, Emperor, 40, 46
Vauchez, Andri, 162
Vaughn, Ellen Santilli, 313
Vico, Giambattista, 8, 11, 316, 318
Victorinus of Petau, Saint, 23
Vigny, Alfred de, 277
Virchow, Rudolf, 266, 270
Vogt, Karl, 261, 270, 271
Vogüé, Eugène-Melchior de, 289
Voltaire, François, 8, 139, 210, 216, 217, 227, 232, 311
Wainwright, Arthur, 17
Waldram, Abbot, 108
Walpurga (Walburga), 107
Walvoord, John, 122
Watt, James, 241
Weber, Max, 87, 148, 184, 300, 301, 306, 317
Wesley, John, 183
Whately, Richard, 157
White, Andrew, 268
Wigbod, 106
Wilcock, Michael, 115
William the Pious, Duke of Aquitaine, 202
Wolff, Christian von, 224
Wollstonecraft, Mary, 239
Woolf, Virginia, 291
Wurmbrand, Richard, 267
Wycliffe, John, 25, 26, 182, 202
Xavier, Saint Francis, 180
Zacharias, Pope, 98
Zeno the Isaurian, Emperor, 53
Zernikov, Adam, 147
Zinzendorf, Nikolas von, 212
Zola, Émile, 290
Zwingli, Ulrich, 176

www.ingramcontent.com/pod-product-compliance
Lightning Source LLC
Chambersburg PA
CBHW071331080526
44587CB00017B/2795